SOLID OBJECTS

SOLID OBJECTS

MODERNISM AND THE TEST OF PRODUCTION

DOUGLAS MAO

PRINCETON UNIVERSITY PRESS

PRINCETON, NEW JERSEY

Library of Congress Cataloging-in-Publication Data

Mao, Douglas, 1966–
Solid objects : modernism and the test of production / Douglas Mao.
p.   cm.
Includes bibliographical references and index.
ISBN 0-691-05926-8 (cl : alk. paper)
1. Modernism (Literature)   2. European literature—20th century—
History and criticism.   3. Material culture in literature.   I. Title.
PN56.M54M36   1998   809′.9112—dc21   98-11863   CIP

To Evelyn Schwarz, my mother

Ein Leben ward vielleicht verschmäht, wer weiß?
Ein Glück war da und wurde hingegeben,
und endlich wurde doch, um jeden Preis,
dies Ding daraus, nicht leichter als das Leben
und doch vollendet und so schön als sei's
nicht mehr zu früh, zu lächeln und zu schweben.

(A life perhaps was spurned, who knows?
A chance at happiness was there and given up,
and yet finally, at whatever price,
this *thing* grew out of it, not easier than life
and yet completed and so perfect — as if
it were no longer too soon to laugh and soar.)

R. M. Rilke, "Die Spitze" ("The
Lace"), *translated by Edward Snow*

In our Father's house there are many mansions, they
taught, and there alone will the incompatible multitudes
of mankind be welcomed and soothed. Not one shall be
turned away by the servants on that verandah, be he black
or white, not one shall be kept standing who approaches
with a loving heart. And why should the divine hospitality
cease here? Consider, with all reverence, the monkeys.
May there not be a mansion for the monkeys also? Old
Mr. Graysford said No, but young Mr. Sorley, who was
advanced, said Yes; he saw no reason why monkeys
should not have their collateral share of bliss, and he had
sympathetic discussions about them with his Hindu
friends. And the jackals? Jackals were indeed less to Mr.
Sorley's mind but he admitted that the mercy of God,
being infinite, may well embrace all mammals.
And the wasps? He became uneasy during the descent
to wasps, and was apt to change the conversation.
And oranges, cactuses, crystals and mud? and the
bacteria inside Mr. Sorley? No, no, this is going
too far. We must exclude someone from our
gathering, or we shall be left with nothing.

E. M. Forster, A Passage to India

CONTENTS

ACKNOWLEDGMENTS

IF THERE IS any truth to the received wisdom that one's work is always deeply "about" oneself, then the existence of this book, which is about the production of objects, seems to attest that I have come to be defined by nothing other than the production of this book. This is not a very happy thought for someone who believes that there should be more to life than work, less so still when it brings to mind a minor but memorably overbearing character in *Mrs. Dalloway* whose "soul is daily secreted" around a single obsession: "Emigration," Woolf writes in wrapping up her sketch of this figure, "had become, in short, largely Lady Bruton." I hope that I have not turned into *Solid Objects*, nor *Solid Objects* into me, but if this is really what happened, I have been spared confronting the painful fact through the grace of those I thank here, people who have made me feel human *and* productive and without whom this book would never have stood a chance of materializing in solid form.

Thinking of the more recent phase of the project, I turn first to Matt Bremer, whose love and affirmation have been astonishing, inexhaustible, and steadfast, and to whom *Solid Objects* and my sanity owe more than either can ever repay. Next, I want to thank Troy Elder and Rex Hatfield, who have endured the genesis of this book with patience nothing short of saintly, and my colleagues in the Princeton English Department (undergraduates, graduate students, and faculty), who have been wonderfully and consistently sensitive to the pressures that finishing it applied. I would also note an additional debt to Maria DiBattista, Jim Richardson, Michael Wood, and Lee Mitchell for their invaluable suggestions anent some of the particular matter of what follows; to Julie Park for her dedicated help in research; and to Princeton University, which provided essential assistance in the form of leave time and research grants. I gratefully acknowledge as well the support of the Princeton University Press staff, especially Mary Murrell, Tina Najbjerg, Suzanne Osborne, and Karen Verde, who have made the path to publication much less arduous and much more fun than it might have been; of the British Library and the Tate Gallery, where I had the chance to review the *Mrs. Dalloway* manuscript and Omega and Vorticist catalogues and prospectuses; and of Gillian Raffles, who graciously provided the cover illustration. Last, I want to thank the many others whose friendship and encouragement have meant so much to me over the past several years but whom space constraints prevent me from naming individually: please know that I think of all of you with the deepest affection whenever I think of this book.

I should also acknowledge those who did so much for me during the earlier phase of this work, beginning with my dissertation directors, Geoffrey Hartman and Jennifer Wicke, who read rigorously yet sympathetically always, and who gave of their time with great generosity. I would also thank Paul Fry, Margaret Homans, and Carla Kaplan, whose thoughtful comments led me to see key aspects of this project in new lights; Patricia Joplin, Harriet Chessman, and the other faculty members whose insights shaped its content from the beginning; and my fellow students, especially Edward Adams, James Najarian, Anne Fernald, Jacinto Fombona, and Jay Dickson, who helped me to think through so many of my argument's contours and details. Finally, I note with gratitude the financial support of Yale University and the Andrew W. Mellon Foundation, without which there simply would have been no dissertation.

I have saved for last my thanks to the book's dedicatee, that extraordinary woman who has had the doubtful pleasure of helping me to stay together in mind and body through both phases of this work. I can never articulate how beautifully my mother's faith and compassion have sustained me in these last years and before; I can only gesture that way by recalling another passage from *Mrs. Dalloway*, one in which Woolf describes the kind of moment when past and present luminously fuse. "For she was a child," Woolf writes of her protagonist, "and at the same time a grown woman coming to her parents who stood by the lake, holding her life in her arms which, as she neared them, grew larger and larger in her arms, until it became a whole life, a complete life, which she put down by them and said, 'This is what I have made of it! This!'" What follows is of course a part of what I have made of my life, Mom, and I hope you will think well of it.

SOLID OBJECTS

INTRODUCTION

Dear H. D.,

I got today some flowers. By chance or intention they are my
favourite flowers, those I most admire. Some words "to greet the
return of the Gods" (other people read: Goods). No name. I suspect you to be responsible for the gift. If I have guessed right
don't answer but accept my hearty thanks for so charming a gesture. In any case,

affectionately yours,

Sigm. Freud

FREUD WAS right about the source of the flowers and about the message that accompanied them. In her *Tribute to Freud*, wherein she
reprints his note (11), H. D. records that in the autumn of 1938, Freud
had received in London some ancient statues of divinities left behind in his
flight from Vienna, and that in honor of their safe passage she had sent
gardenias, accompanied by her commemoration, "to greet the return of the
Gods." She goes on to recall that she saw Freud on only one more occasion,
a somewhat constrained one with others present, when "no words were spoken to recall a devastatingly near past or to evoke an equivocal future," and
that she was in Switzerland "when soon after the announcement of a World
at War the official London news bulletin announced that Dr. Sigmund Freud
. . . was dead" (12).

Given anything more than the most cursory attention, Freud's little story
about "Gods" taken for "Goods" quickly comes to seem freighted with por-
tents and allegories. Issuing in the shadow of catastrophe from the century's
great theorist of misprision, and bringing into suggestive juxtaposition what
are arguably the two great determining tropes of social life since the Enlightenment, it invites us to see in the displacement of religious faith by commodity fetishism the moral of the events before which Freud found himself
driven to a new country, or the framework of the catastrophe that separates
the devastating modern past from the equivocal postmodern future. In the
present scholarly climate, when extrapolating the largest meanings from the
smallest anecdotes is a practice both more common and more subject to
interrogation than ever before, we might hesitate to bring such vast machinery to bear on so casual a reference, to be sure; and yet it is this very

casualness that finally justifies the operation here. For although no overt self-congratulation marks Freud's and H. D.'s moment of solidarity at the expense of misreaders, the air of satisfaction attending their exchange reminds us how naturally to the twentieth-century Westerner comes the idea that we live in an age of Goods amid which, and against which, the enlightened or the sensitive will struggle to secure their loftier Gods. The very minor joke that Freud and H. D. share exceeds the private and contingent precisely because it relies upon a deeply embedded assumption that the elect will strive for a spirit or authenticity purged of the age's ignoble prostration before commerce—an assumption in circulation for as long as there has been an identifiable bourgeoisie, and foundational to the theories and practices that we have begun to think of as so many modernisms.

One reason I begin with H. D.'s recollection is that the reflexive antipathy to the commodity that it betrays forms a significant part of the story that I propose to tell here, which is to say that one of this book's guiding premises is that we have by no means learned all there is to learn about this antipathy's consequences for the writing of the early twentieth century—important recent work on more cordial relations between modernism and the culture of the commodity notwithstanding. But the more specific reason I start with this anecdote is that it speaks so eloquently to the most central topic of this study, which is modernism's extraordinarily generative fascination with the object understood neither as commodity (Goods) nor as symbol (Gods), but *as* "object," where any or all of the resonances of this complexly polysemous word might apply. For the truth is that the opposition between mere Goods and higher Gods is at best secondary, with respect to the affect that presides over the H. D.-Freud exchange, to an opposition between Goods *or* Gods, on the one hand, and, on the other, the little statues regarded as beloved things, treasures cherished when close by and longed for when far away, elements of material life whose significance can be compassed neither by what they stand for nor by their monetary worth. There is simply no way of grasping the intimacy of this moment without acknowledging the peculiar bond that each writer shares with the figurines themselves, quite apart from their status as goods or gods—a bond that cannot be love in one sense, since these pieces of brute matter are clearly incapable of loving back, and yet which clearly must be something like love, since no other term can be invoked without seeming to impoverish description.

This feeling of regard for the physical object as object—as not-self, as not-subject, as most helpless and will-less of entities, but also as fragment of Being, as solidity, as otherness in its most resilient opacity—seems a peculiarly twentieth-century malady or revelation, in any case; or rather, we might say, the open acknowledgment of such a feeling seems one of the minor trademarks of the writing of this period. I will explore this point with more care, and with respect to the broad outlines of Anglo-American modernism, in a moment; but at this juncture it may be enough to suggest how the epigraphs to this book can convey something of what I mean. Consider, for example, Rilke's breathtaking poem on the production of a small piece of lace at the cost of blindness. There is nothing absolutely novel in the fact that it addresses the gains and losses of making, or even in the fact that it centers on an object; but it does seem the very mark of Rilke's modernity that the individual thing in the wonder and terror of its thingness exerts the ultimate moral claim here—here, and throughout the poems of 1907 and 1908 that became known as *Dinggedichte*. The other epigraph makes the point still more tellingly, perhaps, for making it both negatively and indirectly, for what separates this passage so clearly from the discourse of any century before the twentieth is its insistence—unfolded through irony but no less categorical for all that—that the extension of justice to crystals and mud as well as bacteria is at once absurd and morally requisite, the impossible yet necessary terminus of an ideal of love always implicitly sanctified by its own inclusiveness.

Perhaps no writer has articulated the claim of the object on the modern subject with greater precision or candor, however, than Walter Benjamin, whose reflections on the auratic particularity of the work of art remain among his most famous, and whose vision of modernity has seemed for so many readers at once absolutely idiosyncratic and utterly characteristic of his age. In the essay "Unpacking My Library," Benjamin observes that in collecting one discovers "a relationship to objects which does not emphasize their functional, utilitarian value—that is, their usefulness—but studies and loves them as the scene, the stage, of their fate," and that the "most profound enchantment for the collector is the locking of individual items within a magic circle in which they are fixed as the final thrill, the thrill of acquisition, passes over them" (*Illuminations* 60). This reference to acquisition is unsettling, of course, both because it evokes the mercantile sensibility that could mistake the "Gods" of H.D.'s note for "Goods" and because it seems to conflate love with domination; but Benjamin moves to redeem this suggestion, at least partly, a few pages further on:

> [O]ne of the finest memories of a collector is the moment when he rescued a book to which he might never have given a thought, much less a wishful look, because he found it lonely and abandoned on the market place and bought it to give it its freedom—the way the prince bought a beautiful slave girl in *The Arabian Nights*. To a book collector, you see, the true freedom of all books is somewhere on his shelves. (64)

The feeling that acquisition is capture, then, proves inseparable from the feeling (as irrational as any that arise when one begins to think about things in this way) that it is also liberation. Whether an affair of mastery or of freedom, however, this acquisition clearly exceeds the commercial, its foregrounded lack of concern with functionality evoking the Kantian aesthetic of disinterestedness upon which so many confrontations between the commodity and the work of art have been premised, an aesthetic to which Rilke alludes in the first part of the poem on the lace: "Through a rip in fate, a tiny hole, / you extracted from your time your soul; / and it inheres so in this lucid work, / that when I think of 'usefulness' I smile" (93).

What makes Benjamin's statement of feeling especially instructive is that it is both positioned within, and tensely posed against, a larger effort to read through objects to the truth of the social totality that produced them, the project of an archaeological sociology that effectively originates in his work and that of a few others such as Georg Simmel. This is not to say that the attempt to gain insight into some underlying order by way of discrete objects began only in the era of sociology, of course; on the contrary, it finds a precedent in centuries' worth of attempts to disclose the significance or structure of creation by mapping the allegorical meanings of natural phenomena, as Benjamin himself noted in likening the modern encounter with the explosively signifying commodity to the proliferation of arbitrary codes under Baroque emblematics (Buck-Morss 180–82). It is to point out, however, that the twentieth century can appear as the age of the object in the additional sense that it witnesses the birth and flowering of the social analysis of material culture, which is more than merely a matter of research techniques because it has become so thoroughly naturalized among intellectuals and non-intellectuals alike as a way of understanding the relation between present and past. Indeed if we were to suspend our mistrust of grand historical narratives long enough to entertain Foucault's sweeping claim (in *The Order of Things*) that the great epistemic rupture of modernity is to be found in the late eighteenth-century shift from cosmological taxonomies of objects to "the epistemological consciousness of man as such" and the birth of the "human" sciences (309), we might be inclined to say that one of the swerves (if not the break) of our own century is to be found in a new return to objects, now held to illuminate not only the order of the cosmos or distant antiquity but also the immediate human past (and even, in flashes, the dark chasms of the near human future).

One of the several problems attending this kind of speculation, of course, is that in undertaking it we replay the very drifting toward Gods and Goods, and away from beloved individual things, that Benjamin's more intimate reflections were supposed to counter. Yet this consequence is exactly to the point, once again, because it is the tension in Benjamin between cultural history (commodities are our emblems) and Proustian narration (the true freedom of the book is on his shelves) that speaks so acutely to the (or a) modernist vision of the predicament of the object, a vision of the modern age as one in which the particular, the concrete, and the auratic were threatened as never before by habits of generalization and abstraction serving a newly triumphant science. The reading of the discrete thing as representative or symptom of anything other than itself, that is, could become unsettling to the degree that it seemed to partake of the subordination of individuals (humans *and* objects) to system, a process that for the modernists as for their Romantic predecessors represented the essential direction of modernity at its most destructive. And indeed one encounters the tension between interpretation and resistance to interpretation at a pitch of extremity in Benjamin himself, that writer torn so excruciatingly, at times, between the urge to show how his beloved material fragments distill the essence of the world that made them and the wish to abjure any reconstruction in which those fragments might finally be eclipsed—which is to say, any reconstruction at all.

It is worth noting, in this respect, that one of the most rigorous stagings of the contest between auratic particular and quantifying system is to be found in the work of Theodor W. Adorno, not only Benjamin's sometime intellectual associate (Hannah Arendt called him the latter's "first and only disciple" [2]), but also the philosopher and cultural critic who figures for many as mandarin modernism's last great champion. If Benjamin's engagement with the object principally appears in statements of affectionate relation folded into larger projects of reading, for Adorno it materializes in an ongoing campaign against the reasoning subject's inevitable, and inevitably violent, move to reduce every thing in the world to a concept, a campaign in which the role of representative "thing" is frequently played by the individual physical object because the latter's rich phenomenality seems so manifestly diminished by conceptual compression. As an antidote to such reduction Adorno proposes a dialectic of nonidentity that would demand of consciousness an openness to the experience of the object conjoined with a constant vigilance for the deformations introduced by subjectivity, especially in its quantifying mode. In *Negative Dialectics* (1966), which we might fairly call one of the final fruits of philosophical modernism, for example, Adorno writes that to "yield to the object means to do justice to the object's qualitative moments. Scientific objectification, in line with the quantifying tendency of all science since Descartes, tends to eliminate qualities and to transform them into measurable definitions" (43).

This kind of statement offers an unusually pure articulation of a line of reasoning to be found everywhere in the criticism, manifestos, and disquisitions of the Anglo-American modernists, who are especially apt to turn to it when considering the role of art in society; in later chapters, we will see how heavily implicated in the defenses of art mounted by Lewis, Pound, and Williams is the assumption that the work preserves the imperiled particular. We might initiate our exploration, however, by turning to an American writer whose formulation of the problem is nearly as pure as Adorno's, the New Critic, "academic" poet, and quondam Southern Agrarian John Crowe Ransom, who in publishing a contribution from Adorno in *The Kenyon Re-*

view in 1945 described the latter's central interest in a way that would no less fairly capture his own most insistent preoccupations: "the unhappy human condition that has risen under the modern economy, and the question of whether religion and art can do anything about it" (683). Arguing that in regarding an object aesthetically the viewer strives for what "Schopenhauer praised as 'knowledge without desire'" (*World's* 45), and that in writing the poet struggles "to defend his object's existence against its enemies" (*World's* 348), Ransom centers his poetics on the premise that the difference between art and science is the difference between cherishing and devouring: in the scientific mode, he insists, one studies the object in order to see how one "may wring out of it [one's] physical satisfaction the next time," but in the aesthetic one tries to know the object "for its own sake, and conceive it as having its own existence" (*World's* 44–45).

The measure of Ransom's proximity to Adorno, and an indication of the auspices under which Continental philosophy comes together with Anglo-American poetry, fiction, and criticism in the twentieth century, can be taken from the similarity between the two writers' assessments of Hegel. In *Negative Dialectics*, Adorno observes that the "matters of true philosophical interest at this point in history" are "nonconceptuality, individuality, and particularity—things which ever since Plato used to be dismissed as transitory and insignificant, and which Hegel labeled 'lazy Existenz'" (8), before going on to charge that, "all his statements to the contrary notwithstanding, Hegel left the subject's primacy over the object unchallenged. It is disguised merely by the semi-theological word 'spirit' with its indelible memories of individual subjectivity" (38). For Ransom, meanwhile, Hegel figures as "a benign yet extremely aggressive spirit" who intended, by means of the universal, to make over "the objective world . . . even if only a little at a time," effecting a "reformation of nature" that substitutes "modern urban life for the old agrarian life" and finally excludes poetry "because no honor can be wasted on nature. Poetry has already had its day, says Hegel" (*Poems* 167–68).

As passages like these demonstrate, the object could hold a privileged place within certain readings of modernity in part because modernity could be construed as an affair of consciousness gone awry, a phenomenon of subjectivity grown rapacious and fantastically powerful either with the help of or under the sway of science and expansionist capitalism. Within such readings, that is to say, the object functions as the ultimate victim in a drama at once philosophical and thoroughly sociopolitical, something like the synecdoche of endangered nature—where nature would be more emphatically other to humanity than it ever quite was for the Romantics. Indeed if for Wordsworth the natural world figured as a realm that, however alien or resistant, might yet plausibly become the anchor of his purest thoughts and guardian of his heart and soul of all his moral being, for the moderns the object world seemed most compelling when it seemed most marked by impermeabililty to mind, most radically removed from a subjectivity hopelessly infected by *im*moral being and *im*pure thoughts. To read Woolf's depictions of the world without humans, or Lewis's defenses of the concept of the solid object, or Stevens's poems on discrete things, or (somewhat more problematically) Pound's discovery of the indifferent splendor of nature in the Pisan cantos, is to find the modernists crediting the object world not with some immunity to violence or disorder but rather with the profounder innocence of an immunity to thinking and knowing, the noble repose that comes of being out of reach of human persuasion, though not (and herein lay the trouble) out of reach of the human power to destroy. In a sense, then, what the object world represented for modernists above all was a realm beyond the reach of ideology but not secure against the material consequences of ideological conflicts.[1]

I invoke the loaded term "ideology" with a certain hesitation here, because my doing so might so easily be taken for a first step in another attempt to recuperate modernism's frequently discredited politics, or even to revive its bare interest for a literary scholarship that has found it irritatingly resistant to the kinds of analysis that have helped to bring fresh life to the literature of other periods. And yet it seems to me that in this context "ideology" is more adequate than "politics" or "morality," say, because it suggests precisely the point at which modernists (famously allergic to art in the service of propaganda, famously addicted to polemics about art) begin to lose patience with subjectivity itself, which is to say that moment when reflection, speculation, discourse, discussion become so relentlessly partisan as to invite dismissal as *mere* thought, *mere* words—the point at which one grows sick, as Orlando puts it in turning away from humans and back to her beloved woods, of "chatter and praise, and blame and meeting people who admired one and meeting people who did not admire one" (*Orlando* 325). This is certainly not to say that the modernists somehow rose above "ideology" in the Althusserian sense or even that they believed themselves able to transcend embedding in particular sociopolitical loci: Pound would never have thought so, obviously, and neither would Woolf. But it is to say that they turned to the object for relief from the peculiar species of fatigue that the word "ideology" inevitably if faintly connotes, and that the object world represented something like the last terrain of the utopian (or the prelapsarian) for them at times when consciousness itself seemed both the mark and the substance of exclusion from paradise.[2]

To consider modernism in this light is to discover it captivated by radical and threatened difference in a way long obscured by the scholarly tendency to treat the image of the object as victim as an epiphenomenon of some other, more basic, preoccupation, a tendency exhibited even by recent reappraisals of modernism writ large. In his moderately revisionist *Modernisms: A Literary Guide*, for example, Peter Nicholls argues that "*the* recurring problem of the later modernisms" might be identified as a "grounding of the aesthetic in an objectification of the other" (4) which allows the writer to assume an ironic superiority over that other at the cost of the direct "connection between poetic vision and social transformation" upon which Romanticism based many of its aspirations (10). Concerned throughout his book to address the efflorescence of work on modernism and gender of recent years, Nicholls finds the male modernist typically implying that this ironic mastery "is somehow forced upon him by the 'challenge' of the feminine or the natural" (3), and attributes to the line of Anglo-American modernism associated with Pound, Eliot, and Lewis a relentless "fear of 'possession' by an other (be it the past or Woman)" and a detestation of "decadent language . . . which has become somehow 'bodily', a condition which prevents 'objectivity' and which is quickly marked as feminine" (194–96).

Clearly, the foregoing considerations both support Nicholls's claim that the affirmation of subject-object distance is one of Anglo-American modernism's defining gestures and challenge his conclusion that this affirmation arises principally from a need to fortify an "ironically anti-social position" (3) or to defend the self from engulfment by the morass of the external. On the contrary, the preceding points suggest that the affirmation in question at least as characteristically originates with an attempt to ensure the *object's* extrasubjective integrity, to take the part of this radical other without, as it were, resubordinating it to consciousness. The distinction may seem fine enough from some perspectives; and yet a little reflection will show that it inevitably complicates our understanding not only of modernists' more abstract longings (the reposeful utopian of nonconsciousness) but also of their more concrete addresses to changes in art and society occurring around and through them. It requires us, for one thing, to take note of a separation between the challenges of the feminine and of the natural that Nicholls elides; for if modernism appears as essentially patriarchal under his reading (which in spite of his gestures toward pluralism presents women's writing of the period as not "another kind of modernism . . . but rather a deliberate and often polemic disturbance within the canonical vision" [197]), the line of thinking to which I call attention appears as foundationally ecological, difficult to recuperate for feminism and yet clearly removed from the gynophobic mistrust of otherness upon which Nicholls's analysis centers.[3] Further, it invites us to recognize that the formal characteristics most often associated with modernist art—hardness, coldness, impersonality, and so on—only sustain reading in terms of a fear of the feminine when the work of art is presumed to serve as an expressive representative of its (male or masculinized) maker, and that the meanings of these features shift dramatically when the work is regarded as the object in its own right that modernist polemics so often insisted it must be. Finally, this distinction forces us to observe that when modernists took up the object in responding to the (aging) triumph of capitalism, they were concerned not only with the *limitations* upon their abilities to initiate social change (Nicholls's argument), but also—and perhaps more critically—with the troubling *extensiveness* of human power, and with the likeness between their own operations on their materials and the apparently limitless transformations effected by technology.

For the painful truth (which Adorno, above all, recognized) is that it is very hard to think of the work of art as anything but a product of subjectivity's action on the object world. One of the oldest stories about modernism is that of its struggle against the mass-produced commodity on behalf of the handcrafted thing, which can certainly be read as an active effort on behalf of the kind of utopia already described: if to contemplate the object in its unviolated integrity is to catch a glimpse of a serenity beyond ideology and interest, then to produce objects that inspire this kind of revelation might be to bring the world closer to utopia not just as possibility but as reality. The problem, of course, is that as something inevitably marked by the mind of its maker (Eliot's and others' exhortations to impersonality notwithstanding), the work of art, even more than the commodity generated by market forces, must appear at last as a spot or stain of consciousness on the world beyond ideology, a subject-object hybrid (as in Hegel) that infiltrates and compromises the last preserve of radical alterity. This would prove an especially decisive problem for Anglo-American modernists, who, I will argue at length, not only placed extraordinary emphasis on the production of the individual object, but also vigorously embraced production qua production in responding to a wide range of philosophical and practical crises. And indeed if a single claim stands at the heart of this book, it is that Anglo-American modernism is centrally animated by a tension between an urgent validation of production and an admiration for an object world beyond the manipulations of consciousness—a tension that lends modernist writing its dominant note of vital hesitation or ironic idealism, and that leads modernists, as thinkers and artists, to that impasse in which all doing seems undoing, all making unmaking in the end.

I will return to the question of production's liabilities in a moment, but I want first to position this book more fully amid current methodological and historical debates by saying something about two of its fundamental claims: first, that the intertwined stories of the object and of production under modernism cannot be understood adequately apart from each other (though it has seemed to me best to unfold them separately for some stretches), and second, that any efforts to bridge the gap between philosophical readings of modernism and socioeconomic ones must take into account how this interdependence functioned in many modernists' imaginations. I am not quite tempted to say, "in *the* modernist imagination," because this kind of rhetoric has so often been deployed in less than careful appeals to zeitgeist as cause; and yet I do take as axiomatic that something like zeitgeist can legitimately be invoked where there is good evidence that the author under consideration would have had direct exposure to the assumptions, modes of thought, or values in question. My point here is not to wield biography or conscious intention against broader historiography or excavations of the political unconscious, but on the contrary to insist that ideology critique will be most powerful where it integrates conscious and unconscious factors, and that it is better served by the kind of analysis that takes into account the possible mechanisms by which ideas may have been transmitted than by the kind—powerfully operative in some New Historicist work—that maps one discourse onto another without positing any link between them except simultaneity. Indeed another way of situating this study would be to say that it attempts to offer an empirically careful response to Fredric Jameson's call, in *Postmodernism*, for a reintegration of psychology and the economic through a basic attention to "the psychological concomitants of production itself" (316).

That zeitgeist be understood as something like the mediated common denominator of a broad range of psychologies and *not* some free-floating existent is especially important in the case of modernist studies because some scholars have been tempted to read the early twentieth century as uniformly governed by the turn toward "consumption" that occurs in some of the economic theory of the period, as though the astounding range of cultural phenomena produced in these years finds its single source and terminus in a consumptionist frame of mind as pervasive as it was powerful. Against this kind of generalization, needless to say, the book that follows poses a variety of ways in which modernists were affected by certain images of production—above all, the image of the individual maker crafting the individual object. This scene's importance to modernism has long been recognized (see, for example, the title and opening pages of Hugh Kenner's 1975 survey of American modernism, *A Homemade World*), and yet because it does not permeate any readily delimitable area of early twentieth-century inquiry in the way that the scene of consumption permeates political economy and sociology, it may well be lost to scholarship that puts discourses into dialogue with each other without due attention to the channels through which writers absorbed specific facts and values. This is one reason why modernist texts seem to demand an approach that may look more phenomenological than archaeological; but the same demand may well apply in literary and cultural study generally, where a more adequate theorization of such mediation may be the key to badly needed negotiations between historical sweep and historiographical specificity, and between the causal inclinations of materialist reading and the difficult plenitude of cultural forms themselves.

To return, however, to the object world. It is in the retrospective illumination provided by the philosophical approaches to the object just discussed—instances of what might be called the ex post facto theorizing of modernism that went on from the 1930s to the early 1970s—that we can perhaps best begin to understand what happened to Anglo-American literature in the period mainly under consideration here, a period beginning in the 1910s and continuing through the 1950s, when Stevens wrote his last poems and Pound began his final fragments. Imaginative writing in English has always included representations of solid objects, of course, from ekphrastic and allegorical devices anchoring the morals of entire works to ephemeral details generating what Roland Barthes called *l'effet du réel*; but, as has already been suggested, the high modernists introduced into their writings a self-conscious contemplation of the object qua object hitherto only sporadically anticipated. There is very little in previous fiction in English, after all, that resembles Woolf's fascination with the eerily proximate distance of physical things or Joyce's obtrusive catalogues of urban detritus and household debris; nor was there a poet before Stevens who dwelt so insatiably on the scene of mind confronting thing, or one before Williams who so explicitly called for a poetry of the life of the object in all its immediacy. The encounter between Sigmund Freud, *Traumdeuter*, and H. D., *Imagiste*,[4] thus unquestionably figures one of modernism's defining passages, from an older tradition in which the object appears principally as a signifier of something else or a component of scenic plenitude to a newer order in which its value depends neither on metaphoricity nor on marginality.

One of my aims in this book, obviously, is to restore a sense of the significance of this passage, which has been obscured in part by the widely noted importance of object*ivity* to the transformations of poetry that followed from the Imagism of the early 1910s. If "any one term can be said to be a watchword of modernist (American) poetics," Joseph Riddel wrote in 1981, "it is 'objectivity'" ("Neo-Nietzschean" 192); and scholarship has since continued to refine our understanding of the term's significance. In *A Genealogy of Modernism* (1984), Michael Levenson showed how the "objectivity" for which Pound repeatedly called[5] was opposed less to "subjectivity" than to imprecision, how it meant in the Imagist vocabulary "merely a phase of the subjective—namely, that phase where the subject discreetly withdraws, leaving the immediate, uncorrected impression" (119). And more recently, in *Radio Corpse* (1995), Daniel Tiffany has denaturalized the connection between objectivity and precision itself, arguing that while "the discourse of objectivity depends upon the mortification of the subject, and the reduction—even disappearance—of the medium," it also finally includes "a resistance to the object itself" or a "restructuring of the object by nonocular visual practices" (14–16). "Pound's conception of the Image," Tiffany argues, finally "neglects the 'real' and even actively seeks to sever itself from the empirical object" (27), the Image finally implying "that poets do not merely turn a blind eye to what physically exists, but that they represent something invisible, something that lacks a sensible basis in the natural world" (32).[6]

This untangling of objectivity from empirical object clearly represents a salutary clarification, one especially welcome from the point of view of this study because it frees us to encounter freshly the ways in which the idea of the object did in fact operate in modernist theory and practice. Still, it would be unfortunate if the claim that the Image "actively seeks to sever itself from the empirical object" were taken to imply that the scandalous truth of modernism lay in some utter divorce from the object, some choice of the unreal by the very poets taken to be, in J. Hillis Miller's famous formulation, "poets of reality." Pound's seminal first prescription for Imagism, "Direct treatment of the 'thing,' whether subjective or objective" (*Literary* 3) simply leaves no doubt that the Image is at bottom presumptively mimetic (though, as Tiffany and others have stressed, Pound never imagined the operation of art as limited to a simple reproduction of the "thing" treated, and though it becomes difficult to be quite certain of what mimesis entails when the "thing" to be treated is a "subjective" entity such as an emotion). In practice, moreover, the inclusion of "objective" things became one of the hallmarks of Pound's kind of poetry, in part because it seemed extraordinarily difficult—even once one had made the poem formally less ruminative and more lapidary—to conform to the Imagist aesthetic of hardness without turning to images of hard objects, or to dwell on the "subjective" thing without falling prey to the "slither" and "muzziness" that Imagism despised.[7] Indeed by 1916, Pound could be found observing to Iris Barry that "there must be more, predominantly more, objects than statements and conclusions, which latter are purely optional, not essential, often superfluous and therefore bad" (*Letters* 90–91). In the end, the precisely rendered object went on to become a general fixture of the poetry that followed from the Imagist revolution, which is to say of virtually all the poetry in English most influential in the succeeding decades—the same decades that saw writers like Ransom and later Miller elaborating ethical defenses of the giving over of the poem to things. And thus the revolutionary impact of Imagism lay not only in its promotion of heightened precision, but also in the implied reversal of poetic value that made the "objective" thing, with or without symbolic import, not only worth including in poetry but poetry's very marrow.

No more free from entanglement with the solid object than Imagist "objectivity" were the Eliotic catchphrases "impersonality" and "objective correlative," which arguably constituted the other great shaping force on twentieth-century poetry in English, at least from Eliot's rise to preeminence in the 1920s to the rebellions of Robert Lowell, Allen Ginsberg, Charles Olson, and others in the 1950s. Like Pound, Eliot retains a place for subjectivity within a poetics that clearly favors the impermeability of the solid object; and like the Pound disclosed by Levenson in particular he presents subjective and objective as phases in poetry's formation, contending famously in the 1919 "Hamlet" that the "only way of expressing emotion in the form of art is by finding an 'objective correlative'; in other words, a set of objects, a situation, a chain of events which shall be the formula of that *particular* emotion" (*Prose* 48). In "Tradition and the Individual Talent" of the same year, he makes nearly the same point in the no less celebrated comment that the "progress of the artist is . . . a continual extinction of personality" (*Prose* 40), having already rendered the literary work objectlike by insisting that the great works of literature, as "existing monuments[,] form an ideal order among themselves, which is modified by the introduction of the new (the really new) work of art among them" (38–39). For Eliot as for the Imagists, then, the desideratum of object-like form converges with a preference for solid objects over abstractions as referents within the poem, though Eliot was led to this convergence not by a horror of slither but by the sense that thingness, which makes the work enduring and monumental (it outlasts its author) also makes it impersonal (it is not coextensive with its author's subjectivity)—which is to say that chez Eliot the need to extinguish personality in the making of art is undergirded by the very nature of the literary tradition.

One of the most important factors in this shadowing of Pound's and Eliot's transvaluations by the solid object, clearly, was the influence of T. E. Hulme, the éminence grise of the modernist revolution in poetry, whose seminal turn to the classical (which paralleled that of Eliot's more immediate mentor Irving Babbitt) materialized as a rejection of the turn toward intuition and fluidity in art inspired by Henri Bergson. As both Levenson and Alan Robinson have shown, Hulme's 1912–13 reaction against the philosopher whom he had hitherto closely embraced was predicated on nothing other than an epiphany anent the politics of form: the conclusion, to which he was helped by Pierre Lasserre and others, that Bergson's campaign against the logic of the solid might threaten the antisentimental political conservativism to which he was drawn. (Robinson even posits as one factor in Hulme's shift the House of Lords crisis of 1911, which helped to crystallize "the emergence of a new 'Classicism'" of Nietzschean cast in the pages of the periodical with which Hulme was most closely associated, the *New Age* [95].) As the careers of other modernists demonstrate, the privileging of the solid object could be absorbed by or made to align with diverse political positions—including Eliot's somewhat more moderate conservatism, Lewis's antileft, antiright, and anticentrist individualism, Pound's bizarre conflation of Confucianism and Fascism, and Williams's left localism—but in Hulme, politics and phenomenological preference drew close together early on; and it was Hulme who showed that attraction to the object could reach at last to an antihumanism that ached to dispense altogether with the object's other in philosophy and in art. In jottings from around 1907 he was already writing, "Dead things not men as the material of art. . . . And the words moved until they became a dome, a solid, separate world, a dome in the mist, a thing of terror beyond us, and not of us" (27), while in the "notebook" he published in the *New Age* in 1915–16 he elaborated upon his preference for an art that "springs not from a delight in life but from a feeling for certain absolute values, which are entirely independent of vital things" (426).[8]

The naming of Hulme and Bergson calls attention to the fact that what has been said of high modernist poets may sound highly questionable when applied to their prose fiction-writing counterparts, one of whose central interests was the recording of the very experience whose fluidity Bergson championed against the durable world, the life that Woolf described in a famous passage from "Modern Fiction" as "a luminous halo," not "a series of giglamps symmetrically arranged" (*Essays* 2: 106). If in taking Bergson mainly as a negative inspiration the poets were reacting against what they saw as a nineteenth-century weakness for ethereal abstractions, the novelists (as every student of modernism knows) were moving to get out from under the ponderous concretions of those writers Woolf named Edwardian, whose avalanches of furnishings threatened to crush the richness and freshness out of perception itself. And yet it would be a mistake, once again, to assume that an interest in the subject somehow precluded an interest in the object, since for fiction writers the fascination of "internal" life clearly embraced the mystery of its interchanges with the radically other or external. Taking their cues from Flaubert and James (whom Pound also invoked repeatedly in elaborating his objective aesthetic), the novelists sought not to banish the outside world but to register it with a heightened precision, as Stephen Dedalus suggests when in *Portrait* he reflects on Aquinas's *claritas*—reached, in his view, when one sees a thing as "that thing which it is and no other thing. The radiance of which he speaks is the scholastic *quidditas*, the *whatness* of a thing" (213).

Indeed the author whose concerns and emphases most set the parameters of this study is no poet as such but the prose-writing Woolf—and this for several reasons that I will come to in a moment. I want first, however, to note that in beginning with Woolf I proceed under the twofold premise that the earliest or even the most influential formulation of a question need not be its richest, and that a reading of modernism pivoting on Woolf can in some ways tell us more about Lewis, Pound, and Stevens—not to mention Joyce, Forster, Lawrence, Ford, Bowen, Hemingway, Stein, Yeats, Williams, H. D., Moore, Frost, Eliot, Crane, Auden, and so on—than readings centering on these others can tell us about her. It may also be well to note at this juncture that one of the rationales for following Woolf with Lewis, Pound, and Stevens is that, sequenced thus, the four authors form a chain that spans the Anglo-American high modernist field. Lewis was, after all, Woolf's most implacable critic and the loudest of Bloomsbury's detractors; Pound was Lewis's associate in his earliest, most celebrated, and arguably most influential polemical instigations; and Stevens has often played the role of Pound's principal rival for the title of defining poetic figure of the "era" in question here, the master of complex content who balances Pound the formal innovator, or the bastion of ideological neutrality who counters Pound's aggressive political engagement.[9] These writers cannot "represent" modernism in some parliamentary sense, of course, but in sharing direct links like the ones just listed—as well as common acquaintances, correspondents, patrons, and editors—they capture something of the dispersed intimacy of the family of Anglo-American modernists, and for this reason seem to me to provide a strong foundation for arguments that at least gesture toward a characterization (open, imperfect, and incomplete though it must be) of that family as a whole.

If Woolf's fictions bring out with peculiar clarity the stakes of the modernist encounter with the object, they do so in part because they include an especially naked exploration of what has come to be called existential crisis. All four of the writers considered here, but Woolf most visibly, show how the discrete object, as the particular representative or crystallization of nonhuman Being, could exert a powerful hold on the imagination at a time when questions about the meaning of existence seemed unusually pressing, a time when something like a baseline assumption of a secular point of view (among the educated) coexisted with lively memories of an age when religious piety was at least a putative norm. The Romantics, of course, had long ago confronted the question of "how (or whether) to infuse a world of fascinating but chaotic sense-data with transcendent meaning when one is deprived of agreed myths," as Edward Larrissy puts it in his insightful book on twentieth-century poetry, objects, and gender (3), and certainly the Romantic period has proven more attractive than any other for criticism strongly attuned to Continental philosophy in the wake of Existentialism.[10] But it was only with modernism that the possibility of the utter contingency of everything (and every thing) became a major preoccupation of imaginative writing, and it is surely time to reconsider the striking similarity between the questions asked by Anglo-American writers in the early twentieth century and those posed, roughly contemporaneously, by Continental philosophers of existence.

On the side of Goods, rather than Gods, Woolf is also of central importance, because she showed a fascination with the delightful and harrowing processes of consumption matched by no other major writer of the period save Joyce—a point noted lately by a number of scholars reconsidering the relations among modernism, spectacle, advertising, and commodification. As a celebrant of the velleities and perplexities of shopping, clearly, this redis-covered Woolf seems poised to trouble the traditional view that one of mod-ernism's defining features was a loathing of the mass-produced item and an installation of its other, the work of art, as privileged object: for if she em-braces commodity culture so warmly, we are forced to ask, does it make sense to retain the notion that the divide between high culture and mass culture became entrenched with her and her literary peers' alleged disdain for the popular? The answer is, once again, that it does, for although few if any modernists were immune to the pleasures of consumption, most also showed a profound mistrust of the capitalist formations that made what Adorno called a "culture industry" possible, and virtually all promoted the carefully crafted work of art as an alternative to the fruits of mass production and mass marketing. Although the 1913 prospectus for the Bloomsbury-driven Omega Workshops notes that its members "are willing to make use of" modern production "so far as it allows of the expression of their ideas," it insists also on the need to substitute "wherever possible the directly ex-pressive quality of the artist's handling for the deadness of mechanical re-production," and asserts that "[u]ntil the 19th century . . . men used for daily life objects which expressed the joy of the creator and the craftsman and conveyed a corresponding delight to the user," whereas "[m]odern industrial-ism has changed all this." And it is worth recalling too that the final sections of *Orlando* find its protagonist not only fascinated by the department store but also appalled by the commodification of literature.

In this ambivalence, the modernists showed themselves true heirs of the aesthetes of the previous century, who bequeathed them not only a belief in the unqualified importance of art and an aversion to (certain aspects of) Victorian morality but also a complex relation to the culture of the commod-ity in which horror and surrender were not only compounded but, at times, scarcely distinguishable from each other. One of my projects in what follows is to extend further recent scholarship's exploration of this inheritance, and indeed it will become apparent that in the field of literary history aestheti-cism is to this book what Existentialism is in the field of philosophy and, perhaps, what commodification in the field of history proper. Inheritance does not imply a simple reproduction of values in this case, however, and a central point of my argument will be that modernism defines itself in part by rejecting aestheticism's foundational claim that a life well lived can be ori-ented primarily toward consumption, where such an orientation could mean anything from devotion to the sheer experience of the fleeting present (Pater) to professions of self-realization through flamboyant acquisition (Wilde). As Michael Tratner and others have pointed out, the economic theories that modernists found most intriguing (those of Maynard Keynes and C. H.

Douglas, for example) advocated an increase in consumption as the remedy for economic ills, imperialism, and war; and it is very much to the point to suggest, as Tratner does, that modernism's declared liberation from Victorian constraints owed much both to political economy and to sexology, which lent new respectability to what Lawrence Birken names, in the title of his book on the subject, "consuming desire." It is essential to recall, however, that the early rumblings of this respectability coincided with aestheticism's moment rather than modernism's, and that the latter was confronted (far more decisively than was the former) by a variety of counterpressures tending to render consumption in a more abstract sense highly suspect.[11]

Some of these pressures were no less "external" to literary genealogy than Keynes's or Douglas's economic theories: for example, the new exposés of poverty that arrested British and American attention around the turn of the century, after which conspicuous consumption and even wealth in general were attended by a veritably new kind of public suspicion—as Leonard Woolf suggests in remarking that these years found the "capitalist system" and its "sacred rights of property . . . *no longer* compatible with liberty and equality" (127–28; emphasis added). Other pressures had much more specifically to do with literature and its social reception, as for example modernists' felt need to distance themselves from aestheticism's associations with homosexuality, effeminacy, neurasthenia, and degeneracy, a need exacerbated by some male writers' worries that writing had become a thoroughly female or feminized province. In combination, I will argue, such factors made it as difficult for moderns to accept the ethic of relaxation, pleasure, and consumption promoted by late Victorian and Edwardian reformers as it was for them to stomach the work ethic of their mid-Victorian grandparents—indeed made it difficult for them to embrace happily any nineteenth-century attitude toward labor save (intermittently) the promotion of the handcrafted associated with Ruskin and Morris.

In spite of some significant modernist encounters with the theoretical promotion of consumption, then, it is fair to say that modernism shows a reaction against consumption as personal project no less decisive for it than its retention of aestheticism's privileging of the life devoted to art, a reaction that crystallizes in part as a vexed, tentative, and in varying degrees metaphorical turn to production (which appears as consumption's radical other in spite of the interdependence of the two in practice). As we will see, this turn becomes especially visible at moments when modernists reverse aestheticism's tropes so as to emphasize making instead of absorbing, recording instead of experiencing, the enduring instead of the ephemeral, and the solid instead of the fluid; and it is by way of highlighting this shift's central importance that I have drawn the last four words of my subtitle from one of Wilde's most striking formulations of decadent values: his remark, in an essay on Thomas Griffiths Wainewright, that it "is only the Philistine who seeks to estimate a personality by the vulgar test of production. This young dandy sought to be somebody, rather than to do something" (*Intentions* 73–74). For many modernists, by contrast, the test of production—and especially of artistic production—implicitly figured as the test of an individual life's meaning in a world that seemed to furnish subjectivity no other secure source of significance.

This last point, of course, suggests one way in which Goods at last reunite with Gods under modernism, and in which socioeconomic assumptions come together with philosophical anxieties. For the two questions of the existential dilemma—that of how meaning can inhere in Being, and that of how human lives can be lived meaningfully—both seem to find a possible resolution in production, inasmuch as the subject appears to do something meaningful in leaving a material trace on the object world, while the object world appears to accede to meaning through the work of the subject upon it. Neither of these (arguably antithetical) possibilities comes fresh to modernism, of course; in a less rarefied form, they emerge from the literally immemorial habit of valuing material human accomplishment, while in this more abstract incarnation, they arise from a line of philosophy originating, at the latest, with Hegel's disquisition on self-objectification in labor in the "Lordship and Bondage" section of the *Phenomenology of Spirit*. Such a line would then proceed through the early Marx, who in critiquing Hegel in the *1844 Manuscripts* writes that the human being "can only *express* his life in real, sensuous objects" (181), find an American channel of sorts in the pragmatism of William James, and perhaps terminate with Sartre, who devotes an extensive section of *Being and Nothingness* to the psychology of making as an attempt at freedom.[12] And indeed the links between this line and the four writers considered here are readily discernible: Woolf and Lewis were both familiar with, and largely sympathetic to, G. E. Moore's anti-idealism, which was directed against tendencies in British philosophy impossible to imagine without the importation of Hegel into British universities in the mid-nineteenth century;[13] all four writers experienced a transformation of Marx from philosophical specter to vigorous political engine between the 1910s and the 1930s (Lewis, Pound, and Stevens all addressing Marxism in one or both of these aspects quite directly); Stevens, along with several other major modern poets, was a student at James's Harvard, as Frank Lentricchia has recently reminded us;[14] and as I will suggest in the first chapter, Woolf exercised a small but significant influence on Sartre.

Even Bergson enunciated a version of the production imperative, albeit in a formulation more descriptive than prescriptive, in *Matter and Memory*, where his central premise is that the human organism (except, crucially, where memory intervenes) functions as something like a stimulus-response channel in which entering stimuli exit in the form of material action. Bergson condenses this premise in the essential opening lines of his later *Cre-*

ative Evolution, wherein he observes that "the human intellect feels at home among inanimate objects, more especially among solids, where our action finds its fulcrum and our industry its tools"; but in the pages that follow he goes on to expand his earlier reflections on memory into the more radical claim that this logic of solids "is incapable of presenting the true nature of life" in all its fluidity (ix). It is thus that *Creative Evolution* richly supports the evanescent aesthetic of the Nineties, thus that Hulme eventually rejects a Bergson whose philosophy seems so difficult to reconcile with his own preference for the solid and the hard, and thus that Bergson becomes less a positive than a negative philosophical source for the poetic side of the Anglo-American modernist revolution.

In fact, however, modernists on both sides of the generic divide echoed Bergson in finding the imperative of production as profoundly suspect as seductive, though for reasons having less to do with the truth of life than with the devastation wrought by a humanity growing ever more adept at transforming the material world. I have already pointed to the mistrust of Hegel grounding Ransom's defense of the object, and I have at least hinted at how a similar (if not explicitly anti-Hegelian) position can be found in the poetics that begins with Pound, H. D., and Williams—a position emblematized by Williams's famous prescription "no ideas but in things" (*Paterson* 6) and followed attentively by the Miller of *Poets of Reality*, who finds Williams the most modern of modernists, and the call to efface "the ego before reality" and abandon "the will to power over things" (Miller's phrasing) twentieth-century poetry's most characteristic and revolutionary exhortation (8). But a similar concern is also eminently detectable in Woolf's last novels, wherein observations of nature's destructive power give way to anxiety about human violence against the object world; in Lewis's polemics from the late 1920s on, which argue that the disastrous results of Western science are deeply enmeshed with subjectivity's inconsistent attempts both to maintain and to negate the distance between itself and the object; and in Pound's efforts to redeem accumulations of literary and material clutter so overwhelming as to call into question the legitimacy of any further addition to their vastness. Among the authors considered here, only Stevens remains largely unconcerned with the violence and danger of production; but, as I will indicate in my final chapter, his suggestive manner of skirting the question makes him, if not quite the exception that proves the rule, still a highly unusual case who tells us a great deal, in the end, about one of modernism's fundamental anxieties.

Thus it is that Wilde's phrase, with its ambiguous genitive, points to the major argument of this book, which is that if modernists often began by embracing production as a test of meaning, they frequently ended by testing production itself and finding it wanting—finding it, indeed, at least as likely to generate new anxieties as to assist in resolving old ones. It is in this, I would argue, that their work resonates most significantly not only with the Continental philosophers and social critics already mentioned, but also with others whose positions on most questions were dramatically opposed to those of the Frankfurt School. Martin Heidegger is one writer who comes to mind in this context, since in spite of his many differences with Adorno he shared with the latter a sense that the object must be defended against the instrumentalizing tendency of the modern mind and, broadly speaking, the technology that supports a relentlessly expanding industrial production. And another is Jean Baudrillard, who in the early 1970s drew on the anthropology of Marcel Mauss and Georges Bataille to deliver the most radical of critiques of production, though he called for the replacement of production qua investment with a festive and wasteful consumption at odds with Adorno's and Heidegger's more ascetic ecologies. What makes Baudrillard's treatment especially revealing, in this instance, is that it clearly grows out of an earlier work, *The System of Objects* (1968), in which he mounts an attack on the systems and codes (collecting, advertising, marketing, design) that in his view deprive the individual object of its original auratic force—his work appearing in this respect, as in so many others, to represent the final movement of decisively modernist thinking.

This last point, surely, requires me to say something about how this study is positioned with respect to postmodernism, to address the fact that it halts at the frontier of the very period (or style) arguably defined by technological expansion pushed to the very limit of the global. Here I would invoke the critic whom such language inevitably calls to mind, Fredric Jameson, and his observation that the modern-to-postmodern transition can be described as one in which "modernization triumphs and wipes the old completely out: nature is abolished along with the traditional countryside and traditional agriculture; even the surviving historical monuments, now all cleaned up, become glittering simulacra of the past, and not its survival" (*Postmodernism* 311). For Jameson, "the keen sense of the New in the modern period was only possible because of the mixed, uneven, transitional nature of that period, in which the old coexisted with what was then coming into being" (311), whereas "[p]ostmodernism is what you have when the modernization process is complete and nature is gone for good" (ix). This is to say that in Jameson's view the opposition "modern versus postmodern" describes meaningful changes in the concrete conditions of existence, among them a removal from contact with modes of life in which a relatively continuous bodily interaction with a nonrepresentational reality would be the norm; and this means in turn that if we accept Jameson's narrative, we have already come some way toward understanding why it should be that modernism was so much more heavily invested in the pathos of the subject-object relation than its postmodern successor.

Even if we were to take issue with Jameson's generalizations, however, we would still have to admit that the alterations in daily life that he describes could well be implicated in other changes in outlook commonly recognized as postmodern, changes that would include a diminution of anxiety about severings of simulacrum from real, of contemporary from originary, of transient from eternal, and of constructed from organic, along with a new tendency to privilege the formerly devalued term in each of these pairs. The couple of subject and object would not itself fit such a paradigm, since a resignation to their division has been part of intellectual life for at least two hundred years (in spite of many attempts to mitigate it), and since, as has already been indicated, one of modernism's major efforts was to preserve the object's integrity and difference. Postmodernism's close association with the other severings just named, however, does point to its tendency—adumbrated somewhat oddly, but memorably, in Lyotard's remark that the postmodern rejects collective sharing of any "nostalgia for the unattainable" (81)—to be more interested in satisfaction than in desire, or rather to replace the reach for the ungraspable with the play of the immediate. And this choice is keenly relevant to the questions at hand because for *both* modernism and postmodernism the solid object seems, as a matter of knowledge and representation, to fall on the "ungraspable" side of this divide. If the postmodern consciousness tends not to show the anxious affection for the object shown by the modernist, in other words, the reason may lie not only in its more extreme removal from the physical, but also in a difference in its basic philosophical inclinations, which run toward the epistemologically proximate (discourse, say, or information) rather than the radically unknowable and inhuman (as for example Being).

These immense generalizations having been laid out, we might pause to remember that the position of a self-conscious postmodernism is not to be confused with the quotidian conditions of the "postmodern" era, which are notoriously different across nations, classes, and cultures, and that even within the restricted realm of Anglo-American letters the foregoing generalizations are based on the theory and polemic of an avant-garde, or rather self-styled cutting edge, dominated (though certainly not fully constituted) by white men. And if the term "postmodernism" is bedeviled by the conflation of a dominant paradigm with the totality of a period, how much more so is "modernism," which in spite of numerous revisionist histories continues to mean both a period of anywhere from three to six decades in the history of the arts and a very specific body of texts showing certain common preoccupations, impulses, or qualities. The consequence of this double duty of the term, of course, has been to suggest that writing outside this body is somehow not "of" its time, or is behind the times, and thus to legitimate a restricted canon not through an appeal to aesthetic value but through an implicit and highly questionable pronouncement on texts' mode of being. In the book that follows, I use "modernism" or "high modernism"[15] mainly to refer to a body of texts with somewhat fluid boundaries that would usually include writers like Woolf, Joyce, Stein, and perhaps Toomer, while more often excluding writers like Sandburg, Corelli, McKay, and perhaps Toomer; and though I have not always succeeded in keeping this sense of "modernism" as sharply distinct from the other as we might desire, I have tried to stick to terms such as "early twentieth-century" where generalizations about the whole period in imaginative writing are at issue.

These points in turn lead me to note that while this book occasionally suggests how matters of race, gender, and sexuality impinge on the story of the object and production in modernism, it leaves a great many problems in this area unresolved and a great many avenues of inquiry utterly unexplored. One might, of course, object that in omitting these explorations I imply that they are less than essential to the story in question, but this is certainly not my intention; on the contrary, my hope is that this study will provide a meaningful resource for further research along these lines, especially work addressing the pressing question of how the often abstract embrace of difference discussed here could accompany the concrete hostility to other races, genders, and sexualities that has made so much modernist writing seem so hard to write about and so nearly impossible to teach adequately. In this regard, I envision this book as contributing to the project effectively undertaken by scholars such as Robert Casillo, who has charted the figurations of liquid and solid in Pound's anti-Semitism; Marianne DeKoven, who has written on modernism's phenomenology of the fluid and feminine power; James Longenbach, who along with Larrissy, Lentricchia, Nicholls, and others has explored male modernists' identifications of masculinity with empirical precision; and Vincent Sherry, who has traced the associations between antidemocratic politics and an aesthetic of visual distance.

If I have been attracted to questions of class more than to questions of race or gender in what follows—though this book certainly lays no claim to anything like a reading of modernism in terms of class structure or the contradictions of late capitalism—this is so in part simply because class has received less attention than these other factors in the literary criticism, theory, and history of the past several decades. In other respects also the contours of this project have been determined by an urge to avoid, where possible, territories heavily mapped by previous scholarship; and though I hope that this disposition will make what follows fresher and more provocative, I do recognize that it generates certain difficulties of its own as well. It will become apparent, especially, that while the oeuvre of each of the authors considered is treated to a wide-ranging examination, there are in every case some unusual emphases and surprising reticences, important works hardly discussed and marginal texts oddly foregrounded. I can only reiterate, by way of clarification, that the following claims to be not a defining study of modernism, the object, and production (as though any book could be), but rather an attempt to bring together some key moments in modernism's intellectual and affective life, showing broadly and synthetically—but not comprehensively—how certain evidently theoretical problems were connected for modernists to practical confrontations with commodity culture, nature, work, art, suffering, loss, war, technology, love, fulfillment, exhilaration, language, and literature.

Having finished all this prefacing, I find myself facing the question of what, after all, has become of the object in its particularity, to whose defense so much modernist attention was devoted, but which seems on the verge of being submerged, here, beneath an enormous discourse about everything else. Far from the catalogue raisonné of objects in Woolf, Lewis, Pound, and Stevens that I had perhaps once imagined it would be—let alone a retrieval of the stories of these writers' own cherished possessions or habitats—this book moves from individual things to larger issues with an alacrity that I still find somewhat disconcerting, and that the reader out to plunge deep into the materiality of modernism may find much more so. It should be clear by now that in this, *Solid Objects* is both faithful and untrue to the literature that it proposes to examine: faithful, because appearances of individual objects in that literature do adumbrate ideas about the object in general that enrich our sense of the intellectual force of modernist writers; untrue, because the most central of these ideas is that the survival of art, and indeed of society itself, depends upon a reproof to abstraction and a return to the particular. Perhaps the most compelling reason to begin with Freud's note, if also the most perverse, is that the very lavishness of its invitations to interpretation calls attention to the extraordinary difficulty of abandoning the will to power over things, at least insofar as interpretation proves a mode of the exercise of that will (the predicament, once again, of Benjamin). In the end, we may feel chastened by the recognition that like other kinds of love, the love of the object as object—as other, as ungraspable difference—is tampered with as soon as spoken or written about; and yet we must recognize too that this kind of tampering is essential to any imaginable critical production.

Chapter One

VIRGINIA WOOLF

THE TEST OF PRODUCTION

The 22 OCTOBER 1920 ISSUE of the *Athenaeum* carried a short story by Virginia Woolf entitled "Solid Objects," in which a man named John finds a piece of glass buried in the sand at the beach, grows more and more captivated by discarded things, and finally gives up a promising career in politics to devote all his time to the search for alluring fragments of china, odd pieces of scrap iron, and similar treasures. Like many of Woolf's very short stories, "Solid Objects" seems at once intimate and allegorical; like many, its curiously affectless yet earnest mood gives it the feeling of an argument somehow premised on the metamorphosis of vague desire into singular pathology. In this case, however, the pathology in question has something like a tradition behind it, since as a doomed devotee of beauty who forsakes the world's proffered vulgarities in favor of the obscurely fine, John can trace an authentic descent from the Byronic wanderer and the Baudelairean flaneur, from the Huysmanian decadent and the *poète maudit*; and though he may not accede to the glory of one of Shelley's unacknowledged legislators of the world, his choice of the *res* proper over the *res publica* does lend him the distinction of having sacrificed to his profounder calling the chance to become an acknowledged legislator of England. Indeed the narrator takes pains to present John's collecting as a vocation in the richest sense of that term, noting (with something less than Woolf's usual subtlety) that, after years of collecting, John's "career—that is his political career—was a thing of the past" (*Shorter Fiction* 106).

To be sure, the narrator refrains from endorsing John's line of conduct explicitly, so that it is possible to find in the story, as one critic does, an exposition of "the danger of allowing the aesthetic vision completely to overcome the practical vision" (Broughton 54–55). Yet if the aesthetic holds many pains here, Woolf takes care to show that the practical holds few pleasures, in part by providing a foil to her hero in the stodgy and eminently pragmatic Charles, whose exit from the scene closes her tale. In those last moments, Charles looks around John's place

> to find some relief for his horrible depression, but the disorderly appearance of the room depressed him still further. What was that stick, and the old carpet bag hanging against the wall? And then those stones? . . .

"Pretty stones," he said as cheerfully as he could; and saying that he had an appointment to keep, he left John—for ever. (107)

Like a character in a Victorian novel, or rather a reader working with nineteenth-century narrative and decorative codes, Charles tries to determine how John's interior expresses its inhabitant's character; but in this unusual case the room's distinctive elements speak not of an ability to purchase expressive objects but of a profound possession *by* things, where this possession itself might figure as a demystification of Victorian fantasies of self-fashioning through acquisition. The point of these objects is not what they do or say, but their sheer capacity to be appreciated within a setting that conjoins a certain freedom in manner of living to an intense aesthetic devotion—which is to say, amid the kind of domestic informality that was for Woolf the very emblem of passage from constraint, middle-class correctness, and the nineteenth century to freedom, moderate bohemianism, and modernity.

Writing years later of her and her sister's relationship with their father, Leslie Stephen, Woolf remarked in "A Sketch of the Past" that "[t]wo different ages confronted each other in the drawing room at Hyde Park Gate: the Victorian Age; and the Edwardian age. We were not his children but his grandchildren" (*Moments* 126); in a memoir written at about the same time as "Solid Objects," she recalled that at the time of their departure from Kensington (following their father's death), she and her siblings decided that "[e]verything," meaning every social custom, "was on trial" (*Moments* 163). Without question, Charles of "Solid Objects" comes as near as any of Woolf's characters to incarnating the dreary Kensington of her childhood, while John, with his choices of the personally gratifying over the prescribed and of "art" over politics, distills and exaggerates as surprisingly few of Woolf's protagonists some of the essential values of the original Bloomsbury group, of which the Stephen children formed the core. The members of that small coterie hardly removed themselves from politics, of course, but in Woolf's view, at least, they did try to live in consonance with the fundamental tenet (formulated by their absent guru G. E. Moore) that "the most valuable things, which we know or can imagine, are certain states of consciousness, which may be roughly described as the pleasures of human intercourse and the enjoyment of beautiful objects" (*Principia* 188).

The intellectual authority with which Forster, Strachey, Keynes, Fry, Woolf herself, and the peripheral figure of Eliot were eventually invested sometimes obscures the fact that the original Bloomsbury revolution (the move from Kensington) was a rebellion of children against (deceased) parent and, more broadly, of youth against age: "When we both felt that he was not only terrifying but also ridiculous," the passage from "A Sketch" continues, "we were looking at him with eyes that saw ahead of us something . . . so easily seen now by every boy and girl of sixteen and eighteen that the sight is perfectly familiar" (*Moments* 126). This aspect of Bloomsbury did not elude its nemesis Wyndham Lewis, who identified the group as part of the cult of youth that he detested, however, nor is the impulse of the revolutionary child hard to discern in "Solid Objects," wherein the protagonist rejects adult responsibility in order to embrace the magic of the small. While John's fingers burrow into the sand on their way to the fatal lump of glass, "the background of thought and experience which gives an inscrutable depth to the eyes of grown people disappeared, leaving only the clear transparent surface, expressing nothing but wonder, which the eyes of young children display" (103). And when he pockets his treasure, Woolf's narrator observes (in a manner highly evocative of Benjamin's portrait of the book collector) that he may have done so under

> the impulse which leads a child to pick up one pebble on a path strewn with them, promising it a life of warmth and security upon the nursery mantelpiece, delighting in the sense of power and benignity which such an action confers, and believing that the heart of the stone leaps with joy when it sees itself chosen from a million like it, to enjoy this bliss instead of a life of cold and wet upon the high road. "It might so easily have been any other of the millions of stones, but it was I, I, I!" (103–4)[1]

Later, Charles lifts "the stones on the mantelpiece a dozen times and put[s] them down emphatically to mark what he was saying about the conduct of the Government, without once noticing their existence" (106), whereas the child-hero has trouble attending to this discourse because the stones lead him to a secret knowledge such as only children have: he "never talked to anyone about his serious ambitions"—that is, his collecting—because others' "lack of understanding was apparent in their behaviour" (106).

In its address to collecting, above all, "Solid Objects" might be read as a projection of the Victorian childhood onto a modern adulthood, a discreet subversion that takes the nineteenth century at its word (to children) while deploying that word against it. A standard piece of Victorian advice on child-rearing was to make one's child a collector, as for example in *The Complete Home* (1879), where Julia McNair Wright told parents to "encourage Tom to make a museum . . . of his wonderful curiosities; if you talk with him about them, you may make a philosopher of him" (quoted in Briggs 253), or in a little book of 1890 in which C. A. Montresor advised the child reader that "[e]very house ought to possess a 'Museum,' even if it is only one shelf in a small cupboard" (192). It may seem strange that such suggestions could be taken seriously over a quarter of a century after Dickens had mocked the young Gradgrinds' conchological, metallurgical, and mineralogical cabinets ("Go and be somethingological directly," commands Gradgrind mère in a moment of usual impatience [61]), but the idea of the home collection in fact followed from calls for an education based less on Gradgrindian rules than on the visual and tactile examination of natural particulars. "The truths of number, of form, of relationship in position," Herbert Spencer wrote in his 1860 *Education*, "were all originally drawn from objects; and to present these truths to the child in the concrete is to let him learn them as the race learnt them" (100–101). In her biography of Roger Fry, Woolf observes with the hint of an approving smile that Fry's was "a highly scientific family, of a mineral or of a vegetable nature. He went up to bed not with a toy, but with a crystal that his grandmother gave him. 'In return for the Epipactis,' his cousin R. M. Fry writes, 'would you like a specimen of the *Oxalis corniculata*?'" (26).

Leslie Stephen, apparently content to follow the wisdom of his time in this respect, encouraged his children "to botanise as they walked" (Q. Bell 1: 33), but as it turned out Virginia and her siblings developed a passion for insect collecting instead. "Greatly to our relief," she recalled, "instead of scolding and forbidding, mother and, I think, father recognised our mania; and put it on a legal basis; bought us nets and setting boards" (*Moments* 104). The difference between the systematizing Victorian paternal imperative (which acknowledges the respectability of collecting, even as an adult occupation, where it bids to enlarge knowledge) and the "mania" of the younger generation reappears more portentously in "Solid Objects," where what might have been a reasonably healthy interest for a member of that leisure subclass known as middle-class children becomes psychotic in a grown man, a venture into idleness instead of a way of using up idle hours, an end in itself instead of a means of instruction. The transposition of ends and means is figured concretely in the contrast between John's habit of placing his finest discoveries "upon his mantelpiece, where, however, their duty was more and more of an ornamental nature, since papers needing a weight to keep them down became scarcer and scarcer" (105) and Charles's way of using these items to illustrate his points, a contrast presaged earlier in the tale when the two men look at the lump of glass together on the beach. Charles, who has been "skimming flat pieces of slate over the water" (102), sees immediately that the glass is "not flat, and filling his pipe" recommences his discourse "with the energy that dismisses a foolish strain of thought" (103). But in John's realm contemplation displaces action; sheer existence takes precedence over signification; collecting usurps politics; and the ornamental or aesthetic supplants the instrumental.

It is in this transformation of means into ends that John most clearly marks himself an inheritor of those rebellions in which the aesthetes and decadents pitted a doctrine of beauty as terminal value against the renowned Victorian tendency to stress art's powers of moral instruction, and in which loomed large that profoundly secularizing transvaluation according to which "not the fruit of experience, but experience itself, is the end"—in the inadvertently momentous words that made Walter Pater's *Renaissance* a "Bible" for Oscar Wilde (236). In his rapture before found objects, John adheres to Pater's call for discerning perception ("A counted number of pulses only is given to us of a variegated, dramatic life. How may we see in them all that is to be seen in them by the finest senses?" [*Writings* 60]) with a literalness that Pater himself would have found perverse, though the strenuous purity of his devotion would have been much to Pater's taste. Many self-proclaimed followers of Pater, meanwhile, would have applauded John's eccentric trans-valuation of a childhood hobby *because* so perverse and in this sense extrav-agant rather than ascetic; for if Pater's particular vision ran contrary to the assumption that fineness depends on rarity or exoticism, the decadents, whose more congenial genius was Baudelaire, located the substantive virtue of ever more sensitive discrimination in its ability to allay boredom—an ability that tended to give out unless new things were continuously brought before the senses, often at great cost (as in J.-K. Huysmans's *A rebours*). It was thus that the imperative of experiencing finely irresistably shaded into the imperative of acquiring expensively; and it was thus that the anti-bourgeois posture of the decadents would have been resubordinated to the logic of capitalism, with its constant generation of ever new consumer de-sires, even had it not been for the ease (explored by Jonathan Freedman in his revelatory *Professions of Taste*) with which the aesthete-connoisseur's skill itself could be magnificently marketed.

In his devotion to discriminating acquisition, John of "Solid Objects" un-questionably evokes this kind of connoisseur as well as the tormented artist, but because he collects objects with no cachet, his career represents a certain bohemianizing of the already bohemian, indeed a form of collecting that might plausibly elude even commodification's extensive grasp. When Wilde, clearly nodding to the mania for old porcelain that symbolized aesthete hy-per-refinement in the public mind (O'Hara 430), remarked, "I find it harder and harder every day to live up to my blue china" (Ellmann, *Wilde* 45), he may have achieved a certain ironic distance from his own self-fashioning; but such irony can be resisted in turn by a strong claim to take seriously the idea of a moral imperative in things, as in Woolf's note that John's political career suffers its first reversal upon his encounter with "a piece of china of the most remarkable shape" whose "colouring was mainly blue."[2] If Wilde's remark testifies to a recognition that tasteful purchasing could be deployed in the marketing of personality, Woolf's image explodes Wilde's possession more than physically, countering this commodification of the aesthetic with an appeal to the more securely aesthetic realm of discarded things with no exchange value. Woolf even encodes this out-aestheticizing of aestheticism within the story by noting that although the china fragment is mainly blue, "green stripes or spots of some kind overlaid the blue, and lines of crimson gave it a richness and lustre of the most attractive kind" (104), a description beside which Wilde's characterization of his china as merely "blue" takes on the faintest tinge of the philistine.

Woolf's play with the connoisseurship of the expensive in "Solid Objects" is not best understood as a simple move to go aestheticism one better, however, nor is it rightly circumscribed as a case of Bloomsbury's radical chic (or radical dowdiness) taking on Kensington's *haut bourgeois* sobriety. Rather, or in addition, it partakes of a substantive change in values, very roughly coinciding with the turn of the century itself, whose repercussions reverberate through the literature of high modernism—a transformation of basic assumptions under which the relationship between art and wealth, once taken for granted, becomes the object of a fascinated mistrust, and under which leisure-class consumption in general becomes guilty and suspect as it has never been before.

Certainly, the first years of the century were marked by an unprecedented lavishness in leisure-class consumption—"wealth had become virtue," according to A.J.P. Taylor, "and wealth was more rated than anything else by the Edwardians" (2)—but they also saw a significant intensification of public anxiety about the massive gap between rich and poor in England. Although the state of the neediest had been the subject of a number of well known studies since the early 1880s, it first came to be seen widely as a metonymy of the state of the nation as a whole after the shock to English complacency of the Boer War, when the "condition of England" question revived in the wake of revelations that the country's unexpected difficulties were attributable in part to the poor health of its soldiers. A 1902 article claiming that sixty percent of Englishmen were unfit for duty was succeeded by a number of other reports culminating in the 1904 findings of the government's Inter-Departmental Committee on Physical Degeneration, which charged that the English poor were in worse physical condition than ever before, and in succeeding years a literature of outrage blossomed. The most celebrated work in this line, perhaps, was C.F.G. Masterman's 1909 *Condition of England*, in which the well known liberal M.P. "found the plutocrats idle and vulgar, the middle-class suburbanites vacuous, and the workers miserable" (the summary belongs to Samuel Hynes [67]), just as in the 1901 *Heart of the Empire* he had deplored "the listlessness and lassitude so manifest in the people of our crowded streets" and "the anaemia of town life so strikingly prevalent in our city children," while noting how the rich,

> separated from many of the realities of life, . . . are unable to find natural ways of expending their money, and, in consequence, are driven to indulge in sumptuous living or vulgar display. Thousands of pounds representing the toils of years in the cultivation of choice flowers or rare wines are dissipated for the gratification of a

few guests at an evening party. Nor do the owners of this wealth really profit by
their indulgence. . . . [T]heir lives are spent without knowledge of the highest
forms of happiness, with disastrous loss of energy and opportunity—a loss that
falls on all. ("Realities" 23–24; Preface vi; also partly quoted in Hynes 60)

Masterman's references to choice flowers, rare wines, and unnaturalness
clearly evoke the obsessive consumption found in works like *A rebours* and
its British offspring *Dorian Gray*, the transit of such descriptions from exu-
berantly impossible fictions to soi-disant sober social critique figuring, if not
exactly illustrating, how the scandal of elaborate consumption could seem
far more serious when the decay of the nation, not merely a few of its
neurasthenic privileged, appeared to be at hand.[3] If the birth of a decadent
literature in France coincided roughly with the post-1870 sense that the
French nation might already be in decline, self-conscious decadence in England (which was shaped by attitudes imported from across the Channel)
flourished well before the onset of serious indications that Britannia's greatness might be tottering; but it was in the Edwardian era that "decadence"
began to be used routinely in connection with the condition of the whole
country, which in the words of a 1906 commentator exhibited all the "features of a decaying civilization" shown by late Rome, and which according
to another in 1909 had been brought to this pass by a "love of luxury"
(quoted in Porter 133). A 1905 pamphlet called *The Decline and Fall of the
British Empire* listed "The Growth of Refinement and Luxury" as the third
of eight causes of England's decline (Mills 12–14), while naming as the
fourth "The Decline of Literary and Dramatic Taste," with specific reference
to the unhealthy decadent-consumer-addict: "Novels dealing with the mor-
phia or cigarette victim," observed the pamphlet's author, "were more
widely read than the works of Bunyan or Sir Walter Scott" (16), those venerable guardians of moral improvement through fiction.

Certainly, the critique of luxury had been a staple of British imaginative
literature and social discourse for two hundred years,[4] but in some respects
the dividing line of the new century accurately separates earlier forms of
anxiety about consumption from the kind that surfaced with every turn of
British fortunes from the Boer War through World War II. The golden years
of the Edwardian leisured were never as untroubled by guilt as later decades
liked to imagine, once again, and upper-class pangs of conscience only grew
more insistent in the years that followed; the discovery that millions of men
were too unhealthy to be soldiers was repeated in 1917, when another military service survey found "10 per cent of young men totally unfit for service,
41.5 per cent (in London 48–9 per cent) with 'marked disabilities', 22 per
cent with 'partial disabilities' and only a little more than a third in satisfactory shape" (Hobsbawm 165); and the Great War itself made lavish consumption almost more an impossibility than a moral dilemma for those at the

top of the material hierarchy. Even the later return to consumption on a grand scale enjoyed by some of the privileged could not be conducted entirely apart from the knowledge that the very brief postwar economic revival was fizzling, that a ferocious crossfire of blame for this failure was defining British politics, and that a newly intense sense of "labor" as the foundation of economic life was being recorded in the rise of the political party bearing that name.[5] It thus comes as no surprise to find Robert Graves testifying, in his 1940 history *The Long Week-End*, to a general postwar consciousness that even Society now had to earn its money (65–66).

For Bloomsbury, of course, there were reasons more immediate than its association with conspicuous consumption to remain shy of the decadence, among them the latter's ambiguous but never dismissable affiliation with homosexuality. As Perry Meisel notes in his study of Woolf and Pater, "[w]ith Lytton tearing about the country in jealous pursuit of Duncan Grant and Maynard Keynes soon after their graduation, it was probably wisest not to discuss Pater or his school at all, much less to praise him or avow him as an influence" (35)—and this even decades after the Wilde trials had first made the expression of aestheticism's "point of view . . . suspect and distasteful, publicly," to use the phrasing of Osbert Burdett in his survey, *The Beardsley Period* (272). To be sure, the 1925 publication of Burdett's book, which defends aestheticism as England's last meaningful protest against the deadening effects of commercialism, says something about the resurrection of Wilde that took place after the Great War, but it is worth noting also that the twenties Wilde vogue, which centered on a growing aesthete-athlete split at Oxford, Cambridge, and the public schools, in some respects only made allegiances to aestheticism more perilous, by bringing its most scandalous proponent more directly before the public imagination.[6]

Behind even these specifically homosexual associations, however, there loomed the larger anxiety that had made the pale, sensitive, hyperrefined aesthete the unlikely twin of the poorly fed Boer War soldier, the fear that the nonproductiveness emblematized by the life of consumption constituted a danger to the nation as a whole.[7] Bloomsbury clearly absorbed something of this concern, tending to disdain experience unaccompanied by product in spite of Moore's dictum that the most valuable things in life are certain "states of consciousness"; but whereas for the public at large the threat of nonproductiveness bore a largely moral (if not indeed physiological) character, Bloomsbury's tacit disapprobation seems to have been associated more closely with a left-socialist politics opposed on principle to the idea that society should support a class of non-producers—a politics whose ethical origins could be traced, once again, to the watershed of the turn of the century. In his 1939 *Barbarians Within and Without*, Leonard Woolf observed, as noted in the introduction, that what "middle-class liberals and democrats" of the fin de siècle failed to recognize was "that their capitalist system and their sacred rights of property were no longer compatible with liberty and equality"; and he continued, "The chosen people began to burn their sons for burnt offerings unto Baal. It was round about 1890 that Baal worship began to start in England" (127–28). In Woolf's formulation, red-olent in spite of itself of a Whiggish faith in the progress of enlightenment, it was not necessarily that leisure-class consumption grew more extravagant at the close of the century, but that in those years its incompatibility with cer-tain ideals at last grew conspicuous, paving the way for the unleashing of those ideals against the British class structure.

This discomfort of the left-sympathetic wealthy with the life of leisure did not go unnoticed by those on the outside. For one such observer, Wyndham Lewis, this discomfort was not only nothing to celebrate but something to revile, and Lewis filled his works of the late 1920s and early 1930s with denunciations of the supplanting of genuine artists by "revolutionary" rich seeking outlet for their productive capacities. With Bloomsbury (though not Bloomsbury alone) in mind, Lewis wrote in his 1927 *Time and Western Man* that in "the millionaire, and progressive middle-class, Atlantic World, the general temper of revolutionary change has already been thoroughly ab-sorbed," leading to the curious "phenomenon of the 'revolutionary rich,' of a gilded Bohemia" (123) populated by refugees from the guilt, or perhaps the plain vulgarity, of a life of consumption:

> Wistfully, but, oh, so bravely! they exclaim, Times have changed, we must all do something! And, of course, a great many people still possess the means required for such 'little socialist experiments,' as one of these pathetic people described what he was doing—for this thrilling type of idyllic *work*, the necessary capital to return to the Feudal Age as a romantic 'craftsman,' even if that return cannot be effected in the rôle of chatelain. (124–25)

In the new feudalism of the wealthy, as Lewis saw it, the ideals of Owen and Morris figured not as inspiration for a program of meaningful social change, but as motifs in a new fashion under which production itself, engaged in as "experiment" and without the requirement that money be made from it, be-came another form of leisured consumption.

One of the problems with Lewis's formulation is that it lumps together indiscriminately virtually everyone who had more disposable income than he—which is to say, virtually everyone who could be regarded as middle class. In the late 1920s, when Lewis was writing, the Woolfs were only beginning (thanks to a rise in sales of Virginia's books) to make their way out of the financial uncertainties that had formerly kept Virginia's journalism essential to the upkeep of the household; able to maintain two houses and two servants, they were certainly well off in comparison to most members of the working class, but the state of their finances, especially in the 1910s, led them to numerous small economies and some of their friends to anxieties about their situation.[8] Neither they nor any of the other core members of Bloomsbury were "millionaires" (though Bloomsbury could well be associated with the freedom to throw money around to the degree that more marginal figures like Ottoline Morrell or, eventually, Vita Sackville-West illuminated it with their financial blaze); and as Hermione Lee notes, the fact that her income derived in part from "invested, inherited capital" may have made "Woolf—like Forster and Strachey and others of her English friends, and unlike incomers such as T. S. Eliot or Katherine Mansfield—a member of the 'rentier' class," but "it did not make her feel rich" (557). And yet the Woolfs' disposition to leisure-class guilt was not substantially altered by the fact that they had to earn a good part of their living. On the contrary, their writings show clearly that they saw themselves not only as inheritors of the middle-class Victorian intellectual's burden of service, but also (somewhat paradoxically) as members of a privileged class for which times had changed, a class whose responsibility to do something was the more acute now that the days of guilt-free consumption were past.

Lewis's attack on the new bohemia is true to Bloomsbury practice, of course, to the extent that the activity upon which that circle's energies were most intently trained was the making of works of art, and it thus comes as no surprise to find Woolf's concerns about doing something materializing above all in a revision of aestheticism's values under which art-making displaces the consumption of experience. "The mission of the aesthete," Wilde had asserted through his mouthpiece Gilbert in "The Decay of Lying," "is to lure people to contemplate, not to lead them to create" (*Intentions* 216), and in his portrait of Thomas Griffiths Wainewright he had associated the production imperative itself with bad taste, remarking (as noted in both the introduction and the subtitle to this book), "It is only the Philistine who seeks to estimate a personality by the vulgar test of production. This young dandy sought to be somebody, rather than to do something" (*Intentions* 73–74). Even in *Dorian Gray*, wherein the upshot of the battle between Victorian pieties and decadent provocations seems uncertain at best, Lord Henry makes a serious claim when he tells Dorian, "I am so glad you have never done anything, never carved a statue, or painted a picture, or produced anything outside of yourself! Life has been your art. You have set yourself to music. Your days are your sonnets" (393). For the Woolfs and the Bells, for Forster and Keynes, on the other hand, the ideal of life might include sonnet-like days, but it did not embrace the failure to carve, paint, or make, however sympathetic they may have been to Lytton's slowness in writing or Desmond MacCarthy's inability to complete, or even meaningfully to begin, his Great Work. For Bloomsbury, the moral of Wilde in respect to production would have been to do not as he said but as he did.

It was not Wilde's own priorities against which Woolf most immediately and revealingly reacted, however, but rather those of Pater, who has seemed to many critics the most significant late Victorian influence on her writing, and who as celebrant of immediate experience helped to pave the way for the Bergsonian cast of modernist prose fiction. Certainly, no one can accuse modern novelists, least of all Woolf, of turning away from lived experience, but Woolf's emphases and sympathies show clearly how, under modernism, experience seemed to come into its value not as it transpired, but rather as it was recorded or fixed in the work of art. That this was so even beyond the borders of prose fiction is immediately evident if one compares Pater's criticism to that of the early Pound (for example), for if the archetypal moment of Paterian impressionism is the resounding conclusion to *The Renaissance*, "[F]or art comes to you professing frankly to give nothing but the highest quality to your moments as they pass, and simply for those moments' sake" (*Writings* 62), the archetypal moment of Pound's innovation-driven modernism might be his 1912 claim that his "pawing over the ancients and semi-ancients has been one struggle to find out what has been done, once for all, better than it can ever be done again" (*Literary* 11). The difference here goes much deeper than a disagreement about the major function of the critic, of course; it touches directly upon the question of whether art serves aesthetic experience or vice versa, whether value at last resides in the beautiful perception or the beautiful thing, in the passing moment or the enduring object. Hugh Kenner offers perhaps the neatest formulation of the contrast in *The Pound Era*, remarking that Pater says, in effect, "Let us die finely, our life is a long dying, amid which to be conscious is to capture melancholy satisfactions," whereas Pound exhorts, "No, let us write finely . . . if it is our vocation to write, and seize moments in our writing, seize glimpses, there to seize" (71).

Woolf's transformations of Pater illustrate this shift still more strikingly than Pound's, not only because her genre of lyrical prose was Pater's own but also because she redisposes some of Pater's particular tropes in a way that shifts the focus of value from experience to its durable register. "Solid Objects" itself includes just such a repositioning, its narrator evoking Pater's most famous formulation, "To burn always with this hard, gemlike flame, to maintain this ecstasy, is success in life" (*Writings* 60), in the note that John's quest is for any object "more or less round, perhaps with a dying flame deep sunk in its mass," that would remind him of the lump of glass from the beach, which, "almost a precious stone," might if set in a ring become a "dull, green light upon the finger" (104, 103). That the flame imprisoned and almost extinguished in this gemlike thing is a descendant of Pater's flame of experience is confirmed by the essay "Reading," published a year before "Solid Objects," in which Woolf writes of the kind of books one desires in the early morning: "We want something that has been shaped and clarified, cut to catch the light, hard as a gem or rock with the seal of human experience in it, and yet sheltering as in a clear gem the flame which burns now so high and now sinks so low in our own hearts" (*Essays* 2: 26). Even at the core of what might well stand as Woolf's most Paterian essay, the Paterian flame comes enclosed in the solid thing, and "human experience" appears not as a flickering fire but (in a figure evocative of Pound) as an intaglio in a rock.

To say that one of the passages from aestheticism to modernism is the shift from gemlike flame to the gem-hard writing that shelters our hearts' fire, from evanescence with an air of solidity to the capturing of the evanescent in solid form, is not to imply that modernists somehow rejected experience, or that the late nineteenth century showed any lack of interest in the enduring monument. Again, what is in question is only a change in accent that registers the retention of some values as much as the transformation of others. There can be no doubt that Woolf was at least as interested in the moment as Pater, but for her this interest was scarcely separable from the question of how to make "of the moment something permanent," as Lily Briscoe puts it in comparing her own art to Mrs. Ramsay's (*Lighthouse* 161). And though in "Modern Fiction" Woolf complained about the "materialist" bent of Bennett, Galsworthy, and Wells, choosing her own generation's recording of the "incessant shower of innumerable atoms" over the other's catalogues of decor and comestibles (*Essays* 2: 104, 106), it is precisely this emphasis on recording that suggests her distance from Pater's admonition against losing any opportunity for discriminating perception "on this short day of frost and sun," or his impassioned claim that with our sense of the "awful brevity" of our experience "we shall hardly have time to make theories about the things we see and touch" (*Writings* 61).[9]

Perhaps the most telling illustration of Woolf's priorities in this regard is *A Room of One's Own*, in which her professed object is not to bring women writers into the debates and discourses of the day, but to bring women as makers of monuments into the eternal pantheon of artists—to give Shakespeare's sister a chance to live, but to live more for the sake of creating, evidently, than for the sake of living. Arguing that Charlotte Brontë would have written better if she had not suffered the deprivations that infect her writing with bitterness, and that we recognize Shakespeare's greatness by the fact that we can tell nothing about him from his plays, Woolf strongly evokes Eliot's figure of the artist as catalyst and his arguments concerning the extinction of personality in great works of art, while in bringing her narrator repeatedly into confrontations with pages, books, bookshelves, and libraries, she recalls Eliot's image of monumental works forming an ideal order among themselves. Woolf even brings catalyst and monument together in having her narrator remark that a "book which lay open at *Antony and Cleopatra*" (56) led her to reflect on the conditions necessary to freeing "whole and entire the work that is in" the literary artist, and that it was in "turning again to the bookcase" that she came to think how "[i]f ever a mind was incandescent, unimpeded . . . it was Shakespeare's mind" (59).

This ostensible privileging of art over life is not meant to fool anyone, of course, any more than the encounters with the materiality of writing are meant to endorse without irony the patriarchal majesty of archives and tomes. Clearly, Woolf's essay is at least as much about women's status as it is about fiction's, and her appeal to the greatness of literature goes into the service of a call for simple justice. And yet it is important to notice that in turning to monuments of literature for justification, Woolf discreetly natural-izes the premise that a store of monuments *is* indisputably an end in itself, just as in "Tradition and the Individual Talent" Eliot argues for a literary tradition by implying that the idea of such a tradition is itself traditional and, as such, authoritative. To be sure, neither Woolf nor Eliot was doing any-thing too scandalous in taking as a basic premise the importance of main-taining a body of great literature; one need only note the word "treasury" in the title of Francis Palgrave's best-selling *Golden Treasury of the Best Songs and Lyrical Poems in the English Language* to recognize that an assumption of the absolute value of such a body of works, whatever particular works might be included in that body, cut across classes and educational back-grounds.[10] But the mention of Palgrave, the common denominator of whose poetic selections was a capacity to be understood as morally hortatory or inspirational, also helps to disclose how the modernists rang a devious change on this popular piety—namely, by implying that the value of great works arises not from their instructive power or uplifting sentiments but from their sheer status as human achievement, their realization of another kind of ideal.

This is to say that one of modernism's key moves in its own defense of poesy—one so far accorded surprisingly little attention by scholars—was to try to legitimate Nineties aestheticism by, in effect, rewriting it along the lines of mid-Victorian moral earnestness. Retaining the doctrine of art for art's sake, or rather embracing it with a rigor that even the aesthetes seldom showed, they claimed a moral (rather than provocatively immoral or amoral) high ground by turning from aesthetic experience as end, with its threat to the production imperative, to the work of art as fruit of inspired labor and realization of human aspiration. In his 1925 book, Burdett observed of the Georgian poets, "They do not *quote* Gautier or Poe or Baudelaire, and the doctrine that art is an end in itself; but they are as disinterested as their scrupulous care never to offend anyone [will] allow" (282), and this point (altered to accommodate a more complex sense of what offending might entail) applies with even greater force to the high modernists—some of whom, like T. S. Eliot, did quote Gautier, but all of whom effectively pro-ceeded on the premise that the work of art is an end to which one's life might legitimately be devoted. The modernist emphasis on making rather than reception or acquisition thus not only rescued art from its potentially guilty associations with leisured consumption, but also rescued *l'art pour l'art* by transferring it to the domain of production, rewriting that doctrine as something like art for *the work of* art's sake, which could so easily be taken to mean art for the sake of human greatness.

In this respect *A Room* can be said to include another turn of the screw not to be found in "Tradition and the Individual Talent," for against her own presentation of *Antony and Cleopatra* as a touchstone of success in literary art, Woolf poses (in later chapters) the flaws in the play that grow visible beneath the light of engaged, and specifically feminist, analysis: Cleopatra appears amid the gallery of heroines whose power and magnetism obscure real women's historical obscurity, and her mistrust of Octavia is used to illustrate the notable absence, in literature, of friendships between women. That these two views appear well apart from each other and are never explicitly linked by Woolf's persona could suggest, certainly, how treating the literary work as a monument might inhibit one from probing that same work as a representation, commentary, or history—how the text regarded as solid object, complete, could be difficult to reconcile with the messy event of language that, however deliberately or unwillingly, moves to shape the debates and beliefs of its own age or some other. And yet the fact that Woolf does manage to make both views of the play convincing also attests that the modernists found such difficulties far from insurmountable, and in particular that the durability of a work from the point of view of the great tradition did not, in their understanding, necessarily render it impermeable to ideological critique.

Though broad accusations that modernism moved to sever art from history and society inevitably prove absurdly reductive in the end (as any number of studies of the political life of modernism have shown), it cannot be denied that a discomfort with explicit political engagement in imaginative writing was a distinguishing feature of most modernists' understandings of their roles as artists, or that this sense of the boundedness or (to use the charged term at issue here) *autonomy* of the literary work depended in part upon a vision of the successful work as a monument resistant to time's depradations. As *A Room of One's Own*—or for that matter Lewis's criticism, or even Pound's or Eliot's—shows, however, the belief that untransformed polemic might compromise the work's durability was not the same as a belief that artistic monuments were beyond analysis as documents of culture. And as we have just seen, also, the most pressing reason for modernists to treat the work as a solid thing—"so hard, so concentrated, so definite an object compared with the vague sea and the hazy shore" (103), as John describes his admired lump of glass—was not a desire to render art impervious to social conditions, but rather a perceived need to justify art's place in a society apparently unsympathetic to the idea of beauty as its own end but deeply committed to production as moral imperative. The promotion of an aesthetic autonomy whose central emblem was the work of art as bounded monument, then, originated (ironically, we might say) in part as an effort to justify the artist's activity as a part of society's total work, at a time when removal from production no longer seemed to be anyone's prerogative.

In "Solid Objects," this discomfort with nonproduction among the leisure classes is negatively encoded in Woolf's notable avoidance of the question of how her hero will support himself if he continues to devote all his time to his quest. The truth, of course, is that for his story to end in anything other than homelessness and swift death he would have to have an independent income (as the reader might well assume him to anyway, given that he once had hopes of Parliament), but Woolf is spared noting that the vocation of found objects (like the political one or that of the decadent-collector) must prove a prerogative of the leisured by her story's brevity, which lends it a fairy tale's exemption from tedious questions about the mechanics of sustenance. Another reason that John's chosen path seems less permeated by the guilt of sheer consumption than it might, however, is the very fact that it is only "chosen" in the loosest sense. Once again, the story's tone marks John not a dilettante able to satisfy careless whims through the exploitation of others' labor but rather the servant of some inspiration, psychosis, or muse—one who accepts a calling of sorts, whether for better or for worse and whether that calling be noble, ridiculous, or both.

This aspect of the legitimation of John's career is especially important because it anticipates Woolf's later attempts—in the novels of the 1920s, above all—to recuperate certain forms of consumption by rewriting them as artistic production. Many readers of *Mrs. Dalloway* and *To the Lighthouse* have remarked the artistry shown by Clarissa and Mrs. Ramsay as they put together their parties; others have noted that Clarissa's gift extends to that still purer form of consumption known as shopping; and at least one has called attention to the feats of consumption performed by Orlando, the refurnishing of whose ancestral home fills thirty-seven pages of inventory with entries like "seventeen dozen boxes containing each five dozen of Venice glasses" (109), and who enjoys a fascinating encounter with the twentieth-century department store long after his transformation into a woman—that being who had, by the end of the nineteenth century, displaced the aristocrat as the archetypal consumer.[11] "[E]ach time the lift stopped and flung its doors open," Orlando's biographer tells us, "there was another slice of the world displayed with all the smells of that world clinging to it. She was reminded of the river off Wapping in the time of Elizabeth, where the treasure ships and the merchant ships used to anchor" (300–301). Distracted, nostalgic, Orlando succumbs so completely to the whirl of retail display that she fails to bring away what she had come for, but her author makes clear that in the midst of commercial failure the imaginative consumer may attain artistic success. Having observed that nothing more unsettles the time-keeping by which we organize our multiple selves than "contact with any of the arts," she adds, as though to leave no room for doubt on this score, "[I]t may have been her love of poetry that was to blame for making Orlando lose her shopping list and start home without the sardines, the bath salts, or the boots" (305–6).

Clearly, Woolf's rethinking of consumption supports a reappraisal not only of "the" leisure class, but also of another group whose modern history has been shaped by the widespread belief that nonproductivity is its lot either in fact or by divine intention: namely, women in general. In this, of course, Woolf speaks immediately to contemporary scholarly efforts, across the disciplines, to recover not only the significance of women's labor but also the contours of women's intellectual lives—for while any denaturalizing of the assumption that consumption cannot be work will contribute to a reassessment of women's historical roles (by disclosing value in one of the few realms of activity in which women have traditionally been considered dominant), the elucidation of consumption's more aesthetically and cognitively complex aspects bids to argue also for the force of women's minds, or even (far more problematically, of course) for the force of what Woolf, in *A Room*, denominates the feminine mind.[12] The achievements of Mrs. Dalloway and Orlando, along with her sketches of the feminine sentence and the feminine imagination in *A Room*, in fact, find Woolf closer on this point to feminists who have sought to unsettle the traditional privileging of "masculine" or "public" activity than to other writers whose weltanschauungs tend to be much closer to her own—writers such as Simone de Beauvoir, who regarded domestic work as absolutely inferior to projects originating in the struggle for transcendence, indeed virtually meaningless from an existential point of view.

Woolf's position here is complicated, however, by the fact that as a woman and a modern artist, she wrote from what would have been from some angles a doubly feminized, or doubly nonproductive, position. It is by now a commonplace of modernist studies that many male writers, observing the pervasiveness of female "scribblers," internalized a belief that writing itself might be feminizing: Stevens's undergraduate journal entry affirming Homer, Dante, and others against the "effeminate" idea that "poetry is now the peculiar province of women" (*Letters* 26) and Joyce's notebook comment that *The Waste Land* had ended the "idea of poetry for ladies" (quoted in Ellmann, *Joyce* 495) are only two of the better known instances of this belief's casual operation. As the foregoing citations from Wilde in his antiproductionist humor might suggest, moreover, there hovered beside this specter of feminization the possibly still more alarming phantom of *effemin-*

ization localized in the aesthete whose poetry goes unread or even perhaps unwritten (the phantom apparently disowned in *Hugh Selwyn Mauberley* and held at arm's length in "The Love Song of J. Alfred Prufrock"). Together, the figures of the female scribbler and the aesthete dabbler ensured that although the artistic aspect of women's work could under some circumstances be employed to prove that work meaningfully productive, there could always occur a reverse effect under which the success (or failure) of feminine art would call into question the validity of art in general. If according to one kind of reading *Mrs. Dalloway* and "Solid Objects" reveal how collecting and party throwing constitute forms of production, another kind—no less plausible or available—seems to disclose in these works Woolf's doubts about the extent to which art marks a genuine contribution to any community. If the achievements of a tinselly society hostess are art, does this leave the artist a figure of mere tinsel? And what of the myth of the tormented artist if the collecting of trash can be mythologized so easily?[13]

That Woolf did indeed suffer serious anxieties in this area is confirmed at many points in her writing, but perhaps nowhere so strikingly as in a passage from the very late letter-essay "Middlebrow," in which she contemplates working class people queuing up at movie theaters:

> These lowbrows are waiting, after the day's work, in the rain, sometimes for hours, to get into the cheap seats and sit in hot theatres in order to see what their lives look like. Since they are lowbrows, engaged magnificently and adventurously in riding full tilt from one end of life to the other in pursuit of a living, they cannot see themselves doing it. Yet nothing interests them more. Nothing matters to them more. It is one of the prime necessities of life to them—to be shown what life looks like. And the highbrows, of course, are the only people who can show them. Since they are the only people who do not do things, they are the only people who can see things being done. (*Essays* 2: 198)

It is odd enough to find Woolf so lightly designating as "highbrows" makers of movies for 1930s mass audiences, but her presentation of the working-class "pursuit of a living" as magnificent and adventurous is troubling in the extreme, indeed one of the most disingenuous statements on class to be found anywhere in her writing. And yet this passage does illuminate certain painful truths nonetheless, not only in calling attention to social divisions apparently so entrenched as almost to forbid the imagining of a world in which everyone produces "culture," but also in betraying a genuine concern about the degree to which the activities of the highbrows—here identified, strikingly, as "the people who do not do things"—do result in authentic making after all. The very fact that highbrows are not altogether easy to distinguish from "the" leisure class (Woolf's assertion elsewhere in the essay that she knows highbrow charwomen notwithstanding) suggests that even near the very end of her career, Woolf was still working through the question of whether the fashioning of art, or of representations generally, mean-ingfully participates in production—of whether in spite of their earnest talk about *poiesis* and craft, artists qua artists would always constitute, in some essential sense, a leisure class of another kind.

All this said, it must be stressed that mistrust of conspicuous consumption and leisure-class guilt cannot by themselves account for the modernist pro-duction imperative, which clearly partakes of a belief in the importance of doing arguably as old as the literature of heroism, and thus arguably as old as imaginative writing itself. Indeed Beauvoir, whose introduction a few paragraphs ago was not at all innocent, stakes a good deal on the trans-historical validity of such a belief, her position being that of an Existentialist ethics whose address to crises of meaning prescribes productive action on the world in the form of freely chosen projects. On the other hand again, however, we might recall that Existentialism's own treatment of human pro-duction has identifiable historical sources, evolving as it does during the first period of Western history at once visibly dominated by industrial transfor-mation and deprived of authoritative (and customary) assurances of the exis-tence of a God to whom questions of purpose could be referred. That this period would of course include the nineteenth century as well as the twen-tieth reminds us that something like existential crisis really makes its first appearance in English letters around the time of Pater, though it was the innovation of Pater and the aesthetes to suspend that crisis by bracketing questions of telos removed from immediate experience. And this point is crucial to the present discussion because, in resuscitating the production ethic that aestheticism abandoned, modernism also gave life to new crises of purpose—and generated new reasons to turn for resolution to the object world.

EVEN TREES, OR BARNS

In its most authoritative version, that of Sartre, existential crisis begins not with the subject but with the object. Although the narratives of Sartre's ex-emplary Existential novel *Nausea* (1938) and his philosophical monument *Being and Nothingness* (1943) arrive eventually at the problem of the sub-ject's freedom and choice, both begin with the question of appearance and contingency in the material world. The latter commences with the observa-tion that philosophy no longer accepts as legitimate a "dualism of being and appearance" (4) and moves rapidly to an "ontological proof" of the being of the phenomenon (21–24) , while the former opens with its narrator, Roquen-tin, confronting the strangeness of a cardboard box and recalling feelings of disgust on picking up a stone on a beach (1–2). From aversion to this thing, which he describes later as "a sort of nausea in the hands" (11), it seems but a short step to aversion to others—soon he can no longer indulge in his habit of picking up stray objects—and indeed he later recalls that the trouble began when he felt of that stone "that it *existed*" (123). Like John's odyssey in "Solid Objects," Roquentin's begins with a small, hard thing found by the seaside; but it unfolds as an obsession of nausea rather than love, until it culminates in the following revelation in a public garden:

> The word absurdity is coming to life under my pen. . . . This root . . . existed in such a way that I could not explain it. Knotty, inert, nameless, it fascinated me, filled my eyes, brought me back unceasingly to its own existence. In vain to repeat: 'This is a root'—it didn't work anymore. I saw clearly that you could not pass from its function as a root, as a breathing pump, *to that*, to this hard and compact skin of a sea lion, to this oily, callous, headstrong look. (129)

There was no reason for the World to exist, Roquentin eventually recognizes with horror, but "*it was impossible* for it not to exist" (134).

In *Mrs. Dalloway*, published thirteen years earlier, Woolf had written, "It might be possible, Septimus thought, looking at England from the train window, as they left Newhaven; it might be possible that the world itself is without meaning" (88). The language is not quite the same, of course: if Sartre's phrasing is a shade technological, Woolf's is a shade theological; if Roquentin focuses on the brute fact of Being in all its confrontational presence, Septimus emphasizes the absence of something behind the world that would guarantee its legitimacy. Yet even if *Nausea* and *Mrs. Dalloway* had nothing else in common, they would be linked by the sheer nakedness with which they raise the question of why anything, or everything, should exist; and indeed, with respect to the unembarrassed clarity with which they render this anxiety in their fictions, Woolf and Sartre are each other's only peers. Given that critics have long recognized an existential side to Woolf, it is a little surprising to find that only a few—most notably Lucio Ruotolo, who numbers Clarissa Dalloway among "six Existential heroes" in his book of that name (1973) and continues to refer to existential themes in *The Interrupted Moment* (1980)—have devoted serious attention to this connection, although this lacuna is explained in part by the fact that Existentialism itself is only lately showing signs of recovering from the popular success that made it so intellectually unfashionable for so many years.

Some of the most intriguing connections between Woolf and Sartre have gone unremarked, in any case. The similarity between John's and Roquentin's seaside confrontations with small, hard things is one such intersection, and indeed later on in the tale John readily passes from phenomenological fascination to existential questioning: "The contrast between the china so vivid and alert, and the glass so mute and contemplative, fascinated him, and wondering and amazed he asked himself how the two came to exist in the same world, let alone to stand upon the same narrow strip of marble in the same room. The question remained unanswered" (105). Moreover, Woolf's first great rendering of this feeling of strangeness, appearing twenty-three years ahead of *Nausea*, pivots on the word "absurdity," so crucial to Sartre's usage. In *The Voyage Out* (1915), Rachel Vinrace, reading in a chair, is

> overcome by the unspeakable queerness of the fact that she should be sitting in an arm-chair, in the morning, in the middle of the world. Who were the people moving in the house . . . ? And life, what was that? . . . It became stranger and stranger. She was overcome with awe that things should exist at all. . . . The things that existed were so immense and so desolate. . . . The utter absurdity of a woman coming into a room with a piece of paper in her hand amazed Rachel. (125)[14]

Nor is Rachel—whose engagement to the originator of that piece of paper, Terence Hewet, seems somehow to bring on her untimely death—the only one of Woolf's doomed existentialists whose dilemma seems closely to prefigure Roquentin's. We have just seen how Septimus, with apparently minimal affect, poses the great question as the train leaves Newhaven; and when he arrives in London, he becomes, like Sartre's hero, a sitter in a park who encounters something enormous as he looks at a tree:

> He had only to open his eyes; but a weight was on them; a fear. He strained; he pushed; he looked; he saw Regent's Park before him. Long streamers of sunlight fawned at his feet. The trees waved, brandished. We welcome, the world seemed to say; we accept; we create. Beauty, the world seemed to say. And as if to prove it (scientifically) wherever he looked at the houses, at the railings, at the antelopes stretching over the paling, beauty sprang instantly. To watch a leaf quivering in the rush of air was an exquisite joy. (69)

Both Roquentin and Septimus experience a breakdown of particulars that reveals an underlying wholeness, and both find themselves irritated by the loudness of Being. Of the things he sees in the park, Sartre's hero thinks, "I would have liked them to exist less strongly" (127), while it seems to Woolf's that "real things were too exciting" (142). But whereas the tree induces nausea in the one, it leads the other to a jittery ecstasy: whereas for Roquentin, the root of the chestnut is the site at which the dark flower of contingency blossoms, the speaking trees overwhelm Septimus with message, heralding the world's assurance (in response to his earlier question) that, far from being without meaning, it overflows with significance, not to mention love.

In spite of the opposite valences of their reactions to the tree, however, there is good reason to believe that Septimus is Roquentin's authentic park-bench precursor. At the time of the experience that seems to have catalyzed the writing of *Nausea*, Sartre had been lecturing on Woolf, among other writers, in the hall of the Lyre Havraise in Le Havre (Cohen-Solal 94); and the very letter to Simone de Beauvoir (7 October 1931) in which he describes that experience (looking at a tree, he notes, he came to understand "ce que c'était qu'un arbre") concludes with a specific reference to Sep-

timus's author: "Au bout de vingt minutes, ayant épuisé l'arsenal de com-
paraisons destinées à faire de cet arbre, comme dirait Mme Woolf, autre
chose que ce qu'il est, je suis parti avec une bonne conscience" (*Romanesques* 1687–88). Sartre aptly captures Woolf's interest in both the thingness
of the thing itself and the tendency of the mind to make comparisons in the
thing's despite, even extracting from Woolf the possibility that it is only by
making things something other than they are that we manage to keep on
going. Septimus's visionary moments can be seen as just such an effort gone
into overdrive, and indeed if Roquentin's experience of sheer inert existence
represents a neurotic revision of the negative pole of Septimus's psychosis,
Sartre's own experience in Le Havre looks like a philosophical revision of
its positive one.

What links all three episodes so tightly, of course, is the figure of the tree,
which seems the most innocently chosen of natural phenomena only until
one remembers that its banality makes it both a fine provocation to Existential crisis and one of the standard examples of the ordinary object, referent,
or thing-out-there in Western philosophical and literary discourse, its popu-
larity in this area rivaled only by that of the (by now more than a little
creaky) table and chair. To take just three examples: in *The Phenomenology
of Spirit*, the tree serves as Hegel's very first example of a sensuous fact
("'Here' is, e.g., the tree" [60]); in the *Course in General Linguistics*, the
tree appears as the referent in Saussure's crucial diagram of the signified-
signifier relationship, where the Latin word "arbor" stands as the signifier,
and the "concept" of a tree, illustrated by a small drawing of the branched
thing with trunk and leaves, appears as the signified; in *The Body in Pain*,
Elaine Scarry uses the tree existing in the world to exemplify first the natural
as opposed to the artificial object and then, a paragraph later, the real as
opposed to the imagined thing (146–47). Turning to Woolf's own corpus,
we find the tree representing solid reality in *The Years*—wherein Sara Pargiter tries to imagine herself a tree with sunlight shining through its leaves,
only to be recalled by "the actual tree standing out there in the garden"
which "had no leaves at all" (133)—and standing for the raw subject matter
of art in a diary entry recording a dinner with Roger Fry and Clive Bell:

> "D'you know, Clive, I've made out a little more about the thing which is essential
> to all art: you see, all art is representative. You say the word tree, & you see a tree.
> Very well. Now every word has an aura. Poetry combines the different aura's in a
> sequence—" That was something like it. I said one could, & certainly did, write
> with phrases, not only words; but that didn't help things on much. (*Diary* 1: 80)

Nor did Bloomsbury take the tree as archetypal referent only in informal
conversation. In his preface to the catalogue for the groundbreaking "Manet
and the Post-Impressionists" exhibition at the Grafton in 1910, Desmond
MacCarthy, working from Fry's notes, complained that by encouraging the
"artist to paint a tree as it appeared to him at the moment under particular

circumstances," a too passive Impressionism led to works that "failed to express a tree at all," works that lost the "'treeness' of the tree" altogether (9).

In *Mrs. Dalloway*, crises of many kinds occur under the shade of this allegory of a world independent of allegory, this symbol of what comes before the symbolic. In his first appearance in the novel, Septimus sees on the drawn blind of a motor car "a curious pattern like a tree," which seems to him implicated, somehow, in a "gradual drawing together of everything to one centre before his eyes, as if some horror had come almost to the surface and was about to burst into flames," nor can his wife Rezia help looking at the "tree pattern on the blinds" either, though for her the interest lies in whatever lies behind rather than in the depths of the pattern itself: "Was it the Queen in there—the Queen going shopping?" (15). Like most of the other Londoners who see it, Rezia addresses the pattern as the limited signifier of something specific, her manner of reading conspicuously literalized by the fact that in this case the signified lurks physically right behind. But for Septimus, the pattern suggests something about "everything," and does so not as a sign proper but as something more like what Charles Sanders Peirce would call an index, in this case as a part of the drawing together that terrifies him with its prospect of a conflagration.

The difference between Septimus and others is reinforced a few pages later when he and a crowd watch an airplane making smoke letters in the sky. Other observers attempt to form a word from the letters ("'Glaxo,' said Mrs. Coates. . . . 'Kreemo,' murmured Mrs. Bletchley. . . . 'It's toffee,' murmured Mr. Bowley" [20–21]), but Septimus thinks, "they are signalling to me. Not indeed in actual words; that is, he could not read the language yet; but it was plain enough, this beauty, this exquisite beauty, and tears filled his eyes . . ." (21). What others try to read as linguistic signs, Septimus reads first as an index, once again (though what the smoke indexes is the attempt to communicate itself, along with the promise that eventually these indices will be transformed into true signs: "he could not read the language yet"), then as sheer sensuousness apart from any communication except that of "Beauty." A few paragraphs later, he similarly fixes upon the music of spoken language rather than the meanings of the sounds uttered:

> "K... R..." said the nursemaid, and Septimus heard her say "Kay Arr" close to his ear, deeply, softly, like a mellow organ, but with a roughness in her voice like a grasshopper's, which rasped his spine deliciously and sent running up into his brain waves of sound which, concussing, broke. A marvellous discovery indeed—that the human voice in certain atmospheric conditions (for one must be scientific, above all scientific) can quicken trees into life! (22)

Once more, Septimus transforms signification into sensuousness, rendering language richly opaque (indeed doubly opaque here, since the nursemaid has only given him individual letters, which qua letters do not usually signify), and once more he in effect forestalls the collapse of this sensuousness into the purely aesthetic by obscurely and madly connecting it to a force capable of transforming the world (by quickening trees into life).

In a sense, Septimus's horror of the possible meaninglessness of everything marks him less as specifically modern than as generally post-Enlightenment, one of those souls whose visionary experience originates from perplexity before a world no longer readable as a book of divine allegories. Deprived of guarantees of some governing code according to which all things would become legible in the strictest sense, Septimus tries, in recognizably Romantic fashion, to make something of the possibility that meaning might proceed from the object without reference to some ordered system, choosing the symbol over the allegory and Being over cosmos. His response to the problem of meaning in things is complicated, however, by his tendency to render language objectlike: confronting the trees in the park, he believes himself capable of a reading so free of the staleness of prior system that it seems his alone, yet in his response to the smoke letters he inverts the paradigm, attempting not only to treat nature as a book but to put language itself into that book, extending a way to find meaning in objects to a (non)object whose capacity to mean had not, apparently, been in doubt. In "Intentional Structure of the Romantic Image," Paul de Man comments that one of the great Romantic dilemmas is the anxiety that "it is in the essence of language to be capable of origination, but of never achieving the absolute identity with itself that exists in the natural object" (5); in Septimus's vision, the belatedness of language and the potential meaninglessness of Being are both resolved in a vision of a greater reading that embraces language and Being without distinction.

This point is the more immediately relevant to existential questions because in *Mrs. Dalloway* the tree figures not only the nonlinguistic (things as opposed to words), but also the nonhuman or nonsentient (things as opposed to people), thus securing the link between a crisis of significance and the brute facticity of the object world. This second function (to which, as product of nature rather than humanity, the tree is clearly better suited than the table or chair) is confirmed by Septimus's later discovery that "trees are alive," which he thinks profound enough to be worth communicating to the Cabinet (67) in spite of the fact that everyone knows that trees *are* alive, technically speaking. The generous reader, of course, will take Septimus's point to be that trees are conscious—that when they say "we accept; we create" they really mean it—but the transient strangeness that attends his announcement is enough to indicate why it is that trees and other plants make especially useful synecdoches for the nonsentient world here: with their uncanny air of death-in-life, of being nearly but not quite sentient, they foreground the absence of feeling in the object world as few other objects can. (Scarry: "[We] . . . routinely think of trees as not-quite-alive" [174].)

Woolf calls attention to this feature of the vegetal in many of her fictions,[15] but her most brutal and direct such formulation appears in "On Being Ill," where she writes of flowers,

> There they stand; and it is of these, the stillest, the most self-sufficient of all things that human beings have made companions; these that symbolize their passions, decorate their festivals, and lie (as if *they* knew sorrow) upon the pillows of the dead. Wonderful to relate, poets have found religion in Nature, people live in the country to learn virtue from plants. It is in their indifference that they are comforting. That snowfield of the mind, where man has not trodden, is visited by the cloud, kissed by the falling petal, as, in another sphere, it is the great artists, the Miltons and the Popes, who console not by their thought of us but by their forgetfulness. (*Essays* 4: 198)

Published in 1926, this essay comes from the period not only of *Mrs. Dalloway* but also of *A Room of One's Own*, in which Woolf praises Shakespeare by insisting that we know nothing of his personality, just as she suggests here that great artists console by their forgetfulness. Woolf does not say explicitly in "On Being Ill" why artists' or plants' indifference should be comforting, but her image of a snowfield of the mind where man has not trodden suggests that the principal attraction, which would only be enhanced by illness, may have to do with the weariness of human conflicts alluded to in the introduction to this book, a loss of patience with quarrels from which the object world stands apart and into which forgetful authors, blessedly, do not ask their readers to enter.

In *Mrs. Dalloway*, several characters similarly imply that the appeal of plants (if there is one) lies in part in the fact that they demand comparatively little from those who love them—a possibility given more resonance by Septimus's last thought before his suicide: "He did not want to die. Life was good. The sun hot. Only human beings—what did *they* want?" (149). In the third paragraph of the novel, Clarissa remembers Peter Walsh (who longs always for an intimacy whose intensity she rejects) saying, "I prefer men to cauliflowers" (3), while in the closing party scene Peter himself tells Sally Seton that "he did not like cabbages; he preferred human beings" (193). Plants serve as the alternative to people at two other points in that scene alone, first in the thoughts of Miss Parry on India ("her eyes . . . beheld, not human beings . . . it was orchids she saw" [178]) and second in Sally's insistence that "despairing of human relationships . . . she often went into her garden and got from her flowers a peace which men and women never gave her" (192–93).[16] Certainly, it seems that Clarissa's gifts lie in the arrangement of people *and* of flowers; while Miss Parry contrasts herself to her niece in thinking, "Clarissa had always been fond of society" (179), that niece tells the servants that she will "buy the flowers herself" (3) in the first line of the novel, and at the florist's shortly after responds to a combination of human and floral consolations, "as if this beauty, this scent, this colour, and Miss Pym liking her, trusting her, were a wave which she let flow over her and surmount" her hatred of Miss Kilman (13). And yet even she later thinks how "she cared much more for her roses than for the Armenians," a turn that Woolf counterposes quite specifically against a vision of humans as creatures who need: "Hunted out of existence, maimed, frozen, the victims of cruelty and injustice . . . no, she could feel nothing for the Albanians, or was it the Armenians?" (120)

This last is one of those moments that has helped to make Clarissa so understandably unsympathetic for some readers, and matters are scarcely improved by the defensive question that follows, "[B]ut she loved her roses (didn't that help the Armenians?)" (120), which sounds like an attempt to evade social responsibility with the help of a quick moralizing of aesthetics or the Bloomsbury piety that the political is grounded in the personal. Unsettling as it is, however, the admission that she feels nothing for the Armenians does show a certain self-knowledge on Clarissa's part, a knowledge that seems to help focus her resistance to the embracing (but all too theoretical) "love" promoted by Miss Kilman, that absent interlocutor whose actual appearance shortly after seems to lead to the culminating formulation, "[H]ere was one room, there another. Did religion solve that, or love?" (127). Here one room, there another: for Clarissa, neither love nor religion breaks down the boundaries between souls, nor does either change the fact that in the most rigorous sense other people are irremediably objects from one's own point of view. But though roses and Armenians may be equally opaque to some kind of full knowledge, the former can at least inspire in her some feeling that seems genuine, whether because they seem to demand nothing from her or simply because they happen to be much nearer at hand.

That our limited knowledge of other consciousnesses is one of Woolf's central subjects in *Mrs. Dalloway* has been clear to readers from the beginning, in part because this very problem is raised by the book's most notable formal innovations, its unexpected shifts from one point of view to another and its way of alluding to events in characters' lives while withholding explanation of those allusions. We enter the novel through Clarissa's consciousness only to be set at arm's length a few pages later, and leave her mind for the last time twelve pages before the end; nor can we know why the death of her sister was her father's fault, or in what sense she once failed Richard at Constantinople.[17] But the division of subjectivities is not only a "theme" that surfaces for the reader alone above the heads of the characters, for (as just noted) Clarissa herself meditates on the separation of rooms, while Peter Walsh recalls how in their younger days he and Clarissa had agreed that it "was unsatisfactory . . . how little one knew people." And yet, he continues, she did propose a tentative resolution of sorts:

But she said, sitting on the bus going up Shaftesbury Avenue, she felt herself everywhere; not "here, here, here"; and she tapped the back of the seat; but everywhere. She waved her hand, going up Shaftesbury Avenue. She was all that. So that to know her, or any one, one must seek out the people who completed them; even the places. Odd affinities she had with people she had never spoken to, some woman in the street, some man behind a counter—even trees, or barns. It ended in a transcendental theory which, with her horror of death, allowed her to believe, or say that she believed (for all her scepticism), that since our apparitions, the part of us which appears, are so momentary compared with the other, the unseen part of us, which spreads wide, the unseen might survive, be recovered somehow attached to this person or that, or even haunting certain places after death... perhaps—perhaps. (152–53)

Clearly, Clarissa continues to think along these lines as she grows older, for on the very day of the novel and her party, she feels "quite continuously a sense of" her guests' existence and muses that "somehow in the streets of London, on the ebb and flow of things, here, there, she survived, Peter survived, lived in each other, she being part, she was positive, of the trees at home" (122, 9).

With its "transcendental" speculation on an unseen part of us that spreads wide and its evocation of ghosts or *genii loci*, Clarissa's hope of a modest immortality unquestionably invites interpretation along mystical or supernatural lines. As a number of critics have observed, however, her theory can also be understood as an engagement with the epistemological problem of isolated consciousness that only as such allows a reconsideration of mortality, an engagement founded principally on the nonmystical supposition that since perceptions are formative of self, one might recapture something of someone lost by seeing what she has seen. Raising the possibility that "to perceive another means perceiving his perceptions" (as Avrom Fleishman puts it [734]), Clarissa's appears to be "a theory of perception as well as immortality" according to which consciousness is "defined or completed by what it is conscious of" and "individual consciousnesses are related to one another through their perceptions of a common environment" (as S.P. Rosenbaum remarks [336]). Indeed Clarissa's insight into Septimus's anguish, the most apparently magical moment in *Mrs. Dalloway*, seems to follow naturally (in her theory's terms) from the fact that she has just encountered one of the "people who completed" him, Dr. Bradshaw, of whom she thinks even before hearing of his patient's death, "one wouldn't like Sir William to see one unhappy. No; not that man" (182).[18]

Woolf's interest in how perceptions of the phenomenal world mold subjectivity undoubtedly owes something to Pater, who presents an epistemological validation for his emphasis on immediate experience (and the

prose that would register it) in *Marius the Epicurean*, premising the importance of a "diligent promotion of the capacity of the eye" on a Platonic
theory that "supposes men's spirits susceptible to certain influences, diffused
. . . by fair things or persons visibly present . . . into the air around them,
acting . . . like potent material essences, and conforming the seer to themselves as with some cunning physical necessity" (53). But Woolf's interest
in the possibility that subjectivities might be *connected* through objects
seems to respond more closely to some key concerns of the Anglo-American
philosophy of her day, which may have come to her attention through her
friend T. S. Eliot, the author of a 1916 Harvard doctoral dissertation on F. H.
Bradley that begins from the premise that in immediate, unprocessed experience we do not distinguish between subject and object at all.[19] Observing that
"in any cognition there is never more than a practical separation between the
object and that which apprehends it" (25) and that "[a]nother person, and in
its degree another *thing*, is not for us simply an object; there is always . . . a
felt continuity between the object and oneself" (81), Eliot argues that the
possibility of solipsism narrowly defined is only an artifact of according the
subject-object division anything more than merely conceptual validity:

> So far as experiences go, we may be said in a sense to live each in a different
> world. But "world" in this sense, is not the world with which solipsism is con-
> cerned; each centre of experience is unique, but is unique only with reference to a
> common meaning. Two points of view . . . can be said to differ only so far as they
> intend the same object, though the object . . . is only such with reference to a point
> of view. (149)

The isolation of consciousness is understandable, in other words, only with
reference to the very object that would mitigate isolation. And, Eliot concludes, while we may fairly say that we know other subjectivities "only
through the mediation of objects"—that "we have no knowledge of other
souls except through their bodies"—it must also be remembered that "we
have no direct (immediate) knowledge of anything" and that indeed the
"platform of knowing . . . is the assertion of something to be known, something independent of me so far as that knowing is concerned" (151–52).

If Woolf's approach to the separation of souls and the mitigation of distance between them resonates with Eliot and Bradley, her emphasis on the
stubborn distance of an object world that cannot be subsumed by human
knowing more closely evokes the work of G. E. Moore, the presiding philosophical spirit of Bloomsbury. Moore countered turn-of-the-century idealism's emphasis on the experiential continuum with an insistence upon objects' ontological independence of consciousness, attacking the proposition
"that *esse* is *percipi*," for example, in his summary 1903 essay, "The Refuta-
tion of Idealism," which culminates in the rhetorical question, "What reason
have we for supposing that material things do *not* exist, since *their* existence

has precisely the same evidence as that of our sensations?" (*Philosophical* 5, 30). This is not to say that Moore never came close to the position of the Eliotic Bradley; on the contrary, as Rosenbaum notes, he postulated in a 1905 paper the existence of "'sense-contents' (later called sense-data), which would be independent of our private perceptions of them" in trying to answer the question of what reason we might have for thinking that others have particular beliefs or perceptions (Rosenbaum 328). Still, Moore's strong emphasis on the brute facticity of existence would have helped to accentuate, if hardly to inspire, the existential cast of Bloomsbury thought and writing, which (like Existential crisis in Sartre) begins with a sense of the sheer strangeness of the object world. And indeed it would be fair to say that in this respect Woolf's writing constitutes one of the direct links between Anglo-American philosophy of the early part of the century (after William James and before the ascent of ordinary language analysis), and Continental philosophies of existence, between the deployment of solid objects against idealism and the Heideggerian-Sartrean campaign to restore to philosophy the primacy of Being.

Woolf is also linked to these philosophers by her tendency to think about the body less in terms of anything like the mind-body problem (a modernist contrast here would be Beckett's resurrection of Occasionalism) than in terms of further questions about intersubjectivity. Eliot's dissertation observation that "we have no knowledge of other souls except through their bodies" suggests how for him and Bradley, as for Moore,[20] the body is of greatest interest as a third thing that can mediate between minds, and the same is true for Woolf and, in an important sense, for Sartre.[21] In *Mrs. Dalloway*, the separation of rooms submits to a literal (though of course partial) resolution when Clarissa, looking out the window of an empty room, thinks, "Oh, but how surprising!—in the room opposite the old lady stared straight at her!" (185–86), the moment evoking that paradigmatic Sartrean encounter with the other's look in which one becomes aware that one is probably "an object at present functioning as a *differentiated this* for a consciousness" (*Being* 374).[22] Perhaps because the habit of most post-Cartesian, pre-Sartrean reflections on the body in ordinary experience has been to treat it as a housing for the soul rather than a thing for others, however, the mediation performed by things seems more satisfactorily thematized by showing consciousnesses connecting across other kinds of objects, and indeed *Mrs. Dalloway* contains more events of this kind than it does instances of minds meeting through bodies. In the party scene, for example, the *trace* of bodies provides Clarissa a mediation cleaner, though far less profound, than the encounter with the old woman: entering the empty room, she guesses, most likely from the fact that the "chairs still kept the impress of the Prime Minister and Lady Bruton, she turned deferentially, he sitting four-square, authoritatively," that they "had been talking about India" (183).

Woolf foregrounds her concern with objects' intersubjective mediations most strikingly, in this novel, by including a number of scenes in which two people look at the same thing at the same time, among them those celebrated transitions in which the narrator passes from one mind to another by means of a common object of contemplation: the stopped motor car that takes the reader from Clarissa to Septimus, for example, or the skywriting that allows passage through a series of individual subjectivities within the gazing crowd. Common looking is also, notably, a prerogative of lovers and a staple of the talk (or silence) of love: giving Clarissa the roses, Richard cannot "bring himself to say he loved her; not in so many words," and yet it seems that "she understood without his speaking" (118). And when he visits Clarissa at home, Peter shares with her the image of the woman he loves (or believes he loves), and recalls times at Bourton when they would go walking, noticing nothing, "except when she stopped, cried out at a view or a tree, and made him look with her" (154). Such moments appear frequently in the other early novels as well, as in *Night and Day*, where Katharine, looking at Ralph's drawing of a dot with flames around it, tells him, "Yes, the world looks something like that to me too" (493),[23] and in *Jacob's Room*, where Woolf's narrator lightly proposes that paper flowers, as objects of common attention, might pave the way "to the union of hearts and foundation of homes" (83). Nor does common looking inspire only romantic love. In *To the Lighthouse*, Mrs. Ramsay, contemplating a centerpiece arranged by her daughter, observes Augustus Carmichael doing the same and thinks how "looking together united them" (97), while Lily and William Bankes, who do not prove a suitable match, are nonetheless drawn together in gazing at Mrs. Ramsay herself: "Looking along his beam she added to it her different ray, thinking that she was unquestionably the loveliest of people" (48–49).

But although the scene of two people looking together may present the most neatly illustrative case of intersubjective mediation by the object, Clarissa's "transcendental" theory depends for its full impact upon the more complex situation in which the gazers are separated in time or space, and in which, therefore, the object negotiates loss or geographical separation as well as intersubjective distance. These kinds of mediations also are amply represented in Woolf's early fictions, as in *The Voyage Out*, wherein Evelyn is overcome by a feeling of Rachel's personality as she considers a photograph at which the other woman has looked (364), or in *Night and Day*, wherein Ralph, looking through a train window, thinks that "Katharine, too, had seen these gray fields," and imagines something like the haunting suggested by Clarissa's theory (184). In the same novel, Katharine feels almost "better acquainted with" her grandfather and his friends than with her own as she contemplates the books and pictures of the dead (113–14), while the whole energy of *Jacob's Room* seems directed toward the culminating scene in which Jacob's mother and Bonamy confront Jacob's relics, only to be left unsatisfied by this mediation, which can never be substitution: "'Jacob! Jacob!' cried Bonamy" (176).

In *Mrs. Dalloway* itself, the most striking and significant of links between people separated temporally and spatially is forged through a work of literary art. Although Clarissa's feelings about Dr. Bradshaw may explain her recognition of Septimus's suicide as a gesture of defiance, they do not account for the fact that she unknowingly echoes Septimus's "Fear no more, says the heart in the body; fear no more" (139), in silently reciting, "Fear no more the heat of the sun" (186) shortly after hearing of his death; but of course the coincidence becomes less strange when we remember that "as she looked into Hatchards' shop window" that morning she had seen those very words, had indeed been led by them to a vague recollection of "an image of white dawn in the country" (9). The strong possibility, of course, is that Septimus (who had been window shopping in the same area) had paused before the same words in the same book, open to *Cymbeline*; and Woolf strengthens this implication by noting that Shakespeare is important both to him (he "went to France to save an England which consisted almost entirely of Shakespeare's plays and Miss Isabel Pole in a green dress walking in a square" [86]) and to Clarissa (who recalls twice an occasion when she had thought, in Othello's words, "if it were now to die 'twere now to be most happy" [35, 184]).

In *A Room*, Woolf refers Shakespeare's greatness to the fact that "his grudges and spites and antipathies are hidden from us" (58); in "On Being Ill," she observes that "the great artists, the Miltons and the Popes . . . console not by their thought of us but by their forgetfulness"; and in *Mrs. Dalloway*, the linking of Clarissa and Septimus through a very physical *Cymbeline* appears as yet another instance in which the triumph of a work of art seems to have notably little to do with any transfer of the artist's subjectivity to the reader or viewer. Placed as it is in the window of a shop, the volume in question seems less a discourse approached from "within" than a thing regarded from "without," an object that might mediate between two of its beholders as any other object might, but not (at least in any immediately relevant way) something that mediates between either of them and its forgetful author. And thus Shakespeare's appearance in the form of a particular book in a particular location suggests, in the context of the novel's other meditations on objects and intersubjectivity, that the reading of texts might constitute only one species of a more general reading of the object world— the very possibility raised in more extreme or insane form by Septimus's experiences of actually sensuous language and literally articulate trees. If the work of art unites people more profoundly, or even more probably, than other kinds of things, according to this logic, it might be that it does so not because some metaphysical permeation by its maker's subjectivity renders it radically different from other objects, but only because it inspires emotion especially powerfully, or because a similarity in aesthetic judgment could indicate a broader similarity between souls.[24]

If this placement of the material *Cymbeline* among other objects makes sense from the perspective of a certain austere ontology, however, it hardly does so at the level of experience, in which books are clearly distinguished from all nonlinguistic objects by the unusual intensity with which they solicit reading. Just as the tree from which it is made eerily straddles the living and the nonsentient, the book can never quite cease to vibrate with the living voice, no matter how strenuously its reader tries to avoid succumbing to the metaphysics of presence—a point encoded by the very text that links Clarissa and Septimus. As several readers of *Mrs. Dalloway*, most recently Caroline Webb (286), have pointed out, the dirge "Fear no more" proves heavily ironic in *Cymbeline*, since this celebration of a return to the inanimate as a liberation from pain and fear is sung over the body of someone (Imogen) who is not in fact dead but only frozen in a deathlike state; and as J. Hillis Miller notes in one of the first critical explorations of this detail's role in Woolf's novel, part of the resonance of this irony lies in the fact that in existing "within death and within life at once" Imogen resembles writing ("*Mrs. Dalloway*" 101). Against the possibility that meaning in the object world is limited to its function in intersubjective mediation, writing—which may outlive its author and evade that author's intentions yet seem to speak nonetheless—renders it extraordinarily difficult to live the belief that meaning resides only in relations between subjects, never within the thing itself or the realm of Being. And thus the object-*Cymbeline* suggests that if Woolf envisions the work of literary art in monumental terms at certain key junctures, she does so not only in response to a crisis of legitimacy perceived to surround art production but also by way of addressing existential questions about meaning in the object world.

At this point, it will be illuminating to return to *Nausea*, in the final pages of which Sartre suggests that human making might gather its meaning from its effect on other subjectivities, not merely from its operation on the brute expanse of Being, even as he chooses for emblematic production the work of art—or at least the artlike entity of a popular song. Listening to a recording, Roquentin at first dismisses "idiots who get consolation from the fine arts" (174), but he begins to reconsider when he recognizes in the song a thing "beyond—always beyond something, a voice, a violin note" (175) and sees that at bottom he, too, "wanted to *be*"—not in the manner of contingent existents, but "somewhere else, behind the canvases of paintings . . . behind the phonograph records" (175). He then imagines the song's composer:

> But I no longer think of myself. I think of the man out there who wrote this tune, one day in July, in the black heat of his room. I try to think of him *through* the

melody, through the white, acidulated sounds of the saxophone. He made it. . . . It would interest me to find out the type of troubles he had. . . . I don't suppose it would make the slightest difference to him if he were told that in the seventh largest city of France, in the neighbourhood of a station, someone is thinking about him. But I'd be happy if I were in his place; I envy him. I have to go. I get up, but I hesitate an instant, I'd like to hear the Negress sing. For the last time.

She sings. So two of them are saved: the Jew and the Negress. Saved. Maybe they thought they were lost irrevocably, drowned in existence. Yet no one could think of me as I think of them, with such gentleness. . . . [T]hey have washed themselves of the sin of existing. Not completely, of course, but as much as any man can. (176–77)

With this, Roquentin is overwhelmed by "a sort of joy" (177) and imagines, possibly, writing a book that would make its readers "have to guess, behind the printed words, behind the pages, at something which would not exist, which would be above existence," a book that would lead them to think of his life "as something precious and almost legendary," and in so doing help him to "remember [his] life without repugnance" (178).

At first glance, this ending could seem a fairly banal instance of that familiar gesture (at least as old as Schiller and as new as Rorty) in which the philosopher turns to art as a realm of freedom that might provide relief from the dilemmas of a rigorous philosophy; but a little further reflection makes clear that the song represents more than a last resort for Sartre for the same reason that it represents more than a last resort for Woolf (or, for that matter, more than an intermediate one for Hegel). For Roquentin, the song opens up the possibility that another could think of him in the absence of a sense of the contingent facts of his existence, in the presence only of something whose being originates with him alone—which is to say that art (or the artlike thing) seems to promise to redeem the subject from contingency. As in Woolf, moreover, this human production also holds out the possibility of a redemption of Being itself, insofar as it seems to mark some kind of entry of the for-itself into the in-itself's domain. What remains unclear, however, is whether the composer and the singer (or the projected novelist Roquentin) are saved, ultimately, by production or by mediation, by the making of the song or by the fact that the song has provoked a feeling of tenderness in another soul. Like Woolf's fiction, in other words, Sartre's solicits a question of priority: does the imperative of objectification arise only under the sign of the more fundamental need to share something of the self with another subjectivity, or is intersubjective linking through the object merely the by-product of a more foundational drive toward objectification?

Neither *Nausea* nor *Mrs. Dalloway* answers this question decisively, but other writings make clear that their respective authors take rather different positions in the end. In spite of the extensive discussion of the problem of

others and the Other in *Being and Nothingness*, that volume's closing analysis of the impulse to transform the world through making (in the section
"Having, Doing, and Being," where "Doing" inadequately translates "*faire*")
conspicuously omits the question of other subjectivities. In Sartre's view the
aim of making is to achieve a "synthesis of self and not-self" (738) that
would satisfy the foundational and never fulfillable desire of the for-itself
"as consciousness . . . to have the impermeability and infinite density of the
in-itself," the solidity of Being (723), the wish to have and the wish to do
finally collapsing into the impossible desire to be in the mode of a for-itself-
in-itself (to be the *ens causa sui* or God). Put crudely, then, Sartre's position
in *Being and Nothingness* is that however perpetually doomed to failure the
productionist imperative may be, it is at least authentically crucial to making
in a way that intersubjectivity is not. And though in the later *Critique of
Dialectical Reason* Sartre acknowledges that made things do effect a signification of sorts between subjects, this acknowledgment falls in the midst of a
discussion of the practico-inert, the world of transformed matter that con-
strains, instrumentalizes, and sometimes destroys human beings: the defores-
tation that leads to floods, for example, or the gas lighting that apparently
"enabled" employers to extend the working day to sixteen hours but in fact
forced each to do so for fear of losing out to competitors (159–60).

In Woolf's fictions, on the other hand, objects' mediations between subjects appear with extraordinary frequency and visibility, while the requirement of production tends to emerge more sporadically, and less as Woolf's
own creature than as an assumption *en l'air* for reasons suggested in the
previous section. It is worth noting, too, that Woolf draws closest to identi-
fiably masculinist modernist anxieties not in her meditations on intersubjectivity but in her allusions to the need to produce; and it is surely in part
because her stance on the question of women's lives and freedom grew
increasingly radical in the years following *A Room* (as *Three Guineas* attests) that those years also saw her growing less and less comfortable with
the productionist ethic and its patriarchal or imperialist affinities. *Mrs. Dalloway* stands, in fact, as the last novel in which Woolf celebrates making
without including significant counterbalancing doubts, and *To the Lighthouse*
as the first in which she works to articulate a mistrust of production more
closely linked to asceticism than to aestheticism—the first, that is, in which
production is associated with an anxiety that looks more like guilt than like
shame.

PERPETUAL COMBAT

Of "Time Passes," the central section of *To the Lighthouse*, Woolf wrote in
her diary, "here is the most difficult abstract piece of writing—I have to give

an empty house, no people's characters, the passage of time, all eyeless & featureless with nothing to cling to" (*Diary* 3: 76). Nor was the difficulty of giving an empty house merely that of writing absence; it was also that of reversing the habit, common to both novelists and novel readers, of referring descriptions of the nonhuman world either to characters' psychology or to what Barthes would term *l'effet du réel*, a habit of which Woolf herself had made use in attacking Arnold Bennett in "Mr. Bennet and Mrs. Brown" in 1924. Then, Woolf had quoted a long passage of description from Bennett's *Hilda Lessways*, chastising its author for "trying to hypnotize us into the belief that, because he has made a house, there must be a person living there" (*Essays* 1: 330); but in making a house of her own in "Time Passes" she was trying to disrupt rather than to deploy such readerly autohypnosis, as she makes clear when she places her characters' fates in square brackets suggestive of the intrusion of the trivial (128–34), or when she exhorts some unnamed addressee, perhaps Fate or Time, to leave unrecovered the kinds of remnants that John restores to a human context in "Solid Objects": "Let the broken glass and the china lie out on the lawn and be tangled over with grass and wild berries" (138), which in the original manuscript reads, "Let . . . all . . . civilisation lie like broken china to be tangled over with . . . blackberries & grass" (*Lighthouse Holograph* 228). As Cheryl Mares has recently observed, Woolf sometimes denies the attraction of works of art not grounded in "the human element" (74), but at other moments—always highly intriguing ones—she registers an enormous esteem for presentations of the object world from which consciousness is apparently excluded.

In another diary entry, dated 27 February 1926, or about two months before she began "Time Passes," Woolf had written of an experience in which she began to think from the point of view of a world without humans:

> Then (as I was walking through Russell Sqre last night) I see the mountains in the sky: the great clouds; & the moon which is risen over Persia; I have a great & astonishing sense of something there, which is 'it'—It is not exactly beauty that I mean. It is that the thing is in itself enough: satisfactory, achieved. A sense of my own strangeness, walking on the earth is there too: of the infinite oddity of the human position. . . .
>
> Is that what I meant to say? Not in the least. I was thinking about my own character; not about the universe. (*Diary* 3: 62–63)

"The infinite oddity of the human position": Woolf's discovery seems something like the inverse of Septimus's speculation on the possible meaninglessness of the world or Roquentin's nausea before the brute contingency of *l'être-en-soi*, since in regarding the strangeness of the human from the object side, Woolf closes her earlier question, finding the nonhuman "in itself enough: satisfactory, achieved," no longer the excrescence without motivation that anticipates the Sartrean in-itself. And yet this next stage of crisis is perhaps more unsettling than the first, for the completeness of the object world does not necessarily make it meaningful, and meanwhile precisely that which had seemed to give it a second-order meaning before—divided human subjectivity in need of mediation—now seems troublingly superfluous, even guilty. Indeed it is here that one of the disturbing questions implicit in the image of the snowfield of the mind from "On Being Ill" emerges more starkly, for the vision of utter serenity in the world without humans seems to make meaning itself seem a kind of dissonance, a fatal crack in the perfection of innocence. The anxiety betrayed in Woolf's assertion that her own character and not the universe was on her mind, as though these consequential doubts could be brushed aside as passing fancy, suggests that it is not merely literary precedent but also an abhorrence of the possibility of human extraneousness that makes it so difficult to get down in prose the house empty of inhabitants, eyeless and featureless.

In "Time Passes," the conflict between human and nonhuman worlds is amplified by Woolf's rendering of the seductions and subsequent collapse of the pathetic fallacy: spring appears "to have taken upon her a knowledge of the sorrows of mankind" (132), but by late summer, nature looks cruelly indifferent to human "misery, . . . meanness, and . . . torture" (134), the dream that it might offer some answer to human questioning having been revealed as "but a reflection in a mirror" and the mirror itself as "but the surface glassiness which forms in quiescence when the nobler powers sleep beneath" (134). Woolf's phrasing strongly evokes the woman-mirror who reflects man at twice his natural size in *A Room of One's Own*, and as in that closely related text (written shortly after), the fault here lies not with the putative reflector but with a gazer addicted to a self-projection that can take quite violent forms. What makes it difficult to continue "to marvel how beauty outside mirrored beauty within" is the arrival of "an ashen-coloured ship," a thing "out of harmony with this jocundity and serenity," a synecdoche of the Great War that seems a more accurate mirror of humanity than the natural scene threatened by its arrival (133–34). Nor is this the only point in "Time Passes" at which the world without humans appears as a fragile Eden exposed to human violation; in section IV, Woolf notes how the empty house's loveliness and stillness made

> a form from which life had parted; solitary like a pool at evening, far distant, seen from a train window, vanishing so quickly that the pool, pale in the evening, is scarcely robbed of its solitude, though once seen. . . .
>
> Nothing it seemed could break that image, corrupt that innocence, or disturb the swaying mantle of silence which, week after week, in the empty room, wove into itself the falling cries of birds, ships hooting, the drone and hum of the fields, a dog's bark, a man's shout, and folded them round the house in silence. (129–30)

Though such innocence can absorb faint traces of the human (a man shouting, a ship hooting), any more direct intrusion disrupts it, and indeed it can be trespassed upon by perception itself, the very foundation of intersubjective linking in *Mrs. Dalloway* and at other points in *To the Lighthouse*. The "it seemed" beginning the second paragraph both reminds us that such unconscious "innocence" can only be imagined from the postlapsarian standpoint of consciousness and hints at a more literal fragility, preparing us for the arrival of Mrs. McNab, the caretaker who comes "tearing the veil of silence" (130) at paragraph's end.

And yet this woman, who maintains the house in the absence of the Ramsays as best she can and who (with the help of Mrs. Bast) eventually reclaims it for them, seems no despoiler of innocence, but the soul of innocence itself. In the original manuscript, she appears as the "voice of the . . . principle of life," indeed of life in its rawest form: "Oh yes, there had been beauty here, & life here, & Beauty . . . & it was gone, & it was ended; . . . yet the living with their mops & their dusters let issue on the grave of beauty . . . this incongruous song of the twisted the crazed & the thwarted, who . . . had no reason to desire life, no gift to bestow, or give [*sic*] to take," and yet "let rise up" some hope "founded perhaps . . . on the dumb persistency of the fountain of life" (211, 213). Beauty and life had been with the Ramsays; life alone is with Mrs. McNab. Woolf's admirers may well be thankful that the more discreet published version limits itself to likening this working-class woman's song to "the voice of witlessness, humour, persistency itself" (130), but the manuscript is revealing of something besides habits of thought with respect to class; it shows too that "Time Passes" maps the conflict between a possibly superfluous humanity and the satisfactory, achieved object world onto a conflict between "life," understood as human, and the lovely but also uncannily frightening world of nonlife that would include everything else.

It sounds odd to restrict "life" to humanity here, of course, just as it sounds odd for Septimus to declare that "Trees are alive," but we have already seen how significantly this ambiguity reverberates through *Mrs. Dalloway*, and something similar occurs in "Time Passes," which pivots upon the difficulty of separating the inanimacy of the innocent object world from human death, a form of ending that Woolf encountered frequently and always devastatingly in her early life.[25] It seems clear that of the many deaths ravaging her history, the most traumatic for her was that of her mother, Julia Stephen, and her own autobiographical notes indicate (as most students of Woolf know) that this death is the one commemorated in *To the Lighthouse*. Although she was careful to insist that the Ramsays are in important ways quite unlike her parents, her 1939 memoir "A Sketch of the Past" includes the well known recollection that after the novel was completed, she "ceased to be obsessed by" her mother, ceased to hear her voice or see her. "I suppose," she continues,

> that I did for myself what psycho-analysts do for their patients. I expressed some very long felt and deeply felt emotion. In expressing it I explained it and laid it to rest. But what is the meaning of "explained" it? Why, because I described her and my feeling for her in that book, should my vision of her and my feeling for her become so much dimmer and weaker? (*Moments* 81)

One of the most securely installed of critical commonplaces concerning *To the Lighthouse* is that this question is thematized (if not answered) in the novel itself, which ends with a gesture of completion—the final stroke of Lily Briscoe's painting—whose consequences are similar to those of the completion of Woolf's book. Concentrating on her canvas, Lily at last overcomes the emotional turmoil that Mrs. Ramsay has induced in her for so many years:

> One wanted, she thought, dipping her brush deliberately, to be on a level with ordinary experience, to feel simply that's a chair, that's a table, and yet at the same time, It's a miracle, it's an ecstasy. The problem might be solved after all. Ah, but what had happened? Some wave of white went over the window pane. The air must have stirred some flounce in the room. Her heart leapt at her and seized her and tortured her.
> "Mrs. Ramsay! Mrs. Ramsay!" she cried, feeling the old horror come back—to want and want and not to have. Could she inflict that still? And then, quietly, as if she refrained, that too became part of ordinary experience, was on a level with the chair, with the table. Mrs. Ramsay—it was part of her perfect goodness—sat there quite simply, in the chair, flicked her needles to and fro, knitted her reddish-brown stocking, cast her shadow on the step. There she sat. (202)

There is a crucial difference between the novel and the painting, of course, since the book can be said to include a depiction of Woolf's mother, whereas Lily's canvas is quite clearly a landscape: "There was the wall; the hedge; the tree. The question was of some relation between those masses" (147–48). Still, the shadow cast by Mrs. Ramsay on the step does seem to figure into the composition, and the passage just quoted strongly supports the view—again, one widely disseminated through Woolf scholarship—that in painting, Lily lays to rest Mrs. Ramsay's unquiet spirit or completes a work of mourning: as the pain of loss here becomes "part of ordinary experience," on a level with the objects from which one might compose a picture, Mrs. Ramsay loses, or somehow relinquishes, her power to hurt ("as if she refrained").

That Lily should somehow exorcise Mrs. Ramsay's ghost—or, in Mary Jacobus's Kristevan rendering, abject the mother figure[26]—by finishing the landscape makes sense, moreover, because the younger woman elsewhere associates the older with the lovely and still object world, at one point reflecting that a faint thought of her "seemed in consonance with this quiet house; this smoke; this fine early morning air" (161), at another envisioning her as a kind of Demeter figure who "putting her wreath to her forehead" goes "unquestioningly with her companion, a shade across the fields" and drawing from that vision a Wordsworthian comfort: "The sight, the phrase, had its power to console. Wherever she happened to be, painting, here in the country or in London, the vision would come to her" (181). This link between Mrs. Ramsay and the landscape is the more significant because interwoven with yet another elaboration of the existential question, Lily asking "What is the meaning of life?" (161) directly before noting the consonance of thoughts of Mrs. Ramsay with the quiet house. "What does it mean then, what can it all mean?" (145) she had already wondered at the very beginning of "The Lighthouse" (as though making explicit at last the question burningly implicit in "Time Passes"), before transforming Nancy's "What does one send to the Lighthouse?" into a question like that asked by Rachel in *The Voyage Out*: "What does one send? What does one do? Why is one sitting here, after all?" (146).

Woolf's very Bloomsbury answer appears to be that what one does, if anything, is to make art, and that it is toward the final stroke of the painting, if anything, that one's sitting here tends. The coincidence of the closing of the novel with Lily's completed work suggests that in painting Lily addresses not only Mrs. Ramsay's haunting, but also a more general crisis of meaning: both are resolved, if only temporarily, by the fashioning of art, that intervention in the material that sustains the miracle and ecstasy of the human dead and the object world, and yet also brings them into ordinary experience, relieving the one of its capacity to torment and the other of its power to frighten. In making, one finds both purpose and peace, and in Lily's painting the existential question and the imperative of production meet once again—though in this case Woolf seems more concerned with the process and difficulty of making than with the destiny of the made. *Cymbeline* and *Antony and Cleopatra*, not to mention the bowl of fruit that links Mrs. Ramsay and Augustus Carmichael, simply appear and do their work of mediating quite apart from their makers; and although Woolf has shown Clarissa and Orlando in action as artist-consumers, their labors seem a work of love in which they encounter little resistance from their materials. Not so Lily, however, who thinks while painting of how she is

drawn out of . . . community with people into the presence of this formidable ancient enemy of hers—this other thing, this truth, this reality. . . . It was an exacting form of intercourse anyhow. Other worshipful objects were content with worship: men, women, God, all let one kneel prostrate; but this form, were it only the shape of a white lamp-shade looming on a wicker table, roused one to perpetual combat, challenged one to a fight in which one was bound to be worsted. (158)

In spite of her feeling that other worshipful objects, including women, accept devotion without battle, however, something of the wrestling that marks her dealings with the lampshade does indeed inform Lily's confrontation with the specter of Mrs. Ramsay. The resilience of the older woman's image will eventually prove her wrong in thinking, "oh, the dead! . . . one pitied them, one brushed them aside, one had even a little contempt for them. They are at our mercy" (174), but even at this earlier juncture Lily's language registers a certain aggression, and her pun is portentous. At the novel's end, she will indeed brush Mrs. Ramsay aside, or rather into a work of art that neutralizes the older woman's power to torment, and she will register in the tense of her famous final thought, "I have had my vision" (209), the undoing of haunting by making, noting not only how the imagination's more fluid but also more vivid "vision" is diluted by fixing in the work of art ("Why. . . should my vision of her . . . become so much dimmer and weaker?") but also how the otherness of the specter (or the spectralness of the other) is weakened by the completion of a thing that bears the traces of both the once haunted maker and the ghost.

That representation or mimesis takes something away from the represented has been noted from the Hellenistic parable of Zeuxis to Sontag's call for an ecology of images, of course, but perhaps the subtlest such formulation, and the one that responds most directly to the problem of production under modernity, is that of Adorno, whose late *Aesthetic Theory* virtually turns on the acknowledgment that art is at once a resurrection and a murder of its material. "The affinity of all art with death," he writes,

> is most noticeable in the idea of pure form imposed by art on the living manifold, which is thus snuffed out. . . . The grief that art expresses results from the fact that it realizes unreal reconciliation at the expense of real reconciliation. (77)

At first glance, appropriating such a passage for the case of Lily's painting must seem a tricky affair at best, since Adorno is not here referring to anything so specific as the capturing of a person known to the artist in the work of art, nor does the reconciliation of which he speaks occur between people; on the contrary, the "living manifold" in question is more nearly like the object world than an interpersonal one, and by "reconciliation" he means a reconciliation between subject and object in general.[27] In particular, Adorno alludes to the post-Romantic idea that art effects such a reconciliation more or less by fusing matter (the actual material used as well as that which is "represented") with spirit, but he does so admonishingly, arguing that it is precisely when it claims to constitute an opening of the subject to the object world that art is most dishonest—that subjectivity most falls under the spell of its own illusion when it believes that there is such a thing as an innocent transformation that could do anything but displace the nonhuman from priority: "Art stands in for nature by abolishing the latter in effigy" (*Aesthetic* 97).

It is just here, however, that the connection to Woolf becomes apparent, for as we have seen this very sort of abolition is much at issue in *To the Lighthouse*. If Woolf calls attention to the fact that domination will always shadow the work of art, she does so not by anthropomorphizing the object world (a gesture that could be dismissed as a purely sentimental imagining of injustice against that which does not suffer), but rather by linking that world to the human figure of Mrs. Ramsay, who though hardly murdered in Lily's painting is at least arguably mastered by it. This is to say that the exorcism of Mrs. Ramsay helps to foreground the exorcism of the object that always occurs in the making of art, and by extension that Lily's action takes on its full significance only in the twin contexts of her "perpetual combat" with the referents of her painting and Woolf's extraordinary attempt to think from the object side of things, to imagine in "Time Passes" a world innocent of malice (to use Stevens's phrase), if not free from pain. And this is to say also that one of the dilemmas delicately negotiated in *To the Lighthouse* is that of how to indicate this most disturbing aspect of making without quite resorting to terms like "violence" or "aggression" or even "domination" itself, which in spite of their clear relevance all too readily intimate some moral equivalence between this ethically complex facet of art production and the depradations of actual war, imperialism, and exploitation.

For Adorno, art is redeemed at last not because it can ever be anything other than the domination of the object world by an imperialistic subjectivity, but because one social function that it performs (in the modern world) is to call attention to more destructive and direct forms of domination: "By means of spiritualization, which is the radical domination of art patterned after the domination of nature, art corrects the real domination of nature" (*Aesthetic* 166). It is at this point that the question of production proper comes into play, since the principal form of direct domination in question is to be found in the accelerating transformation of the material world required by the productionist imperatives of capitalism, and carried out by means of an ever more refined technological capacity. For Adorno, the work of art exceeds (though it does not fully transcend) the circumstances of its making because, as a gratuitous rather than an instrumental production of the subject, it calls into question the subject's productions in general: art "gives the lie to the notion that production for production's sake is necessary, by opting for a mode of praxis beyond labour" (*Aesthetic* 17). Thus it is not only that art works against domination by "representing" it; it is also that in its very appearance as domination *in play* art offers an alternative to the nonplayful conquest of nature (and, more problematically, of other human beings).

An authentic reconciliation between subject and object, in Adorno's terms, would of necessity be one in which the subject relinquishes the dream of identity in favor of an embrace of difference: "The reconciled condition would not be the philosophical imperialism of annexing the alien. Instead, its happiness would lie in the fact that the alien, in the proximity it is granted, remains what is distant and different, beyond the heterogeneous and beyond that which is one's own" (*Negative* 191). It is not precisely reconciliation that Lily seeks, however, nor can she really allow the object its perfect distance, for while she does recognize that the intrusive demands of her own subjectivity lead to problems of execution ("There was the hedge, sure enough. But one got nothing by soliciting urgently" [193]), her effort is still to fix the moment, to oppose the flux of the world in which she might be content to lose herself were she simply experiencing: "One must hold the scene—so—in a vise and let nothing come in and spoil it" (202). Although she knows that she conquers her demons through the act of painting rather than in the finished work ("It would be hung in the attics, she thought; it would be destroyed. But what did that matter? she asked herself, taking up her brush again" [208]), the prospect of finishing still governs her progress, ruling out the possibility of some thorough surrender to the tide of the things she would represent. And thus Woolf's stress on artistic process here is not simply the embrace of openness that some critics have deemed it, an easy expulsion of what she calls the "damned egotistical self" (*Diary* 2: 14) in the making of art; on the contrary, the language of violence in which Woolf couches Lily's struggle testifies to a certain recognition that the production of a work of art will always involve a subordination or annexing of that which is most radically other to the producing subject.

To the Lighthouse can by no means be said to address directly the transformation of the material world driven by the capitalist production imperative, nor is there much point in trying to portray Woolf as a critical social theorist *avant la lettre*, an agrarian reactionary, or the champion of a green sensibility within cosmopolitan modernism.[28] But it is important to note that in calling attention to the subordination of the object world that shadows all human making (while scrupulously avoiding anthropomorphization of that world, in this case by deploying Mrs. Ramsay as mediating genius of the landscape), Woolf marks a point of continuity between her own work and that of other modernists like Pound, Lewis, Williams, and Ransom, who were much more explicitly troubled by the explosive growth of technology, the fragility of the local and the particular, and the erasure of otherness under a globalizing and quantifying modernity. And if in rendering her anxieties so much more obliquely Woolf appears less closely related to Adorno than these writers, she also resembles Adorno much more nearly than they in combining an unwillingness to exempt art from the violence of appropriation with an operative belief that of all forms of production the making of art must be the least vicious. Thus Noel Annan's comment that the counterindustrial bent of the Frankfurt School writers would have made them as impatient as the Leavises with the "urban polish" of Bloomsbury (31–32), questionable in the first place in its distancing of Adorno and company from the cosmopolitan, also misses Woolf's own anxiety about the impositions of a voracious subjectivity upon a world in itself satisfactory and achieved. What the Frankfurt School and Bloomsbury share above all (and what helps to define both their broad likeness to and their more subtle difference from other modernisms) is an overwhelming attraction to the modern viewed as a pitch of *sophistication* never reached before, along with a sense that devotion to difficult and novel art may be the one way of reconciling this attraction with grave reservations about modernization in general.

The force of this point vis-à-vis some possible map of twentieth-century intellectual life may become still clearer if we return for a moment to Sartre, who as we have seen shares so much with Woolf when it comes to the kinds of questions about human experience that he gives pride of place in philosophical inquiry. Though no less suspicious of technological expansion than Adorno, Sartre was troubled not by the possibility that the attempt to subjugate the object world might succeed but by the evident fact that it inevitably fails (*Being and Nothingness*) or, later, by the inevitability with which human transformations of the material return in the form of new constraints (*Critique of Dialectical Reason*). In the "Doing and Having" section of *Being and Nothingness,* this principal philosophical heir to the Hegelian-Marxist tradition of turning to production as purpose observes that one makes an object in order to be "at the origin of a concrete existence," that one is interested in existence "only to the degree that the bond of creation" established with it gives one "a particular right of ownership over it," and that it "is not enough that a certain picture which I have in mind should exist; it is necessary as well that it exist *through me*. . . . In fact it is this synthesis of self and not-self . . . that I am aiming at and which will establish my ownership of the work" (736–37). The object at issue here is the object made or bought (the painting) rather than the object represented (Mrs. Ramsay), and yet it is precisely Sartre's point, very much in accord with Adorno and Woolf, that making cannot be understood as something disconnected from the attempt to master and absorb the world of the "not-self" as a whole. Continuing his exploration of the continuity between making and possessing, he writes further on that

> to possess is to wish to possess the world across a particular object. And as possession is defined as the effort to apprehend ourselves as the foundation of a being in so far as it is ourselves ideally, every possessive project aims at constituting the For-itself as the foundation of the world or a concrete totality of the in-itself, and this totality is, as totality, the for-itself itself existing in the mode of the in-itself. (762)[29]

Again, Sartre finds at the bottom of all making and acquiring the urge to achieve an impossible synthesis, one that would rival in seamlessness the false reconciliation between subject and object repudiated by Adorno and Woolf. Like both, he recognizes that the longing of consciousness to merge with the object of which it is conscious is inseparable from the desire to master or overcome, even noting that the very independence of the object contributes to the allure of appropriation: "The For-itself," he observes in describing what he calls the "Jonah complex," "dreams of an object which may be entirely assimilated by me, which would be *me*, without dissolving into me but still keeping the structure of the *in-itself*" (739). But whereas for Woolf the problem with production is that it cannot add to the already satisfactory, achieved object world without inevitably subtracting the untroubled distance to which that world is entitled, for Sartre (whose philosophy requires him to take the side of the subject, not the object) what is important is that the in-itself qua in-itself will always escape assimilation—which is to say that the traditional vision of nature as unconquerable force effectively continues valid in his rendering, the amassing of enormous instrumental knowledge notwithstanding. To compare Woolf and Sartre, then, is to note first that perplexity before the contingency of existence has a strong tendency to culminate in meditations on production, and second that the ultimate character of those meditations will be determined significantly by initial assumptions about where the profounder contingency lies: in the human realm, or in the world without a self.

The foregoing does not mean that the Woolf of the middle and later 1920s somehow rejected art—*A Room of One's Own* alone proves the absurdity of such a claim—but it does suggest why and how this period finds her introducing a new note of diffidence into her examinations of the relations among humans, human productions, and the rest of the world of things. Perhaps the most striking such introduction is to be found at the close of *Orlando* (the novel that followed *To the Lighthouse*), when the eponymous heroine imagines interring at the foot of a great oak her copy of her poem on that plant, *The Oak Tree*, begun in the Elizabethan age but only published in the twentieth century. Contemplating this strange burial, she asks,

> Was not writing poetry a secret transaction, a voice answering a voice? So that all this chatter and praise, and blame and meeting people who admired one and meeting people who did not admire one was as ill suited as could be to the thing itself—a voice answering a voice. What could have been more secret, she thought, more slow, and like the intercourse of lovers, than the stammering answer she had made all these years to the old crooning song of the woods . . . ? (325)

Rejecting the material object that mediates (trivially, in this instance) between people in favor of a secret antiphony, Orlando comes close to acknowledging how *The Oak Tree* presents itself as a substitute for the oak tree, how the poem moves to abolish its natural precursor in effigy even as it preserves and transforms it. The imagined interring of the book even draws an air of poetic justice from the fact that the soil—where an acorn will germinate but a book will not, and where printed leaves might become food for oak leaves—seems one of the few places where the original tree (heir of Septimus's trees) seems likely to prevail over the artistic usurper. Of course Orlando is also blessed with something very much like physical immortality, which asset would, one might guess, enable her to relinquish the poetic immortality promised by *The Oak Tree* with unusually good grace; and yet immortality is no more at issue for Lily, who believes that her painting will be hung in attics. The implication of both their stories is at last that, however little addicted to fame, applause, or posterity's admiration the artist may be, the work of making threatens to become the combat of enemies (whether or not it is also the intercourse of lovers) wherever a final fixing is involved— and that among the many forms of art, only perhaps one as open as the unpublished and continuously revised "Oak Tree" (as opposed to the published *Oak Tree*) might constitute a genuine conversation with the object world, a meeting of subject and object in which the distance between the two is respected and preserved.

We might note here that in *To the Lighthouse* Woolf does propose another possible venue for such a meeting. Sitting alone before the lighthouse's beam, Mrs. Ramsay at first seems to indulge precisely the identitarian impulse that Adorno proscribes: "Often she found herself sitting and looking . . . until she became the thing she looked at—that light, for example" (63). Almost immediately, however, this loss of personality is troubled by an intrusion:

> It will end, it will end, she said. It will come, it will come, when suddenly she added, We are in the hands of the Lord.
>
> But instantly she was annoyed with herself for saying that. Who had said it? Not she; she had been trapped into saying something she did not mean. (63)

The feeling of surrender to the thing itself is compromised, almost from the first, by the entrance of a discourse that does not seem to belong to the subject, and yet somehow must, a discourse so markedly proverbial and institutional as almost to give the incident the character of an Adornian fable about how apparent surrender to the object can conceal all manner of ideological investments. For the next two pages, Mrs. Ramsay attempts to regain and refine her communion with the light ("It was odd, she thought, how if one was alone, one leant to inanimate things; trees, streams, flowers; felt they expressed one; felt they became one; felt they knew one; in a sense were one; felt an irrational tenderness thus [she looked at that long steady light] as for oneself" [63–64]) while at the same time wrestling with the doubts introduced by this language that is and is not hers. At last,

[w]ith some irony in her interrogation . . . she looked at the steady light, the pitiless, the remorseless, which was so much her, yet so little her . . . but for all that
she thought, watching it with fascination, hypnotised . . . she had known happiness, exquisite happiness, intense happiness, and it silvered the rough waves a little
more brightly . . . and it rolled in waves of pure lemon which curved and swelled
and broke upon the beach and the ecstasy burst in her eyes and waves of pure
delight raced over the floor of her mind and she felt, It is enough! It is enough!
(64–65)

"Pitiless," "remorseless": the object appears in these crucial negatives
not as the mirror composed by the pathetic fallacy, but as an indifference
across which one might knowingly lay one's emotions ("happiness . . .
silvered the rough waves"), Mrs. Ramsay's sense that the light is "so much
her, yet so little her" seeming to approach that condition in which the alien
remains beyond the heterogeneous as well as the proper, distinct even its
infinite nearness. Could, then, such a retention of difference be possible in
the work of art? Does Mrs. Ramsay's experience imply that Lily could
have painted so as to elude the temptation to dominate, remaining instead
suspended between "so much her" and "so little her"? Woolf's gorgeous
elaboration of the older woman's sense that "it" is enough itself suggests
that the answer must be no, for whether "it" be life, experience, or something else, the thrust of the passage is quite clearly antithetical to the monumental imperative according to which "it" is not enough, unless "it" is
somehow inscribed or memorialized in the form of a production. The ecstatic experience is sufficient; anything more fixed would surely be both
too little and too much.

Mrs. Ramsay's sense of the sufficiency of memory, experience, or life
does not in itself diminish the value of art, but Woolf's extraordinary unfolding of her moment of vision does point to the fact that, in its concern about
the integrity of the object—a concern articulated mainly in prescriptions
respecting art, ironically enough—modernism finally invites the rejection of
art in favor of nature. For if the deformations of subjectivity are to be
avoided as far as possible, then the residue of the subjective that seems to
inform all art, even the most "classical" or "impersonal," will surely make
the work less valid and more suspect, in the end, than any natural thing:
Shakespeare may be quite impersonal, and yet how much more impersonal
must be a tree. To put matters so is, in a way, to compress into the narrow
compass of Hulme at his most extreme what was in fact a wide range of
views—modernists did not categorically reject "expression" or claim uniformly that the least "subjective" works were the best, of course—and yet
the point is far from trivial with respect to modernist theory because it
threatens to undermine that theory's characteristic way of recuperating "art
for art's sake," which included (as we have already noted) an appeal to the

monumental art object, whose poised self-sufficiency suggests at once the culmination and the transcendence of human effort. If the threat of Mrs. Ramsay's ecstasy before the lighthouse beam is the possible priority of transient experience over the fashioned thing, then, Lily's solidification of Mrs. Ramsay in her painting is more than the exorcism of a ghost; it is also a repression of the disturbing possibility that the work of art might not be part of the satisfactory and achieved object world after all, but only an excess, an excrescence of the human subject whose position is infinitely odd.

In this respect, *The Waves* (Woolf's next novel after *Orlando*), might seem to mark a withdrawal from the acknowledgment of violence or excessiveness in human production discernible in *To the Lighthouse*. Toward the end of the long speech that seems the later work's normative summation, Bernard, the most central of the six characters whose monologues compose the book, does briefly take up the effort to think from the side of nature, imagining himself walking through a landscape as a kind of disembodied presence ("how describe the world seen without a self?" [287]); but both the genesis and the termination of this ethereal passage suggest its aberrance within the fiction as a whole. Prompted initially by the feeling of a "heaviness" of "despondency" (285), it gives way (in the novel's final pages) to a yearning not for airy ghostliness but for solidity of self and in things—"I begin to doubt the fixity of tables . . . to tap my knuckles smartly upon the edges of apparently solid objects and say, 'Are you hard?'" (288)—and indeed Bernard makes clear at several points that his project is to oppose flux (and its culmination in biological death) with a fixing figured as an actual solidification of the evanescent. Rejecting ghosts, he speaks of "shap[ing] between [his] hands the story of [his] life" and setting it before his interlocutor as "a complete thing" (289), though he has admitted that the "globe, full of figures" (238) that he wishes to fashion may be at best approximate and fragile. "The crystal, the globe of life as one calls it, far from being hard and cold to the touch, has walls of thinnest air" (256), he observes earlier, as though emphasizing the fearful effort required to protect from the buffetings of a Heraclitean world the "luminous halo," the "semi-transparent envelope surrounding us from the beginning of consciousness to the end" that Woolf had enjoined storytellers to convey in "Modern Fiction" (*Essays* 2: 106).

In his final words, moreover, Bernard presents the struggle against death as an effort heroic and doomed:

What enemy do we now perceive advancing against us, you whom I ride now, as we stand pawing this stretch of pavement? It is death. Death is the enemy. It is death against whom I ride with my spear couched and my hair flying back like a young man's, like Percival's, when he galloped in India. I strike spurs into my horse. Against you I will fling myself, unvanquished and unyielding, O Death! (297)

The passage is followed by the very last line of the novel, "*The waves broke on the shore.*" Italicized in the manner of the natural descriptions that alternate with the six human speakers' monologues, the line is symmetrically paired with the picture of the dawn sea that opens the novel—so that, in conjunction with Bernard's finale, it suggests the triumph over the mortal individual of an inanimate nature, ambiguously associated (as elsewhere in Woolf) with antianimate death. "This is also to show that the theme effort, effort dominates," Woolf told her diary, regarding an earlier version of the ending, "not the waves: & personality: & defiance . . ." (*Diary* 3: 339), indicating that the core of this work would be humanity's struggle against an overwhelming force, not (as in "Time Passes") some attempt to think from the side of the object world or (as in *Orlando*) an effort to envision a dialogue that might form the basis of a happier relation between humans and nature.

The fact that Bernard comes to his battle with mutability so boldly clothed in the trappings of heroism should give us pause, however, if only because we know that after finishing *The Waves* Woolf embarked upon a project that would result in two books, *The Years* and *Three Guineas*, that explicitly repudiate militarism and its iconography. "What connection is there between the sartorial splendours of the educated man and the photograph of ruined houses and dead bodies?" she asks in the latter, and answers immediately, "Obviously the connection between dress and war is not far to seek; your finest clothes are those that you wear as soldiers" (21). Nor was Woolf's abhorrence of the martial merely a drifting with the interwar current: appalled, like the rest of Bloomsbury, by the patriotic fervor accompanying Britain's entry into World War I, she held to pacifism even at the end of the 1930s, when many of her close friends had abandoned it.[30] It would therefore be odd, to say the least, to find Woolf adopting the voice of the soldier without irony or ambivalence, even in a passage as highly stylized as this one; and indeed more careful attention to some moments in the novel suggests that Bernard's casting of the urge to make in terms of military heroism offers a lesson similar to that of Lily's combat with the lampshade—namely, that what appears from one angle as resistance to death appears from another as a domination of the material upon which transformation is wrought.[31]

As in *To the Lighthouse*, Woolf suggests the violent aspect of making by linking the object world to human figures rather than by anthropomorphizing it; but if the exorcism of Mrs. Ramsay was a relatively subtle and gentle business, objectifications of human beings here are attended by a far more decisive aggression. "This shiny pebble is Madame Carlo," says Susan at school, "and I will bury her deep because of her fawning and ingratiating manners, because of the sixpence she gave me for keeping my knuckles flat when I played my scales. I buried her sixpence" (44). In a less overtly violent reflection, but one similarly charged by a bitter sense of subordination, the young Bernard observes that his headmaster "has a nose like a mountain at sunset, and a blue cleft in his chin, like a wooded ravine . . . seen from the train window" before commenting that the man's "tremendous and sonorous words . . . are too hearty be true" (32). Whereas in *To the Lighthouse* the finding of the large scene in the small thing had served to link people in tenderness (Mrs. Ramsay unites with Augustus Carmichael and later soothes her daughter to sleep by imagining landscapes in domestic objects), this encounter evokes a less wholly benign event in the earlier novel—the stealing of the solitude of the pool "seen from a train window" in "Time Passes"—and presses it into the conflict between one phrasemaker and another. Nor does Bernard's handling of others escape the notice of those he objectifies: "Did he not," Neville wonders,

> only wish to continue the sequence of the story which he never stops telling himself? He began it when he rolled his bread into pellets as a child. One pellet was a man, one was a woman. We are all pellets. We are all phrases in Bernard's story; things he writes down in his notebook under A or B. He tells our story with extraordinary understanding, except of what we most feel. For he does not need us. (69–70)

The human being most richly transformed into something else in *The Waves*, however, is Percival, the silent seventh character who in many respects resembles his distinguished predecessor in *To the Lighthouse*. Like Mrs. Ramsay, Percival is generally admired by those who know him, though occasionally disliked precisely for this reason, and like her he appears to have had a counterpart among his author's own lost loved ones: upon finishing *The Waves*, Woolf wrote in her diary, "I have been sitting these 15 minutes in a state of glory, & calm, & some tears, thinking of Thoby [her brother] & if I could write Julian Thoby Stephen 1881–1906 on the first page. I suppose not" (*Diary* 4: 10).[32] Unlike Mrs. Ramsay, however, Percival has no internal life available to the reader, and indeed the other characters agree that the source of his magnetism is his apparent lack of self-consciousness: "He sees nothing; he hears nothing. He is remote from us all in a pagan universe" (6); "Oblivious, almost entirely ignorant, he will pass from my life" (60); "He alone is unconscious of their tricks" (84). Voiceless in a novel that heavily foregrounds subjectivity's need for a speaking "I," Percival seems more like the brute nature of the interludes even than the earth-responsive Susan (notably the only character who seems to elicit any meaningful response from him) and more purely an object while still alive than the matriarch of *To the Lighthouse*. Indeed of all Woolf's characters, Percival perhaps comes nearest to figuring the object world in its sheer otherness to subjectivity, though as a synecdoche for the British domination of India he represents that world in a mode in which it seems (as also in the interludes and Bernard's speech) a force capable of dominating or overwhelming as well as succumbing, an entity whose very reticence contributes to its terrifying power.

The most intriguing of the attributes shared by Mrs. Ramsay and this nexus of the six monologists' desires, however, is a tendency to inspire others to attempt a making permanent. In spite of the fact that his blundering interferes with the attempt "to fix in words," Louis notes, "it is Percival who inspires poetry" (40); and in his last live appearance, Percival will indeed be fixed and made permanent in something like a work of art, just as Mrs. Ramsay is at last captured and tranquilized in Lily's painting. This time, however, Woolf will render the event not in the language of decent interment but in that of ritual sacrifice, as Patricia Joplin has noted, apparently building upon Lucio Ruotolo's comparison of this scene to the ancient rites detailed by Jessie Weston in *From Ritual to Romance* (Lecture; *Interrupted* 153). At the dinner held in honor of Percival's departure for his colonial post (where he will in fact die), Rhoda imagines "the drumming of naked men with assegais" and the decking of "the beloved with garlands and with laurel leaves," while Louis thinks of "[d]eath . . . woven in with the violets . . . Death and again death" (140–41) and of how "the circle in our blood . . . closes in a ring" (145).

What makes this thought so striking in the context of the present discussion is that it slips directly into the rhetoric of making, and specifically that of the transformation of life into globe to which Bernard will return in his valedictory speech. Louis continues:

> the circle in our blood . . . closes in a ring. Something is made. Yes, as we rise and fidget, a little nervously, we pray, holding in our hands this common feeling, "Do not move, do not let the swing-door cut to pieces the thing that we have made, that globes itself here, among these lights, these peelings, this litter of bread crumbs and people passing. Do not move, do not go. Hold it for ever." (145)

Jinny then thinks, "Let us hold it for one moment . . . love, hatred, by whatever name we call it, this globe whose walls are made of Percival, of youth and beauty, and something so deep sunk within us that we shall perhaps never make this moment out of one man again" (145). And shortly thereafter, Bernard remarks how in creating a moment "from Percival" the six have proved that they

> can add to the treasury of moments. We are not slaves bound to suffer incessantly unrecorded petty blows on our bent backs. We are not sheep, either, following a master. We are creators. We too have made something that will join the innumerable congregations of past time. We too, as we put on our hats and push open the door, stride not into chaos, but into a world that our own force can subjugate and make a part of the illumined and everlasting road. (146)

With its faint recollection of the Pateresque moment from Woolf's "Reading" quoted above ("We want something . . . sheltering as in a clear gem the flame which burns now so high and now sinks so low in our own hearts"), Jinny's rendering of Percival as both moment and globe serves as an essential transition between Louis's anxiety about fragility and Bernard's assurance that the friends have fashioned a stay against mutability: in the passage from the one to the other, sacrifice has yielded freedom from flux and death. The problem, of course, is that such a propitiation of destructive time brings death to the victim as well as life to the tribe—that fixing (in the memory, apparently, as in a painting) cannot preserve its object without in some sense destroying it. If we overcome the petty blows we suffer by recording those blows, then in recording our friends, presumably, we likewise overcome them: "oh, the dead! . . . one pitied them, one brushed them aside," Lily had reflected, to which Jinny here adds, "we shall perhaps never make this moment out of one man again."

In his closing monologue, Bernard not only reinforces the connection between fixing and sacrifice but also links both to the haunting that figures so prominently in *To the Lighthouse*. After speaking of shaping his life into a complete thing, he tells his interlocutor that he must "recall things gone far, gone deep," including the "half-articulate ghosts who keep up their haunting by day and night," the "shadows of people one might have been," then goes on to describe "the savage" within him ("the hairy man who dabbles his fingers in ropes of entrails") and to imagine his body as "some cool temple" wherein "the altars stand smoking," before returning at last to the crumbs and peelings that, in Louis's speech, served as the quotidian debris obscurely transfigured by Percival's sacrifice (289–90). Woolf's heavy stylization of ritual violence here teeters on the edge of unintentional camp as well as politically suspect primitivism, to be sure, and yet to dismiss it as either would be to lose sight of the difficult effect that she achieves by having Bernard use a domesticated discourse of savagery (as we might call it) to unfold confessions of whose true brutality he remains unaware. For in suggesting that her performance-conscious protagonist's "darkest" desires in fact prove to be his darkest desires, Woolf not only locates making more securely in the realm of aggression than she had by associating it with the relatively cleaner business of exorcism, but also definitively rejects the possibility that art simply replaces bloody religion as good magic would replace bad, or sublimation replace symptom: "We are creators. We . . . stride . . . into a world that our own force can subjugate," and we sacrifice that world to our creation.

If *To the Lighthouse* had left any doubt, then, *The Waves* confirms that Woolf was intensely, if not continuously, concerned about the element of domination in making, and that this concern lay at the heart of her understanding of the anthropology of art, which is to say her understanding of art's genealogy and indeed its nature. It is thus not enough to note, as Judith Lee does in a recent article, that for Woolf aesthetic activity "involves aggressively acting upon . . . material reality, destroying it if necessary, in order to make room for the world one imagines" (194), or that what in Percival's colonialist "world was antithetical to making—militarism" is in the world of Bernard's creation "a necessary mode of invention" (197): we need to acknowledge also that in Woolf's view subjugation in making remained authentic subjugation, unsublimated because any making compromises the integrity of the object world. Nor is it sufficient to point out that what "involved imposing an inherited order" in Percival's domain "involves defending a self-invented order" in Bernard's (197) without adding that the posture required for such a defense is only illusorily free from the violence of imposition required for order's initial establishment—a problem given historical point, incidentally, by Joplin's reminder that Percival's "apotheosis in the minds of his friends is described in rhetoric chillingly like fascist propaganda in this era" ("Authority" 219), which relied heavily on conflated promises of a defense of order and a return to origins.

This does not mean, of course, that Woolf argues for an actual equivalence between physical violence and the action of rhetoric or imaginative transformation as such, though uses of the word "violence" carrying just this implication have come to appear with troubling regularity in contemporary literary and cultural study. No more than Adorno does Woolf moralize against the artist who willy nilly goes about representing here, reproducing there, stealing life from the innocent world of nature and striking down the human subjects in his path; the "sacrifice" in *The Waves* comes about without direct harm to Percival himself, after all, and Lily's exorcism does nothing to the actual Mrs. Ramsay, long dead. The point is rather, once again, that both writers find in all production, including the fashioning of the work of art, the exercise of a will to power over that which is radically other to the subject, an exercise substantively different from violence, domination, and imperialism in social relations and yet closely related to them structurally and often intertwined with them in practice. Indeed for Adorno, as we have seen, the domination of the object world has desperately immediate consequences, since the tradition that renders it legitimate in idea—the tradition of a "conquest" of nature that Baudrillard describes as man's "continual deciphering of himself through his works, finalized by his shadow (his own end) reflected by this operational mirror, this sort of ideal of a productivist ego" (*Mirror* 19)—underwrites real destruction on a massive scale.

Here a question arises, however, for if Adorno's anxiety about predatory subjectivity gathers its practical significance as part of a history of human consciousness supporting an ecological project (very broadly speaking), then what of Woolf, whose writing seems so removed from such a sensibility and so little occupied with the progress of the mind since Kant? One way of answering this question would be to turn to "Anon," the radically revisionary history of English literature that she began only in the late 1930s and had not finished at the time of her death. In this remarkable fragment, she moves, as Adorno does, to disclose the radical epistemic break that separated modern consciousness from what came before; but whereas Adorno places that moment in the Enlightenment (arguing that the rise of instrumental reason changed the meaning of the manipulation of nature from contest against an overwhelming force to domination of the finally unresisting), she locates the fatal turn at the invention of printing. Having posited as the origin of verbal art an unselfconscious song arising organically and without mediation from human and nonhuman together, Woolf writes that it "was the printing press that finally was to kill Anon," the nameless singer of that original, undivided life:

> Caxtons printing press foretold the end of that anonymous world; It is now written down; fixed; nothing will be added even if the legend still murmers on, and still down in Somersetshire the peasants remember how "on the night of the full moon King Arthur and his men ride round the hill, and their horses are shod with silver". The printing press brought the past into existence. It brought into existence the man who is conscious of the past the man who sees his time, against a background of the past; the man who first sees himself and shows himself to us. The first blow has been aimed at Anon when the authors name is attached to the book. The individual emerges. (385)

Woolf's positioning of printing as the most decisive break in the history of singing and storytelling, or rather her registering of that break as violence ("the first blow"), suggests that "Anon" is in part an interrogation of her own career—that in this valedictory and yet incomplete speculation she came as close as she ever would to questioning explicitly the project of fixing and making permanent so important to her and her fellow modernists, a project whose governing emblem might be the Hogarth Press itself. What is perhaps most remarkable about "Anon," however, is that this questioning occurs not in the mode of moral anguish but in the tones of historical regret, in the rueful acknowledgment of a belatedness that has little do with literary precedent. Positing (in a counterintuitive gesture whose power to astonish is perhaps diminished, for us, by our habituation to such reversals in the wake of Foucault) not that the subject's drive to inscribe itself gave birth to printing, but rather that printing gave birth to the subject, or at least to the authorial subject, Woolf presents the opposition between consciousness and everything else as a historical phenomenon rather than a transhistorical condition, and thus requires us to revise once more our understanding of her interest in the interplay between technology and subjectivity. "Anon," that is to say, is among other things a deliberate reflection upon technology as fatality in the largest sense, according to which the birth of art as we know it coincides not only with the first appearance of "the past" as a phenomenon of consciousness but also with the permanent loss of a prelapsarian past whose perfection (or purity) would be defined, precisely, by the absence of art as we know it. It is thus that the past becomes for Woolf art's first sacrificial victim, killed by the very representation that preserved it, indeed killed by the very fact of preservation; and it is thus that the murderous birth of art is allegorized in every work fashioned since.

BATTLE SCARS

Woolf's treatment of the problem of the object in her last two novels, *The Years* (published in 1937) and *Between the Acts* (which had not undergone final revision but was essentially complete when she committed suicide in 1941), is shaped significantly by the intense concern with the past so strikingly evidenced in "Anon." Certainly, confrontations between subject and object very much like those seen in previous novels still govern important junctures: in *The Years*, for example, Delia experiences a familiar existential shock when on leaving her dying mother's bedroom she encounters "a white jug stained pink by the setting sun" ("Where am I? . . . Where am I? she repeated, looking at the pink jug, for it all looked strange" [25]), while Rose, relieved to find at Maggie and Sara's place a "crimson-and-gilt chair" that had stood in the hall of her cousins' childhood home (165), draws a consolation from this object evocative of many moments in Woolf's earlier fictions. Certainly, too, would-be makers continue to long to capture life in the form of a solid thing: in the same novel, Eleanor recalls Bernard in *The Waves* when she thinks, "Oughtn't life to be something you could handle and produce?" (366), and when she feels "that she wanted to enclose the present moment; to make it stay" (428).

For the most part, however, Woolf's focus shifts in these late books from the process of making itself to the traces of human production in a world grown old, the predominant note of *The Years*, especially, being a feeling of oppression by the sheer weight of accumulated things, an overwhelming that replaces the enchantment of the long ago "Solid Objects" or even the much more recent *Waves*. In the opening pages of *The Years*, for example, Abel Pargiter notes irritably that there are "too many little objects about" his mistress's room (7), and in the course of the narrative characters are repeatedly undercut by their own or others' possessions: "It was a small room, crowded with objects. And I'm too well dressed. . . ." (67); "the Judge . . . looked fretful; no longer immune from human weakness, and she remembered with a smile how very gullible he was, there in that hideous house in Queen's Gate, about old oak" (111); "He was looking round the room. It was crowded. . . . She felt that he was criticising the room and herself too" (262–63). The Pargiters' former servant Crosby seems to harbor a tenderness for objects that other characters lack, but when she places her relics of Abercorn Terrace upon her mantel, Woolf's free indirect discourse exudes at best an impoverished pathos ("it was quite like home") whose dryness is only compounded by an immediately succeeding description of the metamorphosis of Crosby's dog into unliving thing: "at last he refused to open his lips; his body grew stiffer and stiffer; a fly walked across his nose without its twitching" (219).

Even these relics can inspire surprising hostility, moreover, Eleanor taking as her particular nemesis a certain "ink-corroded" walrus of which she thinks at one point, "That solid object might survive them all" (91), and to which she returns, near the novel's close, in rejecting material things in favor of her own ability to solidify experience in memory:

> She shut her hands on the coins she was holding, and again she was suffused with a feeling of happiness. Was it because this had survived—this keen sensation (she was waking up) and the other thing, the solid object—she saw an ink-corroded walrus—had vanished? She opened her eyes wide. Here she was; alive; in this room, with living people. (426)

It is hard to escape the feeling that Eleanor's sense of triumph over a thingly enemy is odd to the point of eccentricity, as though Woolf might be distancing herself ironically from her character at this point—and indeed the joke *is* on Eleanor inasmuch as, unbeknownst to her, Crosby has rescued the walrus from a wastebasket after all. Unlike the element of moral doubtfulness introduced by Bernard's martial language in *The Waves*, however, this irony of fact does nothing to undercut the protagonist's view of the world as a whole; and because Eleanor elsewhere remains largely sympathetic, it seems reasonable to take this moment as confirmation that Woolf has at last abandoned the attempt, initiated at least as far back as "Time Passes," to think from the object side.

And yet the world of objects at issue in *The Years* is not quite the world of objects at issue in *The Waves*. In the later novel, Woolf is concerned not with savage yet innocent nature but rather with the realm of human productions, above all the Victorian overproduction emblematized in *Orlando* by a conglomeration of "the most heterogeneous and ill-assorted objects, piled higgledy-piggledy in a vast mound where the statue of Victoria now stands" in St. James's Park, of which Orlando thinks that she had never "in all her life, seen anything at once so indecent, so hideous, and so monumental" (232). Nor is *Orlando* the only evidence that the Victorian period—regarded as a confluence of industrial expansion, rapacious imperialism, fetishisms of accumulation, and stridently self-righteous patriarchy—encoded for Woolf as virtually nothing else the triumph of a subjectivity that subjugates as it makes: one can find eloquent testimony to the same in *Three Guineas*, "A Sketch of the Past," and Miss La Trobe's dramatization of the nineteenth century in *Between the Acts*. We might, then, recognize in *The Years* Woolf's most formidable attempt to subdue the Victorian, an immense effort to objectify a wantonly objectifying age and to deploy against it its own habit of accumulating detail upon descriptive detail—a habit that, as she indicates in "Mr. Bennett and Mrs. Brown," Woolf found unfortunately out-lasting the Victorian per se. *The Years*, in other words, finally extends rather than confounds the logic of *The Waves*, Woolf turning not against the world of nature at this point but against what stood for her as English history's most astounding eruption of a human production that destroys.[33]

Given this preoccupation with mostly irredeemable making, it should come as small surprise that unlike any of Woolf's other novels, *The Years* contains no genuine artists, nor does it offer much help, most of the way through, in understanding how the work of art might function in the context of this disastrous flooding of the world with things. In the book's final pages, however, Woolf does seem to propose a way for us to share beauty while avoiding the impositions of further production; for as Delia's party draws to its close, a word from Eleanor effects a singular understanding, a much muted version of the seemingly mystical sharing that goes on in *Mrs. Dallo-way*:

> "Listen . . ." said Eleanor, raising her hand. Upstairs they were playing "God save the King" on the gramophone; but it was the pigeons she meant; they were crooning.
>
> "That's wood pigeons, isn't it?" said Kitty. (433)

And a few paragraphs later, Eleanor watches a cab through the window:

> A young man had got out; he paid the driver. Then a girl in a tweed travelling suit followed him. He fitted his latch-key to the door. "There," Eleanor murmured, as he opened the door and they stood for a moment on the threshold. "There!" she repeated as the door shut with a little thud behind them.
>
> Then she turned round into the room. "And now?" she said, looking at Morris, who was drinking the last drops of a glass of wine. "And now?" she asked, holding out her hands to him.
>
> The sun had risen, and the sky above the houses wore an air of extraordinary beauty, simplicity, and peace. (434)

And so the novel ends, with a vision cleansed of the massive detritus of the Victorian human-made world, as though the "simplicity" that transcends such debris must form the natural link between "beauty" and "peace." The alternative to further production—the aesthetic activity that avoids fixing and transforming—presented here is, quite simply, ostension ("There!"), that gesture in which the pointing subject withdraws even as it brings the object into view. The operation is an imperfect one, as Woolf makes clear, since in keeping her attention on the cab Eleanor ignores an ostensive command from Delia ("Look, Eleanor!"), and yet this very imperfection is what saves the whole enterprise: not a gesture of mastery, ostension can be understood as an invitation to share in perception of the object that would avoid the abolition in effigy of the thing in question, as an artlike action that cooperates with life instead of displacing it.

At this point, we may be inclined to pause for a moment, by way of noting that the problem of domination in production seems by now to have grown marvelous attenuated in its capacity to mean anything at all in practice. If Woolf has indeed come to find something blameable in any productive activity much more aggressive than pointing, we might ask, how much of life can be lived so as to satisfy her criteria of correctness, and why should we care? More basically, we might wonder whether such an interest in pointing as alternative is not a little much to extrapolate from the closing scene of *The Years*, even given the positioning of its several ostensions at the conclusion of the novel, which is also a literal and figurative dawn ("And now?"). In response to the first question, we might observe that presenting an ideal alternative is not the same thing as prescribing or proscribing behavior—that Eleanor's pointing is not necessarily a model for living, but rather a logically austere conclusion to a work that explores the costs of a fantastic overproduction.[34] But the more meaningful answer to both objections would be that the possibilities obliquely sketched here are strongly foregrounded in *Between the Acts*, that final work in which Woolf presents a fully realized venture into the art of ostension, even as she suggests how, in a country threatened by war, it can seem almost impossible to separate any action from the work of destruction or complicity therewith.

That the stakes of this last novel are high has been widely noted by its readers, who, whether entranced or repelled, have consistently acknowledged it to be one of Woolf's most difficult texts, in the sense both that its sympathies are often hard to discern and that the conflict-riven world it portrays is extraordinarily hard to accept without grief. What scholarship on this novel has not sufficiently considered is the crucial role, amid the aggressions it unfolds, of violence against nature, though Woolf announces a return to the question of human impositions upon the land five paragraphs in, when Bart Oliver tells the visitors to Pointz Hall that "from an aeroplane . . . you could still see, plainly marked, the scars made by the Britons; by the Romans; by the Elizabethan manor house; and by the plough, when they ploughed the hill to grow wheat in the Napoleonic wars" (4). With its treatment of the land as a wounded body subject to large-scale aggressions, Bart's statement marks the first of several moments in *Between the Acts* in which history is registered as a double violence of humans against one another and of humans against the earth, the first of several in which Woolf calls attention to actual transformations of the landscape rather than the more abstract "domination" inhering in other kinds of making. When Lucy Swithin, evoking "Time Passes," says, "That's what makes a view so sad . . . And so beautiful. It'll be there . . . when we're not" (53), her nephew Giles Oliver grows silently enraged, doubting that even the view can survive the impending human conflict, thinking, "Only the ineffective word 'hedgehog' illustrated his vision of Europe, bristling with guns, poised with planes. At any moment guns would rake that land into furrows; planes splinter Bolney Minster into smithereens and blast the Folly. He, too, loved the view. And blamed Aunt Lucy, looking at views, instead of—doing what?" (53).

Like *Three Guineas*, *Between the Acts* tends overwhelmingly to identify this kind of militarism with a masculine self-assertion at once frightening and ridiculous, but it also seems occasionally to waver on this point in a manner virtually unique in Woolf—perhaps because despair can carry with it a curious openness to all kinds of suggestions. Written largely as Chamberlain's politics of appeasement went into final collapse,[35] the novel records the most severe testing that Woolf's pacifism would undergo, a testing the more strenuous because global events had generated in many Europeans an unusually intense and polyvalent pessimism about human nature. In those years, the Hogarth Press brought out a volume of Freud that included part of *Civilization and its Discontents*, which treatise on the human propensity for aggression (published in full by the Hogarth in 1930) Leonard Woolf cites in *Barbarism Within and Without* (1939) after observing that the "barbarian is, therefore, not only at our gates; he is always within the walls of our civilization, inside our minds and our hearts" (65). And though Bernard of *The Waves* had already spoken of the savage within years before, his author wrote in a diary entry of 9 December 1939, as though first discovering how that phrasemaker's still romantic intimations could be taken to their less appealing but logical conclusion, "Freud is upsetting: reducing one to whirlpool; & I daresay truly. If we're all instinct, the unconscious, whats all this about civilisation, the whole man, freedom, & c?" (*Diary* 5: 250).[36]

Well into the late thirties, Woolf explicitly repudiated the possibility that all humans are innately aggressive, yet Bernard's savage suggests that behind this apparent confidence lay a trace of uncertainty that would flower strikingly in *Between the Acts*. In *Three Guineas*, Woolf had claimed that women "have never felt or enjoyed" the "satisfaction in fighting" that men seem to find (6), and in "A Sketch of the Past" she recalled a moment in her childhood when, in the midst of a fight with her brother Thoby, she "felt: why hurt another person? I dropped my hand instantly, and stood there, and let him beat me" (*Moments* 71). At the end of her final novel, however, she notes that as her tensely married characters Isa and Giles sat together, "enmity was bared; also love. But before they slept, they must fight; after they had fought, they would embrace. From that embrace another life might be born. But first they must fight, as the dog fox fights with the vixen, in the heart of darkness, in the fields of night" (218–19). Transforming the two into archetypes, as if to make certain that they will not simply be mistaken for one aberrantly hostile couple ("The great hooded chairs had become enormous. And Giles too. And Isa too. . . . It was the night that dwellers in caves had watched from some high place among rocks" [219]), Woolf replaces Bernard's savage with an imagining of the primal largely stripped of glamor, in which the savage resides in woman as well as man.[37]

This adumbration of a pervasive aggression is important not least because it proves inseparable from Woolf's elaboration of the possibility that not only making, but all action, might be attended by insoluble moral complexities. In October 1933, the Hogarth Press had published Mussolini's *Political and Social Doctrine of Fascism,* which includes not only an outright attack on pacifism, but also an ominous appeal to spirit evocative of Hegel: "The State is . . . the custodian and transmitter of the spirit of the people. . . . The Fascist State is an embodied will to power and government: the Roman tradition is here an ideal of force in action. . . . If every age has it own characteristic doctrine, there are a thousand signs which point to Fascism as the characteristic doctrine of our time" (21, 25, 26).[38] The Roman tradition as an ideal of force in action makes its appearance in *Between the Acts* in the form of a scar upon the body of the land, as we have seen, and the novel as a whole could well be described as a meditation upon the possibility that Fascism was the characteristic doctrine of its time. But it is the mention of the Fascist state as embodiment of the will that most directly calls attention to the fact that any volitional activity at all could seem suspect in the late 1930s, when many British and Americans (including Stevens) found themselves recanting the belief, evolved just shortly before, that simply because he seemed the only European politician who was doing anything, Mussolini had to be the answer (or at least *an* answer). Making, changing, and doing themselves were tainted by the revelation that their great political avatar could prove so dangerous to the rest of the world, in the end, and if to be *entre deux guerres* was to be between the acts, this was partly because acting had become inseparable from aggression.

But while others, looking toward Italy, were beginning to wonder whether action was not a fatality, Woolf—who had long been concerned about the violence of making, as we have seen—seems to have looked toward a threatened England and begun to wonder whether the refusal of action could continue to be justified. That the old alignments were beginning to dissolve for her is suggested by the fact that Lucy, arguably the most likeable character in *Between the Acts* and certainly the most peaceable, seems curiously out of place in her own story: Alex Zwerdling has commented that this "visionary . . . who makes consoling fictions out of the cosmic emptiness" seems to have stepped out of an earlier novel from a less desperate time (314), and it is hard not to notice how singularly unperturbed by the human capacity to destroy she remains. In assuming that the view will outlast them all, once again, she ignores the mortality of the present landscape as Giles does not, nor does she appear to recognize the ambiguity of a passage from her "favourite reading," an "Outline of History," which leads her to spend hours "thinking of rhododendron forests in Piccadilly; when the entire continent, not then, she understood, divided by a channel, was all one" (8). An optimist who "belong[s] to the unifiers" (118), in the view of her brother, she seems unimpressed by the possibility that a unity of the continent could imply not only an end to conflict but also, as Joplin notes in her crucial article on this novel (211), the absorption of England by Germany, an eventuality for which the Woolfs had prepared by making a suicide pact.[39]

Further, Lucy seems not to notice certain more abstract impositions of the subject upon the land already at work. Her assertion that the "view" might outlast herself and her companions is called into question not only by Giles's practical doubts but also by one of Miss La Trobe's thoughts at twilight: "There was no longer a view—no Folly, no spire of Bolney Minster. It was land merely, no land in particular" (210), the playwright reflects, pointing to the fact that the word "view" only has meaning with reference to human seeing. Lucy's "Outline" also harbors a subtle instance of consciousness annexing the world without a self, in its note that "England . . . was then a swamp. Thick forest covered the land" (218), which by obscuring (however casually) the fact that "England" was not England at the time described reduces all that preceded humans to a mere preface. And this point is reinforced by Woolf's suggestion, elsewhere in the novel, that time itself may be no less anthropocentric a construct than "view" or "history":

> The room was empty.
>
> Empty, empty, empty; silent, silent, silent. The room was a shell, singing of what was before time was; a vase stood in the heart of the house, alabaster, smooth, cold, holding the still, distilled essence of emptiness, silence. (36–37)

Harking back to "Time Passes" and the interludes of *The Waves*, this passage offers to correct the assimilation of the world before ideology to the world after by suggesting that what enables the room to sing of what was before time was is, precisely, its emptiness, its (temporary) freedom from the human makers of "the past."

Sallie Sears has made a strong case for the view that in this novel of extraordinarily fragile hopes women "alone are capable of actions that do not hurt or damage something," that "it is their imaginations that keep alive the sense of the past, the continuity of culture, the interdependence of all living creatures" (216); and yet the case of Mrs. Swithin may lead us to wonder whether particular visions of continuity and interdependence may not be part of the problem, whether the unifiers can unify without forcibly erasing difference. Certainly, Lucy is no more to be dismissed as some instrument of subjectivity's imperialism than is Mrs. McNab of *To the Lighthouse*, nor does it make sense to claim that in *Between the Acts* Woolf simply negates her own pacifism, her faith in human beings, or her suspicion of the urge to do something at all costs. But it can be said that she unfolds in it a complex rethinking of aggression and domination that emphatically continues—if it hardly completes—her earlier reflections on production, art, and nature. And this is so not only because the novel is threaded through with dangers to the land and problematic adventures of consciousness, but also because the work of art upon which it centers, Miss La Trobe's pageant of English history, draws to its close with a quite extraordinary confrontation between humans and object world.

After rendering the Victorian age principally in the form of a policeman who declaims, "Purity is our watchword; prosperity and respectability" (163), La Trobe brings her audience to what she calls in the program "Present Time. Ourselves"—an empty stage, nothing but "the cows, the meadows and the view" (177). On her script, she has written,

"After Vic., . . . try ten mins. of present time. Swallows, cows, etc." She wanted to expose them, as it were, to douche them, with present-time reality. But something was going wrong with the experiment. "Reality too strong," she muttered. "Curse 'em!" She felt everything they felt. Audiences were the devil. O to write a play without an audience—*the* play. But here she was fronting her audience. Every second they were slipping the noose. Her little game had gone wrong. If only she'd a back-cloth to hang between the trees—to shut out cows, swallows, present time! But she had nothing. She had forbidden music. Panic seized her. . . . And then the shower fell, sudden, profuse. . . . "That's done it," sighed Miss La Trobe, wiping away the drops on her cheeks. Nature once more had taken her part. (179–81)

La Trobe's "ten mins. of present time" is, of course, the experiment with an ostensive art obliquely anticipated by the ending of *The Years*, for although the playwright does not explicitly envision her invention as some freeing of the object, she does in practice cede control to the landscape, presenting rather than representing, showing rather than fixing, withdrawing herself to let the thing come into its own. And yet even regarded as a liberation of this kind, the experiment raises problems both in its eventual success in moving its audience and in its initial failure. La Trobe's delighted feeling that "Nature once more had taken her part," for one thing, must compromise any reading of the scene as the triumph of an art of nonidentity inasmuch as it doubly invokes the pathetic fallacy, the punning phrasing here suggesting both that nature has taken La Trobe's side and that nature (as feminine) has assumed her proper role in the play, proving with her spontaneous shower her willingness to give pleasure. And La Trobe's own gesture of "wiping away the drops on her cheeks" is a sort of visual pun that reinforces the verbal one: possibly rain, but possibly tears, the drops in their ambiguity suggest another harmony between the world without and the soul within.

The failure of the enterprise until that shower, meanwhile, follows from the fact that the uneventful ten minutes transpire not in the midst of life, where they might scarcely be noticed, but within the framework of a theatrical presentation, where they drag. The same people content to admire the placidity of the view at other times here grow restive with the sense that something more should be happening, that they may be being had (thus rendering La Trobe's work authentically avant-garde), and above all that decorum forbids them from getting up and walking away. Like Eleanor's closing gesture in *The Years*, this ostensive enterprise resists mediating or displacing its referent, but unlike that gesture it frames the thing presented with some exactness ("the cows, the meadows and the view," not "land merely, no land in particular"), and it relies upon the captivity of an audience upon whom its artist consciously imposes. To use the language of domination in treating the captivity of an audience in for ten minutes of boredom is, of course, to risk obscuring the difference between genuine oppression and the most trivial incident of artistic (mis)calculation, once again; and yet as an exploration of the English past undertaken with an eye toward the possible end of England, the pageant solicits interpretations of this kind with unusual intensity. How, indeed, could anyone imagine the foregrounding of constraint in a scene named for the present time of 1939 to be wholly innocent of such intentions? Critics, certainly, have not missed the force of possible analogies: Judith Johnston, for example, has enumerated several meaningful points of resemblance between La Trobe and Hitler (264–66), while Joplin has shown how "the likeness of woman playwright to fascist dictator" indicates Woolf's recognition "of her own will to power as practicing author" (212)—a recognition that, we might add, has been evolving at least since Lily's painting and Orlando's *Oak Tree*.

And the pageant only gets more aggressive. After the shower, there appear a ladder, a wall painted on a cloth, and a man with a hod on his back, of which tableau an observing reporter writes, "Miss La Trobe conveyed to the audience Civilization (the wall) in ruins; rebuilt (witness man with hod) by human effort; witness also woman handing bricks" (181). The audience applauds "this flattering tribute to ourselves" (182), presumably relieved of the anxiety they express when, encountering "The Present Time. Ourselves" on the program, they ask what La Trobe could possibly "know about ourselves? The Elizabethans, yes; the Victorians, perhaps; but ourselves; sitting here on a June day in 1939—it was ridiculous. 'Myself'—it was impossible. Other people, perhaps. . . . But she won't get me—no, not me" (179). La Trobe does get them, however, for after the hod carrier she unveils her most startling innovation, the cast holding forth toward the audience mirrors, tin cans, candlesticks,

> Anything that's bright enough to reflect, presumably, ourselves?
> Ourselves! Ourselves!
> Out they leapt, jerked, skipped. Flashing, dazzling, dancing, jumping. Now old Bart . . . he was caught. Now Manresa . . . Here a nose . . . There a skirt . . . Then trousers only . . . Now perhaps a face. . . . Ourselves? But that's cruel. To snap us as we are, before we've had time to assume . . . And only, too, in parts. . . . That's what so distorting and upsetting and utterly unfair. (183–84)

This disturbing climax clearly represents Woolf's final great effort to imagine an ostensive art, La Trobe here bringing her audience not the Present Time but Ourselves, a presentation of humanity that complements and surpasses her presentation of a landscape denuded of all intrusions but frame. What is perhaps most extraordinary about Woolf's handling of this moment is that in it domination once again so resolutely proves the order of the day; for although we might imagine a far more benign response to this kind of theater, the audience at Pointz Hall—perhaps too close to the mirrors, perhaps addled by La Trobe's perplexing inventions or by the heat—experiences very little aside from an angry discomfort exceeding that prompted by the ten minutes of present time. Whatever the explanation of its reaction, the effect that Woolf achieves in extending the coercive ten minutes of landscape into the episode of the mirrors is to reinforce the point that no art, not even an ostensive one, can manage to avoid the work of domination—that ostension without compulsion or aggression (Eleanor's gesture) cannot, virtually by definition, be artistic. If the long minutes of "swallows, cows, etc." forced the audience to sense its own captivity under the code of manners required of polite spectators, the mirrors lead it to feel itself captured within the play, to witness its own objectification or even to become at once the viewers and the material of art, oscillating unsettlingly between the voyeur's power and the helplessness of the unwillingly exposed.

Within this bad, however, Woolf still dangles the possibility of a partly redeeming good, suggesting that if art always involves subjugation, it might at least be useful in illuminating how and where such violence operates, teaching painful lessons painfully if it can do nothing peacefully. Indeed the episode of the mirrors seems to offer an exemplary instance of Adorno's claim that domination in the play of art calls attention to real domination, since the audience of this pageant is objectified in a manner unusually rich in political implications. To see "The Present Time" and oneself reified theatrically just after seeing "The Victorian" condensed into a couple of strange tableaux would be to experience a connection with the past of a kind not usually available from historiography, after all; just as to discover, under the threat of invasion, that the transformation from subject into imperial "subject" could be the fate not only of some imagined other but also of oneself is to come to feel the play of international forces with a peculiar intensity.[40] Like the threat of war, La Trobe's culminating ostensions offer to bring the inhabitants of this corner of England into history, where "history" would refer not just to events but also to their representation.

The problem with this relatively hopeful vision of art's operation is not only that it grates against Woolf's late suspicion of all such reconciliations, but also that the pageant does not, in the event, seem to lead its viewers to a new understanding of how artistic or historical representation objectifies its material, let alone to new insights about the imperialism of subjectivity. If the members of the audience feel momentarily what it is like to be radically other, that feeling quickly modulates into a feeling of solidarity with fellow selves from which the absolute object or other may once again be excluded. As Joplin points out, one of the play's most seductive effects is to generate a hostility against a common enemy that closely resembles what both sides in the oncoming conflict sought to achieve through theatrical propaganda (215). More specifically, Lucy's effort to communicate to La Trobe what the play means to her ends in a disappointment that Woolf describes with unusual starkness ("Their eyes met in a common effort to bring a common meaning to birth. They failed" [152]); and her succeeding attempt at recuperation— she tells La Trobe that it made her feel as though she could have played Cleopatra (153)—implies that she has come away with a historical epiphany of a less than profound kind (although La Trobe does interpret her words, resonantly, to mean, "You've stirred in me my unacted part" [153]).

Between the Acts does not find Woolf reconciling herself either to human aggression or to the "violence" of making, then, nor is its moral even that art would be redeemed if it could succeed in teaching about violence of other kinds. Having told Lady Simon in a 1941 letter that she could not see what was to be done about war ("Its manliness; and manliness breeds womanliness—both so hateful"), Woolf added, "This is not a contribution to the problem, only a groan" (*Letters* 6: 464)—a description that would convey something of the feeling of her last novel, were it not for the fact that this "groan" represents so complex a reconsideration of the problem of action, not to mention the point at which Woolf's anxieties about the object world emerge in their most immediate historical significance. Were it not for *Between the Acts*, it would be far easier to argue that Woolf's concern with the predations of subjectivity discovers imperialism at work in a world to which terms like "empire" can never meaningfully apply; but one of the key lessons of this novel—a lesson of La Trobe's pageant for us, if not for its audience—is that the conditions of war (or for us, *mutatis mutandis*, ecological crisis) render strikingly visible how the abstract "domination" of objects can converge with the actual domination of humans and the actual destruction of the object world. *Between the Acts* thus contributes forcefully to the anti-imperalist dimension of Woolf's achievement (lately foregrounded in work by Jane Marcus, Kathy J. Phillips, Patrick Brantlinger, and others) not only because it seems the most overtly engaged of her novels, but also because it shows that the question of domination bears crucially on the sense in which Woolf's career reflects the modern passage—the passage, that is, from the young century's faith in new making (or making new) to the suspicion of all expansion that may be the defining characteristic of the present time, Ourselves.

Chapter Two

WYNDHAM LEWIS

KETTLES AND THE COMMON LIFE

> He gushes about everything he sees. He is enraptured at the qual-
> ity of the curious clumsy country print found on the lodging-
> house wall; at the beauty of cheap china ornaments, a stupid
> chair, a staring, mean, pretentious little seaside house. When with
> anybody, he will titter or blink or faintly giggle when his atten-
> tion is drawn to such a winning and lovely object. (123–24)

THE AUTHOR is Wyndham Lewis, the work *The Caliph's Design*, his 1919 monograph on the state of the visual arts, and the topic the "English variety of art-man," whom Lewis describes as "the heir to the aesthete of the Wilde period: the sort of man who is in the direct *ligné* [*sic*] of Burne-Jones, Morris, and Kate Greenaway" (124). It can hardly surprise us today to find Burne-Jones or the progeny of the aesthetes maligned by an avant-gardist in 1919; what gives *The Caliph's Design* the characteristically counterintuitive vigor of a Lewis instigation is that it groups with the English art-man, as "Interpretive" rather than "Creative" artists, Braque and Picasso, whom Lewis censures for dwelling on "the débris of their rooms" (119) instead of "changing our common life, in every way not only the bigger, but the more vital and vivid game . . ." (119). Nor does Lewis limit his assault to devotees of the quotidian in mimetic art, for though he reaches the climax of his polemic in faulting modern painters and sculptors for taking the pretentious seaside house and its cousins as subject matter, he begins his piece by chastising architects for erecting the house in the first place, and draws to a close with a (scarcely unexpected) dig at Roger Fry's Omega Workshops, offshoot of his archnemesis Bloomsbury:

> Now all the colour-matching, match-box-making, dressmaking, chair-painting
> game, carried on in a spirit of distinguished amateurish gallantry and refinement at
> the Omega workshops . . . was really *precisely the same thing*, only conducted
> with less vigour and intelligence, as the burst of abstract nature-mortism which has
> marked the last phase of the Cubist, or Braquish, movement in Paris. (124)

To paint pictures of banal things or to produce more of them is equally, in Lewis's formulation, to hallow the meanest disjecta of modern life, to choose mere realism over realization, the sordidly existing over the veritably new.

Lewis could not have had "Solid Objects" in mind when he wrote of the latter-day aesthete giggling over cheap china—Woolf's story did not see print until three years later—but *The Caliph's Design* seems nonetheless to speak eloquently to that quirky apology for the Bloomsbury way of life, with its aristocratic bohemianism and its relentlessly exuberant program of locating value just where others might, at least in theory, be least likely to find it. Perhaps Bloomsbury's bitterest detractor, Lewis found its elevation of the small object one of its most typical and grating gestures, famously parodying this tic in a scene from his 1930 satire, *The Apes of God*, in which a caricature of Lytton Strachey named Matthew Plunkett contemplates with stupid fascination the "miniature landscape" of a collection of seashells, until his attention is at last drawn to the impending collision of a cloud and an insect at his window, which he awaits "frowning . . . gazing into the mysterious shadow of Time, dark with 'events,' examining this most proximate exemplar breathlessly" (79–80). For Lewis, this habit of discerning the portentous in the ephemeral was another symptom of the ephemerality of Bloomsbury itself, which in its triple passion for contemplating trivial objects, painting pictures of trivial objects, and making more trivial objects triply abandoned the vital game of changing our common life, the very project upon which the Omega believed itself embarked.[1]

In the scene from *Apes*, the element that perhaps best illuminates what is at stake for Lewis is Plunkett's feeling, as he surveys his shells, of being "on the beach, kicking his heels, it was a midsummer holiday, he was the callow schoolboy," this state of mind evoking the moment in "Solid Objects" when Woolf's John, encountering the piece of glass that launches his obsession, loses "the background of thought and experience which gives an inscrutable depth to the eyes of grown people" to retain "only the clear transparent surface, expressing nothing but wonder, which the eyes of young children display" (*Shorter Fiction* 103). Again and again in his writings of the late 1920s and early 1930s, Lewis insisted that one of the great threats of the modern age (of which Bloomsbury was but a single avatar) was a virulently spreading cult of childhood which, by promising to absolve its votaries of the adult responsibility of political participation, served the aims of world leaders trying with unprecedented thoroughness to turn their citizenries into will-less herds. As the tale of a man who discards a career in government in favor of the satisfactions of the scavenger hunt, Woolf's story explicitly associates childlike attraction to the small found object with the eschewing of political life, thus supporting with quite astonishing precision Lewis's central claim that what the child shares with the most dangerous breed of soi-disant artist is a wonder before the existing material world that modulates rapidly into a passivity before the march of human events. "Solid

Objects," in short, captures perfectly what made some of Bloomsbury's enthusiasms not merely disgusting but positively dangerous chez Lewis, an empiricist conservatism inextricable from a political indifference that might spell the end of freedom itself.

When leveling such charges, of course, Lewis ignored the fact that several members of Bloomsbury participated quite directly in government, just as he omitted to note that in the early 1910s he himself had joined in the attempt to change the world through decoration—first as a member of the Omega, from which he departed after charging that Fry stole from him a commission for a room at the 1913 Ideal Home Exhibition,[2] and then as founder of the short-lived Rebel Art Centre, which produced decorative art for four months before it closed. (The Centre's prospectus promised, "Instruction in various forms of applied art, such as painting of screens, fans, lampshades, scarves will be given if required.") Clearly, Lewis's hostility to the aspirations of decoration owed something to the failures of these enterprises; disparaging the premises of his own unsuccessful projects was one of his trademark strategies, after all, nor can it be a coincidence that his attacks on decoration made their first appearance in *Blast*, the influential but short-lived periodical that he and Pound established following the Rebel's demise. Indeed the first *Blast*, from 1914, shows him already elaborating the connection between the crafting of household objects and Cubist "nature-mortism" that would feature prominently in the 1919 *Caliph's Design*, already preparing the double maneuver by which his more threatening Continental rivals could be damned for likeness to the more irritating ones at home and vice versa. Reviewing an exhibit of cardboard, wood, and string constructions by Picasso, Lewis begins by noting appreciatively how "[t]hese wayward little objects have a splendid air, starting up in pure creation, with their invariable and lofty detachment from any utilitarian end or purpose," but he goes on to comment that the works "do not seem to possess the necessary physical stamina to survive," that they "lack the one purpose, or even necessity, of a work of Art: namely Life," and that a "kettle is never as fine as a man." "This is a challenge to the kettles," he adds, thus suggesting that the aspirations of all incarnations of Arts and Crafts acquire the weakness of "nature-mortism" as it were by association (139–40).

In the second *Blast*, from the following year, Lewis explicitly compares Picasso and Fry, commenting that "the extreme langour [*sic*], sentimentalism and lack of vitality in Picasso's early stylistic work was WEAKNESS, as definite a one as consumption or anaemia" and that the "most abject, anaemic, and amateurish manifestation of this Matisse 'decorativeness,' or Picasso deadness and bland arrangement, could no doubt be found . . . in Mr. Fry's curtain and pincushion factory in Fitzroy Square" (41). One cannot, he goes on to insist, convey the emotion prompted by nature "by imitating her, but only by becoming her," where becoming her evidently does not embrace the making of curtains and pincushions, since it "is always the POSSI-BILITIES in the object, the IMAGINATION, as we say, in the spectator, that matters" (45). What is required, in other words, is not only that one add to the sum of things, but that one add objects both loftily detached from the utilitarian and visibly affirmative of their maker's power to transform the real, objects clearly generated by a strong and healthy subjectivity rather than the anemic aesthete too weak to displace even a feminized nature. (In his note for the Vorticist exhibition catalogue of the same year, he comments similarly that "Picasso in his lastest [*sic*] work is rather in the same category as a dressmaker, he matches little bits of stuff he finds lying about. He puts no life into the pieces of cloth or paper he sticks side by side. . . .") The position Lewis delineates thus partakes fully of the productionist imperative already discussed in conjunction with Woolf, though his justification of the art object relies less upon a standing assumption of the pure good of monuments (as in *A Room*) than upon a (no less reflexive) belief in true creation's superiority to mere replication.

Lewis's position in the *Blast* writings was complicated by the fact that in collaborating with Pound he effectively affiliated himself with Imagism, which could look like yet another variety of insufficiently virile empiricism because it appeared to enshrine discerning perception and accurate transcription as the foundations of literary value. Recent scholarship has shown that so reductive a reading of Imagism is in fact inadequate to the details of Pound's formulations,[3] but it is clear nonetheless that other poets in the Imagist line were uneasy about the passivity that its mimetic investments seemed to imply. William Carlos Williams's later insistence that the poet's work is to imitate rather than copy nature—"To imitate nature involves the verb to do. To copy is merely to reflect something already there, inertly" (*Autobiography* 241)—sounds very close to Lewis's claim that one must not imitate nature but become her, and even in 1915 Pound was still struggling to distinguish Imagism's good (hard, clear) impressionism from Impressionism's bad (blurry, fuzzy) impressionism.[4] The years 1914–15 also found Pound bringing Imagism, a literary mode, under the umbrella of "Vorticism," the new panartistic "ism" (concocted with Lewis) whose governing emblem exuded the will, force, and energy that the term "Image" seemed conspicuously to lack: the Vortex, according to Lewis, "does not deal in reactive Action only" but "plunges to the heart of the Present," rushing "out like an angry dog at your Impressionistic fuss" (*Blast 2* 147, 149); the "Vorticist does not suck up to Life" but "lets Life know its place in a Vorticist Universe" (*Blast 2* 148).

As articulated in *Blast*, Vorticist virility aimed to overcome not only the empiricist languors of Impressionism and Cubism, but also the flaccid abstractions of the expressionists, whom Lewis dismissed in the second number as "[e]thereal, lyrical and cloud-like,—their fluidity that of the Blavatskyish soul" (40). Expressionism, in Lewis's rendering, found its appropriate representative in Kandinsky, who in adopting the premise that the individual subjectivity should serve as a conduit for a superpersonal artistic spirit grew "so careful to be passive and medium-like . . . that he is, at the best, wandering and slack" (40). In this, the second *Blast* once again took a more severe position vis-à-vis artistic rivals than the first, the earlier issue having included a manifesto in which Pound numbered Kandinsky and Picasso among the select ancestors of the Vortex, describing them as "father and mother, classicism and romanticism of the movement" (154), as well as a review of Kandinsky's *Über das Geistige in der Kunst* in which Edward Wadsworth appeared to endorse its author's theories. Whether the second *Blast* altered or corrected these earlier rapprochements as far as Lewis was concerned, it is clear that Lewis regarded Pound's genealogy as a tracing not of the innovations that Vorticism would absorb, but rather of the pathologies of passivity that it would avoid: an impressionist empiricism in which the subject prostrated itself before the external and an expressionist mysticism in which the subject abased itself before a putative great spirit. In both cases, the failure of the resulting work was to be attributed to an absence of strong individual will that Lewis would connect with increasing explicitness, in the writings of the years that followed, to the refusal of political responsibility that he found epidemic in the modern world.

In his painting of the 1910s, as many critics have remarked, Lewis fashioned his achievements out of these avoidances, applying Cubist and expressionist breakthroughs neither to still lives nor to emphatically expressive recordings of the soul, but rather to tableaux in which human material— whether quotidian, as in "Two Mechanics" (1912) and "Gossips" (1917), or fantastic and dystopian, as in the "The Crowd" (1915)—is aggressively transformed under the painter's hand. Lewis also attempted such effects in his fictions, though his efforts in this line are less visible because they differ less noticeably from the norms of the art in question. In the 1918 *Tarr* (the only novel he would publish before 1928), an always surprising diction, a complex and jagged syntax, and the new device of the = sign render less than transparent the language of what nonetheless remains a mimetic narrative, so that Lewis can be said to steer a course between unmediated representation and complete abstraction (or, in Reed Way Dasenbrock's more nuanced formulation, to employ "one as a means to the other" [*Literary* 75]); and yet because language is inevitably referential without being photographic, Lewis's procedures do not depart dramatically from those used in realist fiction. What can look from one angle like a deliberate translation of the terms of visual art into literature, in short, looks from most others like an adherence to precedent modified only by small innovations. In *Rude Assignment* (1950), Lewis himself noted that writing *Tarr* convinced him "that words and syntax were not susceptible of transformation into abstract terms, to which process the visual arts lent themselves quite readily. The coming of war and the writing—at top-speed—of a full-length novel ('Tarr') was the turning point. Writing—literature—dragged me out of the abstractist cul-de-sac" (139).[5]

Still, both the paintings and the fictions from this period do conform to Lewis's own guidelines for valid art inasmuch as they testify to a vigorous subjectivity's power to produce nonutilitarian objects in which nature is manifestly transformed into something else; never mind that the same could be said of Picasso's and Braque's analytic pictures or even, arguably, any novel. What makes these productions more authentically curious, given Lewis's critical prescriptions, is that while their existence clearly conveys the aforementioned lesson anent the capabilities of the subject, their content tells a quite different tale—a tale of large souls thwarted by small, or of what Pound called, reviewing Lewis's *Timon of Athens* series in *The Egoist* in 1914, "the sullen fury of intelligence baffled, shut in by the entrenched forces of stupidity" (*Ezra Pound's* 1: 251). In the paintings, only the faintest energy of personality animates the corporeal and scenic shells upon which the tableaux turn, suggesting the imminent demise of subjectivity amid the robotic herd, while in the fictions Lewis seems able to grant some of his strong heroes survival only at the cost of turning them into flat sketches connected tenuously at best to any reality touchable by the reader. Cantleman of "Cantleman's Spring-Mate" and Tarr himself seem composed more of polemic than of feeling, while Kreisler, whose more intimately related sufferings and adventures fill up the greater part of the novel bearing Tarr's name, is led to his destruction partly by social norms presented as a sort of extreme of bourgeois conventionalism. In the 1910s, in other words, Lewis's formal practice supported his polemics on behalf of the vigorously transforming artist-subject, but in its content his art stressed mediocrity's triumph over the superior individual rather than the artist's ability to reform the common life.

What changes in Lewis's later work—the astonishing output that follows his famous long silence of the early 1920s—is, in effect, that the dominant note of his fictions spreads into his cultural criticism, the 1910s' attitude of exhortation occasionally tempered by fatigue giving way to a more resigned, though still admonitory, voice casting about for the remnants of possibility in a world unlikely to be moved. Although virtually all of Lewis's writing (and most of his painting), early and late, is informed by his peculiar version of the Byronic or Nietzschean tension between the great soul and the exterior forces bent on crushing that superior personality, the production of the late twenties and the thirties regarded as a whole differs from what preceded it in placing the accent more firmly on the crushing than on the resistance, in tending to lament the decline of forceful individuality rather than to consider its prospects for shaping the life around it. The only half-ironic title of his

1926 analysis of culture and politics, *The Art of Being Ruled*, gives a good indication of how the possibility of remaking society had receded for Lewis under the malaise of the English *entre deux guerres*, of how he had not so much relinquished his hopes for change as assented to the impossibility of promoting them with anything like the old energy at a time when both art and politics seemed unusually bare of promise.

Lewis's increasing wariness about romanticizing the figure of the capable authorial subject is especially significant in the present context because it coincides with a shift within his polemics on art, from a vigorous opposition to passive transcription to a vigorous promotion of an art of externals, a dealing in surfaces that would oppose "internalist" proclivities allegedly rampant in the art of the day. Certainly, elements of this later preoccupation are to be found at many key junctures in Lewis's earlier writings, most notably in Tarr's well known verbal manifesto on the necessary deadness of art; and Lewis himself insisted that externalism constituted the very last defense of Imagist clarity and hardness in a world of letters that had unwisely forgotten their value. (He even contrasted himself to Pound, of all people, with the declaration, "I was concerned with the externals of life, in conformity with my innate habit of mind, not with its [life's] mechanics" [*Blasting* 52].) It is essential to recognize, however, that while the externalist campaign marks no change in Lewis's basic affinity for the hard and sharp over the soft and fuzzy, its radical insistence on taking as its *materia poetica* the world as it is, or more specifically the world as it *looks*, brings Lewis much closer than he had been to the procedures of the allegedly more purely empirical art that he had once abhorred. The effects of this change are in fact signally visible in the book that Lewis most frequently used to illustrate the externalist method in action, *The Apes of God*, which has often (if questionably) been faulted for setting its sights not on towering figures but on persons whose inconsequence had never seemed to require the stressing given it by the novel—the kettles and pincushions, in other words, of the satirist's domain.

If the significance of Lewis's shift in emphasis is partly obscured by externalism's ample precedent in his and Imagism's earlier polemics on hardness, it is obscured still more by his insistence that he is and always was an externalist in his very nature, as for example in the remark on Pound just quoted. In *Time and Western Man*, to take another instance, he claims that what made him "a painter, was some propensity for the exactly-defined and also, fanatically it may be, the physical or the concrete" (109), though he goes on to assert that many painters "have no repugnance . . . for the surging ecstatic featureless chaos which is being set up as an ideal" in the visual arts (109–10). In a 1934 essay, meanwhile, he comments similarly that almost any artist will work either in "a starkly articulated fashion" favoring "the hard shell of things" or in "a little blurred and broken, a feebly silhouetted, much less concentrated and compact" manner devoted to "all that is fluid and yielding, misty and mysterious"; and after adding that each is indeed marked from birth as "a 'little Internalist,' or a 'little Externalist'" he places himself on the externalist side (*Creatures* 200–201). What may be the richest formulation of this position, however, appears in a section of *Men without Art*, also published in 1934, entitled "Mr. Wyndham Lewis" and subtitled "'Personal-Appearance' Artist (The theory of the External, the Classical, approach in Art)," in which Lewis, defending *Apes*, writes:

> In contrast to the jelly-fish that floats in the centre of the subterranean stream of the 'dark' Unconscious, I much prefer, for my part, the shield of the tortoise, or the rigid stylistic articulations of the grasshopper.
>
> . . . The massive sculpture of the Pharaohs is preferable to the mist of the automatic or spirit-picture. . . . To put this matter in a nutshell, it is the shell of the animal that the plastically-minded artist will prefer. The ossature is my favourite part of a living animal organism, not its intestines. My objections to Mr. D. H. Lawrence were chiefly concerned with that regrettable habit of his incessantly to refer to the intestinal billowing of 'dark' subterranean passion.
>
> But to return again to Satire: Satire is *cold*, and that is good! It is easier to achieve those polished and resistant surfaces of a great *externalist* art in Satire. (99)

The passage is exemplary in part because it runs virtually the gamut of Lewis's justifications for his partisanship, from personal susceptibility to generic characteristics of the artist to abstract truth, and in part because it contains most of the important catchwords of his binary scheme: rigid, massive, sculpture, shell, cold, polished, resistant, surface, external; dark, unconscious, mist, intestinal, billowing, subterranean, passion. Of all the figures evoked, however, the most freighted is surely that of the stream, which, with its suggestion of the directional temporality that so captivated turn-of-the-century philosophers of consciousness, had served as the ruling metaphor for "internal" experience since the moment of William James. As anyone familiar with Lewis's critical writing knows, it was precisely this post-Jamesian or post-Bergsonian preoccupation (the most seductive of rationales for internalism in art) that Lewis set out to assault in the twenties and thirties, declaring—with all the fury of apostasy—that if the extinction of European civilization was near at hand it owed much to those thinkers and tendencies behind which the "Time-mind" was discernibly at work. The fury of apostasy, because Lewis, like Hulme, had once been strongly attracted to Bergsonian philosophy, but (like Hulme again) had broken with it under the influence of rightist French intellectuals[6]—though whereas Hulme's career was terminated by the Great War, Lewis lived to see Bergsonism triumphant in literature,[7] science, and, worst of all, philosophy itself, which in his view had acquired a new and dangerous influence in spite of philosophers' complaints about their discipline's decline in prestige.

Indeed Lewis's calculatingly paranoiac maneuver in his writing on these subjects was to impute to the philosophy of the Time-mind a capacity to alter daily life that he had never remotely attributed to the kinds of art he favored. The most expansive of his many deployments of this strategy, of course, is to be found in *Time and Western Man* itself, staged as a wide-ranging critique of "the Time-view, from the position of the plastic or the visual intelligence" (xix); and within *Time* the chapter in which alarmist claims attain their highest urgency is one entitled "The Object Conceived as King of the Physical World," in which Lewis claims that the Time-philosophy threatens to alter radically and disastrously the subject-object relation. Confronting Bertrand Russell's suggestion that we should try to conceive of a wallpaper that fades over the years not "as one 'thing'" (401) but rather as many, Lewis writes,

> [I]t would be symptomatic of an almost demented anti-absolutist fussiness to wish to suppress this identity. . . . The objection to the "entity" in the wall-paper of common-sense is an irritable reflection of the disputes of Psychology that have resulted in the elimination of the "mind," "soul," or "psyche." So the "object" is suffering for the sins of the "subject." . . . You would not know, looking at it with the unaided sense, that the wall-paper was in Time at all. . . . If the wall-paper is allowed to be just the wall-paper of "common sense," the conditions of Time-theory are not satisfied. (403)

The alterations that Lewis's priorities have undergone since the 1910s are rendered especially vivid in this passage, for if in *The Caliph's Design* wallpaper as trivial object would have proven a dangerous diversion from more important matters, here wallpaper as continuously existing solid object bears the burden of sanity in a world about to go mad electively. Lewis goes on to warn that Russell's epistemological reorientation is far more than "a mathematician's technical device," that indeed "these conceptions of the external world are intended to supersede those of the classical intelligence and of the picture of the plain-man" and that "it is proposed to teach Relativity-physics and the relativist world-view everywhere in our schools" while "vast propaganda is carried on by popular treatises and articles to impose this picture upon the plain-man and the simple common-sense intelligence" (406). If the Bergsonians have their way, even perception as we know it will succumb to the Time-mind, and the solidity of the entity itself become a thing of the past.

One of the important implications of this chapter of *Time* is thus that a defense of the object's integrity undergirds the whole complex of Lewis's attacks on the Time-mind and internalism in this period—a complex that,

once again, largely displaces his earlier emphasis on the powerful subjectivity's ability to transform the common life through its productions. In this
respect, Lewis's career distantly parallels that of Woolf, whose confidence in
making begins to give way to concern about the domination of the object
world at about the same time; and yet it is essential to take note of the sharp
differences between these two writers' priorities—differences both suggested and repressed in Peter Nicholls's claim that if Lewis favored a version of "mimesis as a process which somehow *supplements* its model" he
did so in order that art might restore a "lost 'otherness' and thereby . . .
inhibit the sort of compound identification which makes us 'all One Fellow'" ("Apes" 431). We might note, first, that Nicholls here conflates the
thrust of the prescriptions of the 1910s (supplemental mimesis) with the
sharper anxieties of the twenties and thirties (identification); but the more
important point is that Lewis's suspicions about identification in fact spring
neither from the anti-interventionist fear of the self's absorption by the Other
that Nicholls (in *Modernisms*) names modernism's defining feature, nor from
the qualms about the violence of a predatory subjectivity that one finds in
the later Woolf. Contra Woolf, Lewis for the most part maintains his alle-
giance to forceful subjectivity, which he views as imperiled rather than imperial under modernity; and contra Nicholls, he cites as the locus of danger
not the power of the Other, at least not in the first instance, but rather a
technological expansion driven by an increasingly powerful instrumental
reason.

This is a strange assortment of negations, certainly, and it invites us to
consider in more detail how Lewis could hold such apparently antithetical
positions simultaneously. Given his combination of alarm about the disappearance of the individual and mistrust of changes in the fabric of life, it
would be tempting to turn for answers to Lewis's right-wing politics, were it
not for the fact that "Lewis's right-wing politics" is more a mythical distillation of contradictory impulses than an entity with real explanatory value. In
this case, invoking it too hastily might lead us to refer Lewis's anxieties
about relativism to a classically Tory agenda under which individuals (regarded as fundamentally nonpolitical) would (ideally) govern their lives according to traditional moral standards, whereas in fact Lewis's solicitude for
the individual is grounded in a vision of the latter as the foundation of a
moral life fully embedded in political conflicts. What is at stake is not some
transhistorical code of behavior but the very possibility of an ethical relation
to the world, as Lewis makes clear in an earlier chapter of *Time* called "The
Subject Conceived as King of the Psychological World" (the complement, of
course, to the "Object" chapter already mentioned). "It is socially of capital
importance," Lewis maintains, that a person "should regard himself as *one
person*," for it is "only in that way that you can hope to ground in him a
responsibility towards all 'his' acts" (341)—most critically, the political re-

sponsibility from whose burden the cult of the child promises to free its adherents. In the present age, "[r]esponsibility and personal will is . . . gladly repudiated. . . . The sense of power, the instinct for freedom, which we all have, would cost too much to satisfy. We must be given, therefore, a dummy, sham independence in its place; that is, of course, what democracy has come to mean" (297).

And it was for this reason, according to Lewis, that "the attack upon the Object" constituted "a political disturbance" rather than solely "a movement of pure intelligence" (382). When in the long passage from "The Object as King" quoted above he remarks that "the 'object' is suffering for the sins of the 'subject,'" he refers to the earlier chapter's depiction of the subject "or ego," as "a sort of primitive king of the psychological world" who "could never have hoped to survive in a democratic environment" because "the INDIVIDUAL has been from the first proscribed" (299–300), and to his narrative of how Jane Harrison, Lange, Freud, Leibniz (somewhat against himself), Schopenhauer, von Hartmann, American behaviorists, and William James have led the subject, the mind, and the self to their present low regard:

> What it *looks like* is that man, as he has been engaged in an internecine war with other men on the grounds of the inequality found among us, has fanatically, at the same time, been engaged in tearing off and out of himself everything that reminded him of the hated symbols, "power," "authority," "superiority," "divinity," etc. Turning his bloodshot eyes inward, as it were, one fine day, there he beheld, with a start of horror and rage, his own proper mind sitting in state, and lording it over the rest of his animal being—spurning his stomach, planting its heel upon his sex, taking the hard-work of the pumping heart as a matter of course. . . . It did not take him long to take it down a peg or two in that respect! (343–44)

The passage is classic Lewis, not only because it focuses upon the *ressentiment* that in his view constituted the most crucial link between philosophy and politics under modernity, but also because it demonstrates one of his great gifts as a cultural critic—a remarkable (and largely unappreciated) ability to denaturalize common assumptions that makes him, perhaps, modernism's premier analyst of the ideological operation of tropes.[8] Showing how anti-individualists have uncritically equated the mind's domination of the body with political domination, he prepares the ground for his later observation that Russell's move to "suppress" the identity of the wallpaper is a specifically "*anti-absolutist* fussiness" (an observation that, by his lights, imports no political charge into Russell's formulation that Russell himself did not put there), and for his claim that this metaphorical equivalence's naturalization has not resisted but in fact supported political authoritarianism and the domination of the object. "After the destruction of the 'thinking Subject,'" he observes in "The Object as King," "the Object became a 'substance' of sorts, and as such is still being attacked . . . 'the mind' being so entangled with the body, it was difficult to destroy one without impairing the other" (382).

Clearly, then, Lewis does align with a number of other modernists in insisting that the division between subject and object must be preserved for the sake of both, and that any putative reconciliations between the two would merely disguise some further domination. This is the philosophy— anti-imperialist in inspiration though certainly not always so in consequence— that also links Woolf, Williams, and Ransom to Heidegger, Adorno, and Baudrillard. Lewis distinguishes himself from these others in several crucial ways, however, among them in his insistence that the collapse of the subject-object distinction represented a concrete prospect for the near future—an insistence that, however hyperbolic, does retain a (very) tenuous plausibility because Lewis situates the anticipated collapse not in the realm of existence but in that of perception. Experiential rather than metaphysical or material, this turn would arise from the implementation of the practical training to see discontinuity that philosophers like Russell, certain educators, representatives of the mass media, and so on were so vigorously advocating, and its consequences would be felt everywhere, day in and day out.

Lewis's distance from the others is also marked by his unwillingness to regard the dissolution of boundaries as a triumph of the subject over the object either in effect or in intention, for although subjects were the provocateurs of collapse in his scenario, the motive of their provocation was not conquest but self-overcoming, a renunciation driven by something like left liberal guilt mapped onto the terrain of epistemology. One of Lewis's most strikingly original claims, in fact, was that the growing dominance of humans over the object world had in fact been abetted by the apparently antithetical critique of predatory subjectivity with which we have become familiar, the reign of technological progress comprehending not only subjectivity's mastery of nature but also the subject's flight before the threat of its own strength. In Lewis's view, science (the "expression of the aggregate or crowd") is a *revolutionary tribunal*," and scientific method a "most admirable guillotine," in the insurgency against the subject as king of the psychological world (*Time* 300, 299), and it was for this reason that the modern could mark both the culmination of the ambitions of consciousness and the moment of the strong subject's demise.

Lewis differs from writers like Woolf and Williams most significantly, however, in that his opposition to the imperialism of subjectivity served not a left politics aimed (however distantly) at liberating the colonized other, but rather commitments (at best ambivalently rightist) aimed first at protecting the intellectually strong from the intellectually weak and second at protecting white Europe from the threats of other states and races. What is tricky about trying to read these projects in light of each other is that they did not in fact operate in parallel, because Lewis's racism was founded not on a conviction that whites were inherently superior, but, on the contrary, on a belief that they put themselves in danger by surrendering any power whatever to nonwhites, who had thus far been inferior only on the point of sheer force and due to utterly contingent events.[9] Haranguing his fellow whites in the notorious 1931 volume *Hitler*, Lewis asks, "When do you think we may expect you . . . to give your best attention to the safeguarding of your famous White Skin, and as a consquence cease sentimentalizing with regard to the Non-White World, of what ever hue or kind?" (121); and in other works of the period he adverts specifically to the dangers of white guilt. In the 1929 *Paleface* he tells his story of "the puritan Palefaces of America and Europe," who, "[h]aving wiped out or subjugated all peoples who had not had the advantage of a christian training . . . naturally were very contrite and tried to make up for it to those who were left. Quantities of edifying books (which were translated into all languages) were produced, pointing out what a beast the Paleface was" (5). And in *Time and Western Man*, his treatment of imperialism and science is subtended by similar references to white Europeans' guilt-generated vulnerability: wherever the European went, Lewis remarks, "people were exterminated and enslaved by him in true Babylonian style. . . . But then, to the stupefaction of the survivors, or of his abject 'native' subjects, he began wiping away a tear from the corner of his eye" (293).

Having thus introduced the factor of self-division within imperialist rhetoric, Lewis comments a few pages later that an illuminating example of this combination of Old Testament behavior and New Testament remorse can be found in European science textbooks, which both acknowledge the horrors unleashed by modern technology and present "melting pictures of 'progress'" in which every colonial subject "becomes a leisured gentleman." Claiming that these alluring images rob "the modern industrial 'savage'" of his power to resist the call of expansion, he concludes by "recalling the immense and unprecedented power of this White Magic, so dangerously broadcast, and now shared in by all races—dangerous, at least, from the practical standpoint of its originators. It represents *power* and nothing nothing else, denuded of its altrustic equipment of humbug . . ." (295). For Lewis, the worst consequence of the tension between the will to dominate and the pull of regret in Western thinking could prove to be the destruction of the West itself, not directly by its own hand, but at the hands of the nonwhites who receive the White Magic of science—a scenario in which the triumph of technology culminates in brutal fact, not merely the suppression of value.

White Europe in this story thus parallels the self-undermining subject in the fable of subject and object, since in both narratives, the mistake of the party responsible for the revolution is to reprove itself for its essence rather than its actions; indeed in *Paleface*, Lewis explicitly analogizes the "invitation to suicide addressed to the White Man" to Russell's "liberalist" attempt "to stir up the tables and chairs against us and lead them in revolt against the overweening overlord, Man, who sits upon them . . . without even asking himself if they may not resent his behaviour" (194–95). Lewis's larger point in making this analogy, however, is to insist finally upon the *limits* of its applicability, which become clearer once we observe that the two stories differ in their endings. In the epistemological tale, both subject and object lose, because the inert object will never gain any kind of volition (no matter how earnestly the self-abnegating subject may desire it), and so will never be able to fill the power vacuum that must follow the subject's abdication; but in the historical tale, the former colonials overcome the white Europeans by deploying against their guilt-ridden former masters the powers of science they have been bequeathed. Whereas Lewis defends the object prescriptively, arguing that the subject's efforts to elevate it will in fact result in its destruction, his positive claim for nonwhites is radically descriptive (if no less alarmist), an impassioned insistence that these Others are more capable and hence more dangerous than Europeans think.

One of Lewis's central claims, then, is that nothing could be more productive of misery for all parties than the white tendency to mistake the "native" under empire for a volitionless object, to take as literal truth what remain only figurative parallels between subject and white European and between object and nonwhite colonial. Finding a peculiar treatment of the object at the heart of a racism that could end in the destruction of white Europe, Lewis presents a lesson similar, in a way, to that of La Trobe's failure to instill vital historical awareness in her audience in *Between the Acts*: in Woolf's fiction, to feel oneself an object does not mean to feel oneself an Other, just as in Lewis's scenario it proves foolhardy in the extreme to treat others as objects without will. To the very crudest approximation, of course, this is also the lesson of Frantz Fanon and so many other interrogators of racist thinking, writers whose agendas and assumptions could hardly be less like Lewis's own; and yet this very fact makes Lewis's writing on these matters more instructive rather than less, an important addition to our understanding of the transactions between modernism and empire. For however repellent and bizarre, these explorations of the epistemology of European domination confirm that the questions of the imperialism of subjectivity and of subjectivity under imperialism had been explicitly connected well before the major phase of colonialism's dissolution—even if Lewis's point was at last that the colonial subject might exact a vengeance of which the Object would be deprived.

AESTHETES AND APES

Among the near kin of "Time-mind" in Lewis's polemical discourse, perhaps no designation is wielded so frequently against other artists as "aesthete," term for that suspect figure who shared with the Time-partisan a tendency to privilege the fluidity of experience, a taste for the gauzy and ethereal, and a common ancestor in the unwillingly revolutionary Walter Pater. Hardly the only early twentieth-century writer to use the term disparagingly, Lewis nonetheless manages to make its capacity to dismiss and denigrate peculiarly his own, from the first *Blast* on ("CURSE WITH EXPLETIVE OF WHIRLWIND THE BRITANNIC AESTHETE" [15]) and even before: in the October 1913 "Round Robin" letter in which he broke with the Omega, he described his former associates as a "family party of strayed and Dissenting Aesthetes" who "were compelled to call in as much modern talent as they could find, to do the rough and masculine work without which they knew their efforts would not rise above the level of a pleasant tea-party, or commend more attention" (*Letters* 49). As such a passage suggests, one reason that "aestheticism" and "aesthete" were especially useful in attack was that they combined suggestions of obsolescence (the nineteenth century against the "modern") with an air of the unsavory that still clung to the memory of Wilde, even—or especially—in those Oxbridge havens where, by the 1920s, that figure was enjoying a limited resurrection. Indeed Lewis could scarcely resist invoking aestheticism's musty trappings even when warning of technology's menace to the white race: in the science-generated heaven promised by socialism, he explains, the gentleman savage would labor only two hours a day, and "the rest of the time he sits in a velvet jacket and paints a field of buttercups, one eye on a copy of the 'Idylls of the King,' while his mate feeds his ear with Puccini and Offenbach" (*Time* 295).

These quotations also suggest a second reason why the figure of the aesthete was so congenial to Lewis's purposes in the late twenties and the thirties, which is that it provided him a way of continuing to condemn the passive or weak artist even after his faith in the actively transforming artistic subject had receded. In the writing of this period, Lewis's contempt for those who treat art as anything other than "rough and masculine work" is encoded most frequently as a disgust with what he insisted was a second coming of the Nineties, as in the 1937 memoir *Blasting and Bombardiering*, where an astonishing representation of Eliot as "the plenipotentiary of the Evil Principle in the Thomistic Heaven of the post-war—despatched there by his satanic majesty (he of the Naughty Nineties)" (282) is premised on what Lewis describes, in a chapter from *Men without Art*, as a "new aesthetic of *art pur*" to be found in the "Eliot-Richards combination" (64).[10] Comparing Eliot's idea of poetic insincerity to "the theory advertised by Oscar Wilde in *The Decay of Lying*" and referring to the "mediumistic account of the transaction" of writing "which this aestheticism exacts" (*Men* 67–68), Lewis notably associates the idea of the author as passive channel not with the Kandinsky reviled in 1915 but with the more colorful and less respectable attitudes struck in the decade during which Yeats was most heavily involved in the

Order of the Golden Dawn. At another point in *Men without Art*, meanwhile, he evokes the image of the emaciated aesthete in claiming that those "influential in the literary world" in the interwar period were moving to "bring into being an imaginary 'time,' small enough and 'pale' enough to accommodate their not very robust talents," in which "anything above the *salon* scale" would be rejected (138)—Lewis in effect finding policy rather than mere prudence in Woolf's assertion (in "Mr. Bennett and Mrs. Brown") that readers would have to reconcile themselves to "a season of failures and fragments" in this revolutionary literary phase (*Essays* 1: 335).

If any of these connotations alone would have made aestheticism one of Lewis's most cherished bywords, however, its authentic preeminence in this role was clinched by its associations with the Nineties aesthetic of the fluid and evanescent, which rendered it immediately serviceable to the externalist campaign. Operating throughout Lewis's critical writing, this resonance comes to the fore nowhere so dramatically as in the Henry James chapter of *Men without Art*, in which Lewis writes early on that "to set up the Shell as your shield, against the Dark Within," to "come down upon the side of what is material," is to compromise oneself forever "with the either disguised or overt doctrinaires of a disembodied, a non-corporeal, artistic expression," the followers of the "internal travellers" Proust and Pater, who have been injurious enough to art. "But James," he continues, as though anticipating that Hugh Kenner's massive reconstruction of the Pound era would commence with the Master,

> is . . . more important than either. For "aestheticism," though in truth rampant and ubiquitous, is on all hands violently disowned: and although the manner of Pater is today constantly imitated, on the sly, and his teaching absorbed along with his style, he is scarcely *respectable*, in the intellectual sense. But there is nothing against James. He has played, in the Anglo-Saxon world, much the part monopolized by Flaubert upon the continent. . . . (120)

Still the most interesting remark follows: James, the author of "great disembodied romances," did not "feel at home with objects—his was a world of men and women" (122).

The comment is arresting not only because it shows once again how Lewis's priorities had altered since the 1910s—the kettle, here, exerts a more vital claim than the man—but also because it suggests the difficulties in which he became entangled when he tried to identify the critique of internalism too closely with a privileging of the object. The internalist preoccupation with the workings of consciousness, after all, hardly precludes attention to the externals of life, nor does living in a world of men and women prevent a writer from feeling at home with things. If Lewis's attack is implicitly directed against the James of the long meditative sections of *The Portrait of a Lady* and *The Golden Bowl*, it ignores the author of Ned Rosier's bibliots and Osmond's objets d'art, of Adam Verver's tiles and the golden bowl itself, not to mention the fabulous spoils of Poynton. Naming James ur-aesthete, Lewis ultimately calls attention to the inadequacy of his own presentation of aestheticism, which for all its associations with the ethereal and fluid also set so much store by the beautiful solid object—the blue china of Wilde that would be transformed into the broken blue china of Woolf's "Solid Objects," or the gems of Dorian Gray or des Esseintes. Indeed it can only be a difficult moment for Lewis when, reading an early book review by James alleged to show how the latter "takes his stand very deliberately upon" the "*inside* method," he comes across James himself saying, "*If you resolve to describe a thing, you cannot describe it too carefully*" (120–21; Lewis's emphasis). Lewis's rather lame way of addressing the line is simply to append the jab, "although that you should want to describe a thing at all, he does suggest, is a little peculiar" (121).

Solid objects disrupt Lewis's critique of internalist fictions no less sharply in the chapter on Joyce in *Time and Western Man*. Having just remarked on his own "propensity for . . . the physical or the concrete," Lewis writes,

> So as far as all that side of the argument is concerned—of ecstatic propaganda, of plunges into cosmic streams of flux or time, of miraculous baptisms, of the ritual of time-gods, and of breathless transformations—I have other views on the subject of attaining perfection. I prefer the chaste wisdom of the Chinese or the Greek, to that hot, tawny brand of superlative fanaticism coming from the parched deserts of the Ancient East, with its ineradicable abstractness. I am for the physical world. (110)

Readers attuned to recent encounters between Joyce criticism and postcolonial studies may hardly be startled to find *Ulysses* associated with Orientalist fantasies, nor will many students of modernism in general be surprised to find Joyce identified with the Time-mind. But the profundity of Lewis's need to stand as the sole defender of the concrete is strikingly attested by his placement of Joyce's fictions on the side of the abstract, a relegation all the more astonishing given that he has just faulted Joyce for creating "an Aladdin's cave of incredible bric-à-brac in which a dense mass of dead stuff is collected," "a monument like a record diarrhoea" or "gigantic victorian quilt or antimacassar" resulting from "an appetite that certainly will never be matched for . . . actual *matter*" (89, 90). Joyce, it would appear, is both too abstract and too material, just as James somehow proves his discomfort with objects in fictions littered with bibliots.

Lewis would surely respond, however, that this apparent contradiction only arises from a misleading conflation of two different levels that we might very loosely call form and content. In Joyce, says Lewis in *Time*, the "torrent of matter is the einsteinian flux," so that while some naturalism achieves an effect of hardness, "the method of *Ulysses* imposes a softness, flabbiness and vagueness everywhere in its bergsonian fluidity" (100–101); and, in *Men without Art*, he arraigns Joyce similarly for allowing "the internal method" to rob his "work as a whole of all linear properties whatever, considered as a plastic thing—of all contour and definition in fact" (99). Taking their cue from Flaubert, James and Joyce cram their fictions with solid objects, but since these objects come explicitly mediated through particular consciousnesses, the total effect of their works (themselves insufficiently firm of outline) will be to undermine the solidity of the perceived world as surely as Pater's Heraclitean paroxysms undo our chances of capturing that which melts before us, or Russell's form of attending to the wallpaper promotes its dematerialization.[11]

For Lewis both pre- and post-silence, then, what is to be condemned is the subordination of the object to a subjectivity enamored of its power to see (in the best tradition of Conrad's preface to *The Nigger of the "Narcissus"*) and frightened by its power to do, a consciousness that can neither restrain itself from trying to reach the external world nor commit itself to the work of genuine transformation. Advocacy of a powerful artistic subjectivity proves consonant with a defense of the object *from* subjectivity, in the end, if one believes as Lewis seems to that the truly new object produced by the strong subject will fully join the object world, whereas the integrity of the work composed of the bare recording of selected perceptions will remain compromised through and through by the all too visible traces of the less forceful subject who fashioned it. Lewis does not unfold this line of logic explicitly, to be sure, but its pertinence is suggested by the fact that he refrains from assigning basic value to any conquest of the world that subjectivity might effect, instead preferring—to use Nicholls's formulation once again—a vision of "mimesis as a process which somehow *supplements* its model." In the end, Lewis's claims for the powerful authorial presence look less like praise of the transcendent human emerging victorious from a combat with nature than like an affirmation of the work of Eliot's catalytic artist, who must have a vivid personality but whose productions, finally nonexpressive and nonexpressionist, do not disclose that personality's contours (except, perhaps, upon the closest and most informed inspection).

Considered in this light, the scene of "the heir to the aesthete of the Wilde period" gushing over the "curious clumsy country print" and "cheap china ornaments" in *The Caliph's Design* (quoted at the beginning of this chapter) neatly demonstrates how what appears to be an elevation of the object can in fact constitute an apotheosis of subjectivity at its palest and most passive. Nor will the effect of such a maneuver be metaphysical only, for what is practically accomplished by affectation of this kind, in Lewis's view, is a promotion of the discernment of the so very effusive "art-man" himself, who appears here in the role not of producer as such but of productively skilled consumer. And indeed another important resonance of "aesthete" for Lewis arises from that term's extraordinarily intimate associations with the connoisseur's attempt to elevate exquisite selection or acquisition to the level of art—associations that Lewis explored in his criticism and fictions through the figures of several aesthetically inclined arch-consumers.

Of all these shady characters, the one who most spectacularly embodies the unjustifiable pretensions of the aesthete-collector is surely Lord Osmund Willoughby Finnian Shaw from *The Apes of God*, a caricature of Osbert Sitwell whose name evokes both Oscar Fingal O'Flahertie Wills Wilde and the brooding Gilbert Osmond from James's *Portrait of a Lady*.[12] Like Osmond, Shaw and his family—whose affiliation with "that wicked, perverse, most clever epoch" when "Wildes, Beardsleys and Whistlers" flourished (353) is noted repeatedly—collect both things and persons, "objects of *vertu* and barbaric fragments . . . from tally sticks to ritualistic pudenda from the Pacific" (494) as well as human oddities of every variety, from a bellowing Finnish poet to retired officers of the British military. One of the notable features of the Shaws' acquisition is that it does not necessarily indicate affection for the things acquired, and is indeed occasionally inseparable from contempt or hostility: they invite the officers to their Lenten party apparently for the sole purpose of deriding them as embodiments of detestable John Bull, and Osmund exhibits a childish tendency to destroy things out of sheer pique. "I have known Osmund to pick a toy to pieces. Once I surprised Osmund putting one of Phoebus's Japanese dancing mice upon the fire!" (496), says the old cook, "the Sib," who elsewhere supplies that rogue "with tit-bits of Gossip arranged with his favourite sauces, the old yellow sauces of the Naughty Nineties" (353), communicates "from afar off among the black Beardsley glades" (360), and delights to see in his visage "the living double of the blank fat mug of Oscar" (497).

The Shaws typify the Lewis aesthete, in fact, in that their collecting proceeds less from a fascination with objects in themselves than from an urge to express their own eccentricity, cleverness, and irreverence through their purchases, thereby (in effect) flavoring the late Victorian imperative of expressive decoration with the romance of the bohemian artist-pariah. It is no accident that Phoebus Shaw has a tower-garret evocative of the haunts of Manfred and Stephen Dedalus, since the family habit appears to be that of borrowing for the superlative connoisseur the trappings of the tormented artist or great soul, nor is it strange that these Bloomsbury satellites feel compelled to bring to their ancestral home so many spectators primed to appreciate their consuming élan: after all, the practical success of any deliberately decadent posture—whether Byronic, Baudelairean, or Wildean—finally depends upon an audience of the admiring and scandalized. Indeed if *Apes* seems to offer a critique of luxury like that mounted in similarly riotous eighteenth-century satires, the reason is not that Lewis disapproved of wealth per se (though he often amply hated the wealthy), but rather that those fictions aimed, as *Apes* did, to resist the transformation of the "public" from a space of accountability into a field for spectacular expression, and in so doing constituted something like anticipatory strikes against the commodification of the Romantic agony.

Yet *The Apes of God* does not repudiate flashy collecting altogether. The longest and most ostentatious list of exotica in the novel inventories not the stores of the Shaws but the Lenten party costume of Horace Zagreus, which includes, among other rarities enumerated over two full pages, "a miniature representation of the Atef crown of Thoth," a "green feather . . . from the crest of Huitzlipochtli," "an Anguinum—egg composed of saliva from the jaws, and froth from the bodies of snakes," and a "calumet with rattan stem, feathered" (334–35). Certainly, this assemblage of arcana serves to advertise well-read cleverness ("My very fly-buttons are allusive," declares Zagreus [337]) no less than the Shaws' chicly pseudoethnographic toys, but there are several reasons for thinking that it receives something like Lewis's approval. For one thing, Zagreus, though hardly immune to satirical assault, serves as critic of the other apes and trustworthy representative of the offstage Lewis-persona of Pierpoint; for another, it turns out that Pierpoint himself is the designer of the costume, which as parodic out-Shawing of the Shaws participates in the satirical project of *Apes* as a whole. The most suggestive of the costume's possibly redeeming features, however, is that it may have been paid for by none other than Osmund (345), so that wearer, designer, and backer are three different people, and it becomes difficult to decide whose personality, if any, it proposes to express. To the extent that the question is unanswerable, the costume undermines rather than participates in the "expression" of the insubstantial consumer-subject, and indeed this may well be its most important function in the carnivalesque masquerade of this narrative, which is finally so much less about the authentic individuals whom Lewis prizes than about apes and their undoing.

In its financing, moreover, Zagreus's attire happily conforms to Lewis's practical prescriptions for the regeneration of art in the twentieth century, which call for a revival of the virtually lost practice of patronage—a practice upon which Lewis depended frequently, if resentfully, over the course of his difficult career. Indeed the central project of *Apes*, as enunciated in Pierpoint's "encyclical" (the text-within-a-text at the polemical core of the novel), is to reveal the illegitimate origins and ominous consequences of the modern trend under which the monied and talentless, who would in other ages have contented themselves with the role of patron, promote themselves as artists. Writing of the usurpation of bohemia by the well-to-do, Pierpoint denounces the fact that in Paris "studios" have become so fashionable for the sham-struggling wealthy that genuinely struggling artists cannot afford to rent them (119–20), and then goes on to note the still more serious problem posed by a subset of the faux-bohemians, an "active minority" (120) who

> produce a little art themselves—more than the inconsequent daubing and dabbing we have noticed, but less than the "real thing." And with this class you come to the Ape of God proper. For with these unwonted and unnecessary labours, and the *amour-propre* associated with their results, envy steps in. The complication of their malevolence . . . redoubles . . . the fervour of their caprice or ill-will to the "professional" activities of the effective artist—that rare man born for an exacting intellectual task, and devoting his life unsparingly to it. . . . It is as regards . . . these *productive* "apes," that I may be useful to you. (121–22)

One problem with productive apes (whether of the Bloomsbury species with which Lewis is largely concerned here or some other kind) is that they are incorrectly *"identified, in the mind of the public, with art and with intelligence"*; but far more troublesome is the simple fact that that they are not *consuming* apes. Unlike "the classical patrons of the renaissance, the great patrons of Turner and Gainsborough or the French Kings," the apes "are careful not to involve themselves economically in a thing they can get as much out of as they require without spending a pennypiece" (121–22), though a passage from *The Art of Being Ruled* suggests that their motive may be less parsimony than the recognition of new social norms mentioned in the previous chapter: "as it is impossible to enjoy openly the privileges of riches in the present period of transition," Lewis asserts, the rich "covet the privileges of the artist, to which . . . they with some reason consider that their *irresponsibility* affects them" (149–50). The result, in any case, is that the rich not only compete with those who must live by their art, but also withdraw one of the great sources of the latter's livelihood. "When you consider," Pierpoint concludes, "that the whole of the graphic and plastic arts have in the past been sustained upon the structure of stable wealth and seigneurial or burgess ostentation . . . then the distress of the artist who is not rich . . . is easy to understand" (124).

The encyclical thus censures not some overextension of the grand-seigneurism of the Shaws/Sitwells but rather its practical diminution, as well as an accompanying erasure of the the line between producers and consumers (which Pierpoint renders nearly tangible in likening the apes to the "gallants who insisted upon invading the Elizabethan Stage—sitting among the actors, to display in that way their personalities to the best advantage" [122]).[13] Pierpoint cautions that he "is not identifying poverty with genuine artistic success, or riches with its opposite" (Cézanne and Manet, he notes, were well off), only reprehending the apes. Yet poverty and talent go together, just as wealth and mediocrity do, throughout Lewis's fictions—from *Tarr*, in which the artist-hero Tarr is contrasted to the pretentious Hobson and the bourgeois Fräulein Lipmann, all the way to *Self Condemned* (1954), in which the reader is invited to share the brilliant Harding's resentment of his mediocre employer, Furber. In *Apes* itself Lewis even suggests that there may be a certain validity to the old chestnut about art requiring suffering and deprivation (pointedly attacked by Woolf in *A Room*) when he describes the Shaws as "a family of 'great poets' . . . where all the exultations of labour, a passionate experience, *and probably a straitened life*, issuing in works of great creative art, are thinly parodied, at great expense" (122, emphasis added). In Lewis's modern world, at least, the chances that means and muse will befall the same person prove extraordinarily slim.

Lewis is therefore not "against" consumption, or even the consumer-subject, in some simple or absolute way. As much as he mocks the Shaws, Pierpoint implies that if they would only acquire the right things, supporting genuine artists instead of trying to be bohemians themselves, one might be generous enough to allow them the fun of "expressing" their (in that case laudable) taste. Even here, however, Lewis's theory does not always survive the assaults of his own bitterness, for he leaves no doubt that the genuine artist is superior as a being to any patron, just as the Creative artist is clearly superior to the Interpretive consumer-aesthete. Mr. Hyde, a very minor character in *The Apes of God*, might seem precisely the sort of enemy that Lewis should desire, for in averring that artists "are all brutes," that he has "never known a man of genius who could tell one piece of food from another," that all "wines taste the same to them" and that they "should all be in a Zoo" (297), he at least reinforces the distinction between artist and connoisseur; and yet it is clear from biography that Lewis could scarcely tolerate such an attitude in the wealthy whom he encountered, let alone assent to the proposition that the sensitive palate and the vital palette might deserve comparable degrees of admiration.[14] Though he frequently faulted a modern epistemology of *ressentiment* for trying to take the overbearing subject down a peg, his own relationships and writings were often troubled by an urge to do as much to the well-to-do, as the number of his patrons—or supporters by other means—with whom this advocate of patronage decisively broke at one time or another testifies. Joyce, Pound, Eliot, the Sitwells, Jessica Dismorr, Kate Lechmere, Edward and Fanny Wadsworth, Richard Wyndham, Christopher Nevinson, Jacob Epstein, Augustus John, Frederick Etchells, Raymond Drey, Robert McAlmon, Sydney and Violet Schiff, Charles Prentice—all fell victim to Lewis's ire or satire, and the list goes on.

A related consequence of the breakdown of the boundary between consumers and producers in the arts, and one no less disturbing to Lewis than the disappearance of support for professional artists, was the decline in artistic standards that must inevitably result (or so it would seem) when the assessors and makers of art, judge and judged, become one and the same. In Lewis's fiction, this latter collapse is embodied most singularly in the ape

Julius Ratner, who goes by the name of the "split-man" for, among other reasons, his division—or rather multiplication—into many steps in the production of books:

> [S]ince Mr. Julius Ratner kept a highbrow bookshop, a certain Mr. R. was able to sell his friend Joo's books—and because as well Jimjulius was a publisher, Joo was luckily in a position to publish his particular pal Ratner's novels and his poems—and on account of the fortunate fact that J. Ratner Co. were the publishers and distributors of a small high-brow review called simply *Man X* it was possible for Juliusjimmie to puff and fan that wan perishable flame of the occasional works of his old friend Jimjulius. It was a concatenation of circumstances such as every author whatever must sigh for. (*Apes* 150–51)

The facile anti-Jewishness announced rather than simply betrayed in the use of "Joo" for Julius, here and throughout the novel, is founded upon a paranoiac imagining of the Jew as a freighted metonymy for finance capital, which vast entity caused Lewis most concern (as we will see below) in appearing to exercise continuously two dangerously connected powers: that of breaking down divisions, preeminently those between nations, and that of forming a self-sustaining cycle beyond the control of the individual consumers and investors that it picks up and drops along the way. The bond between Ratner and finance is sealed late in the novel when the former deploys his finest powers of seduction in rendering the operations of capitalism itself sexy to the eager Jonathan Bell, a character based more on the persona than on the position of Clive Bell, art critic and brother-in-law of Virginia Woolf. "[M]y good honest Jonathan—academic to think of Capital as some solid, non-volatile. 'Capital' is the human heart," coos Ratner, looking to lighten the bank account of this would-be patron of authors by transmuting the "stern and unpalatable facts of economics" into "coarse and juicy morsels" (543–44) likely to appeal to his and his wife's interest in "the gonadal glands of internal secretion" (541). In the world of certain more advanced apes such as Ratner—a world depicted with even more ferocity in *The Revenge for Love*—making and acquiring both take a back seat, in point of glamor, to the business of selling, which requires and sustains a kind of subjectivity beside which the pale aesthete's looks positively vigorous: namely, that of the consumer not taught to discern true value (as the ideal Lewisian patron might be) but rather manipulated into accepting whatever may be presented for sale.

In placing Jonathan Bell in such close proximity to the one-man coterie of Ratner, Lewis alludes to his own tussle over the issue of coterie puffery with Clive Bell, which had unfolded in the pages of the *Athenaeum* in 1920. The dispute began with a 5 March article entitled "Wilcoxism" in which Bell, out to deflate British pretensions to rival the French in contemporary painting, compared the arrangers of the "Imperial Painters" exhibition at Burlington

House to Mrs. Wilcox, the author of a memoir called *The Worlds and I*, who "believed, in perfect good faith, that the crowd of magazine-makers with whom she associated were, in fact, the great figures of the age." Bell complained of having "read in this very paper," similarly, "that Mr. Wyndham Lewis, was more than a match for Matisse and Derain" and even "a match for Lionardo da Vinci" (311). In the following *Athenaeum*, Lewis shot back that "to write one week [6 February] that his friend Mr. Grant is greater than William Blake or Hogarth, and to object the next to your contributor R. H. W[ilenski] asserting that 'Mr. Lewis possesses certain affinities with Leonardo' is just a dull essay in impudence" (349; also *Letters* 117); Bell retorted in turn that Wilenski had not only rated Lewis's sense of humor superior to Leonardo's but also opined that Lewis could beat Matisse and Derain at their own game (379). Lewis concluded the volley with a note suggesting that the *Athenaeum* was not the proper venue for such a quarrel, but two years later he apparently found a suitable spot in the *Daily Herald*: reviewing therein a collection of Bell's essays entitled *Since Cézanne* (which included "Wilcoxism"), he observed that the author

> inextricably mixes up all his personal friends and relations with the great names we all assent to. . . . [F]or the purposes of almost any English public, if you said that Roger Fry was rather better than Braque, but not quite so good as Valmier; or that Vanessa Bell stood midway between Matisse and Chagall, no one would be any the wiser, as all the names dealt with convey equally little. (*Creatures* 77)

And indeed Bell had written in "Wilcoxism" itself that "Duncan Grant holds his own handsomely with Marchand, Vlaminck, Lhote, de Segonzac, Bracque [*sic*], and Modigliani," though Bell would not yet class him with "Matisse, Picasso, Derain, and Bonnard" (311; also *Cézanne* 190).

Suggesting as it does that the true story of modernism is one of rival factions equally well positioned to indoctrinate the undiscerning masses, this interchange tends to obscure a key difference between Lewis and Bloomsbury just beginning to emerge in this period, but increasingly important in later years—that between the mythologizing of a circle of talented friends regarded as amateurs and the mythologizing of a loner whose stance was insistently professional. Even by 1920 Lewis could scarcely have been identified with a particular clique (although the belief that Vorticism was a coherent and indeed extant movement persisted for some time after its demise), whereas most readers of Pierpoint's encyclical would have had no trouble recognizing Bloomsbury as the original of the "select and snobbish club" whose "foundation-members consisted of monied middleclass descendants of victorian literary splendour," that group in which "[a]ll are 'geniuses,' before whose creations the other members . . . must swoon with appreciation" (123).[15] The distinction is especially significant in this case because for consumers at large the appeal of Bloomsbury's amateurism reinforced the attraction of the coterie and vice versa, the inference being that in doing it all for the love of the thing its members had no earthly reason not to praise each other as much as possible, even where the launching of their productions into more public spheres might lay such encouragement open to charges of conflict of interest. And indeed even in this regard the Bloomsberries could well stand to gain rather than to lose, since bias hallowed by friendship could exude a magnetism quite unavailable to dry professional evaluation.

This is to say, in a way, that part of what made the group so attractive was that it seemed to constitute a nearly closed consumption-production system: as Jennifer Wicke notes, it was "an experiment in coterie consumption, which means both the consumption of art by a coterie, the 'Bloomsberries,' and the marketing and consumption of their art (and thought and lifestyle) as produced by a celebrated coterie" ("*Mrs. Dalloway*" 6).[16] To this we might add that the very excesses of admiration decried in Pierpoint's villification of mutual swooning arguably extend rather than subvert at least one general tendency of consumer culture, since, by some lights at least, the archetype of the consumer experience is or should be one in which meticulous evaluation is simply overwhelmed by an exhilaration that leaves reason powerless. For Lewis, of course, such extreme passivity before the impression would indicate all the more plainly why consumer and critic should not be one; and indeed in his review of *Since Cézanne* itself he avers that "Mr Bell's swooning habits" show him "to be a very nice emotional man" but do not "recommend him as a writer on pictures" (*Creatures* 78).

One of the most basic reasons why Lewis's attacks on Bloomsbury tended to focus on the epidemic of monied "artists" and the group's estimates of its own success rather than its theoretical commitments, of course, was that so many of its beliefs about art and art production were hardly distinguishable from his own. In one of the essays in *Since Cézanne*, for example, Bell praises Cézanne for trying "to make of Impressionism 'quelque chose de solide et de durable'" (63),[17] while in another passage that sounds like pure Lewis he applauds Pissarro for approaching everything "in the spirit of a painter," without mushy emotion: "Never for the ugliest harlot, the sorriest thief, or the most woebegone gas-jet did he feel that whimpering, simpering, sentiment that Tolstoy frankly admired" (142). Like Lewis, also, Bell tempers his aestheticism with an acknowledgment that the most successful artists will hardly be aesthetes themselves, commenting that Cubism has little future because in it "conscious aestheticism holds the field" and that "artists must believe that they are concerned with something altogether different" from art, even though they will be wrong about this if they are any good (203).

Indeed Lewis admits at the beginning of his review that his agreement with Bell on a number of points makes it difficult for him to say what he thinks about *Since Cézanne* (*Creatures* 77), which on inspection proves to contain few comments of a general or theoretical nature likely to provoke Lewis's dissent. The exception, here, might be a piece called "Standards," in which Bell seconds Renan's claim that "the proper apology for the old French aristocracy is that it performed the proper function of a leisured class. It maintained standards. . . . Renan recognized that a leisured class is the source of civilization" (153). Lewis's review does not refer to this essay specifically, but it is clear nonetheless that such an observation would have horrified him; for while he would have agreed that the leisure class maintains standards indirectly through the power of the purse, he would just as surely have denied that it therefore constitutes the source of civilization—as though that source were not, rather, artists themselves. Outrageous in its slippage from the claim that the privileged fulfill their role by consuming fastidiously to the implication that, whatever they do, they preserve civilization, Bell's argument would have appeared to Lewis (though not to Bell) the abstract justification for the absurd pronouncements on particular artists delivered in "Wilcoxism." Even were *Since Cézanne* something other than a Bloomsbury product, the treatment of class in "Standards" would surely have led Lewis to some reflections on Bloomsbury; nor is it any wonder that he had some sharp things to say about another volume, published seven years after Bell's book and now securely canonical, in which Woolf seems to make a rather similar claim over the course of a hundred much-read pages. That volume is, of course, *A Room of One's Own*.

A VILLAGE OF ONE'S OWN

> The argument for "amateurism" of any kind is that "professionalism" is the drabbest, most mechanical and sordid affair; which, of course, is true. . . . But that is a one-sided argument; the assumption . . . always is that the amateur is a fresh, capricious and carefully sheltered plant, and as such is relieved of the distorting necessities that dog the professional. The truth is very different from that. Almost without exception the amateur in real life . . . is an imitation-professional. (125)

The Bloomsbury work that Lewis anticipates most directly in this passage from *Time and Western Man* is *A Room of One's Own*, in which Woolf seems to imply that good art will rarely be produced by any *but* amateurs, given that the need to make one's productions marketable will inevitably interfere with the "freedom to think of things in themselves" vital to the creation of great works (39). "Intellectual freedom depends upon material things. Poetry depends upon intellectual freedom," Woolf observes twice in that essay (39, 108), the second time after quoting Sir Arthur Quiller-Couch's note that of the twelve "great poetical names" of the nineteenth century, Keats "was the only one not fairly well to do" (107).

Certainly, *A Room* does not advocate an art of amateurs explicitly: Woolf's narrator concludes her glance at Aphra Behn with the observation that this woman "makes it not quite fantastic . . . for me to say to you tonight: Earn five hundred a year by your wits" (66), and toward the end of the volume Woolf recurs to her female auditors' "chance of earning five hundred pounds a year" (108). But although making money through writing may relieve one from economic dependence in one way ("now that Aphra Behn had done it, girls could go to their parents and say, You need not give me an allowance; I can make money by my pen" [64]), it clearly compromises absolute intellectual freedom in others, a point that Woolf's narrator quite distinctly evades when, in imagining a "very stalwart young woman in 1828" thinking, "Oh, but they can't buy literature too," she applies such self-reinforcement to a defense not against market pressures but against the allure of, "I suppose, some shiny prize" (75) held out by an avuncular patriarch. Perhaps Woolf's most spectacular evasion of the market's effect on intellectual freedom, however, lies in the history of the narrator herself, whose five hundred a year comes not from selling books but from a legacy, which causes "effort and labour" as well as "hatred and bitterness" to cease (38)— and, assuredly, leaves many readers assuming the logical terminus of Woolf's argument to be that the finest work will usually be produced by those who do not have to earn a living by their art.[18]

Lewis could not have addressed *A Room* (1929) specifically in *Time and Western Man* (1927), but he did not fail to attack the essay in short order: in his novel of the mid-1930s, *The Revenge for Love*, he charges it with nothing less than administering the lessons of the old Victorian patriarchs in the guise of a new feminism. It would be difficult to resist pursuing so extraordinary a charge in any context, undoubtedly, but the present one fully warrants such an exploration because Lewis's critique of Woolf on women runs in parallel to a more muted critique of Woolf on aesthetic value and labor, a critique that—as we will see—illuminates Lewis's own difficult position on art production in the modern world. Perhaps more immediately to the point, however, is the fact that the first appearance of *A Room* in *The Revenge* finds Woolf's essay quite visibly linked with what Lewis saw as some of the characteristic behaviors of the apes of god.

Two thirds of the way through the novel, Margot Stamp, almost universally regarded as Lewis's most sympathetic character, imagines stretching out beneath some elms visible from her window with her copy of *A Room*, but her reverie is soon interrupted by her host, Agnes Irons, who (ignoring Margot's poverty) first boasts of the wealth of the people she has been visiting ("Rolls Royces—butler and footmen—pots of money!" [220]) and then points with pride to the fact that she has bought herself a desk out of her golf prizes, which amounted to "over five pounds in vouchers" (217). Her thrill—the thrill of "earning" experienced by one who in fact has no need to

earn—clearly represents another variation on the theme of leisured consumers' dangerous crossing into production,[19] but her way of referring to the
desk of her own responds more particularly to the tone affected by Woolf's
persona as she lectures to women of doubtful incomes on the need to obtain
five hundred a year. Lewis ignores the fact that Woolf's essay is everywhere
suffused by an ironic consciousness of its own mannerisms, of course, and
yet manner is precisely what could make Agnes (and Woolf) so infuriating
from the point of view of the professional artist who could not make ends
meet. For Lewis, Bloomsbury breeziness, like its near relation John Bull
jollity, tended to erase both the hard fact of poverty and the even harder fact
that for many poverty could prove virtually impossible to escape.

Before Agnes's interruption, Margot had been reciting to herself "as she
imagined that great queen among women . . . , her adored Virginia, would
have spoken them" a few lines from Tennyson's *Maud*, lines that Woolf
quotes in *A Room* in a rather unusual moment of nostalgia for feelings of
assurance lost since the Great War. "What poets they were!" exclaims Margot, echoing Woolf, to which Lewis appends, "*They* being those splendid
Victorian monogamists—flowering, as great-hearted passion flowers, hyper-
petalous and crimson red, upon the spoils of the Angloindies and of the Dark
Continent" (215). The suggestion that Woolf's affection for a few lines of
Tennyson implicates her in the violence of imperialism shows Lewis at his
most irresponsible, in one sense: if the comment evokes the Benjaminian
dictum that no document of civilization is not at the same time a document
of barbarism, it obtains none of Benjamin's force because it obscures the
fact that all artists, Lewis the hunter of patrons included, could be similarly
blamed. And yet the comment is highly pertinent in another way, since in
asking (implicitly) how there can be real freedom in art if money never
really comes for free, it only pushes to a troubling pass the arguments for
financial independence put forth by Woolf's persona in *A Room*—a persona
who, incidentally, invites speculation about her own relation to the "spoils of
the Angloindies" in explaining that her inheritance came from an aunt who
"died by a fall from her horse when she was riding out to take the air in
Bombay" (37).[20]

Lewis's more explicit critique of *A Room* emerges later in *Revenge*, however, in a scene in which Margot once again appears in the presence of
nature with book in hand, though in this case the book is Ruskin's "Of
Queens' Gardens." Reading in Ruskin some of the same lines from "Maud"
recited by Woolf's persona ("The Larkspur listens—I hear, I hear! / And the
Lily whispers—I Wait"), Margot whispers again, "*What poets they were!
. . . in the thrilling words of that (for her) incomparable 'queen,' Virginia.
But when she tried to visualize *the garden,* she experienced a slight disillusionment in realizing that it was merely Maud's" (277). Recognizing of a
sudden that she is no royal personage at ease in a garden but rather a resi-

dent "in the camp of the defeated Victors" (Victor being her husband, with whom she will soon be crushed by fate working in consort with political intrigue), Margot turns against Ruskin—who at this point in "Queens'" is concluding his exhortation to women to take upon themselves the salvation of all the unfortunate—and implicitly against Woolf as well: "Without saying it in so many words, and far more in sorrow than in anger, Margot guessed that she had been taken in. The word 'queen' had done the trick!" (278).

Lewis's aligning of Woolf and Ruskin represents one of his more nervily perverse misrepresentations inasmuch as "Queens' Gardens" is in fact the text that Woolf most directly *confutes* in *A Room*, whatever her sentiments about *Maud*. Consulting "the greatest, the wisest, the purest-hearted of all the ages," Ruskin had determined that "Shakespeare has no heroes; he has only heroines," women "steadfast in grave hope, and errorless purpose; Cordelia, Desdemona, Isabella, Hermione" (18: 112–13), and that Scott, Dante, Homer, Chaucer, and Spenser offer further testament to the "guiding function of the woman" (18: 121). In *A Room*, however, Woolf attempts to counter this literature-as-history with a dose of history-as-history, noting that although woman (as represented by Clytemnestra, Antigone, and so on) has "imaginatively" been "of the highest importance; practically she is completely insignificant. She pervades poetry from cover to cover; she is all but absent from history" (43). Lewis thus draws from Woolf's text a moral perfectly antithetical to her expressed point; and yet such critical mischief does disclose an illuminating truth once again. In this case, Lewis cannily amplifies an undercurrent in *A Room* that would become a central element in *Three Guineas*, an affirmation of the value of women in spite of their historical subordination that modulates into praise of marginalization's capacity to engender disinterested activism: "The truth is, I often like women. I like their unconventionality. I like their subtlety. I like their anonymity" (*Room* 111). In Lewis's view, Woolf and Ruskin are both to be faulted for trying to make women believe that the "independent" minds bestowed on them by patriarchal culture are to be counted as blessings; and if to his eye the ruse would have been more transparent in Ruskin (since the Victorian woman's alleged independence from interested calculation was premised on her utter economic dependence), it might well have looked more dangerous in Woolf (where it would have participated in what he saw as a self-proclaimed "democratic" celebration of degradation that in fact threatened to end in the utter erasure of individuality and freedom).

Certainly, Lewis's protest against the reginification of women was motivated far less by a genuine interest in improving women's lives than by his astonishingly resilient disposition to blame feminism for society's problems; but it was also prompted by a sense that in both Woolf and Ruskin a recuperation of disenfranchisement served as the profoundest link between addresses to the question of gender and prescriptions for artistic production. To see how this is so, we need first to notice that in her particular handling of the intersection of "women and fiction" in *A Room* (3), Woolf takes as a second, less foregrounded Ruskinian intertext "The Nature of Gothic"—not only the most famous set-piece from *The Stones of Venice* but also the archetype of Ruskiniana for many readers. In that major pronouncement, Ruskin argues that the Gothic cathedral's strength arises from its origins as a communal project embracing many levels of artistic ability, that it "is, perhaps, the principal admirableness of the Gothic schools of architecture, that they thus receive the results of the labour of inferior minds; and out of fragments full of imperfection, and betraying that imperfection in every touch, indulgently raise up a stately and unaccusable whole" (10: 190). He goes on to comment that "what we have to do with all our labourers" is "to look for the *thoughtful* part of them, and get that out of them, whatever we lose for it, whatever faults and errors we are obliged to take with it" (10: 191), before concluding with the resounding declaration "*the demand for perfection is always a sign of a misunderstanding of the ends of art*" (10: 202). If the author of *The Revenge for Love* felt pressed to ridicule the suggestion that women—everywhere made into mediocrities with no political power—are all queens, the author of *Tarr* and *Men without Art* could only have been appalled by this praise of an art that exalts human limitation (or, rather, limited humans). And indeed in *The Art of Being Ruled*, Lewis mocks this aesthetic and its descendants quite pointedly, dismissing "the democratic humbug of the *What the Public Wants* system" as a "sugar-sweet misinterpretation of the period of mediaeval rebirth, when everything was happy and the workshops were full of songs, and craftsmen jostled with amateur masons" (159).

A picture of this general kind, though one at once grittier and more dignified, appears at the point in *A Room* at which Woolf's narrator pauses to imagine the building of the Oxbridge colleges:

> [W]ith infinite labour the grey blocks in whose shade I was now standing were poised in order one on top of another, and then the painters brought their glass for the windows, and the masons were busy for centuries upon that roof with putty and cement, spade and trowel. Every Saturday somebody must have poured gold and silver out of a leathern purse into their ancient fists, for they had their beer and skittles presumably of an evening. (9)

Woolf's description here is easily passed over, since she goes on to concentrate on how institutions of higher learning for women are conspicuously deprived of the flow of gold that gave the men's colleges their splendor, but the passage's evocation of medieval builders does seem to owe something to Ruskin's vision of communal production nonetheless. Reading the passage with "The Nature of Gothic" in mind, we can see that what the Oxbridge artisan and the artist free to think of things in themselves have in common is a removal from the scene of art's commodification, an immunity to the kind of market demands that might alter the shape of their work in some immediate way. And indeed the modern woman and the medieval artisan with his beer and skittles even seem to find a late conflation in Miss La Trobe, the ambiguously recompensed playwright of *Between the Acts*, who last appears seated before her glass in a pub and whose pageant not only partakes of the local, communal, and imperfect that Ruskin promoted, but also seems suffused by an awareness that it may prove the last work to arise from a world, soon to be destroyed, in which aristocratic patrons still inhabit the land and villages actually have village idiots.

But though Woolf would eventually formulate her own versions of a more communal art in *Between the Acts* and "Anon," and though she seems to assent to the charm of Ruskin's medieval fantasy in *A Room* itself, she directs the economic arguments of her essay as neatly against "The Nature of Gothic" as she poses its feminist ones against "Of Queens' Gardens." As we have seen, Woolf advocates "intellectual freedom" not only because it would allow women to participate in intellectual life, but also, and more emphatically, because it promises to result in more great works of art. Her persona's generous validation of the flawed fictional fiction *Life's Adventure* notwithstanding, Woolf remains centrally interested in making conditions conducive to the production of literary monuments, reinforcing this position, as we have seen, by treating books as solid objects—the volume open to *Antony and Cleopatra*, the bookcase to which she turns—rather than discursive interventions or expressions of personality. For Woolf as for Lewis, Ruskin's insistence that the cathedral is aesthetically superior because of its kinder, gentler production would turn the evaluation of formal success into an attempt to recuperate deprivation, in the process assaulting the independence of the monument as only Victorian moralizing can—a point that Woolf makes implicitly in the Fry biography when she recalls Fry, on a trip in 1932, "waving his hand at the [Venetian] palaces and saying, 'That old fraud Ruskin has chapters about all that. He was too virtuous . . . even those finicky palaces must be morally good, which they're not'" (280). Both Woolf and Lewis, once again, were far closer to *l'art pour l'art* than Ruskin ever was.

And yet although Lewis would have agreed with Woolf on this question of fundamental value, he would also have grouped her together with Ruskin for implying that the best art will not be produced under the modern commercial relation, or indeed under any conditions in which material need impinges on intellectual freedom. For Lewis, Woolf's vision of the (financially secure) amateur was governed by the same fallacy that informed her vision of the (historically oppressed) woman, the idea that a certain independence of mind, tantamount to a moral elevation, could be gained by removal from the rough and tumble of life. In fact, he would counter, such prescriptions join Ruskin's Gothic raptures in inviting the collapse of aesthetic standards, since the rise of the modern artist of independent means implies, for reasons already discussed, the end of disinterested evaluation. Lewis's claim against Woolf is thus not that earning money for one's work dignifies it in some metaphysical sense (he would have attributed this belief to the fictional Agnes Irons or perhaps the real Roger Fry, not to himself) but rather that examination of the actual processes of artistic production and transmission occurring in the real world reveals the comparative virtues of the market. "Since the eighteenth century," he writes in "Pictures as Investments: A Straight Talk" (an essay published a year after *Revenge*), "there are the best of the Impressionists—Manet, Renoir, etc. All good painters. How easy it would have been to substitute Benjamin Laurens, Frith, or Alma-Tadema. But no. Big Business, in this matter, will have the best, and only the best" (*Creatures* 271).

This is not to say that Lewis bore the commercial relation any particular love, however. In *Revenge*, he leaves no doubt of the fallibility of the buyer and the venality of the seller in the art-hawking game, writing of how the owners of a factory for the production of fake masterpieces (the employers, briefly, of the doomed Victor Stamp) would meet at their club "other gentlemen like themselves—agents, publishers, touts, critics (both of art and of letters), shilling-a-liners, experts, museum-officials and moneylenders," with whom they would exchange "tips and gratulatory jokes and messages, and cocky topdog gibes—re such matters as the spot price of American 'mystery' bestsellers, or the heavy backwardation on forward pieces of the early Umbrian school" (232). In "Pictures as Investments," meanwhile, he appends a powerful qualification to the observation that the monetary value of oil paintings saves them from physical destruction:

> Faultless as my arguments have been in favour of the irresponsible commercial mind—willing, not evil, but certainly no good, and yet productive, in spite of itself, of good, up to a point: yet do not let us forget that this irresponsible materialism is a disease as terrible as cancer or leprosy. Its infections not only defile, but endanger, all that it touches. I cannot put my finger on the particular in which, shall we say, El Greco's Annunciation is in danger. It will be saved, undoubtedly, from every fire, shipwreck, air-raid or flood, if that is humanly possible. Yet in our minds these distillations of intellect and emotion, that great pictures are, are numbed, in some way, for us by the position they now occupy.
>
> The solution, of course, would be the passing from our scene of the irresponsible commercial mind and all its works. That is, I expect, an idle dream. (*Creatures* 272)

Among the most moving in Lewis's criticism, this passage reminds us again that from Woolf to Benjamin, from Ransom to the surrealists, one of the hallmarks of modernism was its solicitude for the auratic effect of the art object, which seemed threatened above all by the systematizing and quantifying tendencies of capitalism ("the position they now occupy"); and it makes clear in addition that Lewis's disapproval of amateurs' annexing of artistic production had very little to do with any deep admiration for a world in which the finest objects are produced under the auspices of commerce.

Indeed from the publication of *Blast* on, and even before, Lewis and Pound had vociferated in the strongest possible terms against commodification in art and in life; but whereas Pound eventually arrived at a sentimentalized version of the economic in which Confucius could be conflated with Social Credit theory and Mussolini, Lewis was unflaggingly contemptuous of attempts to find the poetry in money. In this context we might recall his satire on the sexualizing of capital in *Apes*, or consider his attack on the "pretension of Commerce to be *romantic*" in *Time and Western Man*, which he considered important enough to place at the very beginning of the hundreds of pages that make up that volume (4). Or we might turn to another passage from "Pictures as Investments" itself, in which he implies that the market's power to maintain evaluative criteria is both mysterious and counterintuitive: "It is the rarest thing for Finance and Beauty . . . to be associated," he writes, "So when we find that this happy conjunction has occurred, let us indulge in a brief thanksgiving. The fact that Old Masters change hands for stupendous figures is *good*. That is the answer to that question" (*Creatures* 272).

If Lewis's mistrust of capitalism's effect on the arts stayed more or less constant throughout his career, however, his feelings about the possibility of creating alternative conditions for art making had not always been so gloomy. His involvement in the Omega Workshops, the Rebel Art Centre, and *Blast* testify, once again, that in the 1910s he partook of a certain optimism that a new world of possibilities might be coming to birth (slightly delayed) with the new century—though the sometimes clever, sometimes vaguely pathetic attempts at advertising undertaken by all three confederations also show that their projects were informed by exuberant surrender to commodification on a small scale as much as resistance to commodification writ large. Perhaps the most illuminating of Lewis's early speculations on how the visual arts might be promoted, however, appeared in a 1920 editorial called "Art Saints for Villages," in which he proposed a government initiative to make art "a portion of the life of a community" instead of "a curiosity or a precious object in a museum" or "an object of commerce in a dreary market like the Academy":

There are thousands of townships and villages in England—and there are, unfortunately, thousands of artists—that any movement of this sort would have to include.

Let each artist take a village or town. I should be content with a medium-sized one. . . . Each village or town has some characteristic fashion of earning its bread:

Fishing	Carpet-making
Tanning	Tile-making

Why not have, in the centre of its green, park or square, a figure in stone by Dobson, Epstein, or Gill, for instance, emblematic of that occupation? (*Creatures* 62)

Lewis then goes on to imagine architects devising idiosyncratic ways of beautifying their townscapes and to suggest that an "art centre" might be set up in every village (63).

Certainly, this closest of Lewis's approaches to the Ruskinian idea that art might serve a local community is less than perfectly sincere, his signature sarcasm making itself felt in the remark that "there are, unfortunately, thousands of artists," which could be taken to mean either that there are too many good artists going hungry or simply that there are too many artists, including bad and indifferent ones. The editorial as a whole, moreover, seems uncertainly suspended between between a Pound-like desire to help art to some security on the one hand and Lewis's trademark contempt for patronage on the other, and indeed one wonders how Lewis *could* have proposed much of a subordination to the state given his belief in the artist's sheer preeminence. As he has it here, the artist takes the town, not the town the artist, and the phrase "Art Saints" clearly suggests martyrdom to residence in fringe Philistias.

Still, this editorial rings with a note of hope—a sense that art might indeed contribute to a reformation of the world if by some chance it were given the opportunity to do so—quite absent from "Pictures as Investments." The change in tone between the 1920 piece and the 1938 clearly owes much to the general decline in Lewis's faith in art's transformative capability that we have already noted, and to an intensification of his hostility to the idea of communal art-making (the latter expressed most fully in 1925's "Dithyrambic Spectator"); but it also owes something to a further deepening of his mistrust of state power. Looking at domestic conditions in the twenties and thirties, Lewis saw a brief period of postwar optimism about state-sponsored production transformed into the disappointment of an economy hopelessly stalled, while looking abroad he found the Soviet Union a disturbing test case for the effects of enlarged state control over art.[21] In the 1936 *Left Wings over Europe: or, How to Make a War about Nothing*, Lewis asserts that "unfree as . . . countries are, under 'fascist' rule, they are infinitely more free than is Russia, under communist rule" (275); and though he begins by claiming nonpartisanship as usual, he quickly acknowledges that if pressed he would side with "the extremist of the 'right,'" from whom alone "we can

expect any really uncompromising criticism of so-called democratic institutions" (53). Driven by an insistence that leftist compunctions were leading
the British government (in spite of its surface Toryism) to ally itself with
Russia and foment war with the comparatively guiltless Germany and Italy,
Left Wings registers above all a hardening and expansion of the position of
the 1931 *Hitler*,[22] though it also recalls moments in *Time and Western and
Man*, *Paleface*, and *The Revenge for Love*.

In that last work, which as Dasenbrock has pointed out is not the "Spanish
civil war novel" for which it is often mistaken (since it was written in 1934–
35 but delayed in publication ["Wyndham Lewis's" 84]), Lewis villifies
communism's relation to art at least as energetically as he assaults capitalism's, even joining the two in having the communist Tristram Phipps charac-
terize the fake picture business as a "'share-the-wealth' proceeding—performed, of course, at the expense of the capitalist enemy" (235). Margot,
charged throughout with the insight of the doomed innocent, formulates
neatly one of Lewis's own convictions, meanwhile, when she declares toward
the end, "The Reds I meet with Victor have no place for art in their politics—they seem to abominate art" (295). But the set-piece of the book's
anticommunism is a conversation among Victor, Tristy, and Peter Wallace in
which Pete supports his claim that Picasso's is "bourgeois art," its "values
. . . capitalist," first by suggesting that the Cubist "wood-graining racket" is
simply stolen from Braque's father, a house-painter (a house-painter becoming, for Tristy, "a *marxian object* on the spot"), and then by condemning
Picasso as a "classical sensualist" (145, 147, 148). Recognizing the existence
of "another conscience, namely that of that pitiable thing, the artist," Tristy
tries momentarily to hold on to Picasso, but when Victor jumps in to deny
the relevance of Marx to painting, he joins Pete in berating him for uphold-
ing "art for art's sake" and succumbing "to the *sensual* world" (147, 148).

In using the word "sensual," of course, Tristy alludes both to the decadent
pleasures forbidden by a Miss Grundyish caricature of communism—the
luxuries that for an ascetic Marxism would embody the fruits of surplus
value stolen from workers—and to the sensuous dimension of art held sacred by most Anglo-American modernists (and, for that matter, by any apol-
ogists for art drawing on the Hegelian tradition). Presenting his doomed hero
Victor as the lone dissenter to Tristy's comment, Lewis discloses that one of
the primary reasons he found communism so threatening to art was its apparent antagonism to the idea that a work's value inheres partly in its sensuous particulars—the very elements that "Pictures as Investments" had
found capitalism abusing and weakening, but at least preserving in some
form. In Lewis's view, in other words, commerce unquestionably bids to
subordinate auratic immediacy to determinations of monetary value, but
communism's suspicions of high living extend to the utter repudiation of
aesthetic pleasure as such; and this repudiation is backed by a tradition

whose origins predate communism by centuries, a tradition of denigrating both sexuality and sensuality as terrains of (spiritually or materially) non-productive activity—which is to say the same tradition that (in its modern incarnation) links the consumption of goods and the consumption of experience as equally suspect pastimes.

This point is important not only because it indicates something of what Lewis perceived to be at stake in 1930s politics, but also because it reminds us that in spite of his distaste for the weak artistic subject who produces only pale reflections of passively consumed impressions, Lewis repeatedly condemned a productionism that would find in any and all consumption food for *ressentiment*—the kind of thinking that demands continuous action while dismissing every other employment of time as snobbish and wasteful luxury. Parroting this view in "The Object as King" from *Time and Western Man*, in fact, he had written in a memorable passage, "Perception, with its element of timelessness, has . . . a detestable *repose*. Perception, in short, smacks of contemplation, it suggests leisure: only *sensation* guarantees *action*, and a full consciousness that 'time is money' and that leisure is made for masters, not for men, or for the old bad world of Authority, not the good new world of alleged mass-rule (to give this concept its political affiliations)" (*Time* 386–87). It is worth adding that this mistrust of action-at-all-costs also enhanced for Lewis the relative attractiveness of capitalism, which at least had the virtue of being the system presently in place in most of Europe and hence the one that required no action to install. In "The Diabolical Principle" (1931), he wrote, "[R]evolution-for-revolution's sake appears to me irrational—or change-for-change's: for is it not the fashionable philosophy of the worst sort of 'bourgeois,' or better 'bourgeoise'? I cannot believe it to be even an authentic principle of the most enlightened Communism" (149).

In "Creatures of Habit and Creatures of Change," an essay of 1926, Lewis had imagined the leveling spirit of communism whispering into the ear of the millionaire that those who most threatened his supremacy were artists and intellectuals. "The man who is really your rival is . . . the 'brainy' man, the 'high-brow,'" says communism (*Creatures* 141), who then goes on to assure the millionaire that he can put this upstart in his place by going ahead and making some stuff of his own—by becoming, once more, the amateur artist (see also *Art of Being* 172–73). For the Lewis of that essay, capitalism and communism are united not only in their determination to crush those who would stand apart from the mindless herd, but more specifically by the fact that in both cases this urge proceeds from nothing other than *ressentiment*. As we compare "Pictures as Investments" to this earlier statement, what must strike us is that it finds Lewis showing not a more intense dislike of communism than he had expressed twelve years before, but rather a still profounder resignation to a capitalist system that exacts its revenge upon art by keeping great pictures intact in body while stealing their souls. "Pictures as Investments" is written, for the most part, with a certain flippant brio; but the conclusion, of which the last paragraph follows, evokes the fabular grimness of English translations of Kafka as virtually nothing else Lewis ever wrote:

> The solution, of course, would be the passing from our scene of the irresponsible commercial mind and all its works. That is, I expect, an idle dream. Two thousand years ago Christ drove the money-changers from the Temple. But no sooner had they disappeared at one door than they came in again at another. We have no report of this in the New Testament, but it is undoubtedly what happened. (*Creatures* 272)

NONSENSICAL WILL

Most historians of modernism would agree that the passing of "the irresponsible commercial mind" was a consummation for which virtually every modernist writer devoutly wished at one point or another, though most would agree also that the departure of "all its works" would have been a desideratum much harder for the modernists to embrace without hesitation—not only because of their long recognized fascination with technology and lately rediscovered attraction to the spectacular side of commodity culture, but also because a broadly capitalist system had helped to shape the very forms that constituted art as they knew it. As we have seen, Lewis was hard put to imagine any alternative to art as professional enterprise that would not result in the dissolution of aesthetic standards, in spite of his contempt for the commercial mind and its assault upon aura; nor is it easy to find any early twentieth-century artist who went so far as to repudiate utterly all documents of civilization for their share in barbarism. What has gone virtually unrecognized in assessments of modernism's relation to economic systems, however, is that as the archetypal form of doing in the twentieth century, capitalist production itself proved no more possible to abominate *consistently* than its products, even for writers—such as Lewis and Woolf—who posed serious questions about imperatives as basic as making and action. In the last chapter, we saw how Woolf's reservations about material transformation in the nineteenth and twentieth centuries culminate in her rich but inconclusive interrogation of life between the acts; in this final section of the present chapter we will consider how similar, though far from identical, ambivalences about production in the modern age resonate through Lewis's work.

We might begin by noting that in spite of his anticommunist diatribes of the thirties and his resignation to existing conditions governing the making of art, Lewis also excoriated capitalism for its astonishing and perverse capacity to generate human suffering out of the very resources that seemed naturally primed to relieve it. In his 1932 novel *Snooty Baronet*, Lewis's eponymous narrator observes that these

> are times of great and wonderful profusion and plenty and of technical powers of limitless production beyond man's dreams. But upon all that plenty, and that power to use it, is come a dark embargo. . . . By artificial systems of great cunning this land flowing with milk and honey has been transformed into a waterless desert. . . . And it is not *nature* but it is *man* who is responsible for this. (103)

In a *Men without Art* chapter bearing the Ruskinian title "The Artist and the New Gothic," Lewis blames artists for not "insisting that our mad bosses should release their stores of food and clothing, and adjust the credit system in such a manner as to give these brothers and sisters of ours [clerks, factory hands] *work*" (200–201); in *The Vulgar Streak* (1941), the hero Vincent Penhale asserts that the bank is a "licensed *forger* of paper-money" and that therefore "the modern state is based upon organized—*legalized*—Fraud" (204, 205); in an article on Tocqueville of 1946, Lewis writes of the unfairness of blaming democracy, whatever its other failings, for "crimes committed by the greed and cynicism of super-capitalism" (*Creatures* 327). Perhaps the most illuminating remarks in this vein, however, appear in *Left Wings over Europe*, which offers a textbook example in support of contemporary characterizations of fascism as—at least in its principal public self-fashioning—a revolt of the petty bourgeoisie or its nearest equivalent against the super-wealth of financiers (and thus in support, also, of Jameson's contention that in the thirties Lewis's anxieties looked much like those of the typical petty bourgeois). The extreme rightist, Lewis declares in this most rightist of his own books, "announces himself . . . as the champion of the Small Man in his struggle against Big Business, and its intolerable and 'soul-destroying' oppressions: the champion of the creative worker—the damn-fool who *does the work*, whatever that work may be—gripped in the tentacles of 'loan-capital' " (37).[23]

Though Lewis had recognized at least as early as *Hitler* that such references to unjust distribution of resources, loan-capital, and bank-perpetrated fraud resonated with the rhetoric of Continental fascist movements, his own most significant doctrinal points of reference were the Social Credit theories of C. H. Douglas, which first captured Pound's attention around 1919. Although never as close to Social Credit as his erstwhile associate, and indeed never as interested in dwelling upon the details of economic questions, Lewis for a time at least endorsed Social Credit's central recommendation that modern economists should focus on facilitating the distribution of goods rather than on increasing production, a prescription based on the observation that industry was already producing not only enough for all but more than enough, the competition for export markets consequent on this overproduction having given rise to both European imperialism and the Great War. According to Douglas, the solution would be for government to take over the lending function currently performed by the private financial sector, and to distribute the interest it would collect in so doing among the citizenry as a whole, thereby providing the buying power needed to absorb the consumer goods being (over)produced. Lewis's most explicit statement of support for Social Credit appears, not suprisingly, in *Hitler*, in which he proposes to take up the cause of the enlightened minority of "Credit-Cranks" against the prevailing opinion, fostered by "the conventional economist (of the Keynes type)" that "the present miserable impoverished state of the world" is *"natural"* (159–60).[24]

What makes Social Credit theory especially germane to the questions at hand is that, as an "underconsumptionist" alternative to the many schools of "scarcity" economics focused on increasing production and premised on the idea that limited resources are to blame for economic misery, it lies behind some of Lewis's most intriguing analogies between the politicoeconomic and the literary. His assertion—in his chapter on Woolf in *Men without Art*—that certain literati have set out to create "an imaginary 'time,' small enough and 'pale' enough to accommodate their not very robust talents" (138), for example, is supported by a comparison between the naturalizing of economic scarcity and the naturalizing of imaginative poverty. Rejecting Woolf's claim that the postwar period is one "of *Sturm und Drang*, in which new methods are being tried out, and in which the artistic production is in consequence tentative" (the phrasing is his own, not Woolf's), Lewis insists that

> the people who have been most influential in literary criticism, for a number of years now, have been interested in the propagation of this account of things—just as the orthodox economists have, consciously or not, from interested motives, maintained in its place the traditional picture—that of superhuman difficulty—of some absolute obstructing the free circulation of the good things of life. (137–38)

Lewis pursues the same theme in the succeeding chapter, wherein he describes himself as forging a Roman road across the "waterlogged stretch" of "the post-war decade-and-a-half . . . in the field of art and letters," a "purely mental bog" perfectly "coeval with the uninterrupted chain of 'crises' which started as soon as the obscene saturnalia of the war came to a close." Insofar as the economists' "Want-in-the-midst-of-Plenty is artificial, this 'wasteland' is artificial" as well, he insists, in this manner bringing Woolf together with her Bloomsbury cohort Keynes (141–42).[25]

Lewis's efforts to link Bloomsbury to the global evils of capitalism were not circumscribed by the problem of scarcity alone, however, nor were they limited temporally to the interwar period. In the Dantesque 1955 novel *Malign Fiesta* (the last volume of the "Human Age" trilogy), Hachilah, the

Administrative Officer of Hell's "Punishment Centre," gives Lewis's protagonist a tour of sinners under his charge, among them a "Bloomsbury
smart-Alec" become Kenyan (Keynesian?) colonist and sexual predator
whose greatest sin proves to be not sodomy (though that is a punishable
offense) but "the sin against Genius," the "use of money to persecute and
injure a man under the special protection of God" (85–86). All on his own,
this sinner would present a freighted enough conflation of some of Lewis's
antipathies—Bloomsbury, homosexuality, imperialism (whose terminus here
in the Mau Mau rebellion Lewis surely saw as a kind of confirmation of his
late 1920s critique), and wealth ill used—but he takes on additional significance from his proximity to the next sinners on the tour: "the British spirit"
and "something more than a man, a great international spirit" housed in the
same divided cell, whom Hachilah identifies as "International Capital."

As "a blurred national entity; a World Empire," the guide goes on to
explain, Britain is "the only nation in the same category" as the figure of
Capital, that "universal bisector" who splits nations down the middle but has
"no tangible national centre" himself, and who brings immense suffering
upon any "country which is big enough to take him" (87–88). His punishment being to be "treated as Dante treated Mahomet, cleft from the chin,
down the centre" (88), this great spirit is also the descendant of Julius Ratner, the "Split-Man" whose multiple guises conceal a single self-promoting,
endlessly self-perpetuating identity. In succeeding pages, Lewis refers to the
spirit of multinational capital as both "[t]he International Embodiment" and
"the Abstraction," the implication being that one of his alarming powers is to
render himself elusively abstract at need—a power to which René Harding
(the hero of 1954's Self Condemned, which shares several of the obsessions
of Malign Fiesta) alludes in observing that under the expansion of "the
Credit System," one "would sense nebulous spiders, at the heart of wider
and wider webs of abstract simulacras of wealth, suspended over everything"
(90).[26]

The juxtaposition of the Bloomsbury sinner with the spirit of capital in
Malign Fiesta foregrounds the fact that in Lewis's tropology inadequate art,
finance, and sodomy were all linked not only by a common lack of solidity
but also by a common failure to produce solid objects. If in Lewis's scheme
bad art was virtually one with art that failed the test of hardness, and if
global capitalism took on its most threatening aspect in its vaporous abstraction, sodomy could join the insubstantial (in spite of its manifest concreteness as a meeting of bodies) by means of a chain of identifications promul-
gated by (among others) the decadents themselves—a chain that linked
homosexuality to effeminacy, effeminacy to weakness, and weakness to the
ethereal. The more significant fault for which bad artist, financier, and
sodomite all stood condemned, however, was the failure to make anything of
consequence. As we have seen, Lewis found inferior writers linked to finan-

cial powers by a shared determination to perpetuate a myth of scarcity that would excuse a widespread absence of "the good things of life," and the sodomite and the usurer had been connected as nonproducers (the one of children, the other of tangible goods) at least since the thirteenth century, most notably in cantos XIV through XVII of the *Inferno*—a connection to which Pound alludes in essays, letters, and (most famously) the "Tale of the Honest Sailor" from his own twelfth canto, written in 1923.[27] Nor did Lewis himself refrain from denouncing the nonproductiveness of finance throughout the 1930s: in *Hitler*, for example, he noted an "absolute distinction between concrete and productive capital (great or small) upon the one hand, and Loan-capital (as the Hitlerist calls it) upon the other" (147).

It is precisely with respect to the operations of "Loan-capital" itself that this putatively rigid opposition between the concrete and productive on the one hand and the abstract and ungenerative on the other begins to falter, however, because what is truly scandalous about finance capital (as many scholars of Pound have pointed out) is not its infertility but its apparently unnatural capacity to generate wealth out of nothing. Pound seems to suggest as much in canto XII when he places the recitation of the "Honest Sailor" at a meeting of bankers, since the more striking moral of that story is not that sodomy is characteristically ungenerative but rather that under unusual circumstances it can effectively result in a child, thus proving a miraculously productive nonproduction.[28] Lewis, meanwhile, indicates in spite of himself that the fascination of finance capital lies in its unnatural productiveness virtually every time he mentions it—as for instance in another passage from *Hitler*, wherein he notes that the difference between "the *Leihkapital*" and "all that other Capital that is *work*, or that is the product of some concrete act of creation" is discernible as the "significant cleavage between those who own something tangible (like a farm . . . or a factory . . .) and those who own nothing concrete but whose *matière* is the intangible quantities of speculative wealth—the 'financier' pure and simple" (178). The donnée of this statement, after all, can only be that if "speculative wealth" is "intangible" in certain respects, in others it proves a "*matière*" that does something consequential, something whose intervention in reality may be illegitimate but remains thoroughly real for all that.

Even were "true" production restricted to the making of concrete goods, moreover, it could not be said that the "Credit-Cranks" whom Lewis favored in *Hitler* in fact charged private financial interests with stymieing production; on the contrary, Social Credit stressed (as just noted) how large-scale private lending resulted in overproduction and competition among nations for foreign dumping grounds. This is not to say that Douglas never considered how finance capital's powers could give rise to failures of production (indeed the circumstances under which this could occur became increasingly important to underconsumptionist analysis as the depression of the twenties and thirties wore on[29]), but it is to note that in receiving and interpreting Social Credit doctrine, writers like Lewis and Pound were particularly prone to misappropriation when it came to the question of finance's generativity. One reason why this was so, certainly, was the widespread assumption that Britain's interwar economic troubles were caused by banks' refusal to finance industry adequately, an assumption enshrined in the influential report of the "Macmillan" Committee on Finance and Industry, after the release of which this presumptively common feature of business life went under the name of "the Macmillan Gap."[30] But a factor at least as influential on imaginations like those of Lewis and Pound was clearly the plausibility of the figurative scheme just described: since it was hard to *visualize* solid goods (in the sense of solid virtues as well as solid commodities) emerging from unsolid wealth, it was easy to hold to the belief that no such effect actually occurred in real economies. In spite of his striking ability to denaturalize some ideologically potent metaphors, then, Lewis was in this case no more immune to the power of metaphoricity than Pound or Hulme, whose readiness to ascribe political truth to what others might treat as mere vivid analogy has been widely noted.

Thus although Lewis was quick to denounce obsessions with production when they led to attacks on contemplation or eruptions of art making among the well-to-do, he seems nonetheless to have internalized deeply a broad production imperative associated with conventional anxieties about weakness, femininity, and effeminacy and readily deployable against appropriately suspect groups. Indeed Lewis's linking of the aesthete (as well as the sodomite) with the finance capitalist closely reproduces the turn-of-the-century phenomenon, discussed above, in which the refined inactivity of the decadent was implicated in the decline of the nation at large, since both gestures elevate the weakness associated with a failure to produce from a possibly distasteful individual condition to a threat to the well-being of all. And this last point is the more significant because Lewis, like other modernists, found it difficult to purge the specter of the useless aesthete from his thinking about art (no matter how vigorously he insisted on a rigid separation between true artists and worthless dabblers), and like other modernists seems to have been led by such specters not only to provocative questions about the rationale for art but also (in yet another turn of the screw) to encompassing doubts about the very production imperative that rendered the aesthete threatening in the first place.

What is slightly surprising about this strain of uncertainty in Lewis is that it emerges most vitally not, as we might expect, in his attacks on the gilded bohemians, but rather in his diatribes against the reduction of art to a species of politics—as though he could ultimately brush aside those who simply generated inadequate works out of a feeling that in changed times we must all do something, but could not so comfortably answer those who, finding ideology everywhere in art, raised the possibility that *everything* we do is political, and thus in a profound sense (from Lewis's point of view) constrained rather than free. The moment in Lewis's writing that may be most illuminating, in this respect, appears at the end of the Flaubert chapter of *Men without Art*, in an ambiguously ironic exhortation that comes on the heels of a critique of Edmund Wilson's and François Mauriac's avowedly partisan styles of reading. Having reproved the former for basing his praise of Flaubert on that author's politics, and the latter for premising a countervailing attack on Flaubert's irreligion, Lewis observes that "we must allow that a great deal of first-rate art has been performed by persons who have not had the advantage of being Christian salvationists," and then closes by wondering what, if not the urge to promote a particular ideology, *could* motivate one to make art:

> So whether you are a libertine, or devout, you can still be an artist—indeed, you cannot help being that if so you are made. And it is still probably the best manner of kowtowing to the supreme engineer who thought-up the toy, to work well, to function properly: and if you are prone to believe in the miraculous, and suppose that you, a fully-wound-up-toy, got there *out of nothing*—if you are also *a nihilist*—that simply can't be helped. You were in that case so *made*, as to function as a nihilist. And I suppose if you are homicidal, or homosexual, it is the same thing, it is all for the best or worst in the best or worst of all possible worlds. (223)

Studded with reliable indices of Lewis's disapprobation (most notably the reference to the wound-up toy, a staple of his cautionary rhetoric of robots and automatons), these sentiments would seem necessarily ironic given Lewis's usual antipathies to the absorption of individual identity by groups. And yet because the chapter ends here, offering no subsequent retraction or counterproposal, the passage acquires the air of a cranky submission to disagreeable facts rather than an exercise in unadulterated sarcasm, as though its author has found himself up against a doubly irritating reality that he cannot finally compass: not only that the art-making subjectivity always leaves traces of its peculiar conditions on the work, but that these conditions include a shaping by social group that can never be evaded. Indeed Lewis had already conceded earlier in the chapter that, given the referentiality of language itself, it "is perhaps to be expected" that the novelist, unlike the painter or composer, "should take sides to the extent of inclining rather to this political camp than to that" (219–20), where the camps in question would resemble the identities of identity politics today.[31]

Such an affectation of submission is in part strategic, since Lewis's ostensible goal is to persuade would-be engaged artists that there is simply no need to make *consciously* partisan declarations; but to refer it wholly to a strategy teasingly marked as such would be to lose sight of the important irresolution that it betrays. For what is so striking about this passage, along with a number of others like it elsewhere in Lewis, is that it undercuts its own answers to fundamental questions about art's raison d'être in a way that makes those answers seem at once impossible to believe and the best that we can do. Here, the old Lewis model—in which the justification for the valid work of art is its capacity to alter the common life by its very existence—is implicitly rejected as naive, replaced by a thinner formulation in which art-making is legitimated only as a fulfillment of responsibility to one's own nature, where that responsibility itself requires a further justification (kow-towing to the supreme engineer) that Lewis treats lightly at best. Retreating to a defense of art as the mere exercise of a capacity otherwise without purpose, unless it be that of praising a divinity whom we have no reason to respect, Lewis takes his stand on production for production's sake while at the same time administering a critique of productionism that finally leaves art's ethical and even its ontological status uncertain.

This same self-divided rhetoric can also be found at other moments when Lewis contemplates production in general. In an extraordinary passage from the "Subject as King" chapter of *Time and Western Man*, for example, he takes issue with Schopenhauer's idea of Will in the following terms:

> The Will that "objectifies" itself . . . is a will to what? To nothing, Schopenhauer replies. This is, of course his celebrated "pessimism": the picture of a Will that just goes on for some reason "objectifying" itself, resulting in the endless rigmarole in which we participate, and of which (qua Will) we are the witnesses. It produces Charlie Chaplin, the League of Nations, wireless, feminism, Rockefeller; it causes, daily, millions of women to drift in front of, and swarm inside, gigantic clothes-shops in every great capital, buying silk underclothing, cloche-hats, perfumes, van-ishing cream, vanity-bags and furs. . . . It is a quite aimless, and, from our limited point of view, nonsensical, Will. (312)

By his own lights, Lewis is here only objecting to what he takes to be Schopenhauer's sacrifice of the individual consciousness to this "nonsensi-cal" superindividual force (the philosophical parent of von Hartmann's, Freud's, and Lawrence's unconscious and the Bergsonian élan vital), not explicitly announcing his own crisis of meaning: indeed he faults Schop-enhauer for holding "firmly to the *purposelessness* of everything," and for giving the world "the feeblest of Wills with which any unhappy universe was ever afflicted," a Will that "cannot get anything that it wants" (313, 312). But though he can abide neither Schopenhauer's pessimism (the solu-tion of "resignation . . . brightened somewhat by string-quartets" [318]), nor Bergson's optimism (which he reads as Schopenhauer's pessimism minus sincerity), he offers no suggestion of his own as to what the purpose of everything might be, or what a stronger, better Will might comprehensibly seek to obtain.

The passage is of interest not only because it finds Lewis explicitly attacking self-objectification as fundamental value, but also because it shows how existential explorations could be prompted by the spectacles of large-scale production and the modern subject's bombardment by commodities, how profound reflections on purpose could be provoked by daily encounters with an unprecedentedly massive making that had nonetheless failed to lend convincing significance to the long history of human struggle. Phrased thus, of course, such a summary indicates just why production under capitalism will necessarily be excluded from possible resolutions to the questions at issue: Lewis may not know what the human project is, here, but he does know that all this buying and selling is not it. We might note in this context that it is in his book on Lewis, appropriately, that Jameson offers one of his best summaries of the critical side of modernism's relation to mass production, noting that the modernists characteristically found "the concrete determinations of the older social novel—the empirical detail of everyday life, . . . the slow fashion- or furniture-change of the decades, the material coordinates of workplace or mechanical conveyance" to be "so much contingent matter . . . eyed with all the suspicion of a foreign body," against which they posed a "will to overcome the commodification of late nineteenth-century capitalism, and to substitute for the mouldering and overstuffed bazaar of late Victorian life the mystique and promise of some intense and heightened, more authentic existence" (39).

As every student of modernism knows, however, it proved far easier for its practitioners to gesture to the absence that would be authentic existence, or even to describe some of its likely particulars, than to delineate the telos to which such an existence would tend or to determine what necessity it might counterpose to the contingent matter of commodification. Indeed the eminent reversibility of our own formulation of a moment ago indicates why it was so hard for modernists to get away from capitalist production in their attempts to discover a meaningful justification for human action: Lewis knows that all this selling and buying is not the human project, but by the same token he does not know what that project could in fact be, can offer nothing that would circumvent commodity culture's centrality to quotidian life and consciousness or rival in imaginative force the overwhelming massiveness suggested by his heterogeneous list of goods. His primary aim being to ridicule Schopenhauer, it makes perfect sense that his catalogue of objectifications should include mass culture, suspect political formations, and feminine (read: trivial) cosmetics and accessories; and yet it is not hard to see how drastically the sense of the passage would be altered by the substitution of guns and butter for cloche-hats and perfumes—or even how gigantic a void would be left at the heart of modern life should cloche-hats and all their fellows simply disappear. The very plenitude of Lewis's enumeration suggests, in other words, how the effort to generalize about the purpose of human production in some way that would marginalize the proliferation of commodities and technologies or the relentless will-to-more could have seemed an embarrassingly *self*-marginalizing exercise for the modernists, especially given their aversion to fashioning themselves merely nostalgic or regressive.

Like Woolf, in other words, Lewis found the explosion of making made possible by mass production techniques at once stimulating and perverse, its positive grandeur impossible to dismiss, its utter stupid aimlessness impossible to embrace; and like the later Woolf, he was troubled above all by what he recognized to be close associations between this aimlessness and a dangerously restless human will. Having witnessed one world war that seemed a consequence of overproduction (the Social Credit view), he would live to see another apparently driven by a fetishization of Will virtually divested of other trappings, as he suggested in 1942 when, having turned against the fascists, he described his hero Penhale (*The Vulgar Streak*) as "a child of the era of Mussolini and Hitler as much as Sorel was of that of Napoleon: his tragedy being that he has *too much will* (like most Europeans) and is fooled by the idea of *force*" (*Letters* 316). But if anxieties about the goals of production led Lewis to question the validity of the work of art as life project, his related concerns about the expansive designs of subjectivity did not lead him (as hers led Woolf), to the still more disturbing question of whether art might not therefore be implicated in the work of domination. Rather, they brought him, on occasion, to attempt to sever the work of art from the problematic human will altogether—a gesture quite antithetical to the prescriptions of existentialism in its Woolfian and Sartrean forms, but clearly consonant with his own sanctions against an art that would show too plainly the traces of the subjectivity that produced it. One might take almost anything in Lewis's writing on art—from his famous insistence on deadness to his polemics against objectification, impressionism, and expressionism—as testimony to his differences with an existential vision that finally staked a good deal on the bonds between work and subject, but perhaps his most direct statement of divergence is to be found in a letter of 1950. After criticizing André Malraux for "identify[ing] art and life" and the Romans for crucifying "living men upon their stages," Lewis goes on to observe therein that "Sartre, of course, with his philosophy of action, is Malraux's true disciple" (*Letters* 516).

This last comment takes on still greater resonance when considered alongside an essay from 1927 (the year of *Time of Western Man*), in which Lewis makes his deepest foray into problems of interest to Existentialism more narrowly defined. In "The Meaning of the Wild Body," he quotes a passage from William James that resembles very closely Rachel Vinrace's reflection on existence in *The Voyage Out*—"One need only shut oneself in a closet and begin to think of the fact of one's being there . . . to have the wonder steal over the detail as much as over the general fact of being. . . .

Not only that *anything* should be, but that *this* very thing should be, is mysterious"—in commenting on which he virtually states the case for existentialism's central importance to thought: "This sense of the absurdity or, if you like the madness of our life," he writes, "is at the root of every true philosophy" (*Complete Wild* 157). Turning next to the problem of each subjectivity's closure to all others—so crucial in Woolf and Sartre alike— Lewis notes that from one's own point of view "all men are necessarily comic: for they are all *things*, or physical bodies, behaving as *persons*," and then links this point to some observations supportive of his preference for an art of "external" satire:

> To bring vividly to our mind what we mean by "absurd," let us turn to the plant, and enquire how the plant could be absurd. Suppose you came upon an orchid or cabbage reading Flaubert's *Salammbô*, or Plutarch's *Moralia*, you would be very much surprised. But if you found a man or a woman reading it, you would not be surprised.
>
> Now in one sense you ought to be just as much surprised at finding a man occupied in this way as if you had found an orchid or a cabbage. . . . It is just as absurd externally. . . . The deepest root of the Comic is to be sought in this anomaly. (*Complete Wild* 158–59)

That *Mrs. Dalloway* (published two years before) constitutes one of the key intertexts for this essay is suggested not only by Lewis's interest, here, in the particular existential questions that Woolf found most absorbing, but also by the fact that like Woolf he uses the vegetal as a governing synecdoche for the nonhuman object world, even choosing as its representatives the very plants—cabbages and orchids—foregrounded as alternatives to the human in the opening and closing pages of her novel. But if the essay illustrates certain similarities of interest, and even the capacity of Woolf's fictions to infiltrate Lewis's imagination in a manner that the latter would scarcely have cared to acknowledge, it also shows quite forcefully how Lewis abjures the Woolfian and Sartrean scenarios in which the work of art gains its meaning as an intersubjective mediator or as a subjectivity's achieved objectification. For if Clarissa and Roquentin, as reader of *Cymbeline* and auditor of a pop recording respectively, experience the work as an object that forges links between widely separated subjects (and if Sartre leaves open the additional possibility that this mediation is predicated upon the infusion of consciousness into matter), in Lewis's scene the reader is not an experiencing subject but rather an archetypal object, and the book being read the motor of absurdity or meaninglessness instead of a counter to it. The point of Lewis's image is not that we might share something of the beheld reader's subjective life (or something of Flaubert's or Plutarch's) through the medium of *Salammbô* or the *Moralia*, but on the contrary that it is emphatically immaterial to the comic gaze whether we have read these works or not, since the book can only appear to it an object looked at by another object, both of them opaque to knowledge and communication. And the comic view, Lewis suggests, is the one most adequate to reality, the one that responds most acutely to the sense of absurdity or madness "at the root of every true philosophy."

If the denouement of his essay about the comic is itself comic rather than tragic—and if Lewis's other failures to offer a resolution to existential crisis seem less unsettling than similar moments in Woolf—the reason is in part that the mode of existential inquiry did not provoke in him much grief, confusion, or despair, though he certainly entered it with interest and even fervency. As the absence of nonironic representations of intense existential anxiety in his writings indicates, he could not find the absurdity of Being an overpowering source of either fascination or horror, and indeed his philosophy—unlike the philosophies of Sartre, Heidegger, and Woolf—rather surprisingly does not include brute Being's primacy or priority among its fundamental premises. On the contrary, in spite of his extensive defenses of solidity, externalism, and the integrity of the object, Lewis asserts in a key passage from *Time and Western Man* that when it comes to a rigorous epistemology, the objects we encounter are not, as such, solid at all: "'objects' are the finished product of our perceptive faculty," he observes, "the result . . . of the organizing activity of our minds. When we say we see them, in reality what we perceive is not the direct datum of sensation, but an elaborate and sophisticated entity, or 'object.' We do even in that sense 'create' them more than 'see' them" (350).

For Lewis the world is much as it is for Blake, Coleridge, or even Russell (though the figure to whom he traces his own genealogy is Berkeley), but he can still vociferate against the object's absorption by subjectivity because in his view it would be disastrous to try to live each moment—as Russell proposes to—in a full awareness that objects are really creations of our own faculties. In the passage that precedes the one just quoted, he writes:

> The objects of our perception, with their mystifying independence and air of self-sufficiency . . . are far more uncanny than the unity we experience in our subjective experience. These strange *things*, that stand out against a background of mystery, with their air of being *eternal*, and which really appear to be "caused" by nothing that we can hold and fix, and from which we can see them being actually produced, are far stranger than we are, or more brutally and startlingly strange. If architecture is "frozen music"—as it has been rather disgustingly called—what are we to say of these trees and hills and houses? They, at all events, seem far nobler and severer than our minds, or our "inner sense". . . . (350)

In "creating" objects in perception, we "create" things nobler and severer than ourselves, but that nobility and that severity are compromised whenever we take credit for that creation. We cannot do without objects taken to be entities genuinely distinct from us because we need exemplars of virtues that we do not possess as subjects, or at the very least embodiments of a basic alterity or "strangeness" that no subject can exude. That other people can seem to be things is comic rather than tragic in part because things are, in a sense, the morally superior entities: to look around and see not scheming, quarreling, untrustworthy human beings but simply a collection of objects reading, walking, and talking is for Lewis (at least in one of his predominant frames of mind) to see the world filled for an instant if not with goodness then at least with a palpable absence of evil.

This point bears powerfully on the question of art's rationale, finally, because it suggests that the work of art was most fundamentally precious to Lewis insofar as it *was* an object, and as such part of a world existentially or ontologically beyond the pain of human division, even if it could never be removed practically from involvement in ideological conflicts. In Lewis's view, the art object would indeed draw its special power from the fact that of all things it seems the one most intimately entangled with subjectivity, but its function would not be to testify to human greatness or to provide consciousness a reflection of itself; on the contrary, it would come into its own in those moments when in spite of its human making it appears as remote, as hard, as distant as any other thing, thereby reminding us with special force of the difference, the strangeness, and the peace of the nonhuman world. It was surely for this reason, above all, that Lewis found visions of art as expression or self-objectification so destructive; and it was surely because he saw it as an assault on the last preserve of needed difference that he abominated the infusion of subjectivity into matter.

In *The Art of Being Ruled*, Lewis quotes a long passage in which Samuel Butler asserts that "there is no true love short of eating and consequent assimilation," that "we do not really love" our horses and dogs "because we do not eat them," but do love the oyster because "nothing short of its complete absorption into our own being can in the least satisfy us" (253). Lewis retorts that, on the contrary, we do love dogs and do not love oysters (we only find them "'lovely' to *eat*"), and that "[i]t is only when something is independent of us, a non-assimilable universe of its own, that we 'love' it, as we call it" (254). He continues,

> The "superficial contact of exterior form" which characterizes the "love" of the more complex animals is essential to the existence of "love" or "affection"; that is an emotion for something different to the self, that cannot be absorbed into the self, in the sense of be eaten. That *detachment, distance,* and, as it were, chastity, and intense *personal* sensation on our side, is at the bottom of all our *spiritual* values, as we name what about us is independent of feeding and renewing our machine. (254)

The promise or consolation that the object world offers, then, seems to depend upon its retention of its objecthood, which is nothing less than a version of the distance that makes love possible. If Lewis usually said very little about this distance and this love, the reason may be that he wished so earnestly to preserve their tenuous sanctity; and this fundamental deference to the integrity of the object may also explain why he scarcely ventured to elaborate what might have been for him the most satisfying of justifications for art.

This is not to suggest by any means that behind Lewis's unforgiving assessments of his fellow human beings there lurked a person restrained by reverence from expressing his vast love for his kind: on the contrary, when in the Flaubert chapter he writes, "*Human life had better, here and now, and once and for all, be accepted as a very bad business indeed*" (*Men* 213), he seems to be speaking with unusually perfect sincerity, or at least to be recording with truthful directness one of his favored moods. To be sure, it may be this streak of misanthropy more than anything else that has left Lewis the least studied of the great modernist innovators, and left Lewis scholarship as its first task that of stimulating interest in his difficult, brilliant, often repellent work; but the way to begin this process is surely to recognize that Lewis's idealistic disgust offers some complex lessons about the value of otherness and the perils of what can look like love, not to deny this disgust's existence. At the same time again, however, it is important to see that—brutal and paranoid as he appears in so much of his published writing, weary and wounded by life as he so often seems in his letters—Lewis is not always best described as pessimistic. For the fact is that (true to his claims about his predispositions) he thought to an unusual degree in terms of space rather than time, so that terms like pessimism, optimism, and even hope, with their futurative senses, can be applied to his case only with some qualification. If Lewis seems peculiarly immune to existential anxiety, this is so above all because his quest was less for some transcendental signified, purpose, or eschaton than for a sheer alterity already instanced in our own lives by the world of objects—because for him the utopian was less a possibility for the future than a part of the present, though it was almost always to be found precisely where people were not. Even his early dismissal of nature-mortists for failing to change the common life does not alter the fact that the world he sought was never one that would be governed by some radical existential or epistemological reconciliation, certainly not one in which the subject (or the will, or the self) would congeal into the object or the object dissolve into the subject. It was always, rather, one in which the two would remain side by side, each in its proper repose.

Chapter Three

EZRA POUND

THOUGH SCARCELY averse to using the term "aesthete" reprovingly, Ezra Pound dissociated himself from aestheticism neither as loudly as Wyndham Lewis nor with the significant discretion of Virginia Woolf: as he used it, "aestheticism" sometimes designated a past movement of some moment, sometimes an incorrect position taken by contemporaries of minimal importance, but never an evil principle that dared not speak its name. In his early polemics he retained a number of Paterian and Wildean premises, drawing liberally on the catchwords of beauty, emotion, and personality,[1] and in his later writing he occasionally credited aestheticism with breakthroughs whose significance has only lately been generally acknowledged. As Vincent Miller points out in an article on *Hugh Selwyn Mauberley*, Pound had "much more respect for the aesthetic kind of writing than his critics have had";[2] and though in that sequence as in the Pisan cantos he famously laments aestheticism's failures, he also emphasizes those failures' heroic aspect in a way that would prove extraordinarily significant for his art (as we will see). In an essay from 1937, meanwhile, he comments that although aestheticism "took Yeats and Symons one way, and Bro. Ford another," the "literary historian will err if he tries to start the 'revolution of the word' a decade or so later with the emergence of Mr Joyce's epigons [*sic*] and jejune admirers" (*Polite* 50). And whereas Lewis faulted the fin de siècle for the sensationalism of its assaults on sexual morality, Pound praised it—or rather a range of nineteenth-century writers including the Pre-Raphaelites, Swinburne, James, and Hardy—for uniting, as he put it in 1938, "in disgust with the social estimates of their era, in rebellion against the sordid matrimonial customs of England," and in so doing breeding "a generation of experimenters," namely Pound's own (*Guide* 287, 291).

By sordid matrimonial customs Pound clearly meant, in the first instance, love's subordination to (or its deformation by) material interests, as so unsparingly depicted by writers like Hardy and James; and it would be no exaggeration to say that in Pound's own view his most important point of accord with his immediate literary predecessors lay in a continuous fury at the way spirit could be crushed under economic constraints. But if in the works of those predecessors such injustice typically takes the form of a thwarting of happiness or promise that only casually intersects with the vulgarity or bleakness of modern commerce, it was famously one of the habits of Pound's generation to join the two together, in a crusade against what we have seen Lewis calling the irresponsible commercial mind and all its works. In later Pound, of course, this crusade culminates in an epic clash between art and usury (canto XLV, "With *Usura*," for example, or the end of canto LXXIV, where "stone after stone of beauty" is "cast down" by "the useful operations of commerce" [*Cantos* 229, 462]), but Pound can be found denouncing or simply mocking commodification and capitalism generally throughout his career—from sardonic poems of the mid-1910s like "Women Before a Shop" and "The Lake Isle" to his complaint in the *Guide to Kulchur* that as fast as "the state spends a few million on beautifying the highroads and their borders, some foetid spawn of the pit puts up a 30 foot wooden advertisement of synthetic citronade to defile man's art in road-making and the natural pulchritude of the vegetation" (*Guide* 187).

Diatribes against the commodification of literature itself are of course a staple of the Poundian critical store, as in the 1920 article in which he contrasts works by writers like Lewis to the "average novel," to which a "certain commercial interest attaches" (*Literary* 425), or the 1938 manifesto "For a New Paideuma" in which he attacks an "America which treats writing as production of a trade commodity instead of as a communications service" (*Prose* 288). Turning to a series of articles he wrote for the *New Age* in 1917–18 under the title "Studies in Contemporary Mentality," we can even find Pound getting a few laughs simply from composing, with the benefit of his remarkable ear for rhythm, lists of things advertised in current periodicals. In a treatment of one such publication, which he prefaces with the warning, "Reader, pause! We are about to take a jump out of sanity and into the thick of a peculiar, a very peculiar, milieu," he notes that

> Old Moore carries twenty-four pages of ads. Sic: Nerve force, free to the ruptured, asthmas, drunkard saved (18 pictures showing swing of the pendulum), rupture, magnetic girl, whooping-cough, fits, why be fat, pine-forest in every home, children's powders, message to mothers, don't wear a truss, life-pills, test horoscope, no more grey hair, grey hairs, gold watch free, eye ointment, drink habit conquered, neuraliga [*sic*], free offer superior to steel and pennyroyal, ditto, infinitely superior to bitter apple, pills for women, kidney, renal pills, given away: information to the married, pills, pills, £5 notes for correct anwer and stamp, free gift, without medicine, gold watch free, surgical appliance, lung tonic, Eno's.
>
> And some ass has said that the age of faith is dead! (*Ezra Pound's* 2: 303)

In later installments Pound goes over similar ground with the *Christian Herald* ("Why wear a truss, Free book of amazing bargains, Let me build up your normal weight, cough elixir" [*Ezra Pound's* 2: 305]) and the *Church Times* ("'Artificial teeth bought,' jig-saw puzzles, Diabetes, 'Safety from raids—clergyman's wife takes P.G.'s'" [*Ezra Pound's* 3: 12]).

Pound's observation that the true faith articulated here is a faith in the powers of commodities, of course, highlights the fact that the terrain once occupied by religion became, under the modernists' impassioned staging, the site of a struggle between mass-produced cultural forms and authentic art. In the context of this campaign to ensure that Goods did not replace Gods, passages like these seem intensely unsurprising specimens of modernist values in action; and yet insofar as they speak to the question of modernism's own vision of capitalism, they can seem freshly compelling for a literary scholarship invigorated by a return to history, where history is understood not as the "background" or "context" of days of yore but rather as a series of ideological contests and negotiations conducted through many kinds of discourses, including literary ones. Indeed it would be fair to claim that the question of modernism's relation to what Frank Lentricchia calls the culture of capital has lately been installed at the center of modernist studies, though the work that has placed it there has been divided between attempts to deepen our sense of the virulence of modernists' hatred of certain capitalist configurations and rather different efforts to show how their mandarinism was interlaced with accommodation to, and even delight in, the ways of the market and mass culture. If the latter effort has found its gravitational center in Woolf and Joyce, with their exuberant treatments of the spectacle of consumption, the former has not surprisingly settled on Pound, with critics like Lentricchia and Cary Wolfe reminding us—lest we reduce the kind of Poundian tirades just quoted to an effort to deprive "popular" or "mass" forms of their cultural capital—how basic and genuine was Pound's detestation of capitalism and its (in his view) miserably pallid satisfactions.

Without pulling rapprochements from thin air, however, we can still ask if Pound's sense of his own distance from commodification was fully secure, and if so why it should have been: after all, the lists of things advertised in "Studies in Contemporary Mentality" (so evocative, in its way, of Lewis's catalogue of productions of the nonsensical will) do testify to the fineness of the line between the urge to pit goods against poetry and the urge to find the poetry in goods. It is in seeking answers to just such questions that we might appropriately turn to Pound's ambivalent relation to aestheticism, because his anxiety about commodification's ability to materialize just where most defended against is frequently encoded in references to the aesthetes' at once snobbish and subversive devotion to finer things, which in his view could metamorphose into a fetishization of the exquisite with unhappy consequences for art. In an otherwise mostly laudatory 1918 assessment of Henry James, for example, Pound criticizes that great rebel against sordid matrimonial customs for his "dam'd fuss about furniture," advocating a relegation of the master's "cobwebs about connoisseurship" to "the same realm as the author's pyjamas and collar buttons, to his intellectual . . . valeting" (*Literary* 308, 297, 311; see also *Letters* 125); and similar comments litter the rest of Pound's criticism and correspondence. Years later he would write, "When I use the term 'blue china' in abuse, I should define it as 'minor detail' that is NOT being correlated for the sake either of IMMEDIACY or of justice" in composition (*Polite* 102; see also *Letters* 279), a remark that recalls a well known letter to Eliot from 1921 in which he blamed his own failure to produce anything on the order of *The Waste Land* on a constitutional tendency to "go into nacre and objets d'art" (*Letters* 169).

More problematic than its invitation to triviality, however, was aesthetic connoisseurship's affiliation with some of the very forces against which the aesthetic attitude was supposed to contend. "I reject the term connoisseurship," Pound wrote in "The Serious Artist," because " 'connoisseurship' is so associated in our minds with a desire for acquisition. The person possessed of connoisseurship is apt to want to buy the rare at one price and sell it at another" (*Literary* 55). Pound's antipathies here can be attributed partly to the fact that connoisseurship could imply the kind of learned ability to follow conventional evaluations to which he was congenitally hostile; but still more troubling to him was its intimacy with the dramatically conspicuous consumption that made one of the ongoing scandals of the years around the turn of the century, a phenomenon to which we have also seen Woolf and Lewis reacting and which Pound encountered firsthand in Feburary 1907, when a fire at the mansion of Philadelphia department store magnate John Wanamaker (which included a picture gallery) gave him a chance "to observe the destruction of faked Van Dykes, etc." (*Literary* 391). For Pound, the figure of the connoisseur linked aestheticism to a mode of acquisition at once pathetic in its inability to distinguish art from charlatanry and outrageous in its use of spectacular consumption to divert attention from the economic exploitation that supported it: "Mr. Wanamaker was nothing to me, he paid his employees badly, and I knew the actual spectacle was all I should ever get out of him" (391).

In this last remark, Pound renders with unusual clarity a point that he would make frequently in his later poetry, as for example a section of canto XL:

> De banchis cambi tenendi. . . .
>   Venice 1361,
> '62. . shelved for a couple of centuries. .
> "whether by privates or public. . .
>   currency OF (O, F, of) the nation.
> Toward producing that wide expanse of clean lawn
> Toward that deer park toward
> the playing fields, congeries, swimming pools, undsoweiter:
> Sword-fish, seven marlin, world's record
> extracted in 24 hours.

Wd. make the loan, sterling, eight hundred thousand
if Peabody wd. quit business.
    England 1858
IN THE NAME OF GOD THE MOST GLORIOUS MR.
    D'ARCY
is permitted for 50 years to dig up the subsoil of
Persia.

(Cantos 197)

What was "shelved" in 1361 or 1362 (actually 1361), according to an article
by E. P. Walkiewicz and Hugh Witemeyer, was a Venetian plan for a public
bank resembling the kind that the Social Credit movement advocated for
Pound's own century, one whose profits would be recycled through the community rather than going into investors' pockets.[3] Pound here sets up a "subject rhyme" between the initial defeat of that scheme and the more contemporary triumph of financial unscrupulousness exemplified by William Knox
d'Arcy's obtaining of a license to the Persian oil fields in 1901 (see Terrell
155), also rhyming the plunder of a foreign nation's soil (with hints at the
theft of archaeological treasures) with the robber barons' indecently acquired
"wide expanse of clean lawn."[4] Pound then connects these ill-gotten gains to
consumption on a smaller scale further on in the canto, implying through a
catalogue of Victorian bourgeois dream homes, Flaubertian furnishings, and
feminine accessories (for male modernists, apparently, the most irresistable
of tropes for the trivial) that the most ostentatious examples of conspicuous
consumption are as worthless as the most ephemeral:

>   With our eyes on the new gothic residence, with our
> eyes on Palladio, with a desire for seigneurial splendours
> (ÀGALMA, haberdashery, clocks, ormoulu, brocatelli,
> tapestries, unreadable volumes bound in tree-calf,
> half-morocco, morocco, tooled edges, green ribbons,
> flaps, farthingales, fichus, cuties, shorties, pinkies
> et cetera
>   Out of which things seeking an exit
>
> PLEASING TO CARTHEGENIANS: HANNO
>
> that he ply beyond pillars of Herakles
> 60 ships of armada to lay out Phoenecian cities. . . .

(199)

As in "Studies in Contemporary Mentality," Pound uses the form of the
list to advantage, treating the reader passing through it to both the pleasure
of plenitude and the fun of ridicule; but in this case the enumeration of
details appears to serve as a distraction from a serious lacuna in argument, a

failure to balance his condemnation of exploiters with bad taste with some attention to the more morally challenging problem of exploiters with good. While it may be a fairly straightforward business to lament the robber baron's unreadable volumes in expensive bindings, such a complaint says nothing about the patron of really talented artists whose wealth may have originated with no less violent abuses—precisely the problem that Lewis engaged with so much agony in essays like "Pictures as Investments," and precisely the factor that leaves the moral victories of this canto far too easily won, barring some genuine belief that bad business pays only for bad art. And yet it would scarcely be an exaggeration to say that this *is* what Pound believed, his insistence that one can tell the degree of usury prevalent in a society from the quality of its art (treated more extensively below), for example, indicating how he internalized nearly uncritically (as Lewis did not) aestheticism's bourgeois-baiting premise that legitimate art naturally opposes the unlovely affairs of *homo economicus*.[5]

These difficulties are encoded aptly, though surely against Pound's intention, in his reference to the fifth-century B.C. voyage of the Carthaginian Hanno, past the Strait of Gibraltar and around the North African coast, which, though represented as a nobler alternative to the world of imitation Palladio and farthingales, is in fact deeply implicated in the expansionist designs of a famously commercial culture. (And for that matter in imperial violence: Pound includes near the end of the canto his hero's account of how his crew killed three women from an "island of folk hairy and savage" and brought their skins back to Carthage.) Further, even the signifier "Hanno" itself turns out to be bizarrely affiliated with the haberdashery and ormolu of consumption in the decadent mode, inasmuch as it names not only the fifth-century adventurer but also a later Carthaginian general whose excesses Flaubert records in *Salammbô*,[6] a figure as cruel (he kills ruthlessly) and literally degenerate (he suffers from a flesh-devouring disease whose progress Flaubert describes with gruesome relish) as he is posh (he dines on flamingo tongues flavored with poppy seed and sports enormous earrings, necklaces of blue stones, and felt boots sprinkled with silver moons) (Flaubert 99, 43–44, 45). The two Carthaginians are polar opposites in some ways, to be sure—the heroic voyager returns with a map and a record of his travels, whereas the other's only legacy is a novel that Pound elsewhere dismissed as "an old charade in fancy clothes" (*ABC* 74; see also *Literary* 418 and *Letters* 93)—and yet the double name does its damage no less certainly for all that, since the difference between success and failure here does not follow from any sharp distinction between innocence and guilt, peace and violence, or even the visionary and the commercial.

The passages from canto XL further illuminate Pound's relation to modern commodity culture—or, rather, his understanding of modernity as something expressed in the kinds of objects that it unleashed—in that they include two of his trademark responses to contemporary economic life: first, the finding of precedents among the documents of previous eras ("De banchis cambi tenendi. . . . / Venice 1361, / '62. . shelved for a couple of centuries"); second, the finding of alternatives in more nearly mythical histories ("Out of which things seeking an exit / PLEASING TO CARTHEGENIANS: HANNO"). Though the first in effect unmodernizes the modern while the second stresses the unmodernity of the past, both look away from the new world of production by way of denaturalizing contemporary conditions— not, that is to say, in order to revitalize archaic modes of social life as good in themselves, but rather in order to divest the worst aspects of modern modes of their air of necessity. And this point bears closely on a key aspect of Pound's program for art in the twentieth century, his habit of recurring to the scene of the individual craftsman working tangible materials, which is motivated much less by a dislike of modern innovations or a nostalgia for old methods of production as such than by a need to disentangle art from the dominance of commerce, imperial markets, and spectacular consumption.

Pound's position in this regard is neatly captured by his most famous slogan, "Make it new," which works so well as a distillation of his enterprise not only because it encodes his grand project of revitalizing (his own version of) a literary tradition, but also because it balances a delicately indicated preference for individual production ("Make it," which instruction is clearly not addressed to corporations or industrialists) with an insistence that such a turn need not be regressive ("new"). Another fine indication of the nature of Pound's investments can be found in *Patria Mia*, his 1913 prospectus for an American renaissance to be sponsored by enlightened patrons, wherein he praises the night skyline of New York as "our poetry, for we have pulled down the stars to our will" immediately after writing of how in " 'San Zeno' at Verona, one finds columns with the artisan's signature at the base. Thus: *'Me Mateus fecit'*. That is what we have not and can not have where columns are ordered by the gross. And this is a matter of 'industrial conditions'" (*Prose* 107). But the most eloquent testimony to his sentiments on this score is surely to be found in the many manifestos in which he figures the safe poems of popular anthologies as shoddy goods generated for mass consumption while representing poems released (initially) to an appreciative few as the handicraft of the skilled artisan, his refences to craft in poetry (*Literary* 7, 10, 49, 51, 371; *Early Poems* 271, 287; *Prose* 31–34, 111) and to the poet as *fabbro* (*Spirit* 13), craftsman (*Personae* 153, *Early Poems* 209, *Literary* 337), maker (*Early Poems* 213), fashioner (*Early Poems* 249, *Literary* 372), and producer (*Literary* 222, 280) clearly making sense only as strikes against sordid publication practices, not as eruptions of nostalgia for old styles.

In literature as in anything else, however, this recourse to the artisanal could scarcely combat the fatality of commerce in any remotely rigorous way, in part because it so obviously sought to circumvent the systemic change that in the view of Marx and others—including, in a way, the later Pound—would be essential to any escape from commodification. As Wolfe observes, just a trifle hyperbolically, Pound's "antidotes to alienation . . . cannot be class-based but can be initiated only by the particular self whom reform is by and for" because his "defense of the individual is accompanied by a peculiarly American absence of any structural concept of class" (46–47). Orthodox Marxists, or even not very orthodox Marxists, would point out how Pound's refrain in the *ABC of Economics* (1933), "The minute I cook my own dinner or nail four boards together into a chair, I escape from the whole cycle of Marxian economics," justifed on the grounds that "Marxian economics deal with goods for sale, goods in the shop" (*Prose* 239), is symptomatic of his neglect of Marx's insistence that exchange value arises from a total system of social relations, that capitalism in its very nature is not merely "dominant" in the usual sense of that term but pervasive and determining—a point foregrounded, in a way, by the careers of Morris chairs and Omega designs, which showed so clearly the commodity form's adeptness at transforming soi-disant rivals into more instances of itself.

In the late 1910s and early 1920s Pound did, certainly, reflect upon capitalism's globalization, observing in 1918 that "Labour and Capital are in a race towards internationalism" in which "Capital will almost indubitably arrive first" (*Ezra Pound's* 3: 11), and in 1922 that having presented "Ireland under British domination," Joyce had, by extension, "presented the whole occident under the domination of capital" (*Literary* 307). These instances suggest, however, that in this phase Pound tended to imagine the agglomeration of capitalists as one "side," the Manichean other of which might be Labour, or Art, or Artists, or Artisans: in the 1918 article, having praised Capital for its internationalism while noting his mistrust of its tendency to be "very nearly irresponsible," he declares that his thoughts are those "of an amateur in these matters, of one who has turned from the, to him, far more serious matter, that of making poetry, of considering the nature of individual man retired within the recesses of his own subjectivity" (11). And though Pound would later devote all his work to variations on the theme that art cannot be separated from economics, this later position too is governed less by a totalizing approach than by those well known romances of causality or correlation in which usura and artistic failure appear so fatefully entwined, in which (once again) bad business gives rise as by necessity to bad art.

If in their uncritical absorption of pieties associated with subversive aestheticism and their neglect of the problem of totality Pound's economic formulations lack much acutely revolutionary force, however, they nonetheless retain a certain antithetical power at the level of individual choice or intention: after all, even if his "serious artist" can no more ignore the pressures of a "market" broadly construed than Woolf's money-earning writer can think of things entirely in themselves, he can still choose not to put monetary profit ahead of all other goals. And while Pound's emphasis on artisanal making cannot address the alienation of labor as a phenomenon of the total system of social relations, it can address the question of self-objectification in a more ontological sense, inasmuch as the individually crafted item can always be conceived as being "of" its fashioner in a way that the mass-produced item cannot. Neither resale, imitation, nor even the inflation of price attached to craftedness can cancel the fact that such a product comes directly from the hand (or the intelligence) of its maker, the handmade Morris chair being no less handmade for its voguishness, and "Me Mateus fecit" remaining no less true should the column bearing that inscription be taken from its place and auctioned off.

Certainly, it may be objected that since the concept of self-objectification as such arises only with the triumph of the middle class and the theoretician of *bürgerliche Gesellschaft*, Hegel, it cannot be thought apart from capitalism or without naturalizing bourgeois subjectivity; and yet it is worth noting that even Lukács, confuting Hegel and his own younger self in 1967, insisted that objectification and alienation are not the same thing, that the former "is indeed a phenomenon that cannot be eliminated from human life in society" and that "every externalisation of an object in practice . . . is an objectification, that every human expression including speech objectifies human thoughts and feelings" (*History* xxiv). Of course debates of this kind would have been of scant interest in any case to Pound, for whom nailing four boards together constituted an escape from the whole cycle of Marxian economics—and whose concern with self-objectification in art was far from circumscribed by the project of resisting the culture of capital. Even in 1921, when the formerly irresistible aesthete tropes of personality and immortalization had begun to pall for him, he could still write at the very beginning of an essay on Brancusi, " 'I carve a thesis in logic of the eternal beauty,' writes Rémy [*sic*] de Gourmont in his *Sonnets à l'Amazone*. A man hurls himself toward the infinite and the works of art are his vestiges, his trace in the manifest" (*Literary* 441). No pronouncement on artistic production could more audaciously evoke the egotistical sublime, or more sleekly intertwine with Platonism the implication that works of art represent the infusion of spirit into matter (an implication strengthened here by the fact that the essay's subject is a sculptor).

This further articulation of position, however, would itself be misleading if taken to suggest that Pound treated the capacity to crystallize the artist's subjectivity as art's sole or even principal justification; on the contrary, there are many moments at which he appears to take up with alacrity the privileging of object over maker traditionally associated with modernist antiRomanticism, in spite of his highly un-Eliotic affinities for self-promotion, hero worship, and the forceful personality. Even the extreme statement on the thrust toward the infinite just quoted is finally ruled by the functional premise of the essay in which it appears, namely the inherent worth of Brancusi's sculptures, and when Pound goes on to quote with approval T. J. Everets's observation that a "work of art has in it no idea which is separable from the form" (441), he seems to imply that neither the artist nor the infinite toward which he hurls himself is truly prior to the vestige or trace. As we have already noted, Pound's aesthetic was decisively influenced in the early 1910s by the classical, and eventually antihumanist, turn of T. E. Hulme, and though his own strain of Imagism-Vorticism shows little of the mistrust of subjectivism that we find in Hulme or Lewis, its subscription to a similar aesthetic of hardness finally counters expressive effusion in art no less sharply.

What may be Pound's most significant statement in this area appears in the revisionist manifesto "A Retrospect," from 1918, wherein he insists that while "[i]t is tremendously important that great poetry be written, it makes no jot of difference who writes it" (*Literary* 10). The comment falls in the midst of reflections heavy with a language of phallic ambition ("if a man's experiments"; "The mastery of any art is the work of a lifetime"; "technique as the test of a man's sincerity"), and yet it marks virtually the only statement of *fundamental* value or goals in an essay whose major argument is that good poetry can only be produced through careful attention to craft, never as a spontaneous overflow from some poetizing self. By 1934, Pound could write, in a note on an anonymous sixteenth-century pastoral in the *ABC of Reading*,

> The first effort of misguided ink-page scholars would be to FIND THE AUTHOR. Note that the author particularly refrained from signing the poem. *As the great mediaeval architects and stone-cutters refrained from signing their work.* One of the great maladies of modern criticism is this first rush to look for the person, and the corresponding failure EVER to look *at* the thing. (147; first emphasis added)

Discussing the church of San Zeno in 1913, as we have just seen, Pound had written feelingly of the "columns with the artisan's signature at the base," so that it might seem that we witness here a gradual distancing from the seductions of personality occurring over two decades. Yet Pound refers to the San Zeno columns in terms substantially similar to those of the 1913 essay in a number of later cantos (including XLV, LXXIV, LXXVIII, and XCI),[7] which suggests strongly that unless he was simply being inconsistent, he meant to praise medieval art both for authorial signature and for its erasure. And indeed it would be fair to say that the true story of Pound's career is one of a double preoccupation with the heroic maker of the object and the object itself, a story aptly figured by the column in question, with its joining of the trace of the craftsman (Mateus himself, presumably, carved "Me Mateus fecit") to the voice of the work: "Mateus made me," not "I, Mateus, made this."[8]

Pound captures this double vision with disarming honesty in a slightly lefthanded compliment that he paid Williams in 1928, one that evokes tellingly his own statement on Brancusi from seven years before: "Art very possibly *ought* to be the supreme achievement, the 'accomplished'; but there is the other satisfactory effect, that of a man hurling himself at an indomitable chaos, and yanking and hauling as much of it as possible into some sort of order (or beauty)" (*Literary* 396). Pound finally privileges decisively neither the accomplished achievement nor the human yanking of chaos into order, in other words, though he suggests that it may be illuminating for us occasionally to meditate upon what might be at stake in such a choice. Thus while Wolfe is surely right to call attention to the "full-throttled individualism" behind Pound's early rhetoric, to Pound's sense that "it is emotion, the mind, the vortex of the self that makes possible the Imagist" restoration of "heterogeneity in the object world," and finally to the fact that the "Imagist self . . . needed the object world to keep its lyricism honest" (63, 64, 65), the further implication that Pound needed the object world *only* to keep in line a subjectivity that always comes first neglects the extraordinary devotion to things that surfaces (to take yet one final example) in his allusion, in the *Guide to Kulchur*, to his treasured "lists of beautiful objects, made in [his] own head and held before [he] ever thought of usura as a murrain and a marasmus" (109). And this is to say that dwelling wholly on the vision of the forceful maker means losing sight of one of the central dramas of Pound's career, a drama of allegiances divided between the living, producing self, on the one hand, and the captivating leavings of the dead, on the other.

LABORING IN THE TOMBS

Pound's relationship to the making of the beautiful thing was complicated, as Woolf's, Lewis's, and Stevens's was not, by the fact that an essential part of his literary output included translations (foremost among these the 1915 *Cathay*) and critical studies of texts from the distant past (most notably his 1910 volume *The Spirit of Romance*). Of the major modernist careers, Pound's was the only one save perhaps H. D.'s that looks at times truly antiquarian (Eliot's and Joyce's pastiches notwithstanding), which is to say that it shows an unusually resonant encounter with the past conceived as an accumulation of produced matter, and that we should hardly be surprised, given the accelerations of the modern, to find it shaped by a tension between oppression by the weight of this accumulation and anxiety about the world's ability to pass over so rich a store with scant regard. And yet it is a striking feature of Pound scholarship that the complexities to which this tension gives rise have received relatively little attention over the years, in spite of the facts that so much of the published research on Pound concerns his literary appropriations and that scholars continue to explore this poet's sense of the past in lively ways—as recent work by Peter Nicholls and Daniel Tiffany, to take only two examples, attests.

In a suggestive article on lost objects, mourning, and the idea of Italy in the Malatesta cantos (parts of it rewritten into *Modernisms*), Nicholls argues that it is by way of negotiating his discovery that "the poet must reckon with the object as lost" that Pound turns at last to Malatesta's Tempio, a thing whose "continued existence" helps him to evolve a vision of Italy as "both ideal and 'real,' not merely the figure for some original loss, but the actual space in which traces of a recoverable history are pursued" (170; see also *Modernisms* 260). In his own seductive treatment of Pound as mourner in *Radio Corpse*, meanwhile, Tiffany focuses on the irritations of a past too present, noting (twice) that the deceased show "an alarming vitality" (114, 129) in Pound's imagination and considering at length how this unfailingly elegiac author's "infatuation with the dead is always tinged with hostility" (129). Clearly, both of these readings contribute significantly to our understanding of precedent and absence in the Poundian mise-en-scène; and yet in juxtaposition each illuminates crucial lacunae in the other. What Nicholls never really acknowledges is that Pound encountered surviving objects at every turn (and long before the Malatesta sequence), which he was sometimes tempted to wish lost in good earnest because they embodied for him so acutely the fact of how much had already been done (and how little might be left to do) that W. J. Bate has named the burden of the past. And what Tiffany just omits is that the dead were frequently so alarming for Pound not because of their excessive animation but by virtue of the monumental inertness of their traces, a mute yet massive legacy always deeply entangled in Pound's most generative anxieties but frequently hard to incorporate without strain into the figural scheme of haunting that Tiffany favors.

This is to say, in effect, that the tension between affection for the past and hostility toward it so fundamental to Pound's shaping of modernism has everything to do with questions about the object and production, and specifically about how to reconcile the impulse to new making with the sheer quantity of objects already made. That this was a problem for Pound from the beginning is suggested by a 1912 poem (unpublished until 1968) entitled "Epilogue: (To my five books containing mediaeval studies, experiments and translations)," which begins, "I bring you the spoils, my nation / I, who went out in exile, / Am returned to thee with gifts. / I, who have laboured long in the tombs, / Am come back therefrom with riches" (*Early Poems* 209). Testimony to his early fear of being taken for a mere philologist, a mere collector or connoisseur of language, this magniloquent apostrophe nonetheless finds Pound opting to heroicize the activity of recovery instead of figuring his work as new production, as though the latter tactic—in fact used by defenders of *Cathay* from the time of its publication to the present—might invite charges of fraud or heresy in comparison to which even graverobbing would be a minor offense. Presenting himself not as an artisan but as some combination of Marco Polo and conquistador, with echoes of Elgin, Schliemann, and Victorian outcasts-turned-nabobs such as Heathcliff thrown in for good measure, Pound takes on the role of the imperialist-explorer whose claim to notice rests partly upon the sheer splendor of the things themselves ("Behold my spices and robes, my nation . . . I return with devices, / Cunning the craft, cunning the work, the fashion [209]") and partly upon their presumably arduous extraction from the exotic and distant country of the past.

The disproportion between Pound's self-aggrandizing rhetoric and the actual public reception of his work, however, calls attention to the fact that his treasures could hardly partake of the costliness or rarity of real spices or robes, let alone of the mask of Agamemnon or the Elgin marbles, nor could he inculcate appreciation of his "devices" with the kind of facility with which the Cubists, say, established an audience for African and Pacific sculptures. If the latter succeeded in promoting certain objects by praising them for a formal power that had little to do with the histories and cultures that produced them, the foreignness of the language of troubadour songs (and the referentiality of language in general) would have made Pound's similar claims for his own finds much more difficult to sustain, even if the institutional and practical constraints affecting his promotions had somehow been the same. The truth is, of course, that Pound was repackaging items long available from the stock of philologists and second-hand book dealers, a point suggested by an air of glorified hawking in the poem's later lines ("Behold my spices and robes") that seems to confirm him a marketer of connoisseurship in the aesthete mode rather than a heroic explorer donating undisputed treasures to the *patria*. With or without the reference to the trading culture of Phoenicia ("gifts of Tyre") that also muddies the waters for Hanno in canto XL, the poem would notably fail to separate Pound from the kind of salesmanship that he elsewhere deplored in the name of meaningfulness or profundity.

Indeed it is partly its apparent indictment of the absence of such virtues that has made the poem most closely related to the "Epilogue" one of Pound's most famous. In the well known "Portrait d'une Femme," completed by the beginning of 1912, Pound compares the ideas, gossip, and anecdotes that make up the life of a society hostess (possibly Olivia Shakespear) to treasures tangled in the weeds of the Sargasso, concluding:

The tarnished, gaudy, wonderful old work;
Idols and ambergris and rare inlays,
These are your riches, your great store; and yet
For all this sea-hoard of deciduous things,
Strange woods half sodden, and new brighter stuff:
In the slow float of differing light and deep,
No! there is nothing! In the whole and all,
Nothing that's quite your own.
            Yet this is you.

                                                    (*Personae* 57–58)

As in the "Epilogue," descriptions of exotic treasures threaten to overwhelm by their splendor the theme that generates them, but in this case the vehicle is (at least putatively) subordinated to a point about its own vacuousness: the very richness of objects that weakens the other poem seems here transmuted into a moral about the ultimate worthlessness of glittering prizes, a sentiment whose unimpeachability has certainly not damaged the appeal of "Portrait" for anthologists. If the truth is that one likes this poem best because of the sheer gorgeousness of this closing catalogue, one is nonetheless spared having to own up to aesthete infatuations because the list is, after all, unfolded by way of pointing to a missing significance or personality in which more genuine values would be located. Of course this kind of delight in deciduous things is not all that much to confess today: in the wake of Gilles Deleuze and Judith Butler—not to mention a recovered Wilde who revels in freedom from the trammels of essential identity—such an admission sounds more pious than scandalous now. But for modernists and others out to defend individuality (Lewis would have been acutely horrified by the Deleuzian elevation of the schizophrenic over the paranoid) it would have been the element of moral correction in "Portrait"—a quite Victorian poem in some ways, in spite of Pound's well known boast about how its opening consonants offended an editor's Tennysonian ear—that prevented it from slipping into utter triviality.

  To put matters somewhat differently: what the "Epilogue" succumbs to but "Portrait" ostentatiously rejects is a promotion of objects for their own sake that no modernist, no matter how enamored of the object world generally, could quite embrace for fear of relegation to the role of aesthete-connoisseur. For all her defense of the work of art as monument, Woolf frequently insisted on the importance of significant human content or deep spirituality in art literary or otherwise (her praise of the Russians, her dismissal of the Edwardians); and even Lewis, so frequently admiring of the purity of the object world and contemptuous of human behavior, nonetheless wielded the term "deadness" against the work of his rivals as often as he invoked it as a necessary quality of art, his deprecatory usages always imply-

ing that the artist in question had descended to something like the irrelevance that Pound denominated "blue china." For Pound himself in the early
1910s, the danger of succumbing to an absolute privileging of the thing for
its own sake seemed even more serious, as we can see if we add to our field
of view "An Object," a very brief poem also from 1912 in which he excori-
ates an editor for having "a code and not a core" (*Personae* 60), which is to
say for showing only the rigid surface of "an object" instead of the feeling of
a human being. Indeed both this poem and "Portrait" testify to a fear of
people becoming things that Lewis shared in his antirobotic diatribes, though
whereas the latter articulated this fear with an irony bordering on ambivalence, Pound clearly felt compelled to present it in much less nuanced (if
also less explicit) formulations.

One reason for Pound's keen anxiety on this point was surely that Imagism itself could seem ultimately to invite the rejection of human content in
spite of its originator's protestations to the contrary, and indeed it might be
hazarded that the lag (noted by Lewis and dozens of other critics) between
the birth of Pound's revolutionary theories and their implementation in his
poetic practice owes a good deal to a fear that charges of triviality might dog
a poetry apparently bare of human meaning. Indeed the immediately post-
Imagist phase of 1913–15 was the most resolutely psychological, social, and
anthropocentric of his poetic career, its dominant note emblematized by the
1915 "Villanelle: The Psychological Hour," the only poem from his first
decade of publication that he chose to include in his 1964 anthology, *Confucius to Cummings*. An Eliotic *tranche de vie* without quite Eliot's lightness
of touch, this lyric is distinctly unlike the object-centered, "crystalline"
poems produced in this same period by H. D. or Williams (though as a study
of a subjectivity it might fulfill the first Imagist criterion of "[d]irect treatment of the 'thing,' whether subjective or objective" [*Literary* 3]), so that
the reader of *Confucius to Cummings* looking for a striking example of
Imagist hardness in Pound's own work will be rewarded only, if at all, with
the single other inclusion from his oeuvre, the "Envoi" from 1919–20's
Hugh Selwyn Mauberley.

The "Villanelle" is especially interesting, in this context, because it offers
further confirmation (beyond the psychological focus announced in its title)
that the misgivings about objects adumbrated in "Portrait" and "An Object"
were central to Pound's thinking about poetry and life in this period. For one
thing, this relation of a 1913 episode in which Pound waited in vain for the
sculptor Gaudier-Brzeska and his sister to join him for supper can be read as
a story about the failure of the muse of hardness (figured here by the anti-
Rodinian Gaudier) ever to arrive, an allegory of the possibility that Imagism
conceived as a poetry of the solid object had proven or would prove a dead
end. Moreover, the two objects that do figure prominently in this study of
mood *en attendant* Gaudier are implicated in a kind of self-chastising

(faintly evocative of the moralizing in "Portrait") that Pound interweaves with complaint: "With middle-ageing care / I had laid out just the right books," he notes in the first stanza, and in the last, "No word from her nor him, / Only another man's note: / 'Dear Pound, I am leaving England'" (*Personae* 155–56). In this poem about the absence of others, the book is conspicuously positioned to mediate between self and other as object rather than as text, to link two (or three) people by indicating shared tastes or common inclusion among the cognoscenti rather than by serving as a vehicle of communication, but this positioning is clearly marked as an abuse of writing. And thus the other man's note at the close reinforces a double moral: that people should be linked by communication through words, not through the fetishizing of words' material embodiments, and that communicative or not, the text-object is a poor substitute for human contact. The *tristesse* of the "Villanelle" is that of an isolation emphatically remediable by humans alone.

But this sadness, which is finally a matter of circumstance rather than necessity, does not as such quite reach the painful heart of the anxiety that Pound associates with the object, as we can see if we turn to the poem published together with the "Villanelle" in the December 1915 issue of *Poetry*, "Near Perigord." Both the "Villanelle" and "Perigord" present writing as a highly tenuous and vexed link between consciousnesses, but if the former shows Pound looking forward to a meeting of minds prevented only by caprice, the latter considers the far less contingent difficulties of trying to gain access to the psychology of those long dead through the works they left behind. Thinking of the troubadour Bertran de Born's "Domna pois de me no'us cal" (Pound's 1914 translation of which was reprinted with the new work), Pound lays out early the central question, "Is it a love poem? Did he sing of war?" which he had already tried to answer by geographical inspection during a 1912 walking tour of southern France. Having then tested his theory that, in Richard Sieburth's words, "the erotic riddle of the *dompna soiseubuda* [composite lady] in fact veiled Bertran's military designs on the network of castles occupied by each of the ladies whose charms he celebrated" (Introduction xiv), Pound had come by the time of "Perigord" to revise "his earlier positivistic assumptions about the feasibility of reconstructing the actual historical facts of the troubadour's turbulent *vida* from the local lay of the land" (xv). The question, "Perigord" asserts, is unanswerable, and this even if one supplements geography with imaginative reconstruction of the scene of writing—as for example by envisioning Bertran "at a table / Scribbling, swearing between his teeth; by his left hand . . . little strips of parchment covered over" (*Personae* 152).

More striking than this conclusion itself, however, is the poem's suggestion that if such imaginative work by the present-day reader offers no firm answers, it is still no more inadequate in this regard than direct personal contact. In the second section, Pound shows Arnaut Daniel and Richard Coeur-de-Lion trying to guess the motives of the now dead de Born—"Plantagenet puts the riddle: 'Did he love her?' / And Arnaut parries: 'Did he love your sister?'" (153)—but trying in vain, Arnaut in the end none the wiser for having been "born near" de Born (153). If the "Villanelle" seems to suggest that writing does link people, though far from perfectly, "Perigord" further qualifies that claim by pointing out that *neither* reading nor physical proximity can guarantee real knowledge of another person: "Do we know our friends?" seems an antiphonal response to the statement, "Oh, there is precedent, legal tradition, / To sing one thing when your song means another" (153, 151). Spoken language, like written, can by its very nature be used to mislead, so that the opacity of the text-object finally only replicates the opacity of each soul to all others. The poem's closing lines have often been read as a figure for the failure to obtain historical knowledge, but in their more immediate linking of isolation with the figure of immurement they anticipate a footnote to *The Waste Land* in which Eliot conflates Bradley's address to solipsism with Dante's tale of the cruel imprisonment of Ugolino della Gherardesca—which is to say that they suggest again how the deepest anxiety at work here concerns the unknowability of other people, living or dead: "There shut up in his castle. . . . She who could never live save through one person, / She who could never speak save to one person, / And all the rest of her a shifting change, / A broken bundle of mirrors . . . !" (154).

The problem of subjectivities' closure to each other, which we have already seen in Woolf, Eliot, and Lewis, thus assumes a historiographical aspect in "Perigord," which, taken together with the "Villanelle," proposes that mediation between past and present through the text, always tenuous and uncertain, may be an archetype of intersubjective relations rather than a marginal case. But whereas Woolf suggests that such mediation through objects is enough, given the importance of the privacy of the soul, and the doctoral Eliot insists that our sense of separateness between consciousnesses is the after-effect of a subject-object division untrue to immediate experience, and Lewis holds to the vanishing individual so tightly that the absurd thingness of humans occasions not existential crisis but a defense of externalist art, Pound—who questions inherited wisdom about human relations so much less dramatically than most of his modernist peers—seems to find nothing to celebrate, and much to lament, in the division between souls. One of the intimations of "Perigord," in fact, is that in trying to bring the past closer Pound was struggling against his own persuasion that others, alive *or* dead, will always in some sense appear as objects impermeable to full knowledge, even against the possibility that the monuments left by the departed are finally no more mute to us than we living are to each other.

This kind of anxiety clearly figures powerfully in his peculiar combination of yearning for the past and oppression by its material remnants, in which longing and presence remain compatible primarily because the longing in question is a longing for subjectivities, the presence one of objects that (regarded as silent rather than voluble) can magnify the sorrow of separation just as any token of the dead can amplify rather than mitigate feelings of loss. This does not mean that Pound's sense of oppression by the artistic inheritance is free from the feeling of poetic belatedness associated with Bate's burden of the past or Bloom's anxiety of influence; but it does help to explain why he felt most capable of surviving belatedness when the past seemed to him least reduced to its inert material remnants—as in his famous "Pact" with Walt Whitman, in which he addresses the earlier poet as a still active craftsman ("Now is a time for carving") and declares, "Let there be commerce between us" (*Personae* 90). Against our usual habits of thought with respect to hauntings and Oedipal crises (though not, perhaps, against either Bate's or Bloom's more intricate formulations), Pound's relationship to what came before turns out to be one in which the past was far more threatening when still—hence impossible to engage in dialogue—than when invested with life, spectral or otherwise. Contra Tiffany, in short, Pound was far less alarmed by the vitality of the dead than by their impassive deadness.

These points are beautifully illustrated in what have come to be called the Ur-cantos, the next step in Pound's historical speculation[9] and the first of his works to show the double burden of oppression and tenderness in its fully developed form. Published together in 1917 as "Three Cantos," but begun close to the time of "Perigord" (which they closely resemble formally, mixing stretches of Browningesque pentameter with other passages far from pentametric), the Ur-cantos commence with what may be the most explicit and extensive complaint about belatedness to be found anywhere in the oeuvre: "Hang it all, there can be but one *Sordello*!" (*Personae* 229), Pound exclaims, as though having finally readied himself to write an epic about one of his beloved troubadours he has only now noticed that Browning got there first. He eventually asks his Victorian predecessor bluntly, "What's left for me to do?" (231), but soon after arrives at an answer on his own, declaring, "Gods float in the azure air . . . 'Tis the first light. . . . 'It is not gone.' Metastasio / Is right—we have that world about us" (232). There is no belatedness, that is, because we live still in an unfallen world full of originary inspiration, in a place still populated by inspiring genii where we might have thought to find only lifeless matter: "Mid-June: some old god eats the smoke, 'tis not the saints. . . . This is our home, the trees are full of laughter. . . . And the place is full of spirits" (230–31).

It is important to recognize that what Pound needs at this point, for the sake of both the works of the dead and his own writing's future, is a way of addressing Browning's priority that will leave neither himself nor his predecessor valueless, a scheme that avoids the kind of Oedipal (but not Bloom-ian) agon in which the later poet simply displaces the earlier. The first light, then, is not meant to make writers of the past irrelevant, but on the contrary to envelop them and us in a single radiance that confirms the validity of both: "what were the use," Pound asks Browning, "Of setting figures up and breathing life upon them, / Were't not *our* life, your life, my life, extended?" (230). In the succeeding pages, however, it becomes clear that this vision of a spirit-permeated world is not enough, since it cannot address the unsettling fact of fragments of things that do not survive whole, with their ample testi-mony to the myriad ways in which endurance may fail. Ur-canto II com-mences with a vision of the "[d]rear waste, great halls, / Silk tatters still in the frame" of the Gonzaga palace, a place "[a]light with phantoms" (234) that marks a fall in confidence from the sunny image of Verona "full of spirits" (and from full presence to spectral half-presence) bespeaking by now familiar concerns about how the mere passing of time widens the gap be-tween the dead and the living.

The greater part of Ur-cantos II and III, in fact, is taken up with reflec-tions on old texts that dramatize the partialness of our reconstructions: all Pound knows of "one, Joios, Tolosan," for example, "Is that in middle May, going along / A scarce discerned path, turning aside, / In level poplar lands, he found a flower, and wept" (234), because there is only "one stave" saved "and all the rest forgotten. / I've lost the copy I had of it in Paris, / Out of the blue and gilded manuscript" (234). For all those works lost in such ways, moreover, there are as many that lose vitality simply from going unread, for instance Lorenzo Valla's fifteenth-century *Elegantiae linguae latinae*, which once "shook the church. / The prefaces, cut clear and hard," but which might be dismissed today as merely a "dull book" (242), or Camöens's *Lusiads*, which though one of the acknowledged masterworks of Portuguese literature seemed to Pound to require disinterring: "Dig up Camoens, hear out his resonant bombast" (239). This last reference is especially suggestive because immediately preceded by an allusion to the murdered lover of Pedro I, Ignez de Castro, whose body—according to (Pound's reading of) Camöens's third canto—Pedro had disinterred and installed upon the throne: "He and her dug-up corpse in cerements / Crowned with the crown and splendor of Por-tugal" (239). If all such efforts to gather life from books end in only the gruesome semblance of restoration, are they not better avoided? Or is this partial reconstruction rather to be celebrated, considering that we can only know each other, the living know the living, as objects anyway?

Pound seems to refrain from choosing either conclusion until the end of the third Ur-canto, where the encounter with old texts culminates in his translation of the Nekuia (the passage from Homer wherein Odysseus calls up the dead), which he would later place at the beginning of the *Cantos* proper. Noting that the Odyssean ritual "offers an analogue for the act of translation" and that Pound himself reminds the reader that his translation is based on another (a sixteenth-century Latin crib by Andreas Divus), James Longenbach has read this finale as Pound's solution to the problem of how to write poetry including history that would neither ignore "the concrete particulars" of reading and translation nor succumb to the dryness of mere philology (*Modernist* 122). The way to proceed, it would seem, is to acknowledge textual mediation even as one rings transformations on the past, making it new. To this we might add that by foregrounding the mediating text's physicality, Pound also speaks to the problem of the thingness of books, apparently trying to transcend materiality just as he would transcend historical or linguistic mediation, which is to say through incorporation:

"And unto Circe buried Elpenor's corpse."

Lie quiet, Divus.

    In Officina Wechli, Paris,
M. D. three X's, Eight, with Aldus on the Frogs. . . .

(245)

The replication of Odysseus's burial of Elpenor in the bidding of Divus to lie quiet is, of course, meant to be striking: Pound the translator as hierophant-hero is to be seen performing an act of love and holiness, decently reinterring the earlier artist as the Homeric hero buried his friend, quieting the restless ghost. Yet this parallel seems to fall apart almost as soon as we begin to think about it, since Odysseus buries his comrade (that is, ritually acknowledges the material aspect of his friend) in the name of a final silencing, whereas Pound can scarcely incorporate the forgotten Divus into his own new work without effecting a kind of resurrection—a predicament of figuration that comports well with his general discomfort anent the deadness of past works (since under its terms the living writer quiets the literary ghost not by allowing the works to linger in obscurity and mute physicality, but rather by helping them to speak anew). For Pound, Elpenor's unquiet presence must correspond to Divus's silent absence, his ghostly wandering to Divus's going *un*read.

We might ask, moreover, whether the more significant restlessness here does not really belong to Pound rather than to Divus, in the end. For if the work of the past prompts so much anxiety in Pound by appearing as mute, unliving object, then for him to make it speak is for him to render it *less* threatening, not more—which is to say that, from the point of view of an agonistic literary history at least, Pound overcomes the past *by* resurrecting it, even kills it by giving it life. This last way of putting things would be more carelessly overdramatic were it not for the fact that it is neatly suggested by another problematic feature of the passage in question, namely that however affectionately intended, the laying to rest of Divus by his own translator cannot quite fail to resemble attempted murder in the best Oedipal tradition, nor can the injunction "Lie quiet" comport altogether comfortably with Pound's putative attempt to lend Divus voice. Certainly, no raiser of the dead can rid himself of the trappings of mastery, but Pound's peculiarly intense anxieties about the inert lifelessness of the past make his need to tame or subordinate by bestowing life unusually urgent and portentous. As a necromantic summoning to dialogue that is also an attempt to neutralize the text's materiality, Pound's decorporealizing incorporation of Divus invites reading as a charged instance of that move so anathema to modernism in the line of Woolf or Adorno, the effort of subjectivity to compromise the radical otherness of "dead" matter and thereby dissolve the integrity of the mute object world.

When Pound revised the Ur-cantos for inclusion in the *Cantos* proper, he altered the Divus passage so as to omit the burial of Elpenor[10] and removed most of the references to dead books as well: neither Joios nor the *Elegantiae* appears in the early cantos, and the Pedro-Inez story is reduced to a single line in III, "Ignez da Castro murdered." These moves certainly make sense given that negotiations with the material legacy of the past would seem none too appropriate to a work more concerned to affirm the possibility of cultural renewal (this possibility being what Pound earns at the end of Ur-canto III, in Longenbach's reading) than to work through doubts about the resilience of items from the cultural store. Yet Pound's anxieties in this area do, nonetheless, hover over his poetry of the next several years, especially "Homage to Sextus Propertius," another work based on translation that recurs frequently to anticipations of textual immortality, and cantos IV–VII, which are much concerned with the vitalizing and arrangement of history. And of course the past's double burden presides with extraordinary completeness over the *Cantos* as a whole, which constitutes above all a series of attempts to validate both itself and the older texts that it resurrects and reconfigures, so that every canto can be said to retell in its fashion the Ur-cantos' story.

What changes at the end of the 1910s, after the writing of canto VII, however, is that Pound attempts to redeem rather than merely to evade the *Dinglichkeit* of works from the past, and in so doing alters subtly but dramatically the import of the form of his fledgling opus. The primary marker and vehicle of this transition is *Hugh Selwyn Mauberley*, a work read for decades as Pound's postwar farewell to London and ritual exorcism of the aesthete within, but one that also serves as a valediction to the idea that, after the appalling devastation of the Great War, there can be any innocent postponement of the question of what claims "dead" objects can possibly exert over the living:

> There died a myriad,
> And of the best, among them,
> For an old bitch gone in the teeth,
> For a botched civilization,

Charm, smiling at the good mouth,
Quick eyes gone under earth's lid,

For two gross of broken statues,
For a few thousand battered books.

(Personae 188)

Coming from another poet at another point in his career, the last couplet might be taken as nothing more than a striking litotes deployed in a broad attack on the subordination of life to bankrupt traditions, a device in which books and statues function more or less straightforwardly as synecdoches for the Big Idea of civilization. Given Pound's longstanding interest in the past understood as physical accumulation, however, it would be strange for us to try to circumscribe his figuration in this way, even were it not the case that the preceding couplet (on the swallowing of the once living by the earth) imbues these lines with a profoundly material irony, as the works that were supposed to save humankind take the form of unliving matter that reduces "fair cheeks, and fine bodies" (poem IV [188]) to more of the same.

At this point in *Hugh Selwyn Mauberley*, Pound appears to drop this line of reflection on the fatality of art in favor of a rather different one, turning from the present disaster to what would appear to be one source of the "old men's lies" (IV again [188]) responsible for it, the less topically nightmarish but still gloomy world of nineteenth-century aestheticism. In "Yeux Glauques," the Burne-Jones painting "King Cophetua and the Beggar Maid" says less about the happy ending of the old tale than about the misery of its model (misidentified in many guides to the poem as Elizabeth Siddal), whose "faun's head . . . [b]ecame a pastime for / Painters and adulterers" (189). In "Siena Mi Fe'; Difecemi Maremma," next, the speaker encounters "Monsieur Verog," a version of the poet Victor Plarr who, "[o]ut of step with the decade, / Detached from his contemporaries, / Neglected by the young," is found "perfecting the catalogue" among "the pickled foetuses and bottled bones" (an allusion to Plarr's fin-de-siècle *Men and Women of the Time: A Dictionary of Contemporaries*) and talking for hours of the lives and untimely deaths of the lost Nineties (190). After a glance at "Brennbaum 'The Impeccable,'" on whose face the "heavy memories of Horeb, Sinai and the forty years / Showed only when the daylight fell" (191), Pound turns at last to the literary sell-out Mr. Nixon (Arnold Bennett), who puts a period to these tales of woe by advising, "Don't kick against the pricks, / Accept opinion. The 'Nineties' tried your game / And died, there's nothing in it" (191).

If *Hugh Selwyn Mauberley* has inspired more intense interpretive disagreements than virtually any other work by Pound, one of the primary reasons is surely that it takes its major turn at this unlikely point. For in what can seem under hasty reading no more than a flat conclusion to the depressing pageant of art's victims, Pound in fact delivers the least doubtful statement of position to be found in the entire sequence, recuperating the Nineties precisely by placing its dismissal in the mouth of a slave to the market forces that he abhorred, and in so doing reversing the meaning not only of Plarr (and even, arguably against his conscious intention, the stoic Brennbaum) but also of the casualties of war, now aligned with rather than opposed to the dead poets whose tales Plarr tells. As its more discerning critics have noted, the action of *Hugh Selwyn Mauberley* is finally to conjoin the soldier who fought involuntarily for books and statues with the aesthete who fought willingly (if inadequately) in the service of same, its moral finally not that art can be fatal but that at least some people thought it worth giving up their lives for. Those who stress that Pound simply bids goodbye to aestheticism in this work have usually brought forth as their most compelling evidence the protagonist of the poem "The Age Demanded" from the second section, an archetypal aesthete (perhaps Mauberley himself) whose "sense of graduations" is "[q]uite out of place" and whose "mere invitation to perceptivity . . . led him to . . . isolation"; and yet even this figure's defeat is based not on moral failing but on circumstantial failure, an "[e]xclusion from the world of letters" that may be attributable in part to passivity but certainly owes much more to an integrity whose admirableness is never in question.

Indeed it is not in the poems on aesthetes themselves that Pound's recuperations are most sharply tested, but rather in the pendants to the sequence's first and second halves, the "Envoi" and the "Medallion," which raise with unusual directness the familiar question of how to validate the work of art considered as an object. This process commences with the opening line of the "Envoi," "Go, dumb-born book" (195), a conceit that Pound derives from a chain of prior texts (Waller's "Go, lovely rose" and Spenser's address "To His Booke" in *The Shepheardes Calendar*, as well as Southey's Epilogue to the *Lay of the Laureate* and Byron's mockery thereof in *Don Juan* I), but one that will exude a certain oddness whether or not its precedents are recognized. The poet, after all, tells his dumb-born book to say something that its own words do not say, in effect insisting that it can only constitute a mediating object and not a "direct" communication, that it requires the kind of "reading" appropriate to a nonlinguistic object like Waller's rose, which is to die so that Waller's lady "[t]he common fate of all things rare / May read in" it (Waller 164). The speaker then asserts that he would bid his lady's graces "live / As roses might, in magic amber laid, / Red overwrought with orange and all made / One substance and one colour / Braving time" (195), expanding the force of the injunction to the book by suggesting that if a book can no more come into its meaning without an extralinguistic reading than a preserved flower can "live" without some active imagining by its future viewer, full communication through language alone may be no more possible than unmediated seeing of the ambered rose.

This lesson is repeated in less charming form in the "Medallion," which as many critics have noted seems a harder, Imagist version of the "Envoi," just as the second part of the sequence as a whole seems something like an Imagist reification of the first. If the "Envoi" compares the text to a thing that might be "read" as roses are "read" (the pun is relevant, if not essential), then the "Medallion," with its short, hard-edged lines, seems an archetype of the sort of text-object envisioned in that earlier lyric, its own ungiving solidity ("intractable amber" [202]) captured dramatically in its final image of the cameo's eyes, which petrify further instead of coming alive. The "Medallion" appears, in other words, as a poem that demands the difficult engagement of reading-around even more impressively than the "Envoi" (which in spite of its opening conceit might, after all, tell "her that sheds / Such treasure in the air" more or less what the poet instructs it to tell her) while also taking as its subject that very demand.

In these poems, then, Pound seems at least to touch on the possibility suggested by the book open to *Cymbeline* in *Mrs. Dalloway*, namely that the text's way of linking subjectivities finally cannot be divorced from its thingness. But if Woolf seems happy to make an acknowledgment so auspicious for her cherished privacy of the soul, once again, Pound's antipathy to the notion of unbridgeable gaps between subjectivities seems to find expression in the unnerving dryness of the "Medallion"—the moral of which could be that acknowledging a degree of thingly opacity in art might be a first step toward insisting that art *should* be unsympathetic to human interests (Hulme, in a way), or—worse—a first approach to admitting that art never could have saved those who fought to save it, that the true relation between dumb books and the violence of IV and V is a tragic failure to see that there was no positive relation between art and life in the first place. Indeed the "Medallion," as the last poem in the sequence, has seemed to many the climax of a farewell to Imagism as well as aestheticism, a rejection of Imagist hardness *as* the last gasp of aestheticism's deadly preoccupation with the relics of the past.

This reading would seem confirmed by the fact that the work named explicitly in "Siena Mi Fe'," Plarr's *In the Dorian Mood*, extravagantly instances just such a preoccupation, containing as it does a number of poems on material traces whose motifs resonate closely with those of *Hugh Selwyn Mauberley*. In "The Statuary," for example, Plarr envisions an Aegean island whereon a "nameless master of the Pheidian stone" (21), an ancient version of the *sculpteur maudit*, braved public opinion to leave behind but a single perfect statue of a goddess, while his "Ad Cinerarium" asks, "Who in this small urn reposes, / Celt or Roman, man or woman, / Steel of steel, or rose of roses?" (18). "To a Greek Gem," meanwhile, addresses the mystery of a "middle-finger ring whose bezel glows / With the most lovely of intaglios" (17), that preeminent figure of Imagism rejected in Ur-Canto I's "Give up the intaglio method" and, it would seem, in the "Medallion" as well; and in

"To a Dead Student" the speaker seems poised to fail at his project of reconstructing the thoughts of the departed by reading his books: "Alas, for the silenced lips and the dear closed eyes! / They answer me not / Who am seeking for clues and for glosses, tradition and meanings, / Ere the books and the thought be forgot!" (43).

Against all these passionately sentimentalized relics, Pound's sequence poses an age demanding a "prose kinema" (186), the moral of *Hugh Selwyn Mauberley* appearing to be not that art can find no place under modernity, but that to continue meaningful in an age primed to ridicule Plarr's effusions over a dead student's books the artist would have to invent a form that, as far as possible, eschews solidity and thingness in several senses. If art had always lain open to the peril of a fall into "blue china," away from human content and into a triviality that could provoke the interest only of confirmed aesthetes, in other words, how much more crucial it would be to avoid such traps after the first evanescent projection of film, that "prose kinema" which (like the Futurist automobile) could appear as the new century's very essence not only by virtue of its ability to change everyday life dramatically, but also by virtue of its flickering substancelessness, which betokened the sharpest break in sensibility with the ponderous overfurnishing of the old. From this point of view, Brancusi's soaring birds, his "revolt against the monumental, or . . . against one sort of solidity," as Pound described it in 1921 (*Literary* 443), would be charged with all the pathos of a form no longer vital caught in the act of straining to break free of itself—as would Pound's own effort to dematerialize the work of Divus in Ur-canto III.

Yet it is precisely Pound's allusion to *In the Dorian Mood*, and to the aesthetes' affection for the topos of the decontextualized object, that indicates why *Hugh Selwyn Mauberley* proves *not* a rejection of the work of art as solid object after all, but on the contrary an affirmation of the virtues of thingly opacity. As we have seen, more astute critics have long held that this sequence, which Pound described famously as an "attempt to condense the James novel" (*Letters* 180), insists upon the heroism of the aesthetes even as it acknowledges their irrelevance to the age of the prose kinema; but critics have not by and large taken the further step of noting that what *makes* the aesthetes heroic is, almost, their irrelevance. Or rather: that what makes the aesthetic attitude heroic in the modern age is precisely the fact that it "kick[s] against the pricks," that it partakes of the kind of struggle against what the age demands that Pound as latter-day romantic always found irresistible. We might remember, in this context, that it was in the 1938 *Guide to Kulchur*, not in some work of the 1910s, that he praised those Victorian predecessors who out of "disgust with the social estimates of their era" fomented "rebellion against the sordid matrimonial customs of England."

This point bears on the questions at hand because in *Hugh Selwyn Mau-*

berley the heroic struggle against sordidness is inextricably intertwined with a struggle against the unsolid in art, the notion of creating an art resistant to time's depradations inseparable from the idea of resisting the dominant mood (the very anti-Dorian mood) of the present time. In one sense, of course, this is nothing new; Pound had been presenting his campaign on behalf of hardness as a rebellion against prevailing trends since the beginning of the 1910s, so that in a way the only real surprise is that critics have so strikingly ignored the continuity of *Hugh Selwyn Mauberley* with the polemics on hardness that both precede and follow it. And yet in another sense the stance of this work *is* genuinely novel, Pound here linking for the first time the virtues of hardness and artistic heroism with an aestheticism that specifically values the thingness of works of the past *in opposition to* their legibility or transparency. Well aware that all kinds of objects, including books, lend themselves to a form of reading that cannot quite recover the past or bridge the gap between minds, Plarr presents this mysterious illegibility as a source of delight, or at least intense interest, and Pound replicates this move in presenting to the reader, in the "Envoi" and more especially in the "Medallion," lyrical "objects" that arrest the attention through their initial incomprehensibility. Pound thus answers his question about art's value not by pointing to its continued legibility for moral, social, or political inquiry or by stressing the sheer positivity of monumental being, but rather by adding as a third possible foundation of value the entrancing *il*legibility that belongs preeminently to old and intricate things, which can prompt in those who confront them an effort of recovery that would—in an age demanding a prose kinema—constitute a species of genuine heroism. In so doing, he addresses the problem of belatedness never resolved in the "Three Cantos," finding in lateness one source of poetic power absolutely denied the originary mythic world of the first light—namely, the rich negativity of the solid thing rendered cryptic and fascinating by its disjunction from the time that produced it.

It is therefore fair to say that some attention to the figure of the enduring object would be required of any full account of the modernist aesthetic of difficulty, which as *Hugh Selwyn Mauberley* shows is appropriate to (the modernists' version of) modernity not only because it evokes the spiraling complexity of twentieth-century life, but also because it helps to redeem the opacity of the art of the past. It is no accident that Pound arrives at a poetic practice favoring extraordinary difficulty just as he reconsiders what the opaque text-object has to offer the present: unsatisfying and disconcerting the "Medallion" may be, but its very resistance to comprehension can (at least in theory) give it the curious allure of the intaglios and urns that captivate Plarr's speakers—an allure that would continue to inform Pound's own formal practice in the years that followed. For beginning with canto VIII, Pound would attempt to capitalize on the unique power of belatedness by as

it were pre-objectifying his own writing, favoring as compositional technique a presentation of textual fragments that effectively prevents them from
communicating directly to the reader (even though communication remained
his avowed goal).

In his compelling study of Pound, Lewis, and the politics of visual and
aural sensation, Vincent Sherry shows that one reason why the "new epic
muse" to which Pound turned in the years of the Great War "aspires to the
condition of silence" is that the music of language had come to seem so
evidently complicitous with "the public, oratorical culture of total war" (68,
54). Sherry points out, for example, that Pound's 1916 assertion that "The
Seafarer" was "made for no man's entertainment, but because a man believing in silence found himself unable to withhold himself from speaking" is to
be found in a piece suggestively entitled "The Constant Preaching to the
Mob" (54, quoting *Literary* 64).[11] What must be added to this important
recovery of motivations is that Pound's turn was also determined by the
allure of thingly reticence itself, which he had come to connect closely to
one of the varieties of heroism that he could still respect, the engagement
with mystery that led the Nineties generation to devote itself to broken
statues (Plarr's "Statuary") and battered books ("To a Dead Student"). And
thus if the authentic preface to the *Cantos* as a whole is the poet's injunction
to his dumb-born book in the "Envoi," this is so not only because speech had
come to seem dangerous to the future, but also because a new understanding
of muteness had become the means to a redemption of the past.

THE REGISTER OF EFFORT

This is not to say, of course, that Pound ever undertook the recuperation of
what had gone before without an eye to what was to come: even heroic
struggle could lay no claim to validity fully independent of what it set out to
accomplish for society at large, and if allying the opaque work to heroic
resistance provided Pound a way of addressing the past's burden, it did so
only to the degree that it allowed him to rewrite what had seemed confinement amid the nonlife of blue china as an intervention in life after all. In this
regard, the most pressing problem for Pound from the 1920s through the
early 1940s was that the most plausible energies of social change seemed to
him to emanate not from artists but from political leaders, a point readily
confirmed even by a cursory scrutiny of his life and works in this period and
demonstrated most spectacularly in his attempts to defend Mussolini to his
fellow Americans—a series of actions so notorious that Donald Davie was
moved to declare in 1964 that "Pound has made it impossible for any one
any longer to exalt the poet into a seer," that this poet's "disastrous career
. . . will rule out . . . any idea that poetry can or should operate in the

dimension of history, trying to make sense of the recorded past by redressing our historical perspectives" (202). Davie's prediction has since been proven wrong, in a sense, both by literary study's extraordinary recentering on the political unconscious of the texts it examines and by the passage into popular wisdom (often in alarmingly uncritical form) of the idea that historical fictions are somehow truer to history than carefully documented historiography. And yet Pound's political activities do continue to be regarded by many as sufficient grounds for a wholesale rejection of modernism, a proof that modernism's politics was essentially fascistic, patriarchal, or misguided or even a confirmation of the political dangers of modernist aesthetics of *dis*interestedness or disengagement.

This is an old story, of course, and one particularly difficult to combat (on behalf of "modernism" conceived as a body of writing deserving of continued attention within and without the classroom) because it touches on so many vital truths, even if it rearranges them in misleading ways. With respect to Pound in particular, one such truth is that there is indeed a connection between the aesthetic of difficulty and the imperative of heroic action that would eventually lead him to Mussolini; but because modernism's detractors have tended to assume that this connection inheres in a simple opposition between elitist intellectualism and authentically populist politics (an opposition much more relevant to Lewis), the far more vexed and subtle ways in which it does function in Pound have largely been ignored. And this point bears significantly not only on the teaching of literature today, in which debates about the canon (for example) sometimes turn on astonishingly crude equations between complexity in form and complicity with hegemonic structures, but also on the continued production of poetry, which in the view of some critics (for example Vernon Shetley, in his recent *After the Death of Poetry*) has been ill served by the assumption that poets will be able to expand their audiences by jettisoning difficulty. In the pages that follow, we will consider the ways in which difficulty, thingly opacity, and heroism did in fact remain intertwined for Pound for at least two decades after *Hugh Selwyn Mauberley*, which is to say that we will take up once more how the problem of the object shaped the relations among world, text, and critic within one modernist's vision.

No piece of Pound's vast oeuvre depends more emphatically upon the link between the hero and the opaque object than the Malatesta cantos (VIII–XI), begun in 1922, which center upon the fifteenth-century condottiere Sigismondo Malatesta and "his" great monument, the Tempio Malatestiano in Rimini, a gothic church around which, under Malatesta's patronage, the architect Leon Battista Alberti wrapped a neoclassical shell. As Lawrence Rainey has shown in his extraordinary book-length study of these cantos, the Tempio had long been a must-see for the tourist seeking traces of the bloody intrigues and passionate loves of the Renaissance: the visitor using the 1900 or 1908 Baedeker guide to central Italy (which Pound seems to have taken with him on his first trip to Rimini) would have been told of the romantic passion of Malatesta for the divine Isotta, and apprised of its coded indications in the building at hand (35, 117, 180). If the guide gestures toward an elision of the structure itself in favor of its patron's adventures, however, far more dramatic still is the operation that Pound performs in his cantos, which (as Cary Wolfe, among others, has pointed out [135–36]) scarcely mention the Tempio's appearance or contents, concentrating instead on the hero's martial and political struggles and (to a lesser degree) on the logistics of building: "And tell the *Maestro di pentore* / that there can be no question of / His painting the walls for the moment, / As the mortar is not yet dry" (*Cantos* 28); "And stole that marble in Classe" (36); "First: Ten slabs best red, seven by 14, by one third" (38); "The tomb is all done except part of the lid" (40). Indeed we might select as the archetypal sentence of these cantos the long one near the end of VIII that begins, "With the church against him / With the Medici bank for itself, / With wattle Sforza against him," expands through a whole host of modifying clauses, and finally reaches the main clause announcing the essential fact that "[h]e Sigismundo, *templum aedificavit*" only to speed off once more into minutiae of existence in the Romagna of the day (32–33).

Life, it seems, may be more beguiling than art, Pound's infrequent references to the achievement itself ("And he began building the TEMPIO, / and Polixena, his second wife, died" (35); "And Sigismundo got up a few arches" (36)) only enhancing by their very terseness the reader's uncertainty as to whether Malatesta's battles and alliances are supposed to draw their interest from the reflected radiance of the Tempio or, on the contrary, the Tempio is rendered worthy of notice by Malatesta's heroism. Clearly, Malatesta is singled out from hundreds of other petty generals and politicos by reason of his magnificent relic: glossing the line, "He, Sigismundo, *templum aedificavit*," Rainey—who has undoubtedly spent more time with these cantos than any other scholar—comments, "It is in this single act alone— 'he began building'—that Sigismondo's career acquires meaning, articulates its raison d'être, and is consecrated by virtue of its essential harmony with the imperatives of life: 'make it new'" (132). And yet in a note beneath a photograph of Malatesta's seal appearing opposite the title page of the 1938 *Guide to Kulchur*, Pound seems (retrospectively, at least) to accord foundational value to Malatesta's struggle rather than to the finished product: "If the Tempio is a jumble and a junk-shop, it nevertheless registers a concept. There is no other single man's effort equally registered" (2), he writes, though whether the "effort" in question is Malatesta's maneuvering on the Tempio's behalf or the sum of his daring deeds remains unclear.

To be sure, Malatesta as conceived by Pound did share something with the aesthetes of the Plarrian mood who subordinated life to art, kicking as he did against the pricks and gaining a profounder dignity from his devotion to a monument that modern eyes would find singularly rich in the opacity that Pound had come to value. Nonetheless, Pound's consistent emphasis on Malatesta's deeds as leader and soldier indicates how difficult it was for him to hold to a vision of heroism not supplemented by action of a more traditionally virile kind: involvement in events with broad and immediate impact on the life of society, for example, or demonstrations of manly valor (the latter rendered especially striking, in the Malatesta sequence, by Pound's shrewd tempering of grandeur with realism: "And he stood in the water up to his neck / to keep the hounds off him, / And he floundered about in the marsh / and came in after three days" [34]). The problem, of course, is that works so closely uniting political or martial vigor with artistic power are simply not all that easy to find (as Pound virtually admits in observing that no other single man's effort is equally registered); and indeed no monument presides over any other part of the *Cantos* as the Tempio does over VIII–XI.[12] In the *Guide to Kulchur*, Pound would claim that the Malatesta events constitute the first "episode" recorded in his magnum opus, the "openly volitionist" cantos VIII–XI establishing "the effect of the factive personality, Sigismundo, an entire man"; but he names as the second the creation of the Monte dei Paschi explored in XLI–XLIV, which offers a lesson on "the true bases of credit, to wit the abundance of nature and the responsibility of the whole people" (*Guide* 194). After the Tempio, works of art in the *Cantos* look more and more like fragments of superstructure floating above a base of right government and clean economics, their potential to validate or sanctify other kinds of activity dwindling to such flimsy apparitions as Jefferson's hope of finding "a gardener / Who can play the french horn" in XXI. And indeed Pound seems to comment on the turn in his own ambitions when he quotes Jefferson's "I have thought that a passion for music / Might be reconciled with that economy which we are / Obliged to observe" (*Cantos* 97), since those ambitions left him trying to reconcile a passion for art with the economics that he felt (no less passionately) obliged to engage.

In Pound's writing of the twenties, thirties, and early forties, this attempt at reconciliation appears principally in what we might describe as a communal version of the claim that the Tempio registers Malatesta's effort, the assertion that any work of art will index clearly the virtuousness or evil of the society from which it emerged; we have already noted, for example, the *Guide to Kulchur* forecast that "finer and future critics of art will be able to tell from the quality of a painting the degree of tolerance or intolerance of usury extant in the age and milieu that produced it" (27). Pound never relinquished his volitionist faith in the factive personality, but because he increasingly found such powerful shapers of life among politicians as such (or political philosophers) rather than among artists, the location of heroism in art and writing shifted, within his vision, from making itself to the kind of interpretation in which broad social truths could be discerned from the smallest particles of data—a form of interpretation at which, in Pound's view, the ablest political leaders always excelled. This is not to say that Pound now found his heroes in audiences rather than artists, exactly; but it is to observe that he transferred much of his interest from the moment of creation to the moment at which the discerning viewer or reader apprehends the essence of an object whose apparent opacity would make it illegible to the vast majority, a moment that he had described as early as *Gaudier-Brzeska*, telling of how Gaudier (another of the stars in his heroic constellation)

> was so accustomed to observe the dominant line in objects that after he had spent, what could not have been more than a few days studying the subject at the museum, he could understand the primitive Chinese ideographs . . . and . . . was very much disgusted with the lexicographers who "hadn't sense enough to see that *that* was a horse. . . . " (46)

Before considering how these developments crystallize in Pound's more explicitly theoretical writings from this period, we might pause to note that they are demonstrably supported by his formal practice in the *Cantos*—whether or not one is inclined to believe the theory an ex post facto rationalization of a sheer loss of the ability to produce less than inscrutable poetry. From the Malatesta sequence through the China and Adams sections, after all, the cantos are composed largely from pieces of documents that, placed before the reader with far less explanation than they seem to demand, take on something of the ontological immediacy that would accrue to a thing included "in itself" but not to the representation of a thing. Moreover, Pound repeatedly thematizes both the thingness and the opacity of books in the cantos of the late 1920s (which rounded out the first volume to stand as an essentially unretouched whole, *A Draft of XXX Cantos*), as for example in an interchange recorded in XXVIII: " 'Buk!' said the Second Baronet, 'eh... / 'Thass a funy lookin' buk' said the Baronet / Looking at Bayle, folio, 4 vols. in gilt leather, 'Ah... / 'Wu... Wu... wot you goin' eh to do with ah... /'... ah read-it?' " (*Cantos* 139). In this phase Pound also frequently foregrounds his documents' conceptual distance from twentieth-century understandings of the world, pressing for the kind of critical reading-around, the treatment of discourse as message but also artifact, that attends our belief that we "know" previous epochs as they did not know themselves—as in his inclusion in XXV of an attestation to the "miraculous sight" of the birth of three lion cubs "vivos et pilosos" by a fourteenth-century "Ducal notary of the Venetians" who, "by / mandate of the said Doge wrote this / and put it in file" (116).

In the next set of cantos (published eventually as *Eleven New Cantos* in 1934), these operations modulate into a newly intense preoccupation with the fact that the decontextualized text-object, however serviceable to a certain worthy modern epic, could also prove highly vulnerable to employment to bad ends by unscrupulous powers. In XXXI, Pound draws from Jefferson's correspondence a reference to the "care of the letters now enclosed" which "are of a complexion not proper for the eye of the police" (155), and a page later transcribes a remark from the same statesman's discussion of an influential mistranslation with serious legal repercussions: "A tiel leis....en ancien scripture, and this / they have translated *Holy Scripture*... " (156). These reflections effectively culminate in Jefferson's observation, placed at the beginning of XXXIII, that despotism "has never failed to destroy all records, memorials, / all histories which it did not like, and to corrupt / those it was cunning enough to preserve" (160), which in displacing the unfeeling wastage of time with the deliberate manipulations of humans transforms the fragility of documents from an occasion for pathos to a matter of grave political moment. The thingly aspect of texts as it arises here might well cause one to dream one of the dreams of the Enlightenment incarnated in figures like Jefferson and Adams, to long for an utterly transparent language without need of material substrate—or, failing that, to put one's faith in heroes who redeem the danger of materiality with their exceptional ability to "read" the opaque.

In his prose polemics from the thirties and early forties, Pound very nearly conflates these distinct impulses in a way that, odd though it is, clearly accords with some of the other investments we have already encountered in his writing. In "A Visiting Card," his 1942 summary of his economic positions for the benefit of Fascist Italy, he would ask, "Who . . . attacks, continuously, the nerve centres, the centres of communication between nation and nation? . . . I demand, and I shall never cease to demand, a greater degree of communication," having advised his reader a few paragraphs before (as though casting in imperative form Jefferson's comment on despotism), "Suspect anyone who destroys an image, or wants to suppress a page of history" (*Prose* 317). Invariably, however, his pronouncements in this vein come accompanied by a theorizing of communication more amenable to opacity than to lucidity, and specifically by reservations to the effect that the most significant communication is founded not upon the clear, systematic, and logical unfolding of the speaker's or writer's reasoning but rather upon some form of connection that finally exceeds rational articulation. Just before these remarks, for example, Pound comments, "We may write or read explanations, or we may reflect and understand by ourselves, without wasting optical energy deciphering printed pages" (*Prose* 316–17), while in an essay of 1937 he appends to the claim that "[w]riting, which is communications service, should be held distinct from the production of merchandise for the book trade" the note that "the measure of communication was defined by Leo

Frobenius when he said, 'It is not what a man says but the part of it which his auditor considers important that determines the amount of communication'" (*Prose* 75–76).

Pound recognized that this take on language could be understood as an attempt to locate the meaning of a text with form instead of, or rather in addition to, "content": citing the same remark of Frobenius in the *Guide to Kulchur*, he goes on to observe that "STYLE, the attainment of a style consists in so knowing words that one will communicate the various parts of what one says with the various degrees and weights of importance which one wishes" (59). In this, he evokes closely some of the defenses of poetry that would shortly be mounted by the New Critics, especially Cleanth Brooks's argument for the inseparability between a poem's cognitive content and its total form, which eventuates in the rather surprising claim that the poem's unique efficiency as a vehicle of communication has to do not with its transparency but with its *Dinglichkeit*. In "What Does Poetry Communicate?", first published in the Autumn 1940–Summer 1941 number of *American Prefaces* and later included in *The Well Wrought Urn*, Brooks followed his assertion that "the poem is not only the linguistic vehicle which conveys the thing communicated most 'poetically,' but . . . also the sole linguistic vehicle which conveys the things communicated accurately" with a statement of preference for the "old description of the poet" as "a maker, not a communicator." The poet, Brooks writes, "explores, consolidates, and 'forms' the total experience that is the poem," and if "we are willing to use imaginative understanding, we can come to know the poem as an object— we can share in the experience" (74–75).

For the New Critics, famously, the belief that the literary object's peculiarly indirect transmission of experience constitutes a privileged form of communication implied a pedagogy geared to making literati of as many students as were willing to invest some time in learning the techniques of close reading. As we have seen, Pound too believed that the most crucial kind of communication in writing (indeed, in his view, the only transaction worthy of the name) transpired between authors and readers possessed of a literacy beyond the mere capacity to make sense of language, but he showed little of the New Critics' faith that the really literate few could be enlarged to a really literate many. Unable to stomach the idea that right reading might be a matter of learning from hated academics (or for that matter from anyone), he would increasingly treat this skill as the native gift of an elect, in spite of his continued insistence that all his work was directed toward making conditions propitious for a general Euro-American Renaissance. Reflecting on this contradiction in his recent study of the modernist aesthetic of difficulty, Bob Perelman aptly observes in Pound a tension between "a rarified elitism aimed at selecting out the finest readers (or creating the most obedient ones) and a proselytizing that is wildly universal" (17).

Examples of this language of election proliferate unmistakably in the writing of the thirties (where, as Perelman notes, they cohabit uneasily with countervailing gestures toward inclusiveness and instruction such as the *ABC of Reading*). In "Date Line," for instance, Pound asserts that "it is perfectly ascertainable that a number of men in succeeding epochs have managed to be intelligible to each other concerning a gamut of perceptions which other bodies of men wholly deny" (*Literary* 86), while in "A Visiting Card," he glosses his statement, "C'EST TOUJOUR LE BEAU MONDE QUI GOUVERNE," by explaining that

> the best society, meaning the society that, among other things, reads the best books, possesses a certain ration of good manners and, especially, of sincerity and frankness, modulated by silence. *Le beau monde* governs because it has the most rapid means of communication. It does not need to read blocks of three columns of printed matter. It communicates by the detached phrase, variable in length, but timely. (*Prose* 313)

This quote reveals especially neatly how the abstract superiority of Pound's elect could lend difficulty in art a sanction arguably only tenuously tethered, in the end, to the social project that nevertheless had to serve as difficulty's ultimate moral ground. In a move reminiscent of Brooks's arguments about communication in poetry, though far more problematic, Pound conjoins aristocratic reticence with efficiency in the transmission of socially relevant knowledge, suggesting (at a certain limit) that even if most of those who died for battered books (say) were unable to enjoy the full richness of those treasures, their sacrifices would have been repaid nonetheless because right reading helps *le beau monde* to arrange society with greater skill. In this passage, at least, Pound's way of transcribing into ethical terms the mass culture-high culture divide is not to present "the best books" as a source of delight to which anyone might (with some effort) gain access, but to legitimate them as instruments of the social manager, that figure who had by this time replaced the aesthete at the center of his thinking about artistic heroism.

Again, it is important to stress that this governing beau monde was constituted on the basis of what we might call heroic literacy, not on the basis of class—that membership was conferred not by social or economic privilege but by an intuition or skill whose exercise Pound found archetypally exemplified in "the yarn that Frobenius looked at two African pots and, observing their shapes and proportions, said: if you will go to a certain place and there digge, you will find traces of a civilization with such and such characteristics. As was the case. In event proved" (*Guide* 60–61). As Pound himself observes elsewhere in the *Guide to Kulchur*, the attraction of Frobenius—in whose work he became much interested at around the time he began the *Eleven New Cantos*[13]—was that this anthropologist seemed to have "marked out . . . the difference between knowledge that has to be acquired by particular effort and knowing that is in people, 'in the air'" (57), to have deployed to powerful effect a form of cognition that enabled him to stake the very largest claims on the very smallest quantities of data. Ian Bell points out that Pound had valued such an ability at least since 1911, when he had advanced the "luminous detail" as the key to historical study (*Critic* 28); but it was his reading in Frobenius that led him to the conclusion, stated in "Immediate Need of Confucius," the *Guide to Kulchur*, and "A Visiting Card," that finer and future critics will be able to discern from a work of art the degree to which the society that produced it tolerated usury.[14] And it was Frobenius who seemed most forcefully to confirm his feeling that the most essential reading would be a reading of inscrutable things rather than transparent texts. "Frazer worked largely from documents," Pound told T. S. Eliot in a letter of 1940, but "Frob. went to *things*, memories still in the spoken tradition, etc. His students had to see and be able to draw objects. All of which follows up Fabre *and* the Fenollosa 'Essay on Written Character'" (*Letters* 336).

Pound's habit of associating Frobenian insight with the work of Fenollosa is especially enlightening because it points to the peculiar ontology upon which his promotion of intuitional reading and a *dinglich* poetry was finally based. In "The Chinese Written Character as a Medium for Poetry," which Pound had edited and finally published in 1919, Fenollosa grounds his argument that the ideogram allows for a more direct poetic presentation than alphabetic language upon the premise that what we know as individual objects are in fact no more than nodes or crossings of energies that ideograms have a singular power to bring before the reader's gaze: "A true noun, an isolated thing, does not exist in nature. Things are only the terminal points, or rather the meeting points, of actions, cross-sections cut through actions, snapshots. Neither can a pure verb, an abstract motion, be possible in nature. The eye sees noun and verb as one: things in motion, motion in things, and so the Chinese conception tends to represent them" (quoted in Géfin 18). As every student of Pound knows, Fenollosa's theories are utterly inadequate to actual Chinese writing but essential to the method of the middle cantos, which Pound began to denominate "ideogrammic" around 1929, in this making clear that the rationale for his art of the particular lay not in the virtues of particularity itself (as it did for Ransom) but in intuition's capacity to approach a network of connections lying deep in the fabric of the universe, where any compositional procedure more invasive than juxtaposition would tend to inhibit that capacity. As Bell eloquently puts it at the culmination of his *Critic as Scientist*, Pound's principle replaces discursive fullness with "a poetics of 'things', of a non-discursive reality whereby phenomenal objects are simply given and achieve their resonance through their allusion to the full system of completeness that inhabits a ghostly meta-world of coherence, of 'rhymes', behind the text itself" (239).

In practice, Pound took this metaphysics to license an extraordinary arrogation of authority to his own project, as (once again) several critics have observed: Bell, for example, refers to the ideogram's "authoritarian patterns" (*Critic* 245), while Sherry remarks that Pound's ideogrammic clusters "are insignia of presence and authority not open to question" (71), and Perelman, noting that the "ideogram is true for Pound because it is made up of particulars, which in turn are true because they are not abstract," comments that this "circular method grants complete authority to the ideogram's fashioner, who is backed by the irrefutable singularity of the particulars—at the same time as he gets to assign them a more comprehensive ethical significance" (44). But although Pound as a matter of practice deployed the ideogrammic turn to rationalize his poetic choices, *in theory* his work would still have had to submit to the test of the readerly elect, over whom it could wield no arbitrary authority since all those possessed of Frobenian or Fenollosan clarity would necessarily arrive at (the same) correct judgments in confronting significant objects. On the other hand again, of course, it must be remembered that as *le beau monde qui gouverne*, the elect as a group would hold a legitimate authority over those others who do "need to read blocks of three columns of printed matter," who do not communicate "by the detached phrase, variable in length, but timely."

The most disturbing implications of this position emerge when we compare Pound's praise of Frobenius's "knowing that is in people, 'in the air,'" to the allied defenses of his own writing and of Il Duce that appear in *Jefferson and/or Mussolini*:

> I am not putting these sentences in monolinear syllogistic arrangement, and I have no intention of using that old form of trickery to fool the reader, any reader, into thinking I have proved anything, or that having read a paragraph of my writing he KNOWS something that he can only *know* by examining a dozen or two dozen facts and putting them all together. (28)

> Any thorough judgment of MUSSOLINI will be in a measure an act of faith. (33)

> You can't *prove* by Euclid what Mussolini intends to do the year after the year after next but you can use some sort of common sense or general intuition. (93)

As Nicholls points out, the great irony of the cantos of the thirties was that Pound should focus on Jefferson, Adams, and Kung, those eminent defenders of rationality, even as his own political and poetic positions were growing incompatible with any ideal of reason as we know it. And as this set of quotations might suggest, this was an irony of particular moment because the putative power of Frobenian insight allowed Pound to continue to validate his own adherence to Fascism in the face of mounting evidence that Mussolini shared very few of his own views on government and economics; for Pound, "thorough judgment" had become not judgment at all, but "an act of faith."

This much will be obvious even to those whose familiarity with Pound's life and work in the thirties does not embrace *Jefferson*; what may be less so is that this recuperation of Fascism is intimately connected to what proved (by Pound's own lights) one of his most compelling apologies for art. We have seen Pound incorporating into his initial defense of art (in the 1910s) arguments about the imperative of self-objectification and art's resistance to the tendencies of commodification, along with a line of thinking that looks more or less like pure art-for-art's-sake; we have seen how he later fortified this position with gestures toward the mysteriousness that compels interest in the enduring thing and the desirability of registering the factive personality; and we have noted in passing how in the thirties Pound turned toward one further claim that in effect united the several preceding ones under the sign of politicoeconomic reflection or expression. This last, of course, was the claim that the extent of a particular society's usuriousness will always be legible in the art that it produced, and it was this claim that finally secured the Poundian entente of great art, intuitional politics, and terrestrial paradise, inasmuch as it made the aesthetically successful work at once one of the rewards of social justice and the marker by which the just society would be recognized by (Frobenian) readers in later times.

On concluding a brief tour of the monuments of Western art further on in the *Guide to Kulchur*, Pound offers another formulation of this point (a part of which we have also encountered above) that proves exceptionally telling:

> A tolerance of gombeen men and stealers of harvest by money, by distortion and dirtiness, runs concurrent with a fattening in all art forms.
>
> I have not deflected a hair's breadth from my lists of beautiful objects, made in my own head and held before I ever thought of usura as a murrain and a marasmus. (109)[15]

In other words, Pound has lately found his abilities as Frobenian reader confirmed by the historical record, though the form taken by this reading when it was unconscious of its own sociological perspicacity was the aesthetic judgment that engendered a list of beautiful things. The blessing of such intuition, as far its possessor is concerned, turns out to be that it spares him the pain of having to surrender to an enlarged social knowledge the objects or heroes that he loves, love here proving superior to mere connoisseurship not only by virtue of its intensity or elevation, but also by virtue of its utility to the human future. In the case of the thirties Pound, then, the link between Mussolini and difficulty or opacity in art lay neither in some fascistic element inherent in the aesthetic of disengagement nor in an antipopulism inherent in difficult art's affinity for those with greater cultural capital. It lay, rather, in Pound's freighted imagining of an elect whose right to govern would be premised on its ability to locate social meaning in any object (whether "difficult" or not, whether "engaged" or "autonomous"), and in his conviction that, possessing such heroic intuition himself, he might safely embrace a politics from which even reason had been banished.

Plus Always Techne

Before tracing the final phase of Pound's negotiations with the debris of the past, we need to acknowledge the ways in which these were molded by his thinking about capitalist production in general, which means returning to the point in his career at which we dropped this thread earlier: the end of the 1910s, when he would commence his fateful acquaintance with C. H. Douglas, dogged campaigner against overproduction and founder of Social Credit. Much more consequential for Pound than it was for Lewis, Social Credit has been explored amply by many of Pound's ablest critics, but in spite of the wealth of work in this area, only restricted attention has been devoted to the striking convergence between Pound's project of revitalizing works of the past and Social Credit's foundational claim that the central economic problem was not how to increase production but how to distribute the goods already being produced.[16] "[I]n 1918," Pound wrote years later in *Jefferson*, "we knew in London that the problem of production was solved, and that the next job was to solve distribution" (48);[17] and certainly it is not hard to see how a distributionist impulse broadly conceived subtends the *Cantos*, that enormous attempt to put to use the productions of the past while at the same continuing the work of new making.

We might pause here to note that Pound had in fact been bringing questions of distribution and overproduction to the domain of literature even before he and Douglas first met. In "A Retrospect," from 1917, for example, he adds to Carl Sandburg's complaint, " 'It's hell when poets can't afford to buy each other's books,' " the observation that "[h]alf the people who care, only borrow. In America so few people know each other that the difficulty lies more than half in distribution" (*Literary* 13). In a note on "Elizabethan Classicists" from the November 1917 number of *The Egoist* (which also included the last installment of Lewis's *Tarr*), meanwhile, he followed his charge that "[t]he student is told that the classics are excellent and that it is a crime to think about what he reads" with a dismissal of the academy as "[a]n apostolic succession of school teachers" that has, disastrously, become virtually the sole "medium of distribution" for those works (*Literary* 239).[18] And in a letter of 1915, he wrote to Harriet Monroe, regarding the possible "ways of existing in la vie littéraire," that the "problem is *how*, how in hell to exist without over-production" (*Letters* 48), which is to say that even when still working closely with Lewis he was pondering a central problem of professionalism that Lewis consistently skirted, the fact that the professional artist's choice was not always whether to produce or to starve, but more often whether or not to earn a living by turning out second-rate work (as Lewis at times so unapologetically did).

In the early cantos—most emblematically in his deployment of Divus's

Homer in canto I—Pound bids to address all three of these concerns at least analogically, giving his reader (limited) access to works that might well be out of reach, redisposing classics so as to provoke the student to think about them actively, and, above all, trying to reconcile his own urge to produce with an abundance of books so staggering that it could make writing even one new lyric seem a kind of overproduction with respect to the totality of extant literature. Reading Eliot in the context of underconsumptionist economics, Michael Tratner remarks suggestively that art constructed from found materials and old texts "seeks to allow new pleasures from familiar, already-produced objects—or, we might say . . . seeks to sell objects that have been overproduced" (698), and this point of course applies even more resonantly to Pound, who was so much more heavily invested in underconsumptionism than Eliot, so much happier to accommodate himself to the role of impresario and advertiser, and so much less interested in revising the dead (though no less interested in reviving them). Indeed yet another consequence of Pound's need to vitalize the pre-existing while making new works of his own can be discerned in the fact that the total effect of the *Cantos* is so unlike that of Dadaist collages or objets trouvés (which, as Peter Bürger's still cogent reading of the avant-garde has made clear, aimed less at restoring than at problematizing a past embodied in institutions and traditions), surrealist juxtapositions (in which the focus is less the drama of the past than the excruciating comedy of the quotidian present), or even *The Waste Land* (which treats the past to an ironic scrutiny usually well outside the bounds and aims of Pound's quotation-as-rescue).[19]

We might even extend Tratner's scheme, moreover, to note that Pound's intense anxiety about the possible inutility of his beloved objects to the human future led him not only to try to "sell" those objects as consumer goods, but also to position them, eventually, as labor-saving devices within the machinery of literary production. Beginning around 1933, he began to recur frequently to the Social Credit concept of the "cultural heritage," which he defined in *Jefferson and/or Mussolini* as "labour PLUS the complex of inventions which make it possible to get results, which *used* to be exclusively the results of labour, with very little labour, and with a quantity of labour that tends steadily to diminish" (36). In *Jefferson*, Pound uses the cultural heritage to justify fascism as both theoretically and practically superior to communism, arguing that the labor theory of value fails to account for the fact that an item's value does not plunge even when technical advances decrease the amount of labor time required to produce it. In his view, the labor theory, adequate enough in the nineteenth century, was unsuited to the twentieth because it could not accommodate the unprecedented expansion of technology that was the hallmark of the modern: "The 'cultural heritage' as fountain of value in Douglas' economics," he wrote, "is in process of superseding labour as the fountain of values, which it WAS in the time of Marx, or at any rate was in overwhelming proportion" (127).

The most glaring problem with this argument is that the "value" of which Pound speaks seems, in the end, something like a rating of usefulness set by tacit consensus, whereas in *Capital* use-value is effectively removed to the realm of an undiscussable Real almost as soon as it appears. Pound neglects the fact that the labor theory refers to value in exchange as derived from socially necessary abstract labor time, which is tied (as Marx notes explicitly) to the conditions of production normal for a given society at a given time: as Nicholls remarks in his seminal discussion of Pound on Marx, the cultural heritage formulation "left no room . . . for a consideration of the social forms of production or of the conversion of concrete to abstract labour under capitalism" (*Ezra Pound* 57). Perhaps more interesting than Pound's attempt to wield the cultural heritage against Marxism at the purely theoretical level, however, is his effort to show that with its assistance his new economics could supersede communism on the score of community itself. Presenting the cultural heritage as a spontaneous sharing whose sheer facticity renders superfluous communism's attempts to engineer the communal, Pound wrote in "The Individual in his Milieu" in 1935, "The overplus of what a group of men can do acting together, over and above the sum of what they can do each acting alone, is a reality, and no system either of thought or action can be perfect or even reasonably just or complete if it refuse to take count of this reality" (*Prose* 275). Or as he phrased matters in a letter of 1936, with regard to writing in particular, "No real literature will come out of people who are trying to preserve a blind spot. That goes equally for ivory tower aesthetes, anti-propagandists and communists who refuse to think: Communize the product" (*Letters* 277).

The implications of this notion of "acting together" or "communizing the product" most consequential for Pound's own literary production arise from the fact that the cultural heritage allows for an imagining of communities that would unite the living with those no longer alive. In the 1935 essay, Pound faults the labor theory for ignoring the "vast deal" of work "done by men who can no longer eat its fruit, namely by the dead, by Edison, Carleton, and ten thousand others, who have rendered it needless to get up water from wells with buckets" (*Prose* 278); and it is precisely in recasting written works of the past as work done that the cantos of this period mark their difference from those preceding. For if Pound's selection and arrangement of neglected documents in the Malatesta, Ferrara, and Venice sequences can be read as backed by his appropriation of Douglas's emphasis on the distribution of the already produced, his method in the Fifth Decad and especially the China and Adams sections, though unquestionably similar, aligns more provocatively with a vision of the works of the past as congealed labor or energy. In China and in Adams, after all, Pound's procedure is to select and arrange highlights from one major prior work (J.A.M. de Moyriac de Mailla's thirteen-volume *Histoire Générale de la Chine* in the former, *The Works of John Adams* in the latter) that seems to merit attention less by reason of some sheer power to fascinate than by virtue of its accumulation of political wisdom, an amassing of masterpieces and mistakes in the history of governance that renders it invaluable to contemporary social managers. At this point, that is, Pound deliberately precipitates the *Cantos* into the cultural heritage, the Adams section in particular representing a vehicle for the dissemination of material that he believed essential to the American history curriculum but, as he complained frequently, found scandalously difficult to obtain. ("Adams' and Jefferson's thought," he wrote in the *Guide to Kulchur*, for example, "is kept out of the plain man's reach, and out of my reach considering that for three years I have in vain tried to buy John Adams' letters" [162].)

As a project of dissemination, of course, the middle cantos can hardly be regarded as an untroubled success, partly for the very obvious reason that Pound finally subordinates any impulses to broad distribution to the narrower claims of the Frobenian readership, which will respond not to the trumpery of syllogism and explanation but to the opacity of textual fragments laid out like material things. But the inscrutability of these cantos also shows Pound responding to a claim more directly related to the cultural heritage, namely that exerted by technical innovation, which represented for him the central criterion for the canonicity of a work of art, and thus a factor that the middle cantos, *as* art, would have to engage. In the 1929 "How to Read," Pound had insisted that in poetry "there are known discoveries, clearly marked," and placed at the core of his list of required reading in literature "the authors who actually invented something" (*Literary* 19, 23, 27); in the 1934 *ABC of Reading*, he added that "the deliquescence of instruction in any art proceeds" from the "master" who invents a "gadget" to "the paste-headed pedagogue or theorist" who "proclaims the gadget a law, or rule," and thence to "a bureaucracy" that "attacks every new genius and every form of inventiveness for not obeying the law" (200). What governs both this approach to canon and his delineation of the cultural heritage, of course, is Pound's effort to transform the texts that would most constrain the writer of today into those that would most liberate, to rewrite the burden of belatedness as empowerment in accordance with his sense that the dead are best overcome by being revitalized. That this connection between canonicity and assistance to future generations was basic to Pound's thinking even before the advent of the cultural heritage as such is clear from earlier documents like the 1912 "Prologomena" (reprinted in the 1917 "Retrospect"), wherein he asserted that his "pawing over the ancients and semi-ancients has been one struggle to find out what has been done, once for all, better than it can ever be done again" (*Ezra Pound's* 1: 62; also *Literary* 11), or the 1928 letter in which he wrote, similarly, "What a good man gets from another man's work is: precisely the knowledge that the other man has done a job, and that he, the first man, *need not* do that same job or an imitation of it, but is free to do his own job" (*Letters* 221).

It is instructive, in this context, that the rise of "cultural heritage" in the Poundian vocabulary was complemented a few years later by a new affinity for the word "*techne*," which makes it first notable appearance in the free-wheeling reading of Aristotle that bulks out the *Guide to Kulchur*: Aristotle's "dissociation of the 'five' kinds of knowing,'" Pound writes, "is not to be sneezed at. BEGINNING with (1) teXne, skill in an art, in making things" (327). Pound does not pause to say much about the significance of *techne* at this point, but it seems that while the *Guide* was at press, he learned that "'before pore Ari was cold in his grave' the compilers of the so-called 'Magna Moralia' had already omitted TEXNE from the list of mental faculties given in the Nicomachean Ethics" (*Guide* 351), a fact of which he makes much in the midst of a discussion of the ideogram in the 1938 essay "Mang Tsze (The Ethics of Mencius)":

> Greek philosophy was almost an attack upon nature. . . . The school of Kung included intelligence without cutting it from its base. . . . The curse of European thought appeared between the Nichomachean [*sic*] notes and the Magna Moralia. Aristotle (as recorded in the earlier record) began his list of mental processes with TeXne, τέχνη, and the damned college parrots omitted it. This was done almost before the poor bloke was cold in his coffin.
>
> Greek philosophy, and European in its wake, degenerated into an attack on mythology and mythology . . . tries to find an expression for reality without over-simplification, and without scission, you can examine a living animal, but at a certain point dissection is compatible only with death. (*Prose* 86–87)[20]

Considered in light of critiques of instrumental reason, the first and last paragraphs quoted may seem yoked to the middle one only oddly and un-comfortably: the reader with the Frankfurt School in mind will be inclined to ask immediately whether it is not the progress of *techne* itself, the development of ever more encompassing and powerful means for transforming the material, that grounds human "attack[s] upon nature." And indeed, in an important and wide-ranging essay focusing on canto XXXI, Ian Bell has shown that Pound's technological metaphors cannot be separated from the very "functions of abstraction" that Adorno and Horkheimer view as the linchpin of capitalism's dominance and that Pound himself "is avowedly determined to resist," nor can the cut-and-paste technique of the middle and later cantos "be innocent of the paralysed solidity characteristic of the world of technology and commodity that was late capitalism's valorized figuration of Enlightenment materialism" ("Speaking" 164, 174).

One might supplement this Adornian-Horkheimerian account of what Pound was actually doing in addressing himself to technology, however, with a Heideggerian point concerning his intention—namely, that Pound viewed *techne* as akin less to instrumental reason than to something like the positive or authentic *techne* that would shortly appear in Heidegger, a making that follows nature's own instructions anent the revealing of Being, a working with the object world that very nearly amounts to a letting alone. For Pound, what renders *techne* superior to other kinds of knowledge is that it implies a dimension of concrete physical labor on the order of handicraft that requires it to engage the qualities of its materials, whereas the others raise no impediment to the will to abstraction. Nicholls observes that Pound's extraordinary claim for the significance of the elision of *techne* by Aristotle's followers must be viewed in the context of his more general hostility to contemplation untethered to action; but this point might be reversed and remain no less valid, since what enables Pound to present contemplation as a form of inactivity with actively destructive consequences is in part his rendering of *techne*, its alternate, as both the one knowledge that partakes of genuine activity and the one that does not engage in the murderous "dissection" of the thing known. In this, Pound converges not only with Heidegger, but also, strangely and enlighteningly, with Lukács, who in 1922 argued, in effect against the Kantian and Schopenhauerian line eventually adopted by Ransom and Adorno, that only praxis could respond to the particular object in its particularity: "the diversity of subjective attitudes orientates praxis towards what is qualitatively unique, towards the content and the material substratum of the object concerned," he argued in his landmark essay "Reification and the Consciousness of the Proletariat," whereas "theoretical contemplation leads to the neglect of this very factor" (126).

For Lukács, however, *techne* under advanced capitalism would finally align with contemplation rather than praxis because one of the consequences of the rationalization and mechanization of labor was to render the worker's activity "less and less active and more and more *contemplative*" (89), thereby depleting rather than enhancing the worker's will. Pound, on the other hand, would try increasingly strenuously, after the 1910s, to accommodate mass production to a vision of all production as an organic positivity diametrically opposed to the barrenness of finance capital (in this converging, broadly, with Lewis) and would address his attack on contemplation not to the worker but to the social manager—a point illustrated nicely by some lines from the first post-Pisan canto, number LXXXV, published in 1955. "But if you will follow this process" (here Pound places 德, the Chinese character for "virtue" or "awareness"),

> not a lot of signs, but the one sign
>   etcetera
>   plus always Τέχνη

and from Τέχνη back to σεαυτόν
Neither by chinks, nor by sophists,
      nor by hindoo immaturities;
Dante, out of St Victor (Richardus),
      Erigena with greek tags in his verses.
Y Yin sent the young king into seclusion
by T'ang Tomb to think things over,
      that they make total war on CONTEMPLATIO.

(*Cantos* 560)

Pound will mention *techne* explicitly at a few other junctures in the instructions to princes that form the skeleton of the *Rock-Drill* and *Thrones* cantos, but this inaugural moment makes sufficiently clear his major point, namely that this form of knowledge is essential to the right governance by the individual that will be these cantos' preoccupation. One lesson to be drawn here is thus that virtually the same take on subject-object relations that serves a Marxist politics when the normative subject is a member of the proletariat can be absorbed by an anti-Marxist, and in this case lingeringly Fascist, agenda when the subject in question belongs to the class of rulers. It is worth recalling, in addition, that Pound's regression to the archaic form of instruction to princes in these cantos virtually requires him to neglect the changes in the experience of making engendered by mass production, to imagine *techne* (against his earlier habit of opposing the artisanal to the industrial) as a mode of knowledge that operates similarly in handicraft, assembly line work, and government. Viewed in relation to the thinking of a Marxist like Lukács, therefore, this passage shows also how Pound's alignment with Fascism, if in some respects adventitious, was nonetheless supported by a characteristically Fascist transformation of revolutionary rhetoric into a gospel of action founded on historical continuity rather than rupture, and in particular upon an excision (from the center of historical inquiry) of attention to alterations in the conditions of production.[21]

These entanglements bestow a heightened significance upon the material that falls at the end of the *Cantos* as currently published, those late drafts and fragments whose moral strength derives from an element of self-criticism not to be found in *Rock-Drill* and *Thrones*—an element whose appearance even here is tenuous and intermittent, yet no less striking for that. Most crucial in the present context are eight lines first written in late 1959, which appear in the present New Directions edition of the *Cantos* under "Notes for CXVII et seq.":[22]

I have tried to write Paradise

Do not move
   Let the wind speak
      that is paradise.

Let the Gods forgive what I
    have made
Let those I love try to forgive
    what I have made.

                              (816)

As Ronald Bush points out, these lines represent "an affirmation" as much as "a recantation of sorts" in that "they announce a natural site of wisdom" emerging from Pound's lifelong search ("Unstill" 240), but it would be a serious mistake to underestimate the importance of the recantation such as it is. Because it is impossible not to hazard that what requires forgiveness includes Pound's Fascist activities (given their enormous impact on his life and on the situation of American poetry), but equally impossible to read "what I have made" without allowing that the phrase might refer to his entire achievement, the effect of this fragment is to infuse the criminality of Pound's most reprehensible acts into all his works. (In this the fragment differs sharply from other late moments in which Pound emphasizes mixed motives or results: "man seeking good, / doing evil"; "Many errors, / a little rightness" [808, 811].) Even were it demonstrably not the case that Pound here conflates his political activities with the totality of his production, so general an apology for making would still constitute a freighted epilogue to the story of modern art by virtue of its location in the final lyric meditations of the most forceful propagandist for art as making in twentieth-century English letters, a writer who claimed to have adapted his most famous slogan, "Make It New," from an ideogram inscribed on an ancient artifact ("Tching prayed on the mountain and / wrote MAKE IT NEW / on his bath tub" [*Cantos* 264–65]).[23]

In the context of the preceding imperative ("Do not move / Let the wind speak / that is paradise"), moreover, the plea for forgiveness bids to question the validity of human production in general, opposing Romantic conjunctions of inspiration and aspiration (Wordsworth's "O there is blessing in this gentle breeze," Shelley's "West Wind") with the claims of a natural world that might, as other modernists reflected, be in itself satisfactory, achieved. The line's most significant positive intertext, in fact, appears to be "The wind is part of the process / The rain is part of the process" (*Cantos* 449), a statement from the first of Pound's own Pisan cantos (LXXIV) that emblematizes the Pisans' much remarked turn toward natural detail—a turn widely regarded as a late flowering of part of Imagist theory's philosophical armature, and one that made these cantos a kind of trial run (vindicated in a sense by the Bollingen Prize bestowed on them) for the move toward empirical crispness that has dominated poetry in English from the 1950s onward.

Indeed in an early discussion of this shift, Donald Davie emphatically contrasted Yeatsian symbolism to the Pisans' insistence that "the world outside was meaningful precisely insofar as it existed in its own right," observing that the wasp of canto LXXXIII "retains its otherness as an independent form of life; it is only by doing so that it can be a source of comfort to the human observer" (149, 150). Decades after Davie's influential analysis, to be sure, it may no longer need saying that the Pisans include some remarkably powerful illustrations of the modernist preoccupation with the object qua object; and yet Davie's particular phrasing does help to disclose a certain continuity between the Pisan Pound and other modernists who celebrated the radical otherness of the natural world—Woolf, for example, writing in "On Being Ill" that it "is in their indifference that" plants "are comforting," or Lewis insisting that it is "only when something is independent of us, a non-assimilable universe of its own, that we 'love' it." And because this modernist embrace of the object in its distance was frequently subtended by a profound anxiety about large-scale transformations of physical reality, we might take the Pisans to register something of this anxiety as well, a late conversion on Pound's part to what we might loosely call the ecological/anti-Hegelian line of modernism.

The problem with such a gesture toward a harmony of shared doubt is less that Pound continues to validate *techne* in *Rock-Drill* and *Thrones* (which come after the Pisans) than that such a gesture would involve a misreading of the Pisans themselves, which finally do not strike the note of retraction that many readers—including, probably, the 1959 Pound who wrote "Let the wind speak" in a briefer but more genuine palinode—have found in them. The famous "Pull down thy vanity" set-piece, invariably the anchor for assessments that discover in the Pisans a humble acknowledgment of error, proves remarkably self-justifying even on a less than minute examination, as Humphrey Carpenter has observed (680), and its ringing conclusion in particular sounds more like a defense of human endeavor than a dismissal:

But to have done instead of not doing
      this is not vanity

To have, with decency, knocked
That a Blunt should open
    To have gathered from the air a live tradition
or from a fine old eye the unconquered flame
This is not vanity.
    Here error is all in the not done,
all in the diffidence that faltered . . .

                          (*Cantos* 535–36)

"But to have done instead of not doing / this is not vanity" may not be a perfect antithesis to "Let those I love try to forgive / what I have made," but it is surely close enough to one to make a delicate business of any rapprochement between this canto (LXXXI) and "CXVII."

What is in fact accomplished in this crucial passage will become clearer if we turn to the event that it commemorates, a 1914 pilgrimage of Pound, Yeats, Plarr, Masefield, Flint, Aldington, Sturge Moore, and Frederic Manning to the home of Wilfrid Scawen Blunt, whom Pound had called in 1912 "the grandest of old men, the last of the great Victorians; great by reason of his double sonnet, beginning—'He who has once been happy is for aye / Out of destruction's reach'" (*Ezra Pound's* 1: 113). According to Pound's account in a 1914 issue of *Poetry*, the pilgrimage culminated with the presentation of "a reliquary carved in Pentelican marble by the brilliant young sculptor Gaudier Brzeska" containing "verses of homage signed by the committee" (and written by Pound) that concluded, "We, who are little given to respect, / Respect you, and having no better way to show it, / Bring you this stone to be some record of it" (*Ezra Pound's* 1: 224). In his acceptance speech, Pound reports, Blunt observed "that this was the first time in his life that any admiration of his poetry had been expressed to him" (*Ezra Pound's* 1: 225).

The memory in question thus gathers a special poignancy not only from the fact of Gaudier's death in the Great War, which helped to secure the sculptor a permanent place in the Poundian gallery of heroes, but also from its allusion to the gratitude of a man whose poetry had nearly been forgotten, a man whom Pound himself had described as one of several writers "little known to the general public . . . who contribute liberally to the 'charm' or the 'atmosphere' of London" (*Ezra Pound's* 1: 113).[24] And this point is important because it is through poignancy that Pound finally manages his effect here, through just this evocation of tenderness for a fleeting expression of admiration that he chiefly justifies doing and making in general, which in failing to result in anything proof against the wastage of time take on the dignity and heroism of doomed resistance against overwhelming opposition. It is worth noting that the more freighted words in this passage all gesture toward pride in right action combined with humility before a superior power, the aesthete-evoking "fine" being apposed not to a work of art but to a perishable human organ; "decency" betokening a resigned rectitude; and "unconquered" of course suggesting both a moral victory over time and a practical defeat. The metrical scheme elegantly reinforces this mood, Pound weaving pensive "feminine" endings ("open," "tradition," "vanity," "faltered") with "masculine" closes to statelier lines ("knocked," "flame," and the spondaic "not done") in what comes off as an authoritative declamation on the frailty of human authority. And the effect is secured, needless to say, by Pound's omission of all reference to the stone memorial, an elision that suggests how crucial to this negotiation is the suspension of his usual concern with the material burden of the past.

Thus, although the famous sanctions against vanity that precede the last section of LXXXI—"The ant's a centaur in his dragon world. / Pull down thy vanity, it is not man / Made courage, or made order, or made grace"

(535)—do indeed call human achievement into question in one sense, suggesting that it appears incalculably small when compared to the vastness of nature, it is this very reexamination that allows for the recuperation that follows. If prior to the conclusion just quoted Pound uses "vanity" to mean something like "hubris," to which humans have no right by virtue of their relative puniness, he means by his use of the term in "This is not vanity" something like "thoroughly wasted effort," his point being that human making is not pointless in a moral sense, only inconsequential to a nature too vast and powerful to take much note of it. And this means in turn that the conclusion's allusion to struggle heroic, blameless, and doomed partakes of a vision of nature as omnipotent force, rather than fragile victim, that had been suspect at least since Ruskin—a vision that also informs the Pisans' concluding lines, with their Lear-like advice to unaccommodated man and their allusion to the conditions of Pound's internment: "If the hoar frost grip thy tent / Thou wilt give thanks when night is spent" (*Cantos* 554). The final effect of Pound's attention to natural detail, in other words, is not to prescribe restraint in dealings with nature but rather to justify human doing and making on the ground that neither can ever threaten the nonhuman universe's courage, order, and grace in any serious way.

Canto LXXXI's articulation of this position is the more significant because it constitutes the climax of a series of reflections—beginning at the very beginning of the Pisans—that link (or remain uneasily suspended between) macroeconomics and microethics, the morality of individual making and the consequences of global production. Scarcely a page into the first of the Pisans, LXXIV, Pound (already defending the radio broadcasts for which he was arrested) writes:

> Oh my England
> that free speech without free radio speech is as zero
>   and but one point needed for Stalin
> you need not, i.e. need not take over the means of production;
> money to signify work done, inside a system
>   and measured and wanted
> "I have not done unnecessary manual labour"
> says the R. C. chaplain's field book
>   (preparation before confession)
>
>   (*Cantos* 440)

The middle lines of this passage refer to Pound's contention, stated in many of his writings but perhaps most clearly formulated in "The Individual in his Milieu" (published in *The Criterion* in October 1935[25]), that the Social Credit position might be coordinated with the ideas of another marginalized reformer, Silvio Gesell, who reasoned that a government might stimulate "measured and wanted" production and curtail usury by requiring a part of all wages to be paid in the form of scrip ("money to signify work done") that would depreciate rather than accrue interest if not spent. Positioned in this manner, Gesellite economics serves as a superindividual bridge between two individual declarations of innocence: first, Pound's justification of his radio speeches; second, a statement of adherence to Sabbatical prohibitions drawn from one of the few texts to which Pound had direct access during his detention, the camp chaplain's handbook—a statement that speaks in its own fashion to Pound's nonmanual labor on behalf of Mussolini and (by extension, in his own view) against Stalin (who did, of course, "take over the means of production").

What all three parts of this passage have in common, clearly, is that they move to counter possible criticisms of doing and making: in the case of Gesell's formulation, the complaint that the wage scrip would prompt a frenzied consumption leading to a fatal production spiral; in the case of the others, condemnations of untimely work as sinful or criminal. It is thus highly suggestive that a story of punishment for overproduction proper materializes a few lines later, as Pound invokes Wondjina, son of a god in an Australian aboriginal myth, who had the power to create simply by naming:

> but Wanjina is, shall we say, Ouan Jin
> or the man with an education
> and whose mouth was removed by his father
>   because he made too many *things*
> whereby cluttered the bushman's baggage
> vide the expedition of Frobenius' pupils about 1938
>   to Auss'ralia
> Ouan Jin spoke and thereby created the named
>   thereby making clutter
> the bane of men moving
> and so his mouth was removed
> as you will find it removed in his pictures
>   in principio verbum

> (440–41)

This paean to the benefits of traveling light unquestionably testifies to Pound's need to rationalize the deprivations he experienced in the Pisan camp, its positing of a relation between the Australian Wanjina and "Ouan Jin" (or Wen-Jen), the Chinese for "man of letters," pointing to the fact that his books were among the possessions he missed most. Yet this witness to the pain of separation from beloved objects is also informed by Pound's ever mutating anxieties about the burden of the literary past, since the implication of identity between Wanjina and Ouan Jin suggests too that writers share in the guilt of overproduction—or even that the accumulation of words constitutes the originary cluttering of the world ("in principio verbum"). The guilt of making thus spreads at this point from Pound the writer of radio speeches to Pound the writer in general, the bulkiness of whose vast and *dinglich* epic will only be further increased by the Pisan meditations.

In the pages that follow, however, Pound appears to abandon his questioning of the production of physical things in favor of a celebration of an aspect of mental life, filling the void left by the loss of tangible objects with memories—which, whether or not less baneful to "men moving" than material encumbrances, undoubtedly served as the best consolation of a man detained and still. Over the course of the Pisans, Pound will go on to record hundreds of recollections of every description, but he unleashes memory perhaps nowhere more strikingly than in the closing pages of LXXIV itself, which unfold kaleidoscopically a catalogue of anecdotes from his years in England. Launching his retrospective with the memory of Aubrey Beardsley saying "beauty is difficult,"[26] he proceeds through anecdotes from the Oxford of 1913, a thematic quotation from the first Ur-canto ("'ghosts move about me' 'patched with histories'"), recollections of visits to New York and North Africa in the 1890s, evocations of the column at San Zeno with its proud medieval craftsman and of present-day craftsmen in wood and stone, and allusions to a vast array of other experiences, before concluding with the suggestion that his cherished image of invisible pattern in nature, "the rose in the steel dust" revealed by the magnet, might be applicable to the apparent chaos of his memories: "so ordered the dark petals of iron / we who have passed over Lethe" (*Cantos* 458–63).

If one of Pound's efforts in this exercise is to show how a substitute for lost possessions can be found in memory, the effort seems to succeed almost too well, the substitute proving so astonishingly rich in this case that the true crisis of the Pisans seems at times that of a subject discovering not its fragility in the absence of what it loves, but rather its strange self-sufficiency (a point consonant with Pound's post-Pisan biography, which suggests that he found confinement in St. Elizabeth's strangely bearable, the departure therefrom more fraught with uncertainties). And this resolution necessarily implies another, of course, since in demonstrating memory's ability to substitute for absent solid objects, the Pisans also respond to the burden of the past encoded in the error of Wanjina/Ouan Jin, the problem of a world cluttered by human productions. Residing in a space that takes up no space, memory bids to replace the possessions of which Pound had been deprived, above all books, with a far more economical store—which is to say that by offering to provide inexhaustible occupation while adding nothing to the debris of the world, memory cannot but cast doubt on the necessity of fixing consciousness or experience in solid form.

It is important to recognize, however, that calling the necessity of made objects into question is not quite the same thing as calling into question the morality of making; and indeed as it turns out the solid object's loss proves human action's (if not human production's) gain on the terrain of memory as it did on that of nature. We have already seen how at the conclusion of LXXXI Pound vindicated doing by implying that it will always constitute a doomed endeavor whose products are fated to transience before the power of the natural world, and a similar operation comes to light in the same passage if we read it in terms of the far side of Lethe. The event that figures as the archetypal instance of human action at the end of LXXXI is, after all, a dignified and beautiful tribute that (as presented here, with the stone memorial unmentioned) leaves behind no traces, nothing to clutter the world, only the volumeless residue of a recollection that itself acquires a compelling dignity and beauty. The work of this passage, with respect to memory as with respect to nature, then, is to absolve doing of the guilt adumbrated at the beginning of LXXIV not so much by proving its significance as by challenging the reader to find it blameable: "To have gathered from the air a live tradition / or from a fine old eye the unconquered flame / This is not vanity"—for who, indeed, would be so hardhearted as to rebuke a recollection like this one, especially when recollections take up no space and use up no resources? The conclusion of canto LXXXI thus mounts a defense of "hav[ing] done instead of not doing" that proceeds in two stages (which attest, in their very doubleness, to the intensity of the now officially criminal Pound's need to justify action as opposed to "diffidence"): first, the claim that doing of this kind is blameless because it leaves only memories, no addition to the material debris of the world; but second, the implication that such doing would forfeit none of its innocence even if it did leave behind a more concrete record of the event—the stone memorial, say, or canto LXXXI itself—since that record would still be no match for the powers of nature and time.

As Pound presents it here, his recollection of the pilgrimage only confirms the sentiment of the double sonnet that he had praised as Blunt's greatest achievement, "He who has once been happy is for aye / Out of destruction's reach": captured in memory, the pilgrimage issues in a victory over mortality that retains its validity precisely because it remains only a moral victory and not a practical one. But if Blunt's own poetic sentiment evades ironic reversal in LXXXI, the same cannot quite be said for the homage presented by the committee, which asserts that Blunt distinguished himself from his Victorian contemporaries by using a less unnaturally elevated language and thus clearing the way for their own generation's return to hardness and precision. The irony, of course, is that to whatever degree Blunt did indeed initiate a wider turn to earth in poetry, he both replayed Wordsworth's move against eighteenth-century norms and deprived the moderns of a part of their revolutionary force, closing down possibilities for innovation as much as opening them, adding to rather than subtracting from the oppressive weight of past works—a point reinforced rather than not by Pound's and the others' decision to honor a poet who did not, indeed, present much of a threat. In select-ing the Blunt affair as the memory that justifies human doing, then, Pound brings nearly (but not quite) to the surface what must surely count as his most profound anxiety about human action, a fear that any enduring achieve-ment will inevitably exacerbate the error of Wanjina, cluttering the world (in a sense beyond the merely physical) by diminishing the possibilities for in-novation in future production.

It is precisely this anxiety, of course, that Pound dramatically fails to confront in trying to apply the cultural heritage model to the evolution of poetic technique, precisely this problem that he strikingly evades by trying to justify newness in making as necessary progress. To speak of "find[ing] out what has been done, once for all, better than it can ever be done again" is fairly to admit that fewer and fewer things remain to be done as the world gets older (unless the number of things is infinite, a proposition from which even Pound would probably have dissented), while the reference to "known discoveries, clearly marked" cannot but point toward the possibility, how-ever unlikely, that we are in fact heading toward some perfection of effi-ciency in art that would spell art's veritable demise. If in Pound's poetics and economics the cultural heritage proves a vital remedy for the problem of what to do with the things of the past, then, it no less definitively signals the alarming terminus to which all making seems to gesture, namely, the utter cessation of the production of new *kinds* of production, the authentic end of the modern itself. (And if it is true, as Christine Froula suggests, that by honoring Blunt twice over Pound "bypasses the great Romantics to affirm a minor lyric tradition" [236], it must also be said that this affirmation origi-nates less from some profound affection for the truly or deservedly minor itself than from a despair over the shrinking of possibilities for major achievement.)

For Pound, then, what makes production most disturbing (at least at the level of his deeper, less explicitly but still firmly articulated anxieties) proves to be its potentially self-devouring quality—not what it does to some nonhu-man Other, but the possibility that it will eventuate in a foreclosure of the human future that looks, curiously, less like the loss of the paradiso than its utopian arrival. Pound's fears about production were thus significantly dif-ferent from those of, say, Ransom or Adorno, for whom the ultimate danger lay in the reckless transformation of the object world by a subjectivity heed-less of the ends of its actions, and we might therefore be inclined to say that Pound's anxieties were finally far removed from the ecological concerns of critics of instrumental reason. And yet if we were to think of an "ecological" sensibility somewhat more analogically, so as to stress not material transfor-mation per se but rather a structure of thought focused on the amassing of products and the depletion of resources, we could well view Pound as among the most ecologically minded of modernists, one who registers the most genuinely pressing problems of technological expansion in an anxiety about accumulation detectable even where he most fervently represses historical changes in production's governing conditions.

Another way of putting this would be to observe that if there is a sense in which Pound was truer to the crises of his age than Ransom, Adorno, and the other writers considered here, it would be bound up with the fact that he was seldom attracted to the question of whether the individual act of making constitutes an act of violence in some absolute sense, but much concerned (in his way) with the question of how much making can finally be sustained. Never especially sympathetic to the ascesis of philosophical abstraction, never as interested in epistemology or ontology as such as Woolf, Lewis, or Stevens (his references to Aristotle and Richard of St. Victor notwithstanding), he was less inclined than these others to think of the relation between humans and things in terms of a primal scene of subject-object confrontation, but correspondingly more inclined than they to imagine the object among the sum of objects, as an addition rather than an exemplum. If there are affinities between Pound and Woolf on the question of the object world, the Woolf in question would be not the writer of *To the Lighthouse*, *The Waves*, and *Between the Acts*, wherein human activity (including the fashioning of art) comes to seem a strange and disturbing imposition on an innocent landscape, but rather the critic of the overstuffed Victorian age who produced *Orlando* and *The Years*; and if there are affinities between Pound and Sartre, the Sartre at issue would be not the author of *Being and Nothingness* but the originator of the *Critique of Dialectical Reason*, in which transformed matter, in the form of the practico-inert, takes its revenge by imposing ever more appalling constraints upon human life.

Whether Pound was finally more or less modern than the others, or more or less ecologically minded, he seems to have experienced the guilt of production no less intensely than they, and from an earlier point in his career. In a poem of 1911, for example, he can be found wrapping up some fairly standard Paterian ruminations in a way that anticipates (or rather instantiates) some of the generative doubts that make the vastness of his literary output one of the greater ironies in the career of an infrequently ironic poet: "It is enough that we once came together; / Time has seen this, and will not turn again; / And who are we, who know that last intent, / To plague tomorrow with a testament!" (*Personae* 55). In addition, Pound at times showed an anxiety about his admiration for the existing products of human effort that the others for the most part did not share, a feeling deriving partly from the sense that such admiration might endorse the accumulation that caused him so much concern, but also, perhaps, from an intermittent suspicion that no affection in this life can be wholly innocent in the end. In the *Guide to Kulchur*, as we have seen, Pound remarks that in evaluating past societies on the basis of their tolerance of *usura* he had not "deflected a hair's breadth from" his "lists of beautiful objects"; but in his own Pisan cantos, perhaps the most remarkable engagement with guilt in the history of poetry, he offers a less than obliging response to this earlier self's implicit request to be applauded for perspicacity and devotion. At the commencement of the long catalogue of memories that rounds out canto LXXIV, he suggests that even a love of beautiful things quite apart from connoisseurship and possession—even the sheer delight that might separate the truly aesthetic aesthete from the commodifier of taste—cannot be a simple matter in a world in which one can seek good but end up doing evil. For " 'beauty is difficult' sd / Mr Beardsley."

Chapter Four

WALLACE STEVENS

LIFE'S EXTRAVAGANCE

L IKE THE OTHER writers surveyed here, Wallace Stevens was a child of aestheticism, but his aestheticism was not quite the same as theirs. If Woolf and Bloomsbury muted their debts to Pater, Wilde, and the naughty Continent; and if Lewis exposed that legacy even where few others would have detected it; and if Pound ambivalently sanctified the aesthetes as the disruptive force that readied the world for his own generation's achievements, still, the entity to which they were responding was, however polymorphous, at least recognizable as a native growth of the weary and ironical Old World, one that found an appropriately paradoxical figure in Wilde's unnaturally green carnations and the lurid hothouse flowers of des Esseintes. The aestheticism that Stevens encountered, however, was largely the product of a transatlantic transplantation, having arrived in the United States virtually in the form of a single cargo upon a single ship—the ship being the S.S. *Arizona*, which docked in New York harbor on 2 January 1882, and the cargo Wilde himself, who promoted his gospel of beauty in a series of lecture tours that did not conclude until 13 October of that year. Meeting an America primed for an aesthetic vogue but largely without experience of the self-proclaimed "aesthete" in person, Wilde drew audiences partly by proffering initiation into the mysteries of Ruskin, Pater, and Morris, but mainly by generating an atmosphere of sensation and controversy emblematized by the dandiacal knee breeches that he wore when lecturing—or, in the case of his appearance at the Boston Music Hall, pointedly avoided wearing, so as to show up a group of Harvard students who (bent on mocking him) had come sporting breeches of their own (Ellmann, *Wilde* 182–83).[1]

Aestheticism inevitably made its way to Harvard nonetheless, and when Stevens arrived there fifteen years later, he came upon Wilde's American legacy in both less and more profound forms: in undergraduates exhibiting the standard ensemble of decadent ennuis, along with others who lampooned such airs; and in George Santayana, whose name remains associated with the passion for beauty more firmly than that of any other American writer. As Milton Bates notes (in part quoting Stevens himself), the 1890s found many Harvard undergraduates sitting down "with a ready appetite to the feast spread by the French and English *fin de siècle*," locally centered "at Marliave's in Boston, where they could play at being abroad" and repeat "the Decadent commonplace that all the poems had been written and all the paintings painted" (23; see also *Opus* 218). Bates also points out, however, that the Signet society (to which Stevens was elected at the conclusion of his second year) sought deliberately a happy medium between "sportiness" and "preciosity" (25), and it is clear that Harvard in general at the close of the century was far from unrestrainedly precious. The art history professor Charles Eliot Norton—best known to Stevens devotees as the host of a Christmas party that the young Stevens was too dispirited to attend (*Letters* 575)—was no friend to the pretensions of Wilde and the decadents, yet even he complained in 1900 not that students were overrefined but, on the contrary, that "the Cambridge of to-day is a town of prose, and the College is given over to science and athletics" (300). And the point is confirmed by Kim Townsend, who in his recent *Manhood at Harvard* shows that what occasioned copious debate among faculty and administrators around the turn of the century was the proper limitation to be placed on sports (97–100), not some threat of decadent anemia.[2]

Indeed if the pages of the *Harvard Advocate* in the last decade of the century give a fair indication of the campus atmosphere, it would seem that more students were inclined to target the high aesthetic line for satire or critique than were moved to adopt it as a way of life. An 1893 portrait of "The Undergraduate Literary Man," for example, comments that "[i]t's nice to be a cynic" but nicer still "to be a décadent," who can "drink absinthe frappé when other people are having beer" (Flandrau 20), while a number from 1894 features the letters of Theodore Bumford Greene, a fictional *naif* just arrived at the college who recounts to his family his amazement at the customs of a club called the "Rossetti Ring" ("Tea and lemons! I *was* astonished" [Knoblauch 44]). Other issues of the period include poems like "The Ballade of Beardsley" ("So this is our race's heritage,—/ Art where technique is gone insane . . ." [Chamberlin 128]) and the "Ballade of Decadency" ("What odds if squinting cynics prate? / Decayed eyes see all things decayed" [Macy 77]), while an editorial opening the number of 27 January 1896 inveighs against "a spirit of pessimism or *désillusionnement*" manifest in many contributions. The writer goes on to complain that "we are too familiar with the protoplasmic youth in divorce cases or Nordau's diagnoses to be longer attracted by him as a novelty" and to look forward to the day when "those tastes and tendencies which have been arbitrarily classed as *fin de siècle* have altogether ceased to appeal to the imagination of youth" (Editorial 129).

Stevens's own highly flamboyant 1900 contribution to the *Advocate*, "The Ballade of the Pink Parasol," appears on inspection rather uncharacteristic of the undergraduate poetry of its day, and indeed (as Bates notes), uncharacteristic even of Stevens's own undergraduate writing, which includes a number of short stories less concerned with protoplasmic youths in themselves than with the possibility that the ethereal upper classes might be missing out on a rich existence available to the unlettered. "The Higher Life" of 1899, for example, begins with a description of a college student's vest ("embroidered with a multitude of little pink roses" [123]), but consists mainly of that student's restless reflections as he awaits the arrival of some old vulgar friends from the theater (which event he avoids, in the end, by slipping out of his room well ahead of time), while "Part of His Education," from the same year, tells the story of a sort of town-gown reconciliation, heavily implying in its finale that the educated protagonist has learned a lot about life by mixing with the masses. Fairly typical products of the Harvard literatus of Stevens's day, these sketches clearly participate in what Frank Lentricchia (in his chapter on turn-of-the-century Harvard in *Modernist Quartet*) describes as a hedonist and modernist project of allowing "the socially and culturally extraordinary" to become, in imagination, "physical . . . ordinary and ignorant" (8), though we might add that such imagining was less a modernist innovation than a legacy of Naturalism to the Nineties mode, in which the lower classes so often provided the grit of reality as well as the matter of melodrama.

Interested more in a detailed interrogation of beauty than in absinthe and boredom, Santayana—whom Stevens knew well in his Cambridge days (*Letters* 96, 637, 761)—also sought a middle ground between sportiness and preciosity, and for that matter between alternatives that Lentricchia denominates "a radical social conscience" and "the onanism of Pateresque aestheticism" (*Modernist* 6). Recalling many years later his first period of residence at Harvard (as a student), Santayana remarked that the O.K. was the best of the college's literary societies because it included "the class of merely intelligent or even athletic leaders of the College," who in a "commercial civilization . . . were likely to be much *better beings* than the professional scholars or intellectuals," and added—in a manner evocative of the (homoerotically charged) aesthete-admires-athlete pattern that Alan Sinfield discerns in the Oxbridge 1930s—"I liked to feel a spark of sympathy pass from those sound simple active heirs of the dominant class to my secret philosophy: and sometimes the spark did pass, and in both directions" (*Persons* 191; see also Bates 21–22). In *The Sense of Beauty*, the 1896 work that most helped to link him with aestheticism, meanwhile, Santayana (by then a professor) could write without a shudder that the arts "must stand modestly aside until they can slip in fitly into the interstices of life. . . . [Art] must not only create things abstractly beautiful, but it must conciliate all the competitors these may have to the attention of the world . . . " (137–38). And after that book's publication in 1896, Santayana rejected even these kinds of arguments in favor of the view that the aesthetic permeates many areas of life, asserting in *Interpretations of Poetry and Religion* (1900), for example, that "[s]cience and common sense are themselves in their way poets of no mean order, since they take the material of experience and make out of it a clear, symmetrical, and beautiful world" (161).

Santayana's refusal to cordon off the aesthetic from life's other realms, backed as it was by Harvard's prevailing mistrust of preciosity, confirms that the once usual picture of this philosopher as an aesthete who drew Stevens away from his father's hardheaded pragmatism stands very much in need of the revision to which Lentricchia contributes. In his admirable eagerness to restore to us a sense of the social engagement of modernism and its antecedents, however, Lentricchia presents a version of *The Sense of Beauty* much closer to "radical social conscience" and farther from "Pateresque aestheticism" than the text warrants—a point of particular relevance to the question of the object because it turns on Santayana's elusively nuanced definition of beauty as "pleasure regarded as the quality of a thing" (33). In Lentricchia's rendering,

> What Santayana calls the 'objectification' of perception is the creation of that special sort of literary effect that a self-conscious modernist poetics would shortly call the 'image,' . . . not only a form of perception but also a form of expression which integrates feeling and object in a public medium. . . . Santayana's 'sense of beauty' becomes a necessary condition for collective recovery of our sensuous environment . . . : community formed by and for the pleasures of the percept. . . . (*Modernist* 6)

Useful as such a description is in illuminating the connections among Santayana, Imagism, and Stevens's later efforts to develop a community of imagination, it leaves something to be desired as a summary of *The Sense of Beauty*, since "objectification" in Santayana's usage represents not a willed effort to produce an object of shared perceptions or feelings (as Lentricchia's phrasing implies), but rather something like a fortunate mistake that we all make habitually:

> Beauty is an emotional element, a pleasure of ours, which nevertheless we regard as a quality of things. . . . It is the survival of a tendency originally universal to make every effect of a thing upon us a constituent of its conceived nature. . . . [W]hen the process of perception itself is pleasant . . . then we have a pleasure intimately bound up in the thing. . . . We naturally fail, under these circumstances, to separate the pleasure from the other objectified feelings. It becomes, like them, a quality of the object, which we distinguish from pleasures not so incorporated in the perception of things, by giving it the name of beauty. (32–33)

Beauty, in other words, is the subjective feeling of pleasure in perception taken for a quality of the object perceived. And in *The Sense of Beauty* (though not in the later writing) it is explicitly *not* a social phenomenon, Santayana remarking a few pages later that "social feelings, the parental, the patriotic, or the merely gregarious, are not of much direct value for aesthetics" although the rare social need that can become a quality of an object—as for example the concept of "home"—"acquire[s] great aesthetic value" (42, 43).

Lentricchia's misreading is instructive nonetheless because it highlights how Santayana's thinking runs counter to the tendency to associate all art, on the model of sculpture and painting, with the enduring object—a tendency that, as we have seen, was reinforced by modernist attempts to rehabilitate art for art's sake through a naturalizing of the monumental imperative. Instead, Santayana carries his (Paterian) stress on the experience of the aesthetic through to the conclusion that consumability is integral to the very nature of art: in *The Sense of Beauty*, for example, he argues (against Kant) that although the "beauties of nature and of the plastic arts are not consumed by being enjoyed . . . this circumstance is accidental," and points out not only that some "aesthetic objects," such as performances, clearly "depend upon change and are exhausted in time," but also that even "plastic beauties" partake of the consumable because they "can often not be enjoyed except by a few, on account of the necessity of travel or other difficulties of access" (27). (Taking the phrase "not consumed by being enjoyed" out of context, Lentricchia notably inverts its import, suggesting that for Santayana only enduring forms count as stimulants to the aesthetic response [*Modernist* 5].) Santayana also observes in the same volume that if the "art of combining dishes and wines . . . remains in the sphere of the pleasant, and is consequently regarded as servile, rather than fine" (45), this is so not because cuisine's satisfactions are ephemeral, but because we regard the pleasure taken in its "unrepresentable" materials as part of us rather than a quality of those materials (45).

This last contention is of special interest because it shows Santayana refusing to elevate to the status of fully aesthetic enterprise one of the several minor "arts" that the decadents—in a characteristically transvaluative or "perverse" gesture—had championed precisely on account of those activities' traditional affiliations with triviality and luxury. In *Interpretations*, Santayana makes the point still more sharply, distinguishing between poets, on the one hand, and "cooks, hairdressers, and florists," on the other, by way of prefacing his claim that "the greatest function of poetry" is to provide a grounding of the ideal in the concrete, to seize "hold of the reality of sensation and fancy beneath the surface of conventional ideas, and then out of that living but indefinite material to build new structures . . . truer to the ultimate possibilities of the soul" (160, 161). Committed to a philosophical understanding of beauty as subjective experience, but unwilling to find poetry in practices apparently unconnected to the morally or spiritually ideal (but frequently identified with refinement bought at extravagant cost), Santayana shows that the dividing line between his own philosophy and aestheticism at its most daring lay between "consumption" as the activity of absorbing, enjoying, or using up and certain transactions valued by fin-de-siècle provocateurs because they seemed to approach a pure consuming (that is, one without meaningful product, material or moral).

Stevens can be found pondering something like this very division in an intriguing entry from his undergraduate journal that seems actively to resist some of the complacencies of *The Sense of Beauty*. In *Sense*, Santayana concludes at one point that what accounts for the impressiveness of the stars is their evocation of a "sense of multiplicity in uniformity" (68), but in his journal Stevens offers another explanation even as he declares "art for art's sake" to be

> both indiscreet and worthless. . . . To say that stars were made to guide navigators etc. seems like stretching a point; but the real use of their beauty (which is not their excuse) is that it is a service, a food. Beauty is strength. But art—art all alone, detached, sensuous for the sake of sensuousness, not to perpetuate inspiration or thought, art that is mere art—seems to me the most arrant as it is the most inexcusable rubbish. (H. Stevens 38; also quoted in part in Bates 30)

Replacing consumption as enjoyment with consumption as instrument of further productive activity (the intake of nutrients), Stevens betrays a suspicion of pleasure that Santayana did not share, a way of thinking even more removed from *The Sense of Beauty* than that exhibited by the philosopher himself in *Interpretations*. But this entry speaks of more than the confrontation between Santayana's cosmopolitan epicureanism and a residual puritanism in Stevens, for it also shows how, given just a slight shift in philosophical focus, the two kinds of "consumption" somewhat at variance in Santayana can become almost perfectly polar opposites—the term now connoting on the one hand a part of the cycle of production that prevents things from going to waste, on the other an indulgence or excess that would stand as production's moral (if not practical) alternative.

At first glance, these distillations may look a little too finely worked even for the tirelessly subtilizing likes of Stevens and Santayana; but when considered in certain discursive contexts they reveal themselves to be richly and immediately responsive to their historical moment, a moment when preoccupations with "consumption" structured by both of these meanings were shaping social visions across classes and well outside the precincts of academic Cambridge. As Richard Wightman Fox and T. J. Jackson Lears note, "legions of publicists promoted, celebrated, or condemned the centrality of consumption in Americans' lives beginning in the late nineteenth century" (ix), and indeed it was this period that saw consumption achieve its most potent popular apotheoses, while also generating anxieties of unprecedented intensity, on both sides of the Atlantic.[3]

On the English side, as we have seen, these anxieties bore on aestheticism because they tended to locate the peril of the nation as a whole in its corruption by the aesthete's defining vices of overrefinement, physical weakness, cynicism, and nonproductiveness; but one might expect this kind of alarm to have been of limited dissemination in the United States, where the general healthiness of the citizens and the economy (a series of large-scale booms and busts notwithstanding) hardly seemed in doubt. In fact, however, this very vigor generated a closely related concern, since to some observers it appeared—especially when refracted through the conspicuously consuming lifestyles of the nouveaux riches—inextricable from a viciousness fatal to moral progress. Huysmans's typically European suggestion that the enfeeblement of a des Esseintes demands a pedigree stretching back through the centuries notwithstanding, social commentators had no trouble recognizing that a fortune does not require passage down the generations to produce a decadent, and freely speculated that unprecedented wealth poorly used could portend the end rather than the emergence of American greatness.

Responding to Thorstein Veblen's 1899 *Theory of the Leisure Class* in a 1902 article in *The Craftsman*, for example, the Syracuse University art critic Irene Sargent observed that "the ostentatious extravagance and display of the individual are the agents of rapid degeneration and decay in all that stands for good government and civilization" (quoted in Shi 178), not only glancing at The Decadence in the word "decay" but also invoking in the term "degeneration" the pathological reading of the arts that would have made the name of Max Nordau instantly recognizable to the reader of the *Harvard Advocate* editorial quoted above. First published in the United States in 1895 (and lately vigorously revived by historians who find its combination of bizarrerie and social commentary irresistible), *Degeneration* offered to diagnose the psycho-physiological ailments of writers who shared what Nordau called a *"fin-de-siècle"* sensibility, presenting analyses of figures like Nietzsche and Ibsen and naturally not omitting a chapter on "Decadents and Aesthetes," who are condemned specifically for nonproductivity. Having at one point cited with approval Paul Bourget's remark that a decadent society "produces too great a number of individuals unfit for the labours of common life" (quoted at 301), Nordau goes on to observe that Wilde typifies the aesthete in holding "inactivity" to be an "ideal of life," and supports his point with the very quote from "Pen, Pencil, and Poison" that contributes to this book's subtitle: "It is only the Philistine who seeks to estimate a personality by the vulgar test of production" (quoted at 319). For Nordau and for Sargent, degeneration was the consequence of an ostentatious consumption inseparable from a no less ostentatious refusal of production, both of which found their crucial cultural foothold in those literary works that showed, no matter their actual date of publication, the species of weariness that drew its name from an overtaxed century's imminent end.[4]

In his history of the American ideal of the simple life, David Shi quotes

Sargent's remark as one manifestation of a simplification movement vital throughout the United States during the Progressive era, an early instance of alliance between what we might call a green sensibility and a politics of economic justice: "The 'tyranny of things,'" Shi writes (incorporating a quote from a 1904 *Craftsman* article entitled "Duties of the Consumer"), had to "be attacked along with the tyrannies of trusts and boss rule" (176). Within this vogue, aestheticism itself occupied a profoundly contradictory position; for although acquisition in the mode of Huysmans went against the simplifying grain, the necessity of fastidiousness in the work of simplifying properly, along with the suspicion that the vulgar furnishings of arrivistes were conjunct with their bad morals, helped Ruskin and especially Morris (recognizably part of the aesthetic current) to new prestige. Indeed in the United States the Arts and Crafts Movement enjoyed its most expansive flowering after 1900, when through channels like *The Craftsman* it spread more widely than ever the news of interior decoration's role in building health and moral character, and attacked not so much a tyranny of things in general as the kind of cupidity that would wantonly embrace objects in bad taste and excessive number.

By rendering so visible the ease with which the aesthetic could be commodified, however, the Arts and Crafts vogue in another sense only enhanced the delicacy of art's position in the first years of the new century, when social critics were beginning to consider seriously the possibility that beauty and leisure were essentially rather than contingently linked, Ruskin's and Morris's dream of a beautification of the world across class lines notwithstanding. The critique of aesthetics as an epiphenomenon of conspicuous consumption that would take a more developed form later on in the century (in works such as Pierre Bourdieu's *Distinction*) was in fact initiated in *The Theory of the Leisure Class* itself, wherein Veblen observes that because the "cultivation of the aesthetic faculty requires time and application" it tends to change the gentleman's "life of leisure into a more or less arduous application of learning how to live a life of ostensible leisure in a becoming way" (64)—that is, to transform leisure into a form of production (or rather labor) without product. In *A Grammar of Motives,* Kenneth Burke, who was born in 1897, remarks that Santayana's "philosophy of serenity and retirement sounds expensive" and then recalls,

> As an adolescent, when I first read Santayana, I dreamed of a tourist life in white flannels along the Mediterranean. He still means to me something like that, though more circumstantially accurate: reading in the country, on a mild afternoon, after a bit of gardening, or a slow walk in the woods, perhaps with the sound of friends playing tennis in the distance. (216)

The demise of the possibility of maintaining a posture of heroic consumption made the pursuit of beauty seem questionable precisely to the degree that such a pursuit "sound[ed] expensive," where expense would refer to both time and money, to a tendency to compete with other productive projects and a foundation in material resources not available to all.

If consumption as the moral other of production grew highly suspect around the turn of the century in Britain and the United States, however, consumption as the using up of the already produced was the beneficiary of an enormous enthusiasm visible not only in "underconsumptionist" movements such as (eventually) Social Credit, but also in popular hortatory economics and, implicitly, in the very texture of the quotidian. As Miles Orvell has shown in his 1989 study of authenticity in American thinking, an "aesthetic of abundance" is "visible virtually everywhere one looks in the material culture" of the United States between 1873 and 1898, when "the capacities of production were in excess of the market's capacity to absorb goods" (42); and in his earlier pathbreaking work on the late nineteenth-century "loosening of the work ethic" (10), Lears calls attention to, among other texts, the 1907 *New Basis of Civilization*, wherein Simon Nelson Patten celebrates (as he had fifteen years earlier in his *Consumption of Wealth*) the possibilities of consumption in an economy that seemed to have left scarcity behind. Devoted to the project of nudging the lower classes toward happiness and sobriety, Patten writes in the later work that whereas "[b]ack to nature" education teaches "that beauty is in a medieval craftsmanship and ugliness in the machine-made object," an "education that strives to incorporate men into urban civilization gives them contact with men and inculcates respect for civic efficiency" (126). He then goes on to contrast the upper-class aesthetic of simplification to the working-class woman's desire "to add to the number of things," and to praise "the rapid cheapening of commodities" for gratifying "this primary aesthetic longing." One might frown, then, on the working-class home's crowding with "tawdry, unmeaning, and useless objects," but because "each pointless ornament is loved . . . as the mark of superiority and success, and its enjoyment energizes the possessor . . . the aesthetics of addition" should "be supplemented and not reduced" (139–40).

The turn of the century (in both the United States and Great Britain) thus witnessed the rise of something like a benevolently intended double standard among the more progressive privileged, according to which society would benefit from an increase in consumption on the part of the lower classes (where acquisition would assist in both the absorption of abundance and the improvement of behavior) and a decrease in consumption by the well-to-do (where consumption would imply the avoidance of production). If it is true, as Walter Benn Michaels argues, that in the writings of Charlotte Perkins Gilman "commitment to production is a commitment to production in the market," that in them "[f]armers' wives . . . go crazy because the work they do cannot become the empowering work Gilman wants them to do" (17), it is no less true that the urge to engage in this "natural expression of human energy" (3) was also felt by many members of the leisure class (and those who mingled with them, including Stevens), though the realm conferring value in this case was what we might call authentic life rather than the market as such. The conviction that "Times have changed, we must all do something!" had thus been gathering energy for several decades before Lewis formulated it so in *Time and Western Man*; and if such a conviction is detectable in the impulse to physicality that Lentricchia notes in Stevens and Santayana, it materializes still more potently in those turn-of-the-century Harvardians' mistrust of that which is not consumable in one sense (that is, incapable of being absorbed into the circuit of life) and too consumable in another (a distraction from production).

To put matters this way, of course, is fairly to recognize that the kind of thing most naturally poised to excite this mistrust could only be the work of art, whose shadowing by the suspicion that artists in general, not just aesthetes, ultimately fail to engage in true production we have seen attested not only by Stevens, Veblen, and Burke, but also by Woolf and Lewis (and to some extent Pound). We have already seen, that is to say, how a confrontation between the demands of the aesthetic and the imperative of production coalescing at the turn of the century proved influential for several writers who began their careers in earnest in the early or mid-1910s; and in the pages that follow we will consider how a still more striking and complex effect of this kind occurs in the case of Stevens, whom others tended to associate with high aestheticism for decades after the publication of his first and most Nineties collection, *Harmonium* (1923), and who even today remains for many the mauvest of modern poets (thanks largely to anthologists' tendency to draw heavily on that first book for their Stevens selections).

When Pound dismissed Stevens as a "retiring daisy esthete" (quoted in Filreis, *Modernism* 147) in 1935 he was voicing a sentiment whose diffusion had long been abetted even by Stevens's defenders, as for example Marianne Moore, who in a 1924 review of *Harmonium* in *The Dial* cited a passage from "The Comedian as the Letter C" after referring to "the riot of gorgeousness in which Mr. Stevens' imagination takes refuge" and observing that Stevens is "so wakeful . . . in his appetite for color and in perceiving what is needed to meet the requirements of a new tone key, that Oscar Wilde, Frank Alvah Parsons, Tappé, and John Murray Anderson seem children asleep in comparison with him" (21–22). In an article of the following year, meanwhile, Gorham Munson defended Stevens's "dandyism" by insisting that both Stevens and the true dandy are characterized by "correctness and elegance" rather than excess (41), and R. P. Blackmur could be found expanding upon this point even in 1932, arguing that the apparent "preciousness" of Stevens's vocabulary belies an absolutely precise diction (52–80). Perhaps the most characteristic response in this line, however, is a 1925 essay in which Paul Rosenfeld names *Harmonium* "one of the jewel boxes of contemporary verse," but only after observing that the volume does not entirely represent the day. . . . The characteristic note of 1890 was not outworn for us ten years ago; and yet, today, even though nothing in the basic character of life appears transformed . . . we have transcended it. We are somewhat less self-aware; and irritated by what tends to recall us to the old bad consciousness. (40)[5]

Rosenfeld's comment is the more resonant because it evokes closely Amy Lowell's (and others') response to Donald Evans, a friend of Stevens who aggressively promoted a decadent revival in the mid-1910s, wearing a monocle, drinking absinthe, and proclaiming that the "new spirit" of the decade would be the "true child of the brave and battlesome 'Yellow 90s' of England" (quoted in MacLeod 10; see also MacLeod 67–68). "You see I am such an elderly person that I lived during the 1890s. My twenty years saw the annual reappearance of 'The Yellow Book,'" Lowell told Evans in a letter of 1918 concerning his *Sonnets from the Patagonian*, "and these 'mauve joys ' and 'purple sins' were the very 'latest thing' during my adolescent period so that I must be pardoned for finding their manner somewhat dusty, and, indeed, a good deal like a cotillion favor resurrected from a bureau drawer. . . . I confess I think you are better than your pose" (quoted in Damon 458–59 and in part in MacLeod 10). This was the same Amy Lowell who four years later awarded first prize in a contest sponsored by the Poetry Society of South Carolina to an entry by Grace Hazard Conkling, while handing only an honorable mention to Stevens's "From the Journal of Crispin," which after some revision and the addition of two more sections to its original four would become "The Comedian as the Letter C."[6]

It does not require much perspicacity to see how "From the Journal" could have seemed a throwback to the decadent cotillion for the self-appointed custodian of Imagism, nor is there likely to be much serious opposition to the claim that, with the other notably gaudy lyrics in *Harmonium*, "The Comedian" constitutes the most direct and dazzling legacy of the Nineties to modern poetry. With its stylistic pyrotechnics and its weakness for coiffures and like ephemera, the poem (in either version) seems the quintessence of an exuberant aestheticism firmly displaced by the rather different ironies of modernism and hardly to be seen even in Stevens after the early 1920s. And yet this work—not a favorite of most Stevens critics by any means—merits some extended examination both for its decadence and for its modernity, because it demonstrates with unusual intricacy how, in reinventing aestheticism, modernists moved to negotiate both the production imperative and the fear that art might be deeply antithetical to life—a fear at once noted and repressed in the words with which Wilde concluded his American lecture on "The English Renaissance": "We spend our days looking for the secret of life. Well, the secret of life is art" (quoted in Ellmann 166).

After beginning "The Comedian" with a few lines of overwhelming dictional virtuosity, Stevens introduces the fastidious eye of his protagonist, Crispin, as follows:

An eye most apt in gelatines and jupes,
Berries of villages, a barber's eye,
An eye of land, of simple salad-beds,
Of honest quilts, the eye of Crispin, hung
On porpoises, instead of apricots,
And on silentious porpoises, whose snouts
Dibbled in waves that were mustachios,
Inscrutable hair in an inscrutable world.

One eats one paté, even of salt, quotha.

(Poems 27–28)

Embarking on his voyage from the Old World to the New, Crispin immediately attempts to translate his perceptions of the ocean into more familiar
terms—not, perhaps, the most surprising way of crossing the Atlantic, and
yet significant because it affiliates creativity in seeing to an inherited culture
evidently characterized by a certain love of creature comforts but hard to
define further with any certainty. At the beginning of Stevens's first georgic
(which is also, arguably, his first and last epic), in other words, the inspired
perception that will form a cornerstone of his program for the poet in a
secular society appears not only under the sign of European inheritances, but
also under those of coiffure ("a barber's eye," "mustachios") and cuisine
("apricots," "paté"), those minor arts that Santayana had excluded even from
his enlarged definition of poetry.

The apricot is particularly suggestive in this context because Stevens
would still be associating that subtle fruit with a dangerous aestheticism
twenty years later: in the 1940 "Extracts from Addresses to the Academy of
Fine Ideas," he mentions a "maker of catastrophe" who "invents the eye /
And through the eye equates ten thousand deaths / With a single well-tem-
pered apricot, or, say, / An egg-plant of good air" (*Poems* 253). Written
specifically against the aestheticizing of war (a temptation to which Stevens
himself was scarcely immune), the passage inevitably implies a criticism of
the post-Paterian aesthetic attitude in general, which in its radical privileging
of experience or perception could be said to invite, at an extreme, the equat-
ing of an apricot as visual stimulus with the no less stimulating spectacle of
ten thousand deaths. And even if not guilty of this kind of leveling in perception, Crispin on his first appearance nonetheless seems to suffer from a
certain decadent laxity in which sensuous consumption grows so absorbing
as to render the consumer passive before the march of events, Stevens's
syntax repeatedly mixing Crispin's eye into the list of things it observes, and
his diction leaving that eye hanging on those things as though deprived of
substantive control.

Yet the apricot is an ambivalent image, as a glass of absinthe or a cravat,
say, would not be, because juxtaposed to "simple salad-beds" it can be rural
and humble rather than urban and urbane. Viewed from this angle, Crispin

could have less to do with polished and excessive consumption than with the simple life more or less going out of fashion again at the time "The Comedian" was written: no connoisseur of blue china or hothouse flowers, he has an eye rather for "honest quilts" and "simple salad-beds"; as a "general lexicographer of mute / And maidenly greenhorns" he seems to have little in common with the painter of the "mauve joys" and "purple sins" that were the latest thing during the adolescence of Amy Lowell. And yet on the other hand (again), this eye of simple salad-beds is also a barber's (if not a hairdresser's) eye, one that discerns mustachios in the waves and, moreover, comes attached to a lexicographer of mute greenhorns who may be a little too much at ease with words like "silentious." On his debut, in short, Crispin seems suspended somewhere between ironized dandyism and the apotheosis of simplification, an authentically ambiguous descendant of the protagonists of Stevens's Harvard short stories.

What enriches and complicates matters here is the fact that Crispin will, famously, grow into a poet on the model of that celebrated celebrant of local plenitude, William Carlos Williams. Read in the context of this later development, these early lines delicately call attention to the continuity between aestheticism's nuanced discriminations and modern poetry's emphasis on the accurate presentation of the object in verse, highlighting how both depend upon a privileging of discerning seeing ("an eye most apt") and hence upon something like a moralization of connoisseurship. This continuity is curiously reinforced, if at the same time obscured, by the very belatedness with which Crispin's poetic calling or avocation is revealed to the reader, the only references to his writing in the first part of "The Comedian" being his designation as "lexicographer" and the observation that in the immensity of the sea the imagination "could not evade / In poems of plums, the strict austerity / Of one vast, subjugating, final tone" (30). Stevens only makes clear that such poems probably belong to Crispin in the succeeding section, when he refers to his protagonist's "couplet yearly to the spring" and, shortly after, to "the fables that he scrawled / With his own quill" (31), so that what we have seen to be a characteristic modernist shift in emphasis from sensuous consumption to artistic production, from aesthetic experience to its fixing in verse, takes place with a significant absence of fanfare here, as though to suggest that in Crispin's world (or our own) poetry might flow inevitably from an eye for the exquisite.

Given the fantastic allegorical atmosphere of this poem, however, Stevens hardly needed to restrict himself to such veiled indications, and indeed poetic production proves ubiquitous in Crispin's New World in a quite literal sense: the first four sections of "The Comedian" feature virtually no characters except poets, which means that "From the Journal of Crispin," which terminates with section four, has what we might call an all-poet cast. The subject of that fourth section, moreover, is Crispin's dream of a writers' "colony" that would span the Americas from "[f]rom the big-rimmed snow-star over Canada / To the dusk of a whistling south below the south," his vision of a New World inhabited by a race of poets "more true / To its begetting than its patriarch, / A race obedient to its origins / And from the obstinate scrutiny of its land . . . Evolving the conjectural resonance of voice" (*Opus* 57, 56).[7] In Crispin's colony, poetry would continue to flow from inspired seeing, but the process would require active absorption—"obstinate scrutiny"—rather than passive imposition, an intense examination of what is before the eye combined with a vigilant exclusion of the European precedents that are not: "The dark Brazilian in his red café, / Musing immaculate, pampean dits, / Shall scrawl a vigilant anthology, / Not based on Camoëns, but flushed and full" (*Opus* 58).

In the case of Crispin himself, who as of section three becomes a resident of the Carolinas, this obstinate scrutiny focuses on the "rude aesthetic" of a virile quotidian emblematized initially by "rancid rosin, burly smells / Of dampened lumber, emanations blown / From warehouse doors, the gustiness of ropes, / Decays of sacks" (*Opus* 54), though it quickly and strikingly evolves to encompass "shops of chandlers, tailors, bakers, cooks, / The Coca Cola-bars, the barber-poles" (*Opus* 55, 54) as well as "the florist asking aid from cabbages" (*Opus* 56)—which is to say that Stevens here restores Santayana's minor arts of cuisine ("cooks"), hairdressing ("barber-poles"), and flower arranging ("florist") to poetry even as he masculinizes them by association. He continues:

If poems are transmutations of plain shops,
By aid of starlight, distance, wind, war, death,
Are not these doldrums poems in themselves,
These trophies of wind and war? At just what point
Do barber-poles become burlesque or cease
To be? . . .
. . . .
. . . The flimsiest tea room fluctuates
Through crystal changes.

(*Opus* 55)

Linked to the "[g]reen barbarism" that Crispin had sought in section two (*Opus* 49) through the homonymy of "barber-poles," to the rugged world of bad smells by their inclusion within the rude aesthetic, and to the world of momentous masculine action through the transmutation of war, these "doldrums" become "poems in themselves" not as arts capable of building out of "living but indefinite material . . . new structures . . . truer to the ultimate possibilities of the soul," to use Santayana's formulation, but by serving as that living but indefinite material itself. The connotations of excess or luxury that would render cuisine, coiffure, and floral displays per se suspect, in other words, are here suppressed as the baker and company are knit into the fabric of a commercial quotidian that looks like the very antithesis of conspicuous consumption. And yet in its very ordinariness, this humble commerce offers something new: "The bars infect / the sensitive"; Crispin's researches "purify. They make him see how much / Of what he sees he never sees at all"; and this "essential prose" becomes "[t]he one integrity for him, the one / Discovery still possible to make, / To which all poems are incident, unless / That prose should wear a poem's guise at last" (*Opus* 55). This quotidian appears as a new world to (the Williamsesque) Crispin in a double sense, then, not only constituting the essential life of a new continent but also presenting to poetry a territory hitherto unexplored.

In "From the Journal," this redemption of the barber-poles occurs in conjunction with the more prominent redemption of Crispin's barber's eye, which becomes the pivot of a culminating synonymy between the expression of America and the expression of the individual American self. The conclusion of the poem tells how Crispin "requires this end: / The book shall discourse of himself alone, / Of what he was, and why, of his place, / And of its fitful pomp and parentage" (*Opus* 59), so that the poet at last proves the subject of the poem, but with the Whitmanian twist that to discourse of "himself alone" is also to discourse of his place—a moral for which Stevens has prepared the reader in his vision of a colony-continent of poets: "The man / in Mississippi, waking among pines, / Shall be pine-spokesman" (*Opus* 57). Once again, the passage from aestheticism to modernism is enacted as a turn from the consumption of beauty or experience to the production of a transcript (the "journal" whose pages the reader here peruses), and it is the existence of this production that finally confirms the barber's eye's possession of what Stevens would later call a barbarous strength. Or rather: not this production's *mere* existence, but the fact that this existence is indelibly marked as socially freighted via the "idea of a colony," with its intimation that an authentically political dimension inheres in the objectification of self and region. It is thus—through an elision of the boundaries among poet, poem, and place—that "From the Journal" (the most expansive statement on the role and possibilities of poetry to be found in Stevens's early work) moves to counter the "art all alone, detached, sensuous for the sake of sensuousness" that the young Stevens had condemned.

It follows, however, that if the usefulness or validity of the transcript of self and region should somehow fall into doubt, art in general might once again be deprived of its rationale—and indeed this is precisely what happens in "The Comedian," that astounding work of revision in which one of the century's most exuberant advocates of poetry concludes that poetry may be no necessity after all. The turn begins near the very start of the fifth section (the first of the two added to "From the Journal"), as Crispin's ability to record the land is compromised by the land's sheer sensuous power:

Crispin dwelt in the land and dwelling there
Slid from his continent by slow recess
To things within his actual eye, alert
To the difficulty of rebellious thought
When the sky is blue. The blue infected will.

(Poems 40)

When "[t]he bars infect / the sensitive" in "From the Journal," the result is poetry; when the blue infects the will in "The Comedian," the result is poetry's dissolution. If the stealthy appearance of Crispin's writing in the first sections of the poem made the transcription of experience seem the inevitable result of sensitive seeing, this passage quite oppositely suggests that one with a truly sensitive eye might find the will to transcribe sapped by the very intensity of perception—and, further, that the problem might be especially serious in this New World, against whose sensuous riches the mind would have no preformed poetic structures to deploy. In this regard it is worth noting that Stevens excised the concluding reference to the book discoursing of Crispin and his place as he transformed "From the Journal" into "The Comedian," not only replaying in an American context Pater's adumbration of a conflict between perception and production ("With this sense of the splendour of our experience and of its awful brevity . . . we shall hardly have time to make theories about the things we see and touch" [*Writings* 61]) but also suggesting that Santayana's interest in the active dimension of aesthetic experience might be especially *inappropriate* to the overwhelming continent upon which that refined expatriate wrote the books that made him famous.

Nor does Stevens halt at calling into question the validity of the poetic transcript of America; for in constructing an anticipatory allegory of his own withdrawal from writing during the period from 1924 to 1930 (in favor of child rearing and the insurance career that supported this domestic life), he takes pains to suggest that there may be a basic conflict between writing and life itself. Asking if Crispin should "[s]crawl a tragedian's testament" or "[p]rolong / His active force in an inactive dirge," if he should "lay by the personal and make / Of his own fate an instance of all fate" (*Poems* 41), Stevens implies that the answer to these questions is simply no, choosing in preference to the singing of death the conceiving of children, which figures as a virtual silence that says a deeper sooth than the truest expression: "[s]o deep a sound fell down it grew to be / A long soothsaying silence down and down" (42). The last sections of the poem leave Crispin in a humble existence not so different from that in which he began (he turns "to his simple salad-beds again," he builds a cabin), but whereas in sections one and two he was characterized by an apt eye that assisted in the poetic reproduction of self, he now serves an overwhelmed eye whose consequence is a "midwifery so dense / His cabin counted as phylactery," the children in the cabin replacing the sacred writing in its casket. At the close of the poem, he appears as the "[e]ffective colonizer sharply stopped / In the door-yard by his own capacious bloom" (44), this remarkable allusion to Whitman's elegy suggesting not only that Crispin's poetry has been halted by the birth of children but also that Whitman's had been strengthened by the death of Lincoln—and thus (once again) that what proves most antithetical to poetry is life. The poem concludes wittily, "So may the relation of each man be clipped," the modal auxiliary leaving open the question of whether Crispin's fate does turn out to be an instance of all fate, but admitting no doubt that, in this barber-adventurer's epic at least, poetic ambition has been crowded out decisively by "[d]aughters with [c]urls" (43).

Such a rejection of the poet's struggle for greatness has been predictably infuriating to satanic romantics such as Harold Bloom (who names the daughters "grotesque" [*Wallace Stevens* 82]), but it is important to see that this rejection constitutes only one aspect of a far wider and more suggestive reappraisal of production undertaken here. In the finale of "The Comedian," domestic coiffure displaces not only the writing of poetry but also the barber-poles of "From the Journal," and in this instantiates a more general displacement of commerce by agrarian self-sufficiency in the new poem— Stevens's largest excision from the earlier version, in fact, being that of Crispin's tour of "chandlers, tailors, bakers, cooks, / The Coca Cola-bars, the barber-poles / The Strand and Harold Lloyd, the lawyers' row, / The Citizens' Bank, two tea rooms, and a church" (*Opus* 54). The only remnant of the commercial quotidian to be found in "The Comedian" is the trade whose signifiers (warehouse doors, ropes, sacks, rosin) Crispin encounters dockside, and even these are notably left behind in sections five and six, as Crispin plunges into farming and a family unit so self-contained as to admit no need for other people (saving the "duenna" who brings Crispin's spouse). By the end of "The Comedian," in short, Crispin has found both commercial and poetic transactions emphatically extraneous to his existence in the New World—not because barber-poles and poetry have necessarily proven incapable of leading to Santayana's "ultimate possibilities of the soul," but rather because it seems to Stevens that (unlike domesticity, organic cycles, and the raw experience of blue sky) they can be pared away without damaging the essential life that he seeks.

By itself, certainly, Crispin's trajectory from possible aesthete to observer of a pleasant "metropole" to self-sufficient farmer suggests how an initial discomfort with painfully exquisite living could expand to embrace, in the end, everything foreign to a fairly narrow vision of the simple life; and yet something else is indicated by the fact that the rejection of even humble instances of capitalist culture here is intertwined with an abandoning of poetry premised on redundancy, not on luxury as such. It is not, after all, that

Crispin gives up poetry because it seems a guilty pleasure or dangerous indulgence (on the contrary, it is his turn away from poetry that results from the "infected will"); the problem is rather that the poetic transcript seems an unnecessary duplicate of a continent already beautifully articulated and a life already complete. This implies in turn that commerce may be less appealing than the agricultural ideal not because of its tendency toward opulence per se, but because it seems more likely than the self-sustaining farm to give rise to things that, like Crispin's poetic transcript, wind up with no place amid the currents of authentic life. The difficulty, in other words, may inhere in the fact that the commercial system, which often brings its wares into the world before their users are perfectly identified, appears predisposed to generate items that go unconsumed, products that fall out of the production-consumption circuit, residues at last affiliated not with the cyle of life but with the immobility of death.

We might recall, in this context, that when the undergraduate Stevens looked for a term appropriate to art that fails to provide "a service, a food," the word that he came up with was "rubbish"; and we might note too that it was Stevens who would later write what is surely the century's most memorable poem on what to make of collected refuse, "The Man on the Dump." There is a partial irony, then, in the fact that Stevens is widely remembered as the poet of verbal extravagance, since of all the modernists he may have been the one who found extravagance in the sense of waste (though emphatically not in that of richness) most deeply unsettling. True, Pound too shows important anxieties about things that go unused, but as we have seen these arise from a combination of regret on behalf of forgotten objects and fears that overproduction might lead to the end of production itself, where production (at least in principle) remains a good. Stevens's reservations, on the other hand, seem premised on a discomfort with residue as such, a discomfort that discloses, among other things, how Santayana's installation of consumption at the center of the aesthetic constitutes not just an extension of Pater's gospel of experience, but also an early or anticipatory strike against the charge that artists produce useless junk (and therefore, once again, fail to become producers in any meaningful sense). Santayana and Stevens, that is to say, responded to the same post-Nineties crisis of legitimacy that occupied Woolf and Eliot, but in a nearly opposite manner; for whereas the latter rested their defense of art on the image of the great work as monument to human achievement, the former (who in this partake of a characteristically American willingness to embrace disposability, where necessary, on behalf of utility) specifically stressed art's immersion in life as against the repose of an artifact that never fails to gesture to its own gratuitousness. One of the morals of Crispin's final turn, therefore, is that there were good reasons why at least one modernist could *not* find a secure purpose for the individual life in the production of solidly enduring objects—or rather could advance such a possibility only for the briefest of intervals (in this case, between the transcription of self and place that closes "From the Journal" and the revisions of "The Comedian") before withdrawing it.

All this said, it is worth remembering that the analogy between Crispin's story and Stevens's own falters, in point of historical validity, precisely with respect to the possibility of self-sustenance and self-containment, the painful truth being that the energy of the American 1920s was not the energy of a Jeffersonian state, nor Stevens's white-collar provision for his family some departure from the loop of commerce. Even as he wrote this poem, Stevens was well aware that it was becoming decreasingly possible for its pastoral idyll to materialize in real life, and it is this diminishing that gives "The Comedian" a faint *tristesse* evocative of other agrarian nostalgias of the early twentieth century, a feeling of loss quite apart from that associated with its protagonist's abandoning of his poetic career. Indeed the denouement of "The Comedian" is nothing if not a combination of autobiography and flight from reality, a sort of diary entry overlaid with fantasies of escape from the relentless urbanization that imbues even Crispin's "metropole," Coca-Cola and Harold Lloyd included, with the charm of the vanishing small. In the sections that follow, we will see Stevens moving to release poetry, at least, from the problem of production by conceiving of poetic objectification as an abstract or immaterial process; but it is clear that no such efforts could meaningfully address the problem of large-scale production under modernity. If the fates of poetry and commercial production should really be conjoined, as Crispin's story might be taken to imply, then the forecast of "The Comedian" would be not the end of American poetry, but rather its expansion into continents and colonies of which Crispin, even in his most robust fancies, could hardly have dared dream.

IMPOSING FORMS

By the early 1930s, the specific doubts about the possibility of uniting art and life that govern "The Comedian" had themselves come to seem an evasion of life properly understood: Stevens's second volume, *Ideas of Order* (poems of 1930 through 1936), is thick with the sense that the poet may not be entitled simply to live, or to live simply, in a time defined by the miseries that attend a complex society. As James Longenbach observes, the Stevens of the thirties would confront the fact that Crispin's rejection of "both the apocalypse of the isolated self and the apocalypse of a culture's demise" could leave one exposed to an "opposite blindness should the real catastrophe occur," the fact that his choice of "a social and comic vision . . . over the tragedian's lonely fate" might prove dangerous in a world in which the comedy of domesticity could only come to seem the archetype of the "social" under a willed repression of grim public realities (*Wallace Stevens* 93, 97, 93). It was this Stevens who wrote of his poem "Mozart, 1935," "[I]t expresses something that I have very much at heart, and that is: the status of the poet in a disturbed society, or, for that matter, in any society" (*Letters* 292), and it is this Stevens whose richness and subtlety scholarship has notably moved to restore to us in recent years—which has meant supplementing or even replacing the retiring daisy esthete and the satanic-Romantic hero of the imagination with the figure of quite another kind of poet.

In the most famous review of any of Stevens's volumes, the Marxist critic Stanley Burnshaw effectively concurred with Stevens's assessment of "Mozart," describing *Ideas* as "a considered record of agitated attitudes toward the present social order" (Longenbach, *Wallace Stevens* 142), though he pointed out that these attitudes had not necessarily aligned themselves with what he would consider a correct political tendency, or indeed with any tendency whatever. The lesson of some of the poems of *Ideas*, however, is that agitated attitudes can themselves constitute a kind of politics, a lesson especially pertinent in the early 1930s, when brutal impositions of order were supported by anxieties about what seemed an unprecedented and portentous chaos in societies worldwide. The poem "Sad Strains of a Gay Waltz," for example, seems inevitably to carry prescriptive implications in describing

. . . these sudden mobs of men,

These sudden clouds of faces and arms,
An immense suppression, freed,
These voices crying without knowing for what,

Except to be happy, without knowing how,
Imposing forms they cannot describe,
Requiring order beyond their speech.

Too many waltzes have ended. Yet the shapes
For which the voices cry, these, too, may be
Modes of desire, modes of revealing desire.

Too many waltzes—The epic of disbelief
Blares oftener and soon, will soon be constant.
Some harmonious skeptic soon in a skeptical music

Will unite these figures of men and their shapes
Will glisten again with motion, the music
Will be motion and full of shadows.

(*Poems* 121–22)

Whether or not "Sad Strains" was directed primarily at the domestic left, as Burnshaw appears to have thought (Filreis, *Modernism* 218), it was clearly written partly out of a feeling that the politics most vitally responsive to the social turmoil of the era was to be found not at home but overseas, a feeling that if one government in the world was showing "motion," however full of shadows, that government was Mussolini's. This was a feeling common enough in the early and middle thirties even among those Americans who would have thought themselves politically moderate, although as Alan Filreis has recently shown, the editorial position of Stevens's local paper (the *Hartford Courant*) suggests that the poet's "immediate social environment must have been a good deal more hostile to Italian fascism . . . than national surveys indicate" (*Modernism* 25). In 1935, the year in which he wrote "Sad Strains," Stevens commented in an increasingly infamous letter, "But that Mussolini is right, practically, has certainly a great deal to be said for it. . . . Fascism is a form of disillusionment with about everything else. I do not believe it to be a stage in the evolution of the state; it is a transitional phase. The misery that underlies fascism would probably be much vaster, much keener, under any other system in the countries involved at the present time" (*Letters* 295). By the end of the decade, of course, fascist regimes had come to be perceived as practical enemies (in a letter of April 1939, Stevens refers to "so much of Hitler and Mussolini so drastically on one's nerves" [*Letters* 337]), but in the mid-thirties even a fairly hollow heroic rhetoric could sound promising—indeed promising, for someone like Stevens, precisely *because* rhetoric, and as such a shaping of inarticulate longings, "modes of desire, modes of revealing desire."[8]

Stevens's phrasing here indicates lucidly how his understanding of the function of wrought language—be it poetic, demagogic, or that combination of the two about which so much of his poetry from this period circles—had changed since "The Comedian." In the third and fourth sections of that poem, Stevens had called for the transcription of diverse localities and selves in an expressive poetry, but this way of thinking about poetic production had only provided fodder for the palinode of sections five and six, wherein poetry lost the competition between itself and the place that it was to represent in part because, as a duplicate textual body, it could only stand in uneasy relation to the already bodied continent. "Sad Strains," on the other hand, calls for an ordering of desire that, via the figure of giving "shape" to what has gone unarticulated, modulates into an objectification of what does not yet quite exist—not the transcript of a place but the originary reification of a people's (or the people's) longings. It is clear from Stevens's phrasing ("modes of desire, modes of revealing desire"), moreover, that this objectification of longing is itself longed for, as though the need for an object onto which subjective feelings can be projected might be a basic human need—a point Stevens might well have inherited from Santayana's earlier aesthetics, which imply that without such objects we would experience only unfixed pleasures, not the feeling of beauty that seems at times to console by justifying existence itself: "[W]hen the process of perception itself is pleasant . . . then we have a pleasure intimately bound up in the thing. . . . It becomes . . . a quality of the object, which we distinguish from pleasures not so incorporated in the perception of things, by giving it the name of beauty"; "when the world so shapes itself or so moulds the mind that the correspondence between them is perfect, then perception is pleasure, and existence needs no apology" (*Sense* 33, 166).

In "A Duck for Dinner," part of his long and complex 1936 meditation on the role of the poet in society, *Owl's Clover*, Stevens presents even more explicitly his half-skeptical admiration for the demagogue, writing of a "pebble-chewer practiced in Tyrian speech" who

Confounds all opposites and spins a sphere
Created, like a bubble, of bright sheens,
With a tendency to bulge as it floats away.

. . . .

Yet to think of the future is a genius,
To think of the future is a thing and he
That thinks of it is inscribed on walls and stands
Complete in bronze on enormous pedestals.

(*Opus* 93–94)

"To think of the future is a thing": the production of even an imagined objectification of possibility or desire is itself, somehow, an object, and one that transforms the imaginer into a colossus whether or not one feels contempt for the particulars of his imaginative "sphere" (a contempt betrayed in the bathos of "bubble" and reinforced by the "tendency to bulge"). Even his own and America's eventual turn against the actual fascist regimes did not radically alter Stevens's thinking on this matter, for in 1940 he could still write, explaining "A Duck," that "he that imagines the future and, by imagining it, creates it, is a creator of genius and stands on enormous pedestals" and even that the "base of every future" associated with the pebble chewer is poetry (*Letters* 372). We may be inclined to agree with Walton Litz's assertion that it "is a sign of Stevens' uncertainty in *Owl's Clover* that he can seriously consider" the pebble–chewer, "some poetic Huey Long, as a possible and acceptable deformation of the imagination" (222–23); and yet we must also recognize that Stevens never really disowned his sense that demagogue and poet are linked as producers of public objectifications of a community's desires, though in subsequent years he would become more attentive, at least implicitly, to the question of what the community does with those objectifications once formed.

The 1940 letter does indicate one basic difference between its author's hopes for the poet and his more mixed admiration for the artful politician, however, even as it clarifies the difference between his own brand of interest in Mussolini and the investments of others such as Pound. In another passage, Stevens comments with ironic extravagance, "If the future . . . comes to nothing, sha'n't we be looking round for some one superhuman to put us together again, some prodigy capable of measuring sun and moon, some one who, if he is to dictate our fates, had better be inhuman, so that we shall know that he is without any of our weaknesses and cannot fail?" (*Letters* 372). The difference between Pound and Stevens is, clearly, one between an unironic hero worship and an exuberant cynicism, and it is predicated on a more profound difference between a faith that apparently opaque language can serve as an extrarational means for communication among members of a gifted elite (Pound) and a quite different understanding according to which language can be used to order the masses by virtue of another sort of *Dinglichkeit*, a quality of embodying previously unarticulated desires. Whereas the ideogrammic Pound found in a text's thingly character the measure of its truth, where truth would mean adequacy to fact, the Stevens of the same period saw in discourse considered as objectification the achievement of a truth adequate to desire, which may or may not be "true" to present conditions in the world at large.

In the broadest sense, these formulations suggest a certain comfort on Stevens's part with the fact of "ideology" as we have come to think of it since Althusser, which is to say with a sense that "the imaginary relationship of individuals to their real conditions of existence" (Althusser's famous phrase; 162) itself takes on a functional reality as it both forms and is formed by the subject. But the specific historical phenomenon with which Stevens's model resonates most closely is the aestheticization of politics that the Frankfurt School regarded as one of the key innovations of Hitler's Germany, a procedure crucially mediated by a naturalization of aesthetic manipulation no less emphatic than Stevens's own, a vision of art as the accomplishment of nature premised—as Philippe Lacoue-Labarthe has shown (66–70)—on something like a Heideggerian notion of *techne* (making conducted in accordance with the imperatives of Being). It would be fair to say, in fact, that the truth of fiction is no less a political truth for Stevens than it is in the scenarios of Althusser and Lacoue-Labarthe, or at least that it originates as such in those remarkable writings of the thirties in which Stevens justifies collective fictions by naturalizing the desire for ordering objectifications.

In *Ideas of Order* itself, this latter naturalizing is most forcefully undertaken by the poem that gives the volume its title, the 1934 "Idea of Order at Key West," in which a woman singing on the shore prompts the exclamation, "Oh! Blessed rage for order . . . / The maker's rage to order words of the sea," a condensation of an earlier claim that

The song and water were not medleyed sound
Even if what she sang was what she heard
Since what she sang was uttered word by word.

(Poems 128)

There is no doubt that the singer is to be considered a creator of some kind: the poet goes on to observe that she "was the single artificer of the world / In which she sang," calls her a "maker," and notes that "there never was a world for her, / Except the one she sang and, singing, made" (128, 129–30). But it is also clear that her accomplishment can be viewed as a sequencing of words somehow already present in nature (not the book of the divine, but the disordered heap of a book's materials), just as the "shapes" provided by the harmonious skeptic of "Sad Strains" can be seen as a giving of "order beyond their [the mobs'] speech." Whether one regards human making in this poem as a conquest of nature or an achievement of harmony with it, Stevens leaves no doubt that it draws its materials from the natural world instead of producing them *ex nihilo*—so that in this poem, as in the adaptation of *techne* explored by Lacoue-Labarthe, the naturalizing of a fiction includes an appeal to the authority of nature itself.

If in *Ideas of Order* the expressions of person and place once joined in "The Comedian" are split into the sequencing of the physical world's utterances in "Key West," on the one hand, and the articulation of mass desire in "Sad Strains," on the other, the effect of these poems' inclusion in the same volume, a single "record of agitated attitudes," is nonetheless to suggest a continuity between the two activities, and thus to complete the work of naturalization in question. If in *To the Lighthouse* the association between Lily's landscape painting and the exorcism of Mrs. Ramsay calls attention to art's manner of subjugating the object world, a reverse effect occurs here: lacking some equivalent of Woolf's attempt to think from the object side in "Time Passes," *Ideas* does not so much raise questions about the subject's impositions on the object world as lend the authority of natural process to both the masses' desire *for* shape and the leader's desire *to* shape. If the triumph of the harmonious skeptic's will comes encoded in the anaphora of the final tercet of "Sad Strains" ("Will unite . . . / Will glisten . . . / Will be motion . . ."), this will is rendered less drily political by the invocations, in "Key West," of a "maker's *rage* to order," with that word's connotations of uncalculating passion, and of an "[a]rranging, deepening, enchanting" that makes magical the quotidian.

This is not say, however, that *Ideas* fails altogether to remark the more troubling aspects of the craving for order. A more immediately disturbing naturalization appears in "Anglais Mort à Florence," also from 1935, in which a protagonist who has lost the sense of the wholeness that he had once felt, "the pale coherences of moon and mood / When he was young," turns to his once-loved Brahms, "us[ing] his reason" and "exercis[ing] his will" to tell himself:

> He was that music and himself.
> They were particles of order, a single majesty:
> But he remembered the time when he stood alone.
>
> He stood at last by God's help and the police;
> But he remembered the time when he stood alone.
> He yielded himself to that single majesty;
>
> But he remembered the time when he stood alone,
> When to be and delight to be seemed to be one,
> Before the colors deepened and grew small.

(Poems 148–49)

The importance of the penultimate tercet's first line is suggested by the fact that Stevens had originally called the poem "God and the Police," explaining in a later letter that if "men have nothing external to them on which to rely, then, in the event of a collapse of their own spirit, they must naturally turn to the spirit of others. I don't mean conventions: police" (*Letters* 348). Stevens shows his mistrust of God as solacing illusion nowhere more forcefully than in *Ideas of Order*, and in "Anglais" the solace of an order politically imposed (on Florence and the rest of Italy) seems scarcely more attractive; indeed this poem seems the least positive reflection on the urge to order in the whole volume, all that rage and harmonious skepticism here reduced (literally, if "stood" is to be taken literally) to a mere crutch.

In the context of the several other poems in *Ideas* that use music as a figure for an ordering that is also an embodying, this poem's transformation of music into an object irrecoverably separate from the self becomes especially poignant: desire as well as its articulation seem to escape in this diminished world, as though the forms of "Sad Strains" have, in this one man's life at least, already come and gone. Even more explicitly than the others, "Anglais" presents the reaching after order as a compensation, in this case a compensation for loss of a wholeness at least arguably universal in human experience—one that we might compare ontogenetically to the psychoanalytic pre-Oedipal (or to what Freud in *Civilization and its Discontents* calls the primary ego-feeling) or phylogenetically to that seamless oneness of people and earth that Woolf imagines (in "Anon") as the wellspring of poetry until the advent of printing. Indeed "Anglais" suggests that the deeper source of the longing for objectifications is a hope that one might repair the division between self and world by finding something of oneself within that world—a moon, even if an ersatz one, to cohere with internal mood. With its reference to the police, "Anglais" unites this compensatory urge with the political urge to order, Stevens here keeping the perils of such a linkage before the reader by presenting the police not as an attractive remedy for the situation of consciousness but as something like an inevitable (and in this sense natural) recourse in a sublunary in which everything at last gets away from one, an inevitable consequence of our severing from the realm of objects.[9]

The lyrics of *Ideas* were not the first in which Stevens contemplated the division between subject and object or mind and world, of course; he had already done so in many of the entries in *Harmonium*, perhaps most famously in the 1921 trio of "The Snow Man," "Tea at the Palaz of Hoon," and "The Man Whose Pharynx Was Bad." *Ideas* did, however, mark the first appearance of a sustained interest in how the transactions between consciousness and physical "reality" so congenial to his curiosity might be analogized to engagement with social reality, as well as the first strong illustrations of his tendency to shift from the unknowable object world to the infinitely complex world of politics and human suffering, and vice versa, at the most decisive junctures. This is to say that if *Ideas* has provided scholarship its most important opening for the recovery of Stevens as poet of social reflection, it also marks the commencement of negotiations, within the poetry itself, between this Stevens and the one so recently displaced from the center of critical attention, the epistemological puzzler who provoked decades' worth of debate about whether he was essentially a poet of imagination or a poet of reality.[10]

In the books of the half decade following *Ideas*—*The Man with the Blue Guitar*, *Parts of a World*, and *Notes toward a Supreme Fiction*—Stevens would ever more decisively affiliate his reflections on the individual and society to an existential divide between consciousness and matter, or (to put things a little more precisely) ever more readily refer the need for objectifications of desire to a transhistorical alienation of the subject from the object world. The long title poem of the first of these volumes, "The Man with the Blue Guitar" (1937), for example, begins with the question of how the poet might capture the masses in song, the people demanding of the guitarist that he play "a tune beyond us, yet ourselves, / A tune . . . / Of things exactly as they are," the poet-musician responding with "a hero's head, large eye / And bearded bronze" (*Poems* 165); but after about six cantos Stevens seems to abandon the question of how to represent the tribe in favor of reflections on poetry's commerce with the material world. By canto XXII, he can be found glossing the most explicitly doctrinal lines of the poem—"Poetry is the subject of the poem, / From this the poem issues and / To this returns. Between the two, / Between issue and return, there is / An absence in reality, / Things as they are. Or so we say" (176)—with a note that the poem acquires its "true appearances . . . sun's green, / Cloud's red, earth feeling, sky that thinks" (177) from reality—which has thus become, indisputably, a physical rather than a social phenomenon.

Stevens effects this critical slippage from human reality to nonhuman principally at two points in "Man," cantos XI and XVI. In XI, the move from a reality of people to one of things proceeds through a shrewd conflation of the inanimate's power to injure the animate with the process in which the latter actually becomes the former, that of dying:

> Slowly the ivy on the stones
> Becomes the stones. Women become
>
> The cities, children become the fields
> And men in waves become the sea.
>
> It is the chord that falsifies.
> The sea returns upon the men,
>
> The fields entrap the children. . . .

> (171)

This canto's references to the inanimate's power to bring misery upon the living are then expanded in XVI, wherein the earth becomes "not earth but a stone . . . not / The mother" of humans but an "oppressor that grudges them their death, / As it grudges the living that they live" (173). The stage is then set for a revelation of the redemptive power of poetry, Stevens going on to suggest in the succeeding cantos that poetry's work is to make the world the earth again, reconciling the stone (which includes not only nature but also a human-made material reality evocative of Sartre's practico-inert: "Women become / The cities") to humans and humans to the stone through the freshening of perception. In XXII, as we have just seen, the appearance that poetry draws from reality includes a "sky that thinks," and in XXX–XXXI "Oxidia, banal suburb" becomes "the seed / Dropped out of this amber-ember pod . . . the soot of fire . . . Olympia" (182) in the poet's "rhapsody of things as they are" (183). The four-stage logic of the poem is, therefore: (1) reality equals the people demanding to be reproduced in poetry; (2) reality equals the people equals the object world (since, in XI, women become cities and so on); (3) reality equals the object world, which seems to oppress people; (4) the poet's job is to reconcile people to the object world, or reality.

Looking at the passage from *Ideas* to "Man," certainly, we might well trace a crude analogy between American anxieties in the political sphere and Stevensian anxieties in the phenomenological or epistemological: if in *Ideas* Stevens staked much on a parallel between natural disorder and the political disorder of the thirties, he seems here to take up a rhetoric of us versus them (suitable to wartime patriotism) that aligns the foreign human enemy with a now foreign world. Finally far more significant than this correspondence, however, is the simple fact that in the course of "Man" Stevens transfers the question of misery from the political or intersubjective domain to that of subject-object relations, not so much erasing the social as subordinating it to the unconscious brutality of the inanimate, and thus confirming with unusual directness how germane to his oeuvre generally is Bloom's observation that in "The Man Whose Pharynx Was Bad" nature is "*ethos* or Fate, a universe of death" (51). In so doing, of course, Stevens graphs his own trajectory away from explicitly political poetry, though in his view this trajectory does not culminate in anything like art for art's sake: on the contrary, "Man" suggests that poetry will have the definite use of refreshing reality or making it new, of renewing desire where desire had seemed exhausted. And yet as the progress of canto XI shows in miniature, the cost of opening this niche for poetry is an intensified emphasis on alienation from the object world under which the possibility of thinking of the real as social simply disappears.

"The Man with the Blue Guitar" indeed illustrates unusually pointedly how it was that Stevens's existential preoccupations could factor into his attraction for a generation of poets and critics trained to dismiss unmediated engagement with social issues as aesthetically compromising: it shows, in other words, wherein lies the justice of Lentricchia's portrait (in *After the New Criticism*) of Stevens as guru of antihistorical poetics in the 1960s. It would be a great mistake, however, to imagine that Stevens somehow evolved his existentialism in the late 1930s as a refuge from the social, for of course this line of reflection had been implicit from the beginning, in his belief that the subject is inevitably separated from knowledge of the object world in itself, indeed posed against this massive positivity as a kind of Sartrean nothingness. Or rather, it had been implicit in his fascination with this belief—for though hardly unusual among the philosophically inclined in accepting that there is no grasping of the thing undistorted by the mind's associations, peculiarities, and memories, Stevens is perhaps unique among poets in the extent to which his achievement is generated from the poetic possibilities of this impossibility (which, as "Anglais" suggests, appears in his work as the ground or archetype of all relations of desire).[11]

Within "Man," Stevens delineates his own method most strikingly in the penultimate canto, wherein the speaker instructs another poet-musician, or perhaps the people clamoring to be represented,

> Throw away the lights, the definitions,
> And say of what you see in the dark,
>
> That it is this or that it is that,
> But do not use the rotted names.
>
> How should you walk in that space and know
> Nothing of the madness of space,

Nothing of its jocular procreations?
Throw the lights away. Nothing must stand

Between you and the shapes you take
When the crust of shape has been destroyed.

You as you are? You are yourself.
The blue guitar surprises you.

(183)

If the poet is addressed, the instruction is to avoid striving for some dully accurate transcription of the world instead of allowing the poem to be suffused with the jocular procreations available only from darkness, upon which the mind can project without inhibition; if the people are addressed, the point would be similar, except that this trust in subjectivity would be necessary to life rather than to the making of poetry. Either way, the instruction pivots on the claim, "Nothing must stand / Between you and the shapes you take / When the crust of shape has been destroyed," the enjambed ending of the second line momentarily inviting the assumption that "the shapes you take" refers to something like the subject's self-definition, until the full sentence modifies that premise by conflating the subject's own shape with those of the objects no longer apprehended in the dark. The implication is thus that we should make use of rather than reject subjectivity's tendency to mistake its own contours for those of objects if we want to play a tune beyond us yet ourselves—a tune of things as they are according to the truth of desire (which could be knowable) rather than the truth of existence (which cannot be known).

The volume that succeeded *The Man with the Blue Guitar*, the 1942 *Parts of a World*, is remarkable for the doggedness with which it pursues every imaginable variation on the Stevensian ur-tableau of subject confronting discrete solid object across a divide of nonknowing and desire. In "The Poems of Our Climate," "Study of Two Pears," "The Glass of Water," "Dry Loaf," "Dezembrum," "Poem Written at Morning," "A Dish of Peaches in Russia," "Bouquet of Belle Scavoir," and, in a way, "The Man on the Dump," "Martial Cadenza," and "Woman Looking at a Vase of Flowers," the volume reiterates, though it also variously nuances, the simple moral that in contemplating a physical thing one may experience a range of feelings, from the sense that one is perceiving the thing in a clarity undistorted by associations (though in this one would be wrong, strictly speaking) to the sense that one is hardly seeing the thing at all (so densely do associations crowd upon the consciousness). At one extreme we might place "Study of Two Pears," which begins with a rejection of metaphor ("The pears are not viols, / Nudes or bottles. / They resemble nothing else"), proceeds through four quatrains of the most minimal description, including only one usage even arguably figurative ("flowering"), and concludes with the simple declaration, "The pears are not seen / As the observer wills" (*Poems* 196–97). At the other extreme might reside "A Dish of Peaches in Russia," which, after weaving back and forth between the immediate and the remembered or imagined, concludes with a surprisingly violent rendering of the power of association: "Even the drifting of the curtains, / Slight as it is, disturbs me. I did not know / That such ferocities could tear / One self from another, as these peaches do" (*Poems* 224). If the pears in the other poem resist being seen as the observer wills by refusing associations, the peaches here do so by inviting them, apparently setting the imagining self at odds with the perceiving one and in so doing preventing the subject from grasping the object in anything like a perfect knowledge.

In most of these poems, Stevens conveys his epistemological moral through static tableaux rather than vital narratives, but in "Bouquet of Belle Scavoir" the impossibility of seeing without the deformations of subjectivity appears convincingly as one of the despairs, and one of the hopes, of romantic love (even between nonphilosophers). The scene seems to be that of a man contemplating a bouquet sent by the woman he loves, and deploring the fact that he has the roses rather than the beloved: "The sky is too blue, the earth too wide. / The thought of her takes her away. / The form of her in something else / Is not enough." And yet, in the sixth and final stanza, he thinks:

> But this she has made. If it is
> Another image, it is one she has made.
> It is she that he wants, to look at directly,
> Someone before him to see and to know.

(Poems 231–32)

If the last line implies that the desire really at issue here is the desire to gain noumenal knowledge through the phenomenal, then fulfillment would seem forbidden in advance by the other poems on objects, with their moral that all seeing is transformed by the figurative projections of the viewer. And yet if metaphor seems likely to preclude satisfaction here, metonymy may offer a compensation, the flowers bringing the woman nearer not because they resemble her, but because her choice of them is a material embodiment of her own desire, and in this sense possibly more truly she even than her body. Governed by a "But" that casts the final stanza in the mode of recuperation, the closing lines may illustrate not the failure of intimacy but one of its sanctuaries in Stevens's epistemologically rigorous world, telling not of unfulfilled desire but of the satisfaction of roses that become someone to see and to know.

Perhaps more explicitly than any other Stevens poem, then, "Bouquet of Belle Scavoir" entertains the promise of closeness offered by Woolf in *Mrs.*

Dalloway and evoked at moments by Lewis and Pound as well, the promise of communion through an object seen in common, especially one chosen, transformed, or created by a subject. Yet if the scene of two people looking together is a standard feature of the Woolf novel, "Bouquet" seems almost bereft of companions in the oeuvre of Stevens, for whom subjects' uniting through an object of common attention usually has little to do with intimacy, let alone romantic love. As we have seen, the common perception that most interests this poet is the more abstract drawing together of a mass of people around an objectification of their desires, a phenomenon that in the mid-thirties usually took the form of an order beyond the speech of mobs, but which in *Parts of a World* appears principally in the figure of the hero, already heralded in the man with the blue guitar's offer to sing "a hero's head, large eye / And bearded bronze . . . / And reach through him almost to man."

If in that earlier poem the hero was abandoned in favor of a disquisition on poetry as freshening of life, however, he takes center stage—himself becoming the freshening of life par excellence—in "Examination of the Hero in a Time of War" (1942), the poem that Stevens clearly regarded as the culmination of *Parts*:

> They are sick of each old romance, returning,
> Of each old revolving dance, the music
> Like a euphony in a museum
> Of euphonies, a skin from Nubia,
> A helio-horn. How strange the hero
> To this accurate, exacting eye. Sight
> Hangs heaven with flash drapery. Sight
> Is a museum of things seen. Sight,
> In war, observes each man profoundly.
> Yes. But these sudden sublimations
> Are to combat what his exaltations
> Are to the unaccountable prophet or
> What any fury to its noble centre.

> (*Poems* 274)

Evoking the never quieted specters of "Sad Strains," the figure of the old revolving dance points to one of the more dismal consequences of the fact that perception is never free from the mind's interventions, namely that the stores of memory can give rise to the staleness of repetition: three times "sight" hovers on the edge of expectation at line's end and three times seems both disappointed and disappointing. But enter, then, the hero (descendant not of Crispin the poet but of Crispin the subject of the poem), who like the poem takes on the "true appearances" of reality and yet clearly exceeds reality so as to renew those appearances, surprising the jaded eye and invigorating with sublimations a too comfortable euphony.

What allows the hero to seem at once part of reality and other to it—what allows for paradoxical formulations such as, "It is part of his conception, / That he be not conceived, being real" (279)—is, of course, Stevens's epistemology, according to which any perception is always part fiction for the perceiver:

> There is no image of the hero.
> There is a feeling as definition.
> How could there be an image, an outline,
> A design, a marble soiled by pigeons?
> The hero is a feeling, a man seen
> As if the eye was an emotion,
> As if in seeing we saw our feeling
> In the object seen and saved that mystic
> Against the sight, the penetrating,
> Pure eye.
>
> (278–79)

The hero may be a feeling, but no perception is not part feeling: we always see something of our own feeling in the object seen, and hence as percept the fictive hero might differ from the two pears or the bouquet of belle scavoir only in degree, not in kind. But these moments in "Examination" do more than represent the culminating tableau of mind confronting object in *Parts*; they also disclose the political consequence of the shorter lyrics on objects, which lies in their naturalizing of what Stevens would shortly call "[t]he final belief . . . in a fiction, which you know to be a fiction, there being nothing else" (*Opus* 189; see also *Letters* 430, 443). If in *Ideas* the (possibly unconscious) feeling of an absence of wholeness leads to a longing for objectifications that appear to install our own desires in the external world, in *Parts* a full consciousness of the epistemic divide between subject and object undergirds a way of making use of objectifications fully understood as our own projections. The point, of course, is not to take the hero for truth as the pebble–chewer's audience might have taken his promises for truth, but to understand the hero as true to desire and in this strictly limited sense "real"—as though we might deploy to advantage our ability to invest a larger-than-human figure with humans' best qualities (precisely what Feuerbach condemned as the essence of religion) as long we never mistake our fictional hero for an actual god.

What happened in the interval between *Ideas* and *Parts*, clearly, was that Fascism's increasingly visible threat forced Stevens to abandon his admiration for the demagogue's artistry (an admiration whose ancestor was surely the venerable American love affair with the confidence man) in favor of an exploration of objectifications plausibly immune to demagogic manipulation. As Longenbach observes, Stevens discovered a need for "the hero who cannot become the dictator because he is never more than theoretical—and yet a hero who speaks to real rather than theoretical people" (*Wallace Stevens* 186). Seeking an alternative to that dangerous state of affairs in which the embodiment of desire and the genius of that embodying converge in a single object of unskeptical belief, Stevens prescribed for a United States at war a dose of what we might call ideology at once demystified and retained: a recognition that imaginary relations to real conditions take on a functional reality, combined with a willingness to hold on to some of those imaginary relations on the assumption that we can never have nonimaginary ones—that we can never fully know our real conditions—anyway. And thus another way of describing the manner in which the poems on objects support "Examination" would be to say that the impossibility of "knowledge" of the physical thing in itself here underwrites the (arguably antiutopian) conclusion that it is impossible to know the social "object" in itself, as well as the collateral recommendation that we embrace certain fictions in their fictionality.

The danger (or one of the dangers) of enlisting this basic epistemology in the service of social prescription, of course, is that it invites the less careful reader to forget that power is never purely a matter of belief. While suspending the urge to move beyond imaginary relations may suit admirably the construction of a hero in time of war, it clearly works less adequately when we turn our attention from the fictive hero to the real demagogue or, invoking "Anglais," to the actual police, who may always require ideological support in one sense and yet may also, like the natural forces named in "The Man with the Blue Guitar," enjoy powers that do not depend directly upon anything like a communal imagination. This is not to say that Stevens explicitly advocates applying a skeptical epistemology across the entire terrain of political life, but it is to take note once more of something that gets lost in his characteristically rapid transits from social "object" to material object and back again. "If men have nothing external to them on which to rely," he had written in reference to "Anglais," "then, in the event of a collapse of their own spirit, they must naturally turn to the spirit of others. I don't mean conventions: police." What might get lost, as this comment itself suggests, is the recognition that although some social objects may figure as virtually pure objectifications, others are features of reality that may affect people enormously even where no one seems to believe in much of anything at all.

Notes and Nuances

> Begin, ephebe, by perceiving the idea
> Of this invention, this invented world,
> The inconceivable idea of the sun.

You must become an ignorant man again
And see the sun again with an ignorant eye
And see it clearly in the idea of it.

Never suppose an inventing mind as source
Of this idea nor for that mind compose
A voluminous master folded in fire.

(*Poems* 380–81)

Perhaps the least surprising thing about *Notes toward a Supreme Fiction*, Stevens's most expansive wartime opus and unquestionably his best known and most discussed longer work, is that it opens with a lesson on the distance between subject and object. Seeing something clearly in the idea of it does not mean knowing that thing in itself, the instructor tells the ephebe (who may be an aspiring poet or simply anyone interested in poetry's relation to life), but means rather beholding it in what Stevens will call, in the next poem of *Notes*, its "first idea," glossed in a letter to Henry Church (famous as the dedicatee of the volume) as follows: "If you take the varnish and dirt of generations off a picture, you see it in its first idea. If you think about the world without its varnish and dirt, you are a thinker of the first idea" (*Letters* 427). The object seen in its first idea might appear in something like the ascetic bluntness of the pears of "Study of Two Pears," in other words, except that in this case perception would be more overtly influenced by volition: the sun would not be "seen as the observer wills," but the will to see cleanly would affect seeing, as though with a little effort one might be able to close up one's associative "museum of things seen."

The demand of poem I of "It Must Be Abstract" is thus that we (as ephebes) try to imagine the sun as it would be without the intervention of consciousness, while at the same time keeping in mind that consciousness is in fact performing that imagining. Such a charge may be impossible to fulfill, certainly, but nonetheless it represents Stevens's major delineation of an *epochē*, part of the grounding for his claims on behalf of the fiction known to be a fiction, which is to say part of the naturalizing of objectification that once supported the demagogue's sphere of bright sheens but now supports the figure of the hero who must not become a god. Or rather: most recently supported that figure, for the action of *Notes* is clearly to shift attention to poetry and away from the hero, who may partake of poetry and share its ability to freshen life, but who finally remains too specific to the situation of war to count as the supreme fiction considered here. When Stevens goes on to disdain gods explicitly in "Abstract" I, he does so less in order to defuse the power of Feuerbachian projections per se than by way of initiating his argument that poetic fictions must replace untrue religious "truths" as our primary way of addressing the separation between humans and world:

Never suppose an inventing mind as source
Of this idea nor for that mind compose
A voluminous master folded in his fire.

.   .   .   .

Phoebus is dead, ephebe.

(381)

"Never suppose an inventing mind as source / Of this idea": in a negative imperative of extraordinary compression, Stevens manages to warn against both belief in a divine creator and an extreme idealism that would treat objects as mere projections of the mind. But Stevens is doing more than exhibiting his virtuosity here, as he makes clear in "Abstract" IV, where he affirms the interdependence of these two prohibitions in a seminal reformulation of his proposal that we need poetry because we inhabit a material Being utterly unlike us, utterly inhuman and independent. "From this the poem springs: that we live in a place / That is not our own and, much more, not ourselves" (383), he declares, refining the thesis of "The Man with the Blue Guitar" by suggesting that our alienation from Being is predicated not so much on a general sense of the nonhuman world's distance as on a specific intuition of its self-sufficiency—on something like Woolf's feeling that "the thing is in itself enough: satisfactory, achieved," her sense of "the infinite oddity of the human position." Indeed in the lines just preceding he attempts a second *epochē* of sorts that evokes Woolf's attempt to give "an empty house, no people's characters" in "Time Passes": "There was a muddy centre before we breathed. / There was a myth before the myth began, / Venerable and articulate and complete" (383). Poetry's necessity, it appears, has to do not with some lack on the part of the world without humans but rather with that world's unsettling lack of lack, which bids to leave everything in the human realm (including, presumably, poetry itself— witness Crispin's transcript of the New World) condemned to secondariness: "We are the mimics. Clouds are pedagogues" (384).

From this formulation, however, it seems possible to draw either of two inferences about what the supreme fiction should attempt. It might be that poetry should try to reach toward Being so as to absorb, if possible, some of its priority; but it might be, alternately, that it should try to remove itself from the muddy center as dramatically as it can, the better to revel in and redeem the secondariness that is its (and our) lot. Part of what makes the opening of *Notes* so difficult is that in it Stevens seems to try to have things both ways: "The poem refreshes life so that we share, / For a moment, the first idea," he writes in III; "It satisfies / Belief in an immaculate beginning / And sends us, winged by an unconscious will, / To an immaculate end. We move between these points: / From that ever-early candor to its late plural" (382). Does poetry's luxuriant trajectory away from austere Being, then, paradoxically bring it into closer contact with that austerity? Stevens has already raised this possibility at the end of poem I:

Phoebus is dead, ephebe. But Phoebus was
A name for something that never could be named.
There was a project for the sun and is.

There is a project for the sun. The sun
Must bear no name, gold flourisher, but be
In the difficulty of what it is to be.

(380–81)

As nearly every critic writing on this poem has noted, the joke is (of course) that the pedagogue names the sun "gold flourisher" just after saying that it must not be named.[12] And this is to say that in this passage—another instance of the astonishing compression that makes the beginning of *Notes* so rich—Stevens not only insists upon the sheer difficulty of purging the operations of association from our perceptions of objects, but also intimates that poetry might somehow draw us closer to the muddy center by seeming to take us further away, mediating in a way that undoes mediation, naming in a way that throws away the rotted names.

In suggesting so much, he appears to carry on a debate (on his own terms) with William Carlos Williams, who among his modernist peers was the one who embraced most avidly the idea that poetry allows the thing to emerge in its immediacy, and it is therefore not surprising to discover that the opening of *Notes* recalls closely a 1918 poem (included in *Harmonium*) entitled "Nuances of a Theme by Williams." Beginning that early lyric by quoting in full Williams's four-line "El Hombre"—in which Williams tells the morning star that it gives him "a strange courage" and asks it to "[s]hine alone in the sunrise / toward which [it] lend[s] no part"—Stevens goes on to dilate,

Shine alone, shine nakedly, shine like bronze,
that reflects neither my face nor any inner part
of my being, shine like fire, that mirrors nothing.

(*Poems* 18)

As Longenbach observes, Stevens "undermines the call" to shine alone "with the vigor of his own language" (*Wallace Stevens* 55), deconstructing with a knowing wink his own "nuances" of Williams's theme just as the pedagogue of "Abstract" I names what cannot be named. Rushing into similes that compromise the aloneness he demands, Stevens shows how self-contradictory must be "shine alone" or any other apostrophic command to refuse apostrophe; and in continuing, "Lend no part to any humanity that suffuses / you in its own light / Be not chimera of morning, / Half-man, half-star" (18), he suggests how Williams succumbs to the temptation to anthropomorphize (another intrusion of subjectivity) three times in a very short poem, not only apostrophizing the inanimate but also naming it *"el hombre"* and (arguably) imputing to it a courage of its own.

Williams's response to the critique that Stevens offered implicitly in "Nuances," and explicitly in other expressions of dissent from around this time, is instructive. In the prologue to *Kora In Hell*, which was first published in the *Little Review* in April 1919 (four months after "Nuances" appeared in that same magazine), he remarked:

> The true value is that peculiarity which gives an object a character by itself. The associational or sentimental value is the false. Its imposition is due to lack of imagination. . . . The attention has been held too rigid. . . . It is to loosen the attention, my attention since I occupy part of the field, that I write these improvisations. Here I clash with Wallace Stevens.
>
> The imagination goes from one thing to another. . . . [T]he thing that stands eternally in the way of really good writing is always one: the virtual impossibility of lifting to the imagination those things which lie under the direct scrutiny of the senses, close to the nose. It is this difficulty that sets a value upon all works of art and makes them a necessity. (*Essays* 11)

This passage is then followed by a quote from a letter in which Stevens criticizes the collection that included "El Hombre" (*Al Que Quiere!*) for its "casual character," observing that "to fidget with points of view leads always to new beginnings and incessant new beginnings lead to sterility" (11–12).

Needless to say, Stevens agreed with Williams that the work of poetry was to lift sensible things to the imagination, but for him this could never happen without the transformations of association and sentiment, nor for that matter could the senses be altogether "direct" in their "scrutiny" if directness implies some capture of the thing in itself. Elsewhere in the prologue to *Kora* Williams observes, in the tones of Coleridge at his most Johnsonian, "Although it is a quality of the imagination that it seeks to place together those things which have a common relationship, yet the coining of similes is a pastime of a very low order, depending as it does upon a nearly vegetable coincidence" (16). Sensitive to the tendency of likenesses to spring up unsought, Stevens would no doubt have agreed on the provenance of simile, but would not have followed Williams in denigrating its power, nor would he have accepted Williams's later claim (in some notes of 1927) that it is thanks in part to "the bastardy of the simile" that in almost all verse the "truth of the object is somehow hazed over, dulled" and "the vividness which is poetry by itself" lost (*Essays* 67–68).

Williams reveals how much is at stake in this debate a little further on in the prologue, when he writes of how the poet witnessing the chicory flower and realizing its virtues of form and color . . . gives his poem over to the flower and its plant themselves, that they may benefit by those cooling winds of the imagination which thus returned upon them will refresh them at their task of saving the world. (17)

The vocabulary of imagination and refreshment, and poetry participating in no lesser work than that of saving the world: for all their friendly (and sometimes less than friendly) bickering over poetics, Williams and Stevens were dramatically united in 1918 in their sense that the key to all better futures lay in a renewal of perception, and they stayed united on this point throughout their careers. In this, of course, the two only disclose the continuing force of Paterian (or for that matter Santayanean) aestheticism, as well as the sense in which modernism made those fin-de-siècle values modern: new perception, ever new, could be looked to for the accomplishment of great things, because the malaise of the world was at last nothing other than the museum of things seen. Yet the peculiar syntax of part of this passage also brings out with special force the fact that the two ultimately located salvation in different places. Whereas for Stevens salvation was the gift of the poet, who, as he put it in a 1941 essay, "fulfills himself only as he sees his imagination become the light in the minds of others" (*Necessary* 287), for Williams it was the work of the object, the "task of saving the world" belonging in some essential respect to the chicory flower and its plant.

That this passage finds Williams's poet giving his poem "over to the flower and its plant themselves" also makes clear that his and Stevens's differences anent the source of salvation have an epistemological source, for whereas Stevens locates the power that refreshes with the poet in part because the flower's effects will always be modified by the poet's consciousness, Williams can speak of the thing's power to save because for him the poet (or another sufficiently attuned perceiver) really *can* surrender to the thing in its immediacy, transcending the deformations of association. As Stevens and Williams made their ways through the upheavals of the Depression, the rise of Fascism, and World War II, moreover, these differences of epistemology absorbed a certain social charge, as we can discern from a letter of Williams to James Laughlin written at the tail end of what we might call the long thirties. Apropos of his own *Paterson*, Williams remarks in this 1943 correspondence that whereas "Stevens speaks of *Parts of a World*, this is definitely Parts of a Greater World—a looser, wider world where 'order' is a servant not master. Order is what is discovered after the fact, not a little piss pot for us all to urinate into—and call ourselves satisfied" (*Letters* 214). To the extent that Williams accuses Stevens of celebrating the imposition of order for its own sake, of course, he neglects or misunderstands the latter's basic premise that the deformations introduced by the subject are an inevitable aspect of knowing, not a matter of choice; and yet his formulation reminds us once again how in the Stevens of the mid-thirties the positing of an inherent rage to order served to naturalize visions of possible imposed social orders, if not such impositions themselves.

The letter also highlights the fact that these disagreements between Stevens and Williams finally have to do with ontology as well as epistemology; for if Stevens usually has little to say in favor of the idea of a natural order existing apart from what humans think they see, Williams announces quite explicitly that an order exists spontaneously, apart from the imposed constructs of mind—and not only in the physical universe (as in Pound) but, provocatively enough, in human society, even when society seems most chaotic. Indeed in 1937, even as Stevens was beginning to turn away from imposed orders to develop a mature defense of poetry unburdened by affinities for now clearly hostile regimes, Williams was looking toward discovered order by way of justifying the idea of a humanity free of political parties. Proposing to "define the connection between the poet and the mob" in an essay of that year, Williams insists that the only principle in "matters of the imagination" is "the rediscovery in people of the elements of order" (*Essays* 189), and that this rediscovery is the province of the artist, who is "the truthfulest scribe of society . . . when he is left free." He continues:

> Who shall tell him how or what he must write? His very function as a servant of society presupposes his ability to see clearly beyond the formulations of his day and to crystallize his findings in a durable form for social confirmation, that society may be built more praiseworthily. . . . The facts are enclosed in his verses like a fly in amber. (193–94)

Both the Williams and the Stevens of this period envision the social work of the artist as an objectification of sorts ("crystallize his findings"), but if for Stevens the accent is on desire, for Williams it seems to rest on fact: if Stevens affiliates art to an imagining of order that might give form to incoherent longings, Williams suggests rather that the artist as "truthfulest scribe of society" can register in his verses an actual order underlying the apparently disorderly mobs. When in a statement of two years later ("Against the Weather") Williams refers to the artist as "a man of action" who "perpetuates his deed and records himself as a reality in the structure of his work" (*Essays* 204), he also makes clear that this self-recording introduces no significant distortion into the transcript of social life, since the true artist, unlike the political parties of the day, discovers rather than imposes forms:

> We live under attack by various parties against the whole. And all in the name of order! But never an order discovered in its living character of today, always an order imposed in the senseless image of yesterday. . . . Then let those who would force the artist to conform to their party—in the broadest sense—but especially let

such poets realize, such pretty orderists as seek to impose a fixed order from without, that the . . . brutalities and bigotries of the various segmentary regimes are a
direct moral consequence upon their own faithless acts of a generation previous. . . . (210–11)

Williams goes on to remark that Chamberlain's decision not to defend "a
Spain that does not fit that 'order' which conveniences England" was "a
choice no artist could make without sacrificing his status as artist," and that
this illustrates the "sharp cleavage between the true and the false in art." The
artist, he declares at last, "can never be a liar" (211).

After poststructuralism and Language poetry, which have helped to make
revolutionary politics, disruptions of literary form, and a mistrust of language's pretensions to reproduce an "exterior" reality seem indissolubly
united, it is easy to lose sight of the fact that Williams conjoins and promotes the first two members of this triad while at the same time rejecting the
third. It would not be too much to say, in fact, that his constant insistence on
revolutions in society and literary form served, and were served by, one of
the most highly mimetic poetics in modernism, along with a faith in language's referential capacity virtually beyond recapturing today. Certainly, it
can be astonishing to recall that writers in what Paul Hamilton calls "the
radical tradition of British thought from Bacon to Bentham" (99) allied their
visions of human progress to the dream of a transparent language perfectly
adequate to the world it would be used to describe; but Wiliams and his
followers, though more enamored of the vocabularies that we already have,
and the expressive possibilities thereof, believed in a similar alliance between a faithful correspondence of words to things and a politics of far-
reaching social change. And as goes language, so go all human works for
this poet, for whom the accumulated weight of tradition—with its carping
critics, impotent academics, entrenched regimes and parties, and general resistance to the new—was wrong not only because traditional, but also because untrue, in the strictest sense, to the immediate life of the world in all
its wonder and possibility.

Trite as this last observation will inevitably sound to anyone familiar with
Williams, it is worth making here because it helps to bring out something
implicit in both his attribution of salvational power to the chicory itself and
his insistence that an order awaiting elucidation resides in the masses. This
something is a moral element in his ontology that locates value with existence, or rather nature, itself, where nature would include an ambiguously
contoured human nature as well as the inanimate world, would indeed mean
the totality of what is—minus, only, those entities (parties, traditions) clearly
generated by a consciousness somehow gone awry, somehow grown out of
tune with the rest of the universe. In a compelling discussion of Stevens,
Williams, and the politics of the real in the mid-1930s, Filreis points out that

the objectivists saw themselves as "providing the link between the imagist revolution . . . and the social revolutionist's immediate 'object,' presented rather than mediated," and that Stevens's attachment of terms like "romantic" and "sentimental" to the objectivist side of Williams was arguably a way for Stevens to "make facticity palatable" to himself, now that he was feeling the need to turn to a difficult reality (*Modernism* 143).[13] Alongside, or even in tension with, this power of poetry to reproduce chaotic or miserable social conditions, however, we need to place Williams's feeling that a poetry made from the humblest materials also captures the essential good of the real world in general, including a natural human arrangement submerged or displaced by aberrant cultural or political orders (an arrangement that Stevens, uncomfortable with "facticity" partly for epistemological reasons, once again would have regarded as yet another projection of desire).

This double devotion to Being and truth helps to account for those moments when Williams seems to demand both that poetry be faithful to the thing represented and that it be a thing in itself ("To imitate nature involves the verb to do. To copy is merely to reflect something already there, inertly" [*Autobiography* 241]) or, as Edward Larrissy puts it, that the poet render "a world of things . . . with impeccable accuracy, but nevertheless according to a fresh, imaginative ordering" (69). The problem that emerges when belief in the goodness of accurate recording is subtended by belief in the basic goodness of the world so recorded is, once again, that of the possible superfluousness of poetry, which as mere replication of the world might hold only a second-order claim on the attention, or (even worse) reveal itself as another of the unnatural products of bad or dissonant consciousness. As we have seen, this problem was far from unique to Williams; we have already encountered it in Lewis's advice to the artist to become nature rather than imitate her, in Pound's efforts to distinguish Imagism from passive empiricist transcription, and in Stevens's poetic version of Williams himself, Crispin in "The Comedian as the Letter C," who at last finds life as such too full to leave room for a poetry that would duplicate an already embodied continent.[14] But the most illuminating point of comparison (or rather contrast) here is surely the poetics that Stevens developed in the thirties and forties, with its interlocking premises that the poet can give shape to what had not been articulated before and that existence, though sufficient unto itself (whole, complete), can never be sufficient for us, remaining alien because unknowable, frightening because alien, and in need of mediation because frightening. This is to say that if Williams seems to proceed from an ontology of sufficiency to a corresponding epistemology, Stevens proceeds from an epistemology of lack (for *us*) to a corresponding ontology: if Williams's assumption of the goodness of Being leads him to posit the goodness of truth, Stevens's assumption that true knowledge of Being is not our province (hence alien to us) leads him to the belief that Being itself is not our province (hence alien to us). Thinking of the sun in "the remotest cleanliness of a heaven / That has expelled us and our images" brings us to the acknowledgment that "we live in a place / That is not our own and, much more, not ourselves"; and this admission leads to an explanation of why life is "hard . . . in spite of blazoned days" and the discovery that poetry "springs" from such misery as by necessity (*Poems* 381, 383). The counterpoint of Williams thus helps to clarify Stevens's position in *Notes*, which is not that poetry reaches the "articulate and complete" world of things as such, but rather that out of our distance from such completeness it makes something that cannot be assessed in the same terms as primary Being. When Stevens writes "From this *the poem* springs: that we live in a place / That is not our own and, much more, not ourselves," he really means the poem, and not merely the necessity for poetry.

This point is made nowhere more movingly than in poem X of "It Must Give Pleasure," in which remarkable conclusion to the *Notes* Stevens addresses the earth as a "fat girl":

Fat girl, terrestrial, my summer, my night,
How is it I find you in difference, see you there
In a moving contour, a change not quite completed?

You are familiar yet an aberration.
. . . .
             . . . You
Become the soft-footed phantom, the irrational
Distortion, however fragrant, however dear.
That's it: the more than rational distortion. Yes, that.

                               (406)

It must be said that the poet's progress through *Notes* toward this redemption of the muddy center is by no means a steady one; on the contrary, a closer relation to the place not our own seems to emerge only fitfully, as at the mention of the "easy passion and ever-ready love . . . of our earthy birth" in "It Must Change" VII (395), or the nuptials of Bawda and the captain in "Pleasure" IV: "They married well because the marriage-place / Was what they loved" (401). But if the ground of reconciliation between poet and earth is not to be discerned among the anecdotes of *Notes* proper, it can be found in the moral that these anecdotes purportedly illustrate, namely that the supreme fiction must be abstract, must change, and must give pleasure—or, more precisely, that abstraction and change serve the cause of pleasure, while pleasure reconciles us to abstraction and validates change.

Less a blazon than an effort to work out a fitting blazon's terms, "Pleasure" X finds the poet recognizing that the never quite completed changefulness of the earth, the continuous elusiveness of a planet as abstract as any object under his epistemology, gives rise to nothing less than the greatest of pleasures and the best of loves. In this most winning of his statements of affection for the elusive object world, that is, Stevens transforms the gap between subject and object from the cause of coldest loneliness to the source of warmest intimacy, offering something like his version of the distance between people so prized by Woolf, or the "emotion for something different to the self, that cannot be absorbed into the self" that Lewis associates with love and all spiritual values. By the end of *Notes*, the world appears no less beloved of Stevens than it is of Williams, but this is a beloved proper to the Stevensian world of desire, not the Williamsian one of plenitude or satisfaction—a beloved ever elusive, ever beyond the pale of knowledge, and though not meaningfully false never knowably true. And yet beautiful as this resolution is, it seems in its own way to come at the cost of the supreme fiction's own raison d'être; for if the earth is already a fiction or more than rational distortion, what function can poetry fulfill? If our sense of a gap between subject and object has been redeemed in the discovery that this gap is itself the source of pleasure, what can be the use of the poem to life?

Stevens offers his answer, which involves a reintroduction of the social backed by an extraordinarily shrewd deployment of metaphor, at the end of "Pleasure" X:

> They will get it straight one day at the Sorbonne.
> We shall return at twilight from the lecture
> Pleased that the irrational is rational,
>
> Until flicked by feeling, in a gildered street,
> I call you by name, my green, my fluent mundo.
> You will have stopped revolving except in crystal.

(406–07)

The penultimate tercet, in which "they" have gotten some hugely general "it" straight, suggests that the mise-en-scène of this closing address is something like utopia, achieved when reason has quelled its adversaries and the citizens are "pleased"—Stevens having already laid the ground for this move in the earlier phrase, "Civil, madam, I am," a punning reminder that *Notes* has never quite abandoned the question of the role of the poet in the *civitas*. Having reflected that meaning and pleasure originate in the imperfect that is our paradise, the poet then suggests that in an achieved political paradise the necessity of the supreme fiction would only be the more apparent; for if the professors were to stop the earth's revolving in one sense (that is to say, to halt its revolutions political and otherwise), the earth revolving in the imagination's crystal of fiction would be the only earth capable of generating fresh pleasure because the only one still suffused by the exhilarations of change. In the aforementioned letter, what Stevens says exactly is, "The fat girl is the earth: what the politicians now-a-days are calling the globe, which somehow, as it revolves in their minds, does, I suppose, resemble some great object in a particularly blue area" (*Letters* 426). That politicians should imagine the earth as both some object in the blue and the encompassing sphere of the political suits Stevens perfectly, because he can use this duality to slip back and forth between social reality and physical reality once more, this time making use of the social sense in which the earth might stop revolving in order to confirm that poetry remains necessary to freshness in life.

Its logic followed out, however, Stevens's remedy would appear to create new problems for poetry in any world—as for example our own—in which utopia has not yet arrived: solving one difficulty by shifting from the physical world to (the end of) history, "Pleasure" X seems to create another inasmuch as the historical events that we still have in abundance evidently provide the change that Stevens would name the supreme fiction's province. As though anticipating this difficulty, Stevens had remarked the year before, in "The Noble Rider and the Sound of Words" (from which comes the reference to light in the minds of others quoted above), that the work of the poem is that of "resisting or evading the pressure of . . . reality," where the pressure in question would be "the pressure of an external event or events on the consciousness to the exclusion of any power of contemplation," and where reality would be not a "collection of solid, static objects" or the "external scene" but rather "the life that is lived in it" (*Necessary* 27, 20, 25). Not the elusive object world but the intrusive sociopolitical globe, which renders reflection impossible in the age of newspaper and radio (except within the contemplative haven that poetry provides), reality would in this scheme be constituted by events like the revolutions that the professors have not succeeded in halting, but it would make poetry more necessary rather than less.

One curiosity of "The Noble Rider" is that in it the social appears to take over the domain of the real, the very realm from which it is normally excluded under Stevens's binary existential ontology (humans versus earth as stone); but what makes this regrouping still odder is that it appears to position poetry itself in opposition to the social, just where one might least have thought to find it given Stevens's antipathy to art that fails to touch other spheres. And indeed it seems that it was far from Stevens's principal intention to enforce such an opposition. As Filreis has shown, his aim in this period was in fact to stress the "idea that a poet must make 'an agreement with reality,'" and in his Mount Holyoke lecture of 1943 he tried to "modify his 'pressures of reality' thesis so that his interest in the threatened actual world would be unmistakable" (*Actual* 100, 97). It was therefore supremely ironic, in one sense, that "The Noble Rider" should become one of the linchpins of those early critical accounts depicting Stevens as an advocate of utter poetic autonomy; and yet this development could hardly be unexpected given that the essay's central image presents poetry not in transit between world and mind (as in, say, "Man" XXII), but pushing back against an invasive reality as a kind of bulwark of beleaguered consciousness.

It would be easier to dismiss all this as a case of mere carelessness in phrasing were it not for the fact that Stevens makes a very similar move in the epilogue to *Notes*, wherein the consciousness and world so harmoniously married at the end of "It Must Give Pleasure" appear once more in conflict, with poetry as the mind's weapon of choice:

> Soldier, there is a war between the mind
> And sky, between thought and day and night. It is
> For that the poet is always in the sun,
>
> Patches the moon together in his room
> To his Virgilian cadences, up down,
> Up down. It is a war that never ends.
>
> (407)

We could hazard that what Stevens "really" means is once again that the poet's job is to reconcile mind and reality, of course, but only at the cost of significant violence to the metaphor at hand, since the business of the soldier to whom the poet is explicitly compared a few lines later ("war for war, each has its gallant kind") is not to make the treaty but to fight for one side against the other. Of the several ingenious methods for dealing with this finale that critics have proposed over the years, the most appealingly direct may be that of Filreis, who, following Helen Vendler, simply dismisses it as a poorly conceived effort to convince readers that *Notes* is a genuine war poem: "We must assume that it causes an undeserved break between itself and the thirtieth canto of the poem proper, a far more appropriate conclusion to its argument" (*Actual* 143).

Yet such a move only begs the questions of why Stevens should make this particular *kind* of slip in both "The Noble Rider" and the epilogue and of whether these moments' incompatibility with the idea of poetry as happy commerce between world and mind indexes a more profound dissonance within Stevens's thinking. We might answer in a general way simply by noting how short a step it is from Stevens's existential premises (his habit of positioning mind in opposition to everything else) to tableaux in which subject-object conflicts are figured in terms of intersubjective combat; but a complexity so far left implicit in the foregoing discussion of his poetics allows us a much more specific and pointed response. For the truth is that the strain between "Pleasure" X and the epilogue only highlights a tension in operation at least since the maneuvers of "The Man with the Blue Guitar" XI and XVI, a tension between the claim that poetry allows us to objectify our desires—and thereby, in a sense, resist reality—and the claim that it redeems our alienation by making a kind of commerce between subject and object worlds out of the very gap that separates them. In "Anglais," to be sure, Stevens had suggested that objectification itself constitutes something like such commerce in that it allows us to find our own desires in the external; and yet it is precisely this suggestion that indicates why the two aspects of poetry's work cohabit at best uncomfortably—Stevens having also made clear in *Ideas* that this putative discovery of our longings in the world is (rigorously speaking) illusory, the objectification of desire being "true" only to desire and not to the facts of Being or society prior to or apart from desire's appearance. For Stevens, once again, the order of the harmonious skeptic does not already exist among the masses, occluded but waiting to be disclosed (as Williams would have it), nor is there a pattern in nature whose true contours poetry reveals. In Stevens's scheme, any human vision, demagogic or poetic, must prove an uneasy combination of reconciliation and combat with the external world precisely because desire, by its very nature, will always both spring from and seek to alter what is.

What the figurations of "The Noble Rider" and the epilogue to *Notes* suggest, then, is not only that Stevens could never quite cease to associate nature with "*ethos* or Fate, a universe of death," but also that he could never quite rid himself of a fear that the world and our objectifications are intrinsically at odds—that the veritable archetype of our transactions with the real might be not the poem benignly returning with the appearances of a "sky that thinks" ("Man" XXII) but rather the infecting of Crispin's will by the vastness of the blue. It is instructive, in this context, that the figure for the oppositional world presented in the epilogue is none other than the sky, that immense metonymy of a universe beyond human manipulation, that (former) residence of gods whom mortals could not conquer: "Soldier, there is a war between the mind / And sky, between thought and day and night." The war between mind and sky is indeed a conflict between us and the place not our own, and it is one in which Stevens consistently sides with us—not a choice to cause much astonishment, perhaps, until one thinks of how modernists like Woolf and Lewis favored the innocence of the vulnerable object world over the depradations of a brutal subjectivity, or of how Williams tried to redeem consciousness by implying that only some aberrant deformations thereof disturb its harmony with a world of things in itself perfect.

In *Wallace Stevens and Poetic Theory*, B. J. Leggett explores the debt of "The Noble Rider" and *Notes* to Charles Mauron's *Aesthetics and Psychology*, in which Mauron argues that the aesthetic attitude is characterized by a contemplation that disdains utilitarian employment of the object in favor of present pleasure in the thing regarded for itself. Mauron's position closely evokes the Schopenhauerian aesthetics emphasized by Ransom and others in this period, of course, but it derives most immediately from Roger Fry, whom Mauron regarded "as his master," in Leggett's words (73), and who, according to Woolf in her biography of her friend, found in Mauron the kindred intellect with whom he "was to carry on the most fruitful of his aesthetic arguments" (223). Stevens's theoretical connection to Woolf's circle is therefore unusually direct in this case, and Leggett's fine exploration of Stevens's receptivity to Mauron helps to remind us that even his and Santayana's anxieties about useless art were rooted in the belief that the aesthetic qua aesthetic implied a removal of the object from use as ordinarily understood. And yet "The Noble Rider" illuminates a vast gap between Bloomsbury solicitousness about violence against the object and Stevensian anxiety on behalf of the human nonetheless, for its work is to rescore Mauron's points in a more aggressive key comporting closely with the martial epilogue to *Notes*—to present contemplation not as a relaxation from action but as a different kind of force, and poetry not as a defense of the object world against subjectivity (as in Ransom) but as the weapon of a fragile humanity against an externality never free of threat, no matter how fragrant or dear. "For a long time," Stevens told Robert Pack a dozen years later, "I have thought of adding other sections to the NOTES and one in particular: *It Must Be Human*"; but he added that he had held off out of feelings "that it would be wrong not to leave well enough alone" and that he could not "imagine anything more fatal than to state" one's intention "definitely and incautiously" (*Letters* 863–64). Perhaps his belief in poetry's necessary humanness was rendered as evident as he found desirable by the epilogue, with its drama of the war between mind and sky.

THINGS GOING AS FAR AS THEY CAN

As critics have recognized for some time, the major thematic venture of Stevens's postwar work is an effort to engage the real more intense and consistently complex than any to be found in the earlier poetry, a venture whose specific terms are anticipated by "The Noble Rider" and *Notes* inasmuch as both decisively position poetry against the background of a reality whose most striking feature is its sheer power. Of those two works, however, only the *Notes* constitutes an authentic prologue to this final phase, because the paradigmatic form of reality for the postwar Stevens proves to be not "the life that is lived in" the "external scene," the totality of human events discussed in the essay, but a physical world regarded alternately as the *Ding-an-sich* whose elusiveness to consciousness provides the basis for poetry and as the universe of death that destroys humans and their works. This is not to say that the poems from the end of the war and after somehow resist historically inflected reading or that Stevens invested none of them with engaged content at the level of allegory (Filreis shows in *Wallace Stevens and the Actual World* that he did); but it is to say that they almost always present the social as a component of a total reality whose typical threat is the violence of the inanimate against the human, not the violence of humans against each other.

This direction is effectively announced by "Esthétique du Mal," a 1944 meditation apparently prompted by the war, whose donnee is nonetheless the object world's ability to inflict suffering on sentient beings, tersely summarized in the observation that "[e]xcept for us, Vesuvius might consume / In solid fire the utmost earth and know / No pain" (*Poems* 314). The poem's major turn occurs when its protagonist recognizes this nonsentience for a basic innocence rather than the malevolence that we so easily believe it: that he "might suffer or that / He might die," the poet declares, "was the innocence of living, if life / Itself was innocent" (322), just as in the closely related "Auroras of Autumn" the menacing auroral lights prove an "innocence of the earth and no false sign / Or symbol of malice" (*Poems* 418). As a war poem, "Esthétique" makes especially noticeable not only Stevens's tendency to evade the hard fact of intersubjective violence (surfacing here in the form of the notorious canto VII on the "soldier's wound," which culminates in "a summer sleep, / In which his wound is good because life was" [318–19]) but also his habit of applying to intersubjective situations solutions more appropriate to the subject-object relation. Here, Stevens offers as a recuperation of suffering the by now familiar proposition that the divide between consciousness and Being allows for the delights of imaginative encounter, making

> . . . out of what one sees and hears and out
> Of what one feels . . .
> So many selves, so many sensuous worlds,
> As if the air, the mid-day air, was swarming
> With the metaphysical changes that occur,
> Merely in living as and where we live.

> (326)

In "Esthétique," as in so much of Stevens, the preeminent source of metaphysical changes is the physical world, which stimulates consciousness not as informational overload (the pressure of news) but as a plenitude of sensuous particulars; and this poem's kind of trajectory, in which the poet at first fears the object world's power to overwhelm and then celebrates its ability to invigorate, can be found in virtually all the major poetry of the final years. The 1946 "Credences of Summer," for example, turns on the question (vital since Crispin's encounter with the sky) of how to grasp the sensuous world when the mind is deluged with its richness, figured here by exact midsummer, "green's green apogee" (*Poems* 373). In the pivotal seventh canto of that poem, some "they" who want to sing of summer in the fields, reaching "an object that was near, / In face of which desire no longer moved," find that they can only sing of the fields when they leave them for another habitat: "Far in the woods they sang their unreal songs, / Secure. It was difficult to sing in face / Of the object. The singers had to avert themselves / Or else avert the object." Only out of the presence of the thing itself, it seems, can the "thrice concentred self" grip the object "in savage scrutiny," make it captive, "subjugate / Or yield to subjugation," and "proclaim / The meaning of the capture, this hard prize" (376). But the reward for this swerve from midsummer abundance may be a happiness richer even than "youthful happiness," because deepened by an oscillation between immediacy and distance, between nostalgia and plenitude (378).

In the 1949 "Ordinary Evening in New Haven" (to take just one other example), Stevens makes clear that the desire for the "poem of pure reality, untouched / By trope or deviation, straight to . . . the object / At the exactest point at which it is itself" (*Poems* 471) can never be satisfied, and that part of the object world's strength in its combat with subjectivity lies in its ability to slip the mind's hold: "It is not in the premise that reality / Is a solid. It may be a shade that traverses / A dust, a force that traverses a shade" (489). If reality is a force, this is so in part because it can be a shade, possessed of a ghostly immunity to mastery; and yet once again it is just this reliable unreliability, this "permanence composed of impermanence," that makes the phenomenal delightful, rendering "gay the hallucinations in surfaces" (472) by allowing for the play of the imagination. Arguably the supreme statement of Stevensian epistemological doctrine, "Ordinary Evening" refracts through an astonishingly various series of anecdotes the key features of Stevens's late address to reality: the proposition that our compensation for being born into a place not ourselves is pleasure in the changes of that fluent mundo, and a newly strenuous insistence on the sheer priority of the muddy center that was before we breathed.

Nothing would be more inadequate, however, than to claim that in this last phase Stevens simply chooses reality over the imagination or the object world over subjectivity, whatever that would mean; for if he shows a willingness to grant primacy to the real in the realm of power, necessity, and fact, he balances this concession with a newly explicit insistence that pre-eminence in the realm of *value* belongs to the imagination—indeed that human perceiving and describing confer upon the object world any value that, rigorously speaking, it can be said to have. Professor Eucalyptus in "Ordinary Evening" XIV, for example, "seeks / God in the object itself," but this quest culminates in his own choosing of "the commodious adjective / For what he sees . . . the description that makes it divinity, still speech . . . not grim / Reality but reality grimly seen / And spoken in a paradisal parlance new" (475). For the late Stevens, poetry is indeed description (as also in "Description without Place") but description is re-creation: not the reproduction of the world in nonliving form that long ago led Crispin to reject poetry, but the seeking of "a possible for its possibleness" (481), the bestowing of meaning upon its otherwise meaningless sprawl. Offering perhaps the archetypal enunciation of this position at the conclusion of "The Rock" of 1950, Stevens calls the rock the "starting point of the human and the end," but only after insisting that poetry would be a "cure of the ground," that "the poem makes meanings of the rock" until "its barrenness becomes a thousand things / And so exists no more" (*Poems* 528, 526, 527).

Almost any of the later poems could be enlisted to reinforce this point, but two eloquent instances should suffice for our purposes here. In 1952's "Looking across the Fields and Watching the Birds Fly," a Mr. Homburg begins by reflecting on the priority of a nature "free / From man's ghost, larger and yet a little like, / Without his literature and without his gods," noting that the "external" world is our "[o]bscurest parent" and that "[w]e think, then, as the sun shines or does not" (*Poems* 517–18). Dismissing decisively the ambivalent formulation of a 1942 poem entitled "Desire and the Object" ("It could be that the sun shines / Because I desire it to shine or else / That I desire it to shine because it shines" [*Opus* 113]), he concludes that "[t]he spirit comes from the body of" a world

Whose blunt laws make an affectation of mind,
The mannerism of nature caught in a glass
And there become a spirit's mannerism,
A glass aswarm with things going as far as they can.

(519)

Offering to correct the mistake of the protagonist in "Madame La Fleurie" of the year before, who had "looked in a glass of the earth and thought he lived in it" (*Poems* 507), Mr. Homburg envisions consciousness as the mirror of a prior nature—but not just any mirror, for this is a magic glass, swarming with metaphysical changes, in which the things that began amid the blunt laws of the world's body race toward the ideal or transcendent. In "The World as Meditation," from the same year, Penelope mistakes the sun that wakes her for Ulysses, but instead of drawing despair from her misprision relishes her vision of a sun-Ulysses ever distant and yet "coming constantly so near": "It was Ulysses and it was not. Yet they had met, / Friend and dear friend and a planet's encouragement" (*Poems* 521). As Stevens's phrasing suggests, this encouragement must belong in one sense to the planet (at once the sun and the totality of the world as rock) that prompts it; and yet of course it is only Penelope who makes it possible for the sun to become Ulysses or for a planet to feel, only Penelope who, taking courage, gives meaning to this break of day.[15]

What allows Stevens to present such redemptive resolutions mostly by implication, and without straining credibility, is nothing other than the secular humanist tradition of separating the realm of value from the realm of fact, so as to make the human the measure of all things while at the same time acknowledging the manifest power of the material world. Stevens shows his investment in this tradition—one that, shorn of its more overtly self-congratulatory rhetoric, remained alive and provocative for much of the twentieth century[16]—at many points in his poetry and essays, but perhaps nowhere more distinctly than in a letter of 1943, in which he cites with approval a *Partisan Review* essay by John Dewey entitled "Anti-Naturalism in Extremis." One of a group of defenses of secular rationalism and liberalism collectively entitled "The New Failure of Nerve," Dewey's article argues that supernaturalists, extranaturalists, and religionists of all varieties habitually identify naturalism with "materialism" and then "employ the identification to charge naturalists with reduction of all distinctive human values, moral, esthetic, logical, to blind mechanical conjunctions of material entities," whereas in fact "naturalism finds the values in question, the worth and dignity of men and women, founded in human nature itself" as well as the material world dismissed by antinaturalists as "thoroughly corrupt" (32, 38). Recommending the essay to Henry Church, Stevens noted that he had hoped to read the number of the *Review* in which it appeared with "more care" than he did ("I have gone through [it] once, but without quite making everything in it my own" [*Letters* 441]), thus suggesting not that the article influenced him in its details but rather that it accorded broadly with his basic beliefs.[17]

This point is suggestive not least because the proposition that value resides with the human while sheer priority belongs to the object world undergirds the vast philosophical drama of Sartre, with its polymorphously elaborated encounter between an in-itself or Being without meaning and a for-itself or consciousness that longs for Being's brute facticity. Stevens's version of this opposition is not the same as Sartre's, to be sure, but it is similar enough to make less than outlandish his early readers' tendency to view him through an existentialist lens, and to render instructive the points of divergence between these writers' ontological speculations—the most significant of which stem from the fact that Sartre regards the for-itself as the logically immanent negation of the in-itself, whereas Stevens treats the two as something like separate elements that meet very nearly contingently in the moments of perception (or imagination) and death. In "Madame La Fleurie," for example, Stevens gives us a protagonist whose "grief" is that the "crisp knowledge" he has acquired in life will be "devoured" by the earth upon his death, that his terrestrial "mother" will "feed on him, himself and what he saw" (*Poems* 507). The poet does not decide whether what we have seen and known really returns to the earth with our dust, but that Stevens raises so bizarre a possibility at all attests to his tendency to think of consciousness as a substance somehow apart from the rest of the material world (at least during the life of the subject), as though the universe might be comprised of two "things," matter and mind, set side by side. A still cleaner articulation of this point appears in the ironically titled "Metaphor as Degeneration" (1948),

in which metaphor proves no degeneration from reality because "being /
Includes death and the imagination" (*Poems* 444)—which is to say that consciousness and world (presented here in the metonymies of death, or world's
action on mind, and imagination, or mind's action on world) can be conceived as two positive terms that together add up to the greater whole of
Being.

The relevant Sartrean contrast to "Metaphor as Degeneration" appears in
the final pages of *Being and Nothingness*, wherein Sartre asks whether the
fact that consciousness must be consciousness *of* something implies that the
for-itself "is articulated with the in-itself so as to constitute a totality," and
whether it is "not this totality which would be given the name *being* or
reality" (790). "[T]he Greeks," writes Sartre,

> were accustomed to distinguish cosmic reality, which they called To παν, from the
> totality constituted by this and by the infinite void which surrounded it—a totality
> which they called To ολον. . . . [H]ere as in Greek philosophy a question is raised:
> which shall we call real? To which shall we attribute being? To the cosmos or to
> what we called To ολον? To the pure in-itself or to the in-itself surrounded by that
> shell of nothingness which we have designated by the name of the for-itself? (791)

For Sartre, the answer returns to the fact that the dream of a substantive
union of in-itself and for-itself can never be separated from the dream of the
in-itself-for-itself, the *ens causa sui*. From the perspective of that inevitable
but unlivable dream, he notes, it can only seem that the real is "an abortive
effort to attain the dignity of the self-cause," that "[e]verything happens . . .
as if the world, man, and man-in-the-world were presented in a state of
disintegration in relation to an ideal synthesis" (792). Because the synthesis
that would be greater Being (corresponding to To ολον) must be impossible,
in other words, trying to conceive of it forces us to acknowledge a frustrat-
ing and constant slippage in the universe, a "perpetual failure": "the ολον
we are considering is like a decapitated notion in perpetual disintegration. . . . There is here a passage which is not completed, a short circuit"
(793).

For Sartre, then, the in-itself and the for-itself are enmeshed with each
other in a logical relation that effectively forbids us from simply adding
them together, whereas Stevens conceives of mind and world as entities
whose sharing of the universe is comparatively contingent. And it is this
divergence that finally accounts for the difference in mood between Sartre's
unfolding of *la condition humaine* and Stevens's; for where Sartre sees the
for-itself conferring value upon the in-itself in its nature but always thwarted
in any of its particular efforts at transcendence, Stevens emphasizes how
those contingent meetings of mind and world that we call perception and
imagination themselves take on a positive value as events in which value is
conferred (and in which delight is generated).[18] As we saw in the first chap-

ter, the Sartre of *Nausea* entertains the possibility of transcending mere Be-ing through the production of imaginative representations, but the Sartre of *Being and Nothingness* finds all such attempts haunted by an inevitable fail-ure, discerning behind the drive to make anything at all a version of the doomed urge to become the self-cause. Stevens, on the other hand, cele-brates the transformation of the barren rock of the world and, by extension, praises the poetic leaves that cover it as an intervention in material reality, a triumph of mind over world in the realm of fact after all.

Or does he? Does this "by extension" in fact prove adequate to the po-etry? Certainly, much of the critical literature seems to take for granted that Stevens, like many of his fellow modernists, found in such making the hu-man activity par excellence, and that he casts the poet in the role of *artifex* with an alacrity broadly typical of twentieth-century poetics. Yet we might observe immediately that even in "The Rock" itself Stevens resolutely insists upon the metaphoricity of the poetic leaves, moving swiftly to a reflection on what would occur "if they broke into bud, / If they broke into bloom, if they bore fruit, / And if we ate the incipient colorings / Of their fresh culls" and then explaining flatly, "The fiction of the leaves is the icon / Of the poem, the figuration of blessedness" (526). Dissuading the reader from supposing the rock to be made less bare at the level of pure Being, Stevens emphasizes that when "the poem makes meanings of the rock" this "barrenness becomes a *thousand* things," as though even the time-honored metaphor of the leaf becomes risky to the degree that it drifts toward a Williamsesque poetics in which the poem-object would be installed as a material thing among material things. And indeed one of the subtle surprises of Stevens (though one for which we have been prepared by his earlier writings' inclination to enlist art in the service of life's transactions, as against the residues of death) proves to be that the poem as made object does *not* figure significantly in his re-sponse to the division between humans and world—or, more broadly, that his belief in the conferring of value on Being by consciousness is premised neither upon the Sartrean relation of logical necessity *nor* upon a privileging of material transformations of the object world.

A superb demonstration of this point can be found in 1952's "Two Illus-trations That the World Is What You Make of It," in the first part of which a man who thinks "within the thought / Of the wind" fails to understand that this "thought / Was not his thought, nor anyone's," does not know that he breathes "the breath of another nature as his own," although this is a "nature still without a shape, / Except his own—perhaps, his own / In a Sunday's violent idleness" (*Poems* 513–14). The moral, of course, is that the poem's punning title is both true and false, since although the world comes mediated through associations (so that it is "what you make of it," what you imagine it to be), the process of perception alters consciousness itself (so that you are what the world makes you). This first illustration thus asserts once more the priority of Being in the realm of fact and of imagination in the realm of value; and so does the second, in which the same or another character declares "that everything possessed / the power to transform itself, or else, / And what meant more, to be transformed." Discovering "the colors of the moon / In a single spruce" when the sun breaks upon him and "sensuous summer [stands] full-height," this "master of the spruce, himself, / [Becomes] transformed" (514–15), the physical world once more changing the perceiver at the level of existence but itself undergoing change in the domain of perception.

The added complexity of this second scenario lies in its introduction of the work of art as solid object, in the form of "half a shoulder and half a head" left by the master of the spruce "[t]o recognize him in after time," which "lay weathering in the grass / When . . . the change / Of summer and of the sun, the life / Of summer and of the sun, were gone" (514)—when, in short, the sensuous intensity of the intensest season, and perhaps the life of the artist as well, had passed. The illustration closes with the master's mastery having "[l]eft only the fragments found in the grass, / From his project, as finally magnified" (515), a finale emphatically Stevensian in that it leaves the work of art resisting nature's power in one sense while succumbing to that power in another: the fragments survive to be "found," and yet remain "only" fragments after all, the failure of this attempt to elude mortality encoded by the sculptures' own representation of the divided human body. Certainly, Stevens allows that the existence of the marbles leaves material reality altered; but the profounder moral is that such a local alteration in the object world can scarcely count as a human conquest of that large, powerful, and always prior realm.

This second illustration of how the world both is and is not quite what you make of it thus evokes Sartre's stress on the impossibility of producing a transformation that would extend across the entirety of the in-itself, as well as the humility before the power of nature that Pound describes in the Pisans. As we have seen, however, Pound's anxieties about accumulation at least touch on the possibility that the making of art could stand as a synecdoche for a general human production that would leave no part of nature unaltered, and Sartre would go on to make the problem of the earth's transformability one of the centerpieces of the Critique of Dialectical Reason. Stevens, by contrast, shows virtually no concern with subjectivity's potentially radical and devastating large-scale transformations of the physical world, or indeed with the ways in which even individual instances of making might represent a mastery of matter or an infusion of subject into object. Nor is this omission (the more striking in view of his strong interest in actual monuments, to which Michael North calls attention in The Final Sculpture) merely characteristic of his last phase. On the contrary, it is notably in evidence as far back as "Anecdote of the Jar," arguably the most famous ekphrastic poem of the twentieth century, and yet one in which, as W.J.T. Mitchell has pointed out, the "narrator does not make the jar; he 'places' it." It is "not production but distribution and observation of the ekphrastic object" (704) that Stevens presents; and when the poet credits the object with transforming its surroundings ("It took dominion everywhere"), the implication is that this transformation occurs within the mind of the observer, not as a material rearrangement of the landscape ("The wilderness rose up to it, / And sprawled around, no longer wild" [*Poems* 76]).

Another way of putting this would be to say that a highly significant absence in Stevens—one disclosed by his whole poetic career, but most visible in the late poetry, with its continual insistence on the precedence of reality—is that of a strong interest in production as a possible point at which subject might meet object *in a relation other than that of perception or knowledge*, in praxis or poiesis considered as a decisive material operation. And indeed Stevens's one notable use of the latter term in his late poetry exemplifies perfectly his tendency to distance making from intervention in the material. In "Large Man Reading" (1948), ghosts who "would have wept to step barefoot into reality," who "would have wept and been happy, have shivered in the frost / And cried out to feel it again" gather around the reading man, hearing

> The outlines of being and its expressings, the syllables of its law:
> *Poesis, poesis*, the literal characters, the vatic lines,

> Which in those ears and in those thin, those spended hearts,
> Took on color, took on shape and the size of things as they are
> And spoke the feeling for them, which was what they had lacked.
>
> (*Poems* 423–24)

There is no suggestion, here, that poiesis might be less than a genuine creation, and yet the curiosity of this making is that it is also a disembodying. Ignoring Stevens's crucial modal "would have," critics commenting on this poem have tended to treat it as a story of corporealization, but what in fact happens is that the red man of earth changes the "literal characters," which at least have body in print, into forms for a world of ghosts, forms with the color, shape, and size of physical things, and yet apparently without their weight or solidity, indeed without material substrate. Poiesis turns out to be the fashioning of imaginary objects within the imaginations of phantoms, not the production of physical objects in a physical world.

Certainly, Stevens's point is that reading as incitement to the imagination is a genuine making after all, not that all making is a rendering intangible; but it is nonetheless a vivid index of his commitments that incorporeal fashioning is the principal kind treated in his poetry. In the closely related poem "A Completely New Set of Objects," a protagonist envisions flotillas bearing "[s]hadows of friends" who bring "[f]rom the water in which he believed and out of desire / Things made by mid-terrestrial, mid-human / Makers without knowing, or intending, uses," things that prove nonetheless "the exactest shaping / Of a vast people old in meditation" (*Poems* 352–53). Works of art thus seem to transcribe the truth of the tribe in the manner of Williams or to articulate communal desire as per Stevens's own formulation in "Sad Strains," and yet the fact that these "objects" are borne by shadows renders the scene spectral, as though to remind us that the objectifications of which Stevens made so much in *Ideas* and *Parts* were never solid objects, always rhetorical ones. Even more extraordinary, perhaps, is that when Stevens does turn to the durable work of art, he suggests how it can seem unsatisfactory *qua object* by virtue of the very fact of its having been made. "So-And-So Reclining on Her Couch," from *Transport to Summer*, includes the observation that a woman in a painting "is half who made her," in part the objectification or expression of the artist, in part a transcription of (perceptions of) the real; but instead of celebrating this joining of subject and object, the speaker turns, perhaps with relief, to the natural world. "But one confides," he concludes, "in what has no / Concealed creator. One walks easily / The unpainted shore, accepts the world / As anything but sculpture. Good-bye, / Mrs. Pappadopoulos, and thanks" (*Poems* 296).

Similar disruptions occur in the poem "Prelude to Objects," from *Parts of a World*. Having asked what purpose art serves, given that (as "So-And-So" also suggests) we find reflections of ourselves in everything, Stevens answers that "the guerilla I should be booked / And bound," thus announcing fairly straightforwardly that one of the needs of the self is to be objectified in the work of art. In the second part of the poem, however, he instructs the poet, described as "patting more nonsense / Foamed from the sea," to conceive "the diviner health / Disclosed in common forms," and declares, "We are conceived in your conceits" (*Poems* 195), effectively undercutting his most explicit positing of self-objectification as imperative by sanctioning, in the next breath, at least three rival rationales for poetry: the need to give voice to the object world, as in "Key West" ("nonsense / Foamed from the sea"); the need to forge intersubjective bonds around objects of common attention, as in the poems on the hero and the supreme fiction ("common forms"); and the need to shape or even create humanity as such ("We are conceived in your conceits"). That Stevens did not view self-objectification as a singular or outstanding justification for making is confirmed by the fact that "Prelude to Objects" comes from the period of "The Noble Rider," wherein he writes not only that the poet's job "is to make his imagination theirs [people's]" and to see "his imagination become the light in the minds of others" but also that the poet "has immensely to do with giving life whatever savor it possesses" (*Necessary* 29–30)—thus conflating the imperatives of projection, enlightenment, and pleasure.

One reason why Stevens has so much difficulty with the booking and binding of the guerilla "I," of course, is that such fixings in solid objects or fashionings of durable residues seem to run counter to the crucial desiderata of abstraction, pleasure, and change. In "It Must Give Pleasure" IX, Stevens answers the preceding poem's question, "These external regions, what do we fill them with, / Except reflections, the escapades of death" by declaring,

> These things at least comprise
> An occupation, an exercise, a work,
>
> A thing final in itself and, therefore, good:
> One of the vast repetitions final in
> Themselves and, therefore, good, the going round
>
> And round and round, the merely going round,
> Until merely going round is a final good,
> The way wine comes at a table in a wood.

(405)

A triumph of connotative synonymy as poetic device, the second line of this passage first plays upon the double sense of "occupation" to naturalize an equation between necessary work and mere exercise (busywork), then uses the double sense of "a work," which can mean either "an occupation" or a completed thing, "a thing final in itself," to show that an exercise is a thing final in itself and, therefore, good. Stevens would deploy a similar formulation in "The Lack of Repose," from *Transport to Summer*, which concludes, "And not yet to have written a book in which / One is already a grandfather and to have put there / A few sounds of meaning, a momentary end / To the complication is good, is a good" (*Poems* 303). The shrewdly ambiguous syntax leaves unclear whether not yet having written is to be identified with putting there a few sounds of meaning or with *not* putting there a few sounds of meaning, but either way, the not-yet-having-written, the failure to have yet fixed, is a good—a genuinely good good, the evanescent kind, not the durable commodity that one might trade.

Stevens's clearest professions of his belief that meaning does not depend on durability, however, appear in some of the last lyrics of his final phase. In "The Planet on the Table," one of several luminous valedictions to his life and career, his persona Ariel thinks with pleasure of his poems, but feels that it "was not important that they survive" (*Poems* 532); and in "Note on Moonlight," which by happy disposition directly precedes "The Planet" in the *Collected Poems*, it seems in the moonlight as if "being was to be observed," as if "the purpose that comes first . . . is the purpose to be seen." This purpose is "empty / Perhaps, absurd perhaps, but at least a purpose, / Certain and ever more fresh," the poet declares, before concluding (as though relishing his suspension in doubt), "Ah! Certain, for sure . . . " (531–

32). "Purpose," "absurd": the answer even to the existential question (if there is one) seems to be that meaning lies in the going round of perception, in the pleasure of an evanescent meeting between mind and world that, occurring all the time, confirms in the most festive terms how life—where truly life—is always extravagant yet never wasteful. In "The Snow Man" of decades before, Stevens had made the approach to the first idea the exclusive province of those who have been cold a long time, but in "Ordinary Evening" he observes that the sense of "cold and earliness is a daily sense," and that to "re-create, to use / The cold and earliness and bright origin / Is to search," just as "to say of the evening star" that "it is wholly an inner light, that it shines / From the sleepy bosom of the real, re-creates, / Searches a possible for its possibleness" (481). This later Stevens, in other words, proves more than content to place poetry along a continuum with description and perception, justifying the poem not as an enduring transmutation of the universe of fact but as an especially inviting fulfillment of the purpose to be seen, where this purpose remains notably free of the implication that crystallizing the self for posterity is a necessary ambition ("It was not important that they survive").[19]

If, as Harold Bloom asserts (glossing the well known close of "The Well Dressed Man with a Beard"), the early Stevens felt that the mind "cannot be satisfied . . . because it wants to assert its power, its *pathos*, over the humming of the sea, and no assertion can convince it of a finality in that exercise of its will" (*Wallace Stevens* 166), then one of the crucial insights of the late phase is that the more meaningful mastery of reality (if mastery it is) lies in the seeing and imagining that goes on constantly, even apart from a vigorous will or any work of physical transformation. And thus although it is true, as Alan Filreis argues, that the late poem "Description without Place" tips "the seeming-being scale irrevocably toward seeming" (*Actual* 184), Stevens's statement that description is the "difference that we make in what we see" (*Poems* 344) does not mean that "actuality, the world of reference must become . . . the goal or end point (the finale) of seeming," as Filreis claims (184). For Stevens, once again, the difference that we make in what we see is made in the seeing itself; and it is precisely because this poet's interest slackens just at the idea of intervention in the material real that "Description" cannot be the endorsement of an "official American notion of a reconstructive moment" that Filreis names it (in exploring how this 1945 Harvard Phi Beta Kappa Poem relates to Sumner Welles's Harvard Phi Beta Kappa Oration of the same year [*Actual* 184]). Nor does saying all this mean holding to a "belief in Stevens's . . . devotion to imagination unspoiled by reality" (240), as Filreis seems to think; rather, it means acknowledging that a claim for reality's necessity to imagination need not imply that the latter's value is confirmed only in decisive transformations of the actual world.

This point has consequences also for Lentricchia's central claim (advanced in *Modernist Quartet*) that Stevens's greatest fear, especially in his later years, was that desire might wear out, or satisfaction prove fatal to the endless possibilities of possibility. Stevens, Lentricchia argues, combated this anxiety preeminently in two ways: on the production side, by balancing the urge to write "poems that will not be preliminary" with an urge to refrain from doing so (his double desire being "to *want* to write poems of real significance and, at the same time, not to want to *write* them" [154–55]); and, on the consumption side, by collecting things (pictures, statuettes) in such a way as to leave most of the final decisions to others, thereby maintaining in his acquisition a component of serendipity. The poet "went to extraordinary lengths to will the innocence of his efforts as a collector," writes Lentricchia, "and to conceal from himself the intentional character of his hobby," just as he wanted poetic composition to occur "as surprise, expression as a gift of spontaneity from some unknown benefactor" (171–72). In this most invigorating of recent reappraisals of his life and works, then, Stevens appears (rather against expectation) as the modern poet who adumbrates more resonantly than any other the central experiential elements of life under capitalism: the constant restlessness not only of desire but also of metadesire, the impossible hope of a thoroughly spontaneous consumption, and the impulse to a continuous production that would stave off the finality of production completed.

Without denying the extraordinary force of Lentricchia's reading, however, we might notice how some of the arguments advanced here necessarily modify its overwhelming emphasis on the desire for desire as prime Stevensian motor. We might observe, for example, that Stevens's hesitancy about completing a definitive magnum opus could arise not only from an anxiety that desire might fail but also (or alternately) from his sense that the work of art is most vulnerable to consignment to the world of waste objects, to the junk heap of items that have fallen out of the cycle of life, when it seems most narrowly monumental—in which case the problem of closure would pertain not only to his own relation to his work but also to his works' reception in the world and even to art's basic ontology. Similarly, we might note that, to the degree that it succeeds, Stevens's effort to obscure his own role in acquisition renders this kind of consumption more nearly like perception, so that his willed "innocence" figures as, among other things, a removal from material intervention in harmony with his elevation of imaginative seeing (over physical transformation) as the principally interesting relation between subject and object.

What links these two points is again Stevens's belief, formulated most fully toward the end of his career, that the purpose to be seen is indeed a real purpose, and that seeing itself can be thought of as an achievement rather than a distraction from, or postponement of, some putatively more authentic production. And this is to say, in effect, that what Lentricchia's compelling narrative least succeeds in compassing is the quiet but vital shift of Stevens's last years, in which the poet of transient imaginative satisfactions comes to emphasize the satisfaction rather than the transience, to grow less fearful that desire will decay, to speculate that the cycles of longing and fulfillment might be daily cycles—and to find in all of these changes of view, perhaps, the deepest satisfaction of all. This is a movement already anticipated at points such as "Pleasure" X, wherein the elusiveness of the object world brings forth love and even a kind of peace by sustaining imaginative encounters; but it finds what may be its most confident figuration in the daybreak scene of Penelope in "The World as Meditation," the moral of which Lentricchia misreads only inasmuch as his stress on the costs and limits of Stevens's resolution seems willfully to neglect the poem's extraordinary serenity: "Yet they had met, / Friend and dear friend and a planet's encouragement. / The barbarous strength within her would never fail" (521).

It is Helen Vendler, perhaps, who brings out most eloquently how consciousness bestows value in Stevens, commenting with respect to "Ordinary Evening" XVII, "The things of this world are beholden because they are beheld: they are saved, and grateful, because we have looked on them and immortalized them" (288)—though we might add that we have done so, paradoxically, only in the sense that we have given them value for the moment of seeing. And it is in this elevation of seeing as doing, finally, that the profoundest influence of Santayana on Stevens's poetry may inhere, for if there was in both the later Santayana and his young friend a strong aversion to the idea of an art without purpose, there was never in either a strong attraction to the idea that production might be intrinsically more valuable than perception. Certainly, there can be no question of the need to jettison the old picture of Stevens as an aesthete heedless of the dangers of living without doing; but as a new, more engaged Stevens emerges, it would be unfortunate to lose sight of his poetry's striking and voluble *lack* of interest in making as material transformation, or of the ways in which this particular form of disengagement was supported by the philosophy of a man whose life Stevens once described as one "in which the function of the imagination has had a function similar to its function in any deliberate work of art or letters" (*Necessary* 147–48). We might think, for example, of "objectification" itself, which as Santayana deploys it refers not to the creation of a tangible new object, but to an aspect of experience in which the subject encounters itself in the mode of otherness through projection upon an already existing thing.

Apposite here is the larger context of Burke's remark about Santayana's philosophy of serenity and retirement, a section of *A Grammar of Motives* in which Burke draws an extended contrast between Santayana and Marx considered as representatives of contemplation and praxis, respectively. "Whatever speculation and investigation may precede Marxist assertions," writes Burke, "there is the pressure to make them serviceable as a Rhetorical in-

ducement to action on the part of people who have slight interest in speculation and investigation *per se*. Santayana, on the other hand, cultivates a *lei-
surely* approach . . . " (215–16). A few pages later, Burke notes that reading
Santayana, "we do feel that it might be enough to cultivate the contemplation of essences, simply through love of dwelling in the vicinity of terms at
rest and at peace, terms that would serve as much as terms can to guide us
through a long life of euthanasia" (223)—or, for that matter, through the
Paterian short day of frost and sun. Burke's indirect gift to contemporary
Stevens scholarship, we might say, is the reflection that a way of swerving
from the expansive logic of capitalism (though not, as the contrast to Marx
suggests, a way of combating it) would be to take the promise of bliss in
"consumption" so seriously as to feel it actually fulfilled—or at least that a
way of liberating oneself from the guilt of nonproduction, and hence from
the production spiral, would be to find truly satisfying satisfaction in the
"consumption" of experience and to accept that satisfaction as good.

This is a direction suggested both in the conclusion to Pater's *Renaissance*
(the original intersection between aestheticism and the simple life, as it
were) and in Stevens's later poetry; and it is also, in a sense, the direction of
Stevens's life in Hartford, whose pattern was determined in part by the
poet's unusually ample capacity to be interested in the fluctuations of the
weather and the minutiae of the natural world around him, which he expressed most vividly in a letter of 1951:

> I like a world in which the passing of the season (or the passing of the seasons) is a
> matter of some importance; and I have often wondered why newspapers did not
> contain wires from Italy reporting flights of storks; or from Buenos Aires reporting
> on the Argentine spring; and most of all I have wanted in winter daily dispatches
> on the front page of the Tribune describing the dazzle over the Florida keys. How-
> ever, today General McArthur [*sic*] is more important than the sun. (*Letters* 721;
> see also 805, 819, 843)

What Stevens moves to do here is, in effect, to recuperate nature-as-fate by
showing how fate's daily details might provide continuous food for surprise,
how the object world might offer literally endless satisfaction even to the
gourmand of perception if that gourmand's mind could only be attuned sufficiently to the world's nuances. Indeed we might even say that such records
of Stevens's last years, like Crispin's story, offer to show how the cycles of
nature might replace the cycles of commerce with no sacrifice of the pleasure of consumption.

If such a proposal fails to convince in practice, of course, this is so preeminently because the relishing of the seasons at issue here is no more innocent of dependence on production than the acquisition of objets d'art:
Crispin had to farm his land as well as look at it, after all, and Stevens's
enjoyment of weather, which presumed installation among an array of com-

forts that most would unhesitatingly label bourgeois, was manifestly supported by his insurance career at the Hartford. As Lentricchia stresses, moreover, Stevens would always think of his poetry as a reward for labor in this
other sphere (one notably not burdened by art's suspicious claim to find true
use in inutility and true virtue in the failure to become a paying proposition),
no matter how central to the life of society he might claim the supreme
fiction to be; and it was surely this other work, above all, that made less
urgent for him the anxiety that art might have to justify itself in a transformation of the world, instead of simply in the purpose to be seen. It was
surely in part because Stevens the insurance executive could manifestly support his family and take a hand in the economic life of his country, in other
words, that Stevens the theorist of poetry could remain relatively free of the
guilt of nonproduction, dispensing with the imperative of durable making
more easily than full-time artists such as Woolf, Lewis, and Pound. (By the
same token, of course, we have to bear in mind that his longstanding mistrust of removal from the cycle of life was undoubtedly one of the factors
that led Stevens to a non-artistic career in the first place.)

Stevens's sense that authentic production could be achieved apart from
material transformation would, moreover, have been reinforced rather than
weakened by his engagement with the particular kind of nonpoetic work that
supplied him his living. For most modernist writers, the archetypal scene of
artistic making—and hence the typical scene of their vocation, broadly conceived—remained the fashioning of the plastic work of art, in which the
sensuous fabric of reality is immediately and visibly transformed, and in
view of which it becomes difficult to separate meaningful accomplishment
from the image of the made thing. Stevens, by contrast, was involved every
day in a kind of labor whose consequence (both for the world and for himself) could scarcely be doubted in spite of the fact that it was at least as
abstract as the writing of poetry, consisting essentially as it did in an interpretation and manipulation of discourse in which even the sensuous dimension of language did not normally impinge. From his job, in other words,
Stevens would have gained not only a general security that his life had
meaning, whatever the fate of his art, but also a specific assurance that one
need not act directly on material reality in order to affect the lives of others.

This point is immensely important in turn because other modernists' discernment of an element of violence or domination in their own work was
founded in part upon a confrontation with subjectivity's most destructive
interventions in the object world, above all industrial expansion and war—
because, that is to say, it was only in the face of physical changes on the
largest scale that one of the defining features of modernist self-positioning
could become a double bind under which life without production seemed
meaningless while life with production looked profoundly wrong. We have
seen this double bind at work in the tension between Woolf's axiomatic

embrace of monuments and her anxieties about the ways in which the making of art subjugates the object; in the strain between Lewis's contempt for the pure consumer and his hostility to the premise that everyone must do something (as well as the conflict between his dislike of the will-less masses and his distaste for the nonsensically generative will); and in Pound's negotiations with the burden of the past, in which the imperative of making new comes to blows with a powerful intuition that far too much has been made already. If Stevens escaped this difficult condition, clearly, the major reason lay in his resistance to conceiving of production in material terms, which can be regarded as either a cause or a symptom of his notably untroubled confidence in the power and permanence of the natural world.

Nor does Stevens's relative freedom from guilt on this score illuminate his departure from the line of his fellow Anglo-American modernists only, for it also figures instructively as another respect in which he both evokes and diverges from Sartre, that philosopher whose career illustrates perhaps more neatly than any other how production could mutate from primary purpose into principal evil. To consider Sartre's shift in emphasis from *Being and Nothingess* to the *Critique of Dialectical Reason*, after all, is to witness a more properly existential dilemma giving place to a more fully ecological one, to observe the making to which each individual is impelled returning as the origin of a devastating range of communal catastrophes—though, to be sure, Sartre never associates production with full mastery (either desired or achieved), instead stressing in both visions how the ambitions of the for-itself are bounded or curtailed by the in-itself's brute facticity. In the first scenario, however, this is so because an unbreachable Being can be compassed by no human action, however immense; here, the appearance of reflections on το ολον just after the section on the urge to make suggests how heavily Sartre's culminating vision of an essential slippage in the universe depends upon the image of the discrete fashioned object, which in its limitedness of spatial extension seems to emblematize the profounder limitations of all human projects. In the second scenario, by contrast, human ambitions fail because the world of matter, all too locally manipulable, comes back to haunt its manipulators in the form of the practico-inert ("every object . . . will in its turn become exigency through the mode and relations of production, and give rise to other exigencies in other objects" [*Critique* 189]), possible fatality in this case residing in the made thing understood not as simple failure but as consequential intervention.

It is significant, in this context, that the *Critique of Dialectical Reason* seems so clearly to mark a point of transition from the modern to the postmodern; for if the governing argument of this book has been that modernism was decisively shaped by a tension between the assumption that the individual life finds its meaning in making and the sense that all making is complicit with global disaster, one of its corollary claims is that such a crisis has

been of far less moment to postmodernity, under which the dangers of production have become more incontrovertibly visible and the guilt of nonproduction has appeared to recede. Another, less obvious, corollary is that
this tension was also more crucial to the first part of the twentieth century
than it was to the ninenteenth, though it can hardly be denied that individual
ambition and anxieties about the degradation of nature joined to set the
agenda of the Romantics and the more romantic Victorians. We might recall,
for instance, that Wordsworth, who attributed the genesis of his magnum
opus to anxieties about his own poetic output ("Far better never to have
heard the name / Of zeal and just ambition" [*Prelude* 35]), had already noted
in the preface to the *Lyrical Ballads* how "the encreasing accumulation of
men in cities" was helping "to blunt the discriminating powers of the mind,
and unfitting it for all voluntary exertion to reduce it to a state of almost
savage torpor" (*Prose* 128). Yet as this latter quote itself reminds us, the
crisis of material transformation for the Romantics (and even Ruskin) was at
least in the first instance a crisis of injury to human consciousness, the clear
remedy for which was poetry itself—an antidote to instrumentalization in all
its forms, in Shelley's vision, and for Wordsworth (in the same part of the
preface), a tonic that might "produce or enlarge" the mind's capability of
"being excited without the application of gross and violent stimulants"
(*Prose* 128). For cosmopolitan modernism, by contrast, the problem was not
urbanized consciousness specifically but a subjectivity that seemed, in including disruptive material transformation and imperialism as well as the
making of art among its capacities, to leave no production guiltless in the
end. It is telling, in this respect, that the modernists largely avoided the
rhetoric of therapy or healing in promoting poetry; and it is telling also that
Stevens is the modernist who most nearly retains it, in visions of the poem
as both cure of the ground and freshening of life.

To mention subjectivity, however, is also to invoke the sense in which
Stevens's vision of an epistemologically inexhaustible reality proves not the
exception to the modernist rule but one of the fullest articulations of modernists' preoccupations. For the truth is that while nature per se may be
fragile, the object world as such—whatever is not subjectivity, the world
outside the mind no matter how blighted or mastered—will remain a resource for contemplation as long as consciousness continues to find something compelling in that world's immunity to perfect knowing: this is the
final otherness that can be undone by no human activity, however forceful or
relentless. While modernists categorically rejected or repressed the belief
that art's primary service to society might lie in moral instruction, they
tended quietly to retain one of that belief's key premises, namely that imaginative literature expands the reader's understanding of self and others,
thereby mitigating otherness; and yet such mitigation was, as they recognized with a kind of bittersweet satisfaction, restricted to the human sphere.

Language, even literary language, could hardly diminish the opacity of the nonhuman thing, which—in spite of the enormous poetic output it might generate in a writer like Stevens—seemed at last (as Stevens himself noted repeatedly) to evade anything more penetrating than meticulous description or play at the level of the phenomenal, to exceed the subject's power to know most signally, perhaps, in exceeding words' power to contain. And it was without question this epistemological security, as much the aforementioned physical insecurity, that led Woolf, Lewis, Pound, Stevens, and their contemporaries to find in the object so striking a source of interest for imaginative writing.

Detractors of modernism have long charged it with a certain deficiency in feeling, a cold aloofness from the struggles and perils of a suffering world to which it allegedly offered only—inadequately—the autonomous work of art, and there is no point in trying to obscure this claim's ample foundation. A sometimes dangerous fascination with authority, a frequently troubling confidence in art's need (and ability) to rise above transitory conflicts, and a tendency to associate disenfranchisement with vulgarity are too obviously woven into the works of all of the high modernists, even the most politically engaged, to make such an attempt much more than futile in the end. And yet in their approaches to the object—which they almost invariably treasured as something out of the reach of subjectivity, something vibrantly independent, different, apart—modernists show how partial is the truth of this indictment, with its unwarranted assumption that love always demands the closeness of joining and holding, never the distance of respect and longing. It has also been said, as noted in the introduction, that modernism tended to look toward beyonds or ideals that postmodernism partly defines itself by relinquishing, and here the modernist admiration for the object's ungovernable excess and irreducible distance confirms the claim. Indeed one of the lessons of the solid object is that modernists' most striking expressions of tenderness are often scarcely separable from their most significant enunciations of ideals, where both turn on a powerful sense of the virtues of radical alterity.

This allure of the object world, casually possessed of something that neither the subject nor language can ever have or know and yet constantly threatened by subjectivity's practical power to transform, is adumbrated nowhere more movingly, perhaps, than in "The Planet on the Table," that late lyric in which Stevens rather uncharacteristically imagines the poem as a kind of thing—and yet also as not a thing, resisting with a certain humility the thought that his work might fully grasp some quality to which the object world alone can lay claim. Looking back on his career from the vantage of its very end, the century's great poet of desire most movingly affirms his satisfaction not by praising his poems as monuments, but by noting his hope that they partake, even slightly and mediately, of that quality which with characteristic precision he names "affluence." "Affluence": in spite of

Stevens's own unusually secure faith in the resilience of the place not our own, this word as used here—with its suggestion of both plenitude and limitation, of an ampleness that gestures toward infinity but cannot reach it—captures perhaps better than any other the object world in its modernist moment, a moment of transition from power and inexhaustibility to fragility and diminishment, or rather one in which an inevitable resistance to human knowledge is posed tensely against the possibility of losing everything else to human violence. We have already seen how Ariel, glad that he had written his poems, acknowledged that their survival was not what was important. "What mattered," Stevens goes on to explain,

> was that they should bear
> Some lineament or character,
>
> Some affluence, if only half-perceived,
> In the poverty of their words,
> Of the planet of which they were part.

(532–33)

NOTES

INTRODUCTION

1. From the point of view of a rigorous philosophy, of course, such a vision may seem to unite illegitimately (at least) three very different kinds of "object": the object of knowledge, the object as opposite to "the subject," and the object as discrete physical entity. As Vincent Descombes points out, under a careful philosophical grammar the "object" of knowing can only be a proposition ("I know that x"), not "some thing, an object in the sense in which the knowing subject, by virtue of knowing, is projected onto something other than himself" (128), which is to say that it can be neither a perfect "not-subject" nor (a fortiori) a material thing as such. But Descombes also shows that philosophy since Kant has been shaped decisively by a tendency to conflate the object of knowing, the other to the subject, and the physical thing; and the same conflation informs modernist literature, where the recognition that one cannot "know" an inanimate object even to the degree that one can "know" a person—though one can love, make, and destroy material things—gives rise to some of the most crucial strands of reflection to be found in the writing that I examine here.

2. These points also help to clarify why the term "fetishism" has not seemed to me very useful in the context of this study. As William Pietz has shown, "fetishism" as originally coined (in 1757, by Charles de Brosses) meant "the worship of terrestrial, material objects," which was understood by the *philosophes* to disclose at "the origin of religious belief" a "primitive causal reasoning: a mode of thought deriving not from 'reason' but from 'desire and credulity'" (131, 137). What virtually all later usages, including Marx's and Freud's, share with this acceptation is the implication that the fetishizer mistakenly attributes to the object a power that it does not have: in David Simpson's formulation, for example, "fetishism occurs when the mind ceases to realize that it has itself created the outward images or things to which it subsequently posits itself as in some sort of subservient relation" (xiii; see also 9–20), while Wendy Steiner finds in Marxian and Freudian fetishism "a confusion of the power an object represents with the object itself" (81–82). Although the affinity for the object discussed here does at times negotiate a sort of felt experience of animism, it more usually emphasizes either the epistemological distance between object and subject or the power of human beings over the object world (rather than the reverse), so that in a narrow sense it would be quite unlike the kind of magical thinking denominated "fetishistic." Certainly, such an affinity might be considered "fetishistic" where the term is used to indicate a mistaken, questionable, or simply obsessive investment of longing or hope in a particular thing (the American right fetishizes states' rights, poststructuralists fetishize language, the culture of therapy fetishizes therapy), but of course the breadth of this usage means that it will be of little help in articulating the specific kinds of relations to objects that this book sets out to explore.

3. It could be argued, of course, that this putatively ecological anxiety in fact serves as an alibi for more devious attempts, on the part of a masculinist modernism, to contain the feminine—that the writer threatened by the New Woman and in need of something helpless for which to feel solicitude finds a handy candidate in the

object world, over which he casts the very net of imperial subjectivity against which he claims to be struggling. Certainly, when Ransom (for example) believes himself to be speaking of the integrity of the object, he is engaging in a work of objectification that demands further interrogation; but to insist that either gender or material transformation is the "real" problem for which the other serves as a screen is surely to impoverish our sense of history and to resign ourselves to chicken-and-egg debates that can never be resolved. Nicholls, incidentally, seems to assign gender a distinctly secondary role, arguing that "the feminine" appears as "a suitable surrogate for social relations in general . . . because the illusion of some absolute otherness is required to protect the poet's self from the full recognition of identity with other people" (4). This claim clearly combats rather than affirms Gilbert and Gubar's contention that "'modernism' is itself—though no doubt overdetermined—for men as much as for women a product of the sexual battle" that raged with particular violence around the turn of the century, "set in motion by the late nineteenth-century rise of feminism and the fall of Victorian concepts of 'femininity'" (Gilbert and Gubar xii).

4. In H. D.'s well known account of the birth of Imagism, Pound, having hastily edited a page of manuscript by his friend in the tea room of the British Museum, scribbled "H.D. Imagiste" at the bottom and promised to send it to Harriet Monroe at *Poetry* magazine. Three poems signed "H.D., Imagiste" did indeed appear in the January 1913 number, and the movement, or quasi movement, was underway (Carpenter 187–88). Both "Imagism" and "Imagisme" have been used by writers within and without Pound's circle; I stick to the former for the most part, but take up the latter at one or two points when Pound's artful promotion of his and his associates' work is at issue.

5. In a letter to Harriet Monroe of 1915: "objectivity and again objectivity, and expression . . . nothing that you couldn't, in some circumstance, in the stress of some emotion, actually say" *(Letters* 49). In 1913, he complimented Ford Madox Hueffer by observing that he "believes in an exact rendering of things," in "getting a precise meaning," and is therefore "objective" *(Ezra Pound's* 1:112; also quoted in Levenson 106).

6. Levenson himself, it should be noted, applies the description quoted here only to what he calls the impressionist or Fordian phase of Imagism, which lasted through early 1914, arguing that in the months that followed, the influences of T. E. Hulme and debates in the visual arts led Pound away from an investment in mimesis and toward an aesthetic of autonomous form. As Levenson notes, however, Pound retained his emphasis on the importance of emotion and individual expression even in this latter phase (135).

7. In 1914, Richard Aldington, who joined H. D. and Pound in forming the triad of original "Imagistes," listed "[a] hardness, as of cut stone," as the third among the six Imagist prescriptions, though this was not one of the three principles included in Pound's 1913 manifesto in *Poetry* (Harmer 45). This preference for the hard over the soft, which has been discussed amply by many scholars, can be found throughout Pound's writing: in a 1914 essay, for example, wherein he deplores literary partisans of "Monet's softness" in favor of "Flaubert's definiteness" *(Literary* 400); or in a review of that year in which he praises a Yeats whose work was "becoming gaunter, seeking greater hardness of outline" *(Literary* 379); or in a letter of that same year again in which he tells Amy Lowell that Imagisme "stands, or I should like it to stand

for hard light, clear edges" *(Letters* 38). Perhaps his most honest formulation in this line comes from the slightly mellower vantage of 1918, when he wrote in "The Hard and the Soft in French Poetry" that while softness is not always a fault, hardness is nearly always a virtue *(Literary* 285).

8. This is not to say that in his antihumanism Hulme took the part of the object world per se; his primary interest was rather to restore a sense of the "anti-vital" element in religion, to combat the conflation of biology and theology that he came to associate with Bergson. It does seem, however, that Hulme's more developed formulations were fed by an early interest in an object-centered poetry, some statements of which evoke Ransom's later claims for contemplation as against predatory action (see Hulme 40, 70, 189, 194–97).

9. With respect to the form-content split, the central text is of course Marjorie Perloff's 1982 article-question, "Pound/Stevens: Whose Era?" Certainly, the effort of virtually all the major Stevens scholarship of the past decade, including Perloff's, has been to overturn the myth of Stevens's distance from politics and history, a myth arguably installed by the Bollingen Committee's decision to award its second annual prize to Stevens (a year after its recognition of Pound's *Pisan Cantos* was greeted with an explosion of denunciations), and ratified by Stevens criticism of the fifties and sixties. But the habit of opposing Pound to Stevens has not yet been forgotten, and continues to provide critics a useful paradigm against which to define their own positions.

10. One of Larrissy's central arguments is that modern and contemporary commentators have underestimated the extent to which the habit of regarding "[a]ccurate description" as a touchstone of poetic value is in fact a legacy from the Romantics; another is that they have overstated the extent to which "an easy merging of mind and matter" is to be found in Romantic poetry (1, 12). True, Larrissy writes, "natural objects" have for the Romantics "the function of filling" a "split in the self" (and thus become, in Robert Young's formulation, versions of the Lacanian *objet a*), but in many Romantic encounters these objects prove unable to fulfill this role convincingly, and in so doing ultimately reveal the split's "ineradicability" (18, 24, 18). The difference between Romanticism in its less affirmative mode and modernism, then, would lie not so much in opposing positions anent the success of the attempt to join subject and object as in differing views on what valence should be attached to that attempt's inevitable failure. (In *Language as Living Form in Nineteenth-Century Poetry*, Isobel Armstrong argues similarly that modernists most signally misunderstood nineteenth-century poetry in mistaking for mere expressions of "subjective life" what were in fact rigorous efforts "to de-mystify the relation between subject and object," efforts in which "a primal unity on the part of the perceiving mind" was not assumed [xiii].)

11. With respect to many if not all of the revolutions that Tratner associates with modernism, in fact, it seems proper to point out that the aesthetes got there first, and with far less hesitation. Discussing Wilhelm Reich's work as a context for modernist innovations, for example, Tratner writes that "Reich's conclusion is thoroughly consumerist: feeling pleasure becomes the best method of production" (705); but of course this line of thinking appears, arguably, as far back as Pater. Certainly, Reich's own case confirms that the twentieth century could believe that it was making for the first time discoveries of which the fin de siècle had been aware, but as it happens Anglo-American high modernists did not lose sight of aestheticism's (and even Ro-

manticism's) precedents in this regard; and indeed one of this book's major arguments is that modernists decisively turned against their predecessors' habit of rewriting experience as production, even where they found more concrete forms of production gravely problematic.

12. A few further notes are required here. First: Hegel's notion of realization through labor represents more than just another stage in the unfolding of *Geist* insofar as it constitutes the basic figure that makes all the other self-realizing turns of Hegel's progression comprehensible; even were it not for the legacy to Marx, it would make sense that this unusually concrete section of the *Phenomenology* has elicited a disproportionate amount of commentary. Second: at the point in the *1844 Manuscripts* just quoted, Marx is arguing against Hegel that human activity is "the activity of an objective, natural being"; the full quote runs: "To say that man is a *corporeal*, living, real, sensuous, objective being full of natural vigor is to say that he has *real, sensuous, objects* as the objects of his being or of his life, or that he can only *express* his life in real, sensuous objects" (181). (A brilliant and far-reaching argument for the utter centrality of a faith in making to all of Marx's thought can be found in Scarry 243–77.) Third: the remarks on Sartre must be taken with the understanding that for him meaning in the secular universe is always, as we will have occasion to note again, more or less provisional.

13. In *The Sensible Spirit*, F. C. McGrath argues that this Hegelian wave, along with its neo-Hegelian progeny, profoundly affected Pater, who encountered it as an undergraduate at Oxford, as well as Yeats, Eliot, and Joyce (79, 130ff). In McGrath's account, the late nineteenth-century British Hegelians "typically rejected Hegel's absolutism along with its transcendental foundations" (130), although aspects of Hegel's idealist vision of history can be detected among the moderns nonetheless.

14. See *Modernist Quartet*, especially 15–46, in which Lentricchia argues that with "James, modernism was born in America as an anti-imperialist project" (19) and that this anti-imperialism undergirds James's advocacy of "the liberation of the small, the regional, the locally embedded, the underdog" (22) as well as his view of interpretation as domination (45). Lentricchia's portrait, which clearly marks James a defender of the particular, should remind us (as should Bergson's career or even Sartre's, in a rather different way) that praxis-centered philosophies need not necessarily hold mastery to be the normative or most desirable relation between subject and object.

15. It seems to me that although "high" may once have implied a judgment of superiority in some absolute sense, the present antihierarchical disposition of scholarship across the humanities makes so uncritical an understanding of the term virtually impossible today. I like "high," in fact, not only because it is already in use, however irregular, but also because it records rather than erases a change in the way in which value has been envisioned by literary scholarship. More generally, I would endorse Rita Felski's point that it will be useful to retain the term "modernism" as a designation for texts showing certain "formally self-conscious, experimental, antimimetic features . . . while simultaneously questioning the assumption that such texts are necessarily the most important or representative works of the modern period" (25).

CHAPTER ONE
VIRGINIA WOOLF

1. The magic of small things for the child, or for the adult recalling childhood, is eloquently captured in a 1936 letter from Woolf to David Cecil. Groping, against fatigue, for a suitable metaphor for Cecil's 1935 Leslie Stephen lecture on Jane Austen, Woolf writes: ". . . what figure do I want? I'm so sleepy I can't think; but I'm dreaming of a lovely little toy that used to lie in a workbox: a nut, full of green silk" (*Letters* 6: 22).

2. The preeminence of china as a collectible in general, at least by the end of the nineteenth century, is attested by the very first paragraph of an 1897 volume called *The Connoisseur*: "What do lovers of art collect? There is a large proportion of persons who . . . would be unable . . . to suggest anything beyond the accustomed phrase, 'Pictures and old china'" (F. Robinson 1). In the book's third chapter, however, the author aims to set such persons straight: "There has never, perhaps, been such a rage for collecting anything and everything as at the present time" (30).

3. It should be made clear that in the view of the contributors to the anti-imperialist *Heart of the Empire*, imperialism had disastrously derailed the important social reform impulses of the 1880s—so that for Masterman and his coauthors there lay a disturbing irony in the fact that imperialist sentiment was spurring the return to such reform (as the more powerful imperialist Liberals, led in effect by Lord Rosebery, promoted the idea that an empire such as the British required "a race vigorous and industrious and intrepid" [quoted in B. Gilbert xx; for more on this turn, see Gilbert xi–xxi]).

4. For the definitive treatment of eighteenth-century attacks on luxury, see John Sekora's *Luxury: The Concept in Western Thought, Eden to Smollett*.

5. Hobsbawm: "At all times between 1921 and 1938 at least one out of every ten citizens of working age was out of a job. In seven out of these eighteen years at least three out of every twenty were unemployed, in the worst years one out of five. . . . For the first time in history, a proletarian party became and remained the major alternative government party, and the fear of working-class power and expropriation now haunted the middle classes" (208–09). "Not until the Conservative era of the middle 1950s," Hobsbawm observes elsewhere, "did the confidence which flaunts its wealth in public return" (275).

6. On the aesthete revival, see Sinfield 131ff. Graves notes that in 1925, newspapers like the *Daily Express* could be found attacking modern youth for a fashion-conscious effeminacy (128), and claims that in the early part of the decade, at least, "[d]isillusion—a hard, cynical, gay disillusion" was the "new keyword" (127), though Burdett asserts that in the twenties fashionable "disillusion" had "been replaced by indifference" (290). Burdett's was not the first book-length recuperation of the aesthetes and the decadents, incidentally: in *The Eighteen Nineties: A Review of Art and Ideas at the Close of the Nineteenth Century* (first published in 1913), Holbrook Jackson abjured the posture of the scandalized to offer a balanced, even sympathetic, consideration of their lives and works, writing in a typical sentence from his introduction, "It was an epoch of experiment, with some achievement and some remorse" (14). The book reappeared in a revised edition (cited here) in 1923.

7. Nonproductiveness was registered as an aesthete trademark in both promotions and satires of aestheticism—which were, of course, often hard to tell apart. For the archetypal instance of the former, see Wilde's quotation from "Pen, Pencil, and Poison" below. One moderately amusing example of the latter can be found in G. S. Street's *Autobiography of a Boy*, wherein the protagonist, the young would-be aesthete Tubby, remarks the "utter unreason and irrelevancy" of his father's demand that he earn some money and protests unconvincingly that, "if need be," he might "live on a crust in an attic" (46, 48).

8. On the Woolfs' finances, see Bell 2: 38–41, 160; King 105–106, 370–71, 400, 429; and above all Lee 556–62.

9. For a somewhat different version of this story, see *Aestheticism*, in which Leon Chai argues that "the origins of Aestheticism," as in Baudelaire, Burckhardt, and Pater, "involve a preoccupation with the beauty of impressions, while the end of the movement," as in late James and Proust, "attempts to give such impressions a form . . . an ideal architectonics that would relate an impression to all the others in an individual's existence" (xi). Accepting Chai's account, one might be tempted to conclude that the shift in emphasis from experience to recording was more gradual than has been argued in the foregoing, and better described as internal to an aestheticism that would embrace some or all of what we have come to call modernism. Yet such a conclusion finally seems problematic in (at least) two respects: first, in that although Chai's readings of individual authors are uniformly intriguing, they largely fail, on close analysis, to support his overarching narrative; second, in that while there are some respects in which modernism is rightly seen as a late aestheticism, Chai's scheme encompasses neither the self-conscious distancing from aestheticism undertaken by writers like Woolf and Pound nor these writers' emphasis on material rather than ideal forms—so that in the end that scheme would not bear on the "modernism" treated here even were it more internally persuasive.

10. In "How to Read," Ezra Pound noted that at one point an "academic press . . . had ventured to challenge Palgrave" with a new anthology; "they had been 'interested'—would I send back my prospectus? I did. They found the plan 'too ambitious.' The said they might do 'something', but that if they did it would be 'more in the nature of gems'" (*Literary* 18).

11. On the artistry of parties, see for example Naremore 105 and Caughie 28; on Clarissa's shopping, see Wicke, "*Mrs. Dalloway* Goes to Market" and Abbott; on Orlando see Abbott 208–209; on the woman as archetypal consumer, see Bowlby 18–34, Felski 61–90, and Wicke, *Advertising* 158–69.

12. On these questions as they relate to Molly Bloom and Clarissa Dalloway—but also on the dangers of limiting such readings of consumption to their implications for gender history and polemic—see Wicke, "Who's She When She's at Home?" and "*Mrs. Dalloway.*"

13. On masculinity and the modern writer, see Bowlby, *Just Looking*, especially 11 and 89–90; Felski 91–114; and Huyssen 44–58. On women, art production, and modernity, see Felski 47–49.

14. Although he neither calls attention to the term "absurdity" here nor brings Woolf and Sartre together in his reading (his preferred interlocutors for Clarissa being Heidegger and Wittgenstein), Ruotolo does take note of this passage in both of the books just mentioned, observing that it marks an instance of the "critical moment of

absolute doubt" central to Woolf's work (*Six* 13) and that it suggests how Rachel—virtually a born critic of all that exists—is bound to become "an outsider by virtue of her eccentric view of things" (*Interrupted* 21).

15. In *Night and Day*, Katharine Hilbery notes that for her flowers are "variously shaped and colored petals, poised, at different seasons of the year, upon very similar green stalks," while to her fiancé Ralph they are "living things endowed with sex" (330); in "The Mark on the Wall," the narrator says that it is pleasant to think of trees because "they grow, without paying any attention to us" (*Shorter Fiction* 88); in "Kew Gardens," in E. M. Forster's terse summary, Woolf "sees men, sometimes looking at flowers, and flowers never looking at men" (*Abinger* 108); and in *To the Lighthouse*, the brightness of the day is made strange by "the trees standing there, and the flowers standing there, looking before them, looking up, yet beholding nothing, eyeless, and so terrible" (135).

16. This remark recalls Mrs. Thornbury's observation, in *The Voyage Out*, that "she had taken up the study of botany since her daughter married. . . . It was a good thing to have some occupation which was quite independent of other people . . . when one got old" (324–25).

17. This strategy of omission is at least as important in *Jacob's Room*, where the narrator continually calls attention to the necessary incompleteness of any depiction of character and to the fact that people know so little about one another: "It is no use trying to sum people up" (31, 154); "Each had his past shut in him like the leaves of a book known to him by heart; and his friends could only read the title, James Spalding, or Charles Budgeon" (64–65); "It seems that a profound, impartial, and absolutely just opinion of our fellow-creatures is utterly unknown" (71).

18. As Rosenbaum points out (331–32), Woolf offers ample foundation both for readings that stress the element of mystical continuity in her fiction and for Forster's claim that it would be utterly mistaken to read in *Mrs. Dalloway* or any of her works "mysticism, unity beneath multiplicity, twin souls" (*Abinger* 111). Woolf's position is perhaps best characterized as the view that while experiences of extraordinary joining do occur, they are infrequent at best and (however powerful) understood better as revelatory feelings than as divine revelations.

19. Eliot was not merely following Bradley's ordering in beginning his treatment with experience: *Appearance and Reality* does take experience as the foundation for further inquiry, but this foundation is won only after some struggle. "I am driven to the conclusion," Bradley writes 130 pages in, "that for me experience is the same as reality" (128).

20. See, for example, *Principia Ethica* 203.

21. In *Being and Nothingness*: "Pierre's body is in no way to be distinguished from Pierre-for-me. The Other's body with its various meanings exists only for me: to be an object-for-others or to-be-a-body are two ontological modalities which are strictly equivalent expressions of the being-for-others on the part of the for-itself" (454).

22. In a recent article testifying to the continuing attraction of the problem of knowledge of others in Woolf, Martha Nussbaum argues that in *To the Lighthouse* Mr. and Mrs. Ramsay "know one another as we know them—by reading. Having lived together for a long time, they have gathered a lot of information about patterns of speech, action, reaction" (745). Characteristically, Nussbaum rewrites in the mode

of sharing or love (for the Ramsays submit to each other's reading willingly) what in Sartre is founded in a certain anxiety about the power of the other.

23. At this point, the two have already "compared their respective tastes in the matter of trees and lakes," and found that "[w]hile talking exclusively of what they saw . . . the compact between them was made firmer and deeper" (339)—Woolf faintly gesturing here at those courtship scenes in eighteenth- and nineteenth-century fictions in which the justness of another's aesthetic observations implies fineness of character and a mind in harmony with one's own. Even Moore felt compelled to note how the third thing figures in bonds of affection, if not of romantic love: discussing the relation between affection and aesthetic appreciation, his two incontrovertible goods, he wrote in the *Principia Ethica*, "Admirable mental qualities consist very largely in an emotional contemplation of beautiful objects; and hence the appreciation of them will consist essentially in the contemplation of such contemplation" (204).

24. Indeed, in the original manuscript of *Mrs. Dalloway*, Woolf seems to mark both the allure and the futility of the belief that in reading a book one meets its author inasmuch as she includes just such an expectation in one of Septimus's delusions. Imagining himself climbing up to the levels of the great dead, Septimus at one point tells himself, "I shall hear Shakespeare talking," to which thought a "general voice" replies, "In time" (*Hours* 64).

25. The problem of keeping the nonliving separate from the no-longer-living is adumbrated metonymically in *Mrs. Dalloway*, in Peter Walsh's recollection that Clarissa's sister had been turned into an unliving thing by a falling tree, and metaphorically in "Time Passes," in which the bracketed mention of Andrew Ramsay's death follows directly the note that "there seemed to drop into this silence, this indifference, this integrity, the thud of something falling" (133).

26. "*To the Lighthouse* inscribes the movement of abjection without which there could be no subjectivity, and no signification either. . . . If Lily's line at the end of the novel is the emblem of minimal but fixed difference which secures her self-inscription, the price Lily pays for finishing her picture is the casting out of the mother, her beloved Mrs. Ramsay" (118).

27. In his 1990 *Late Marxism*, Jameson claims that in Adorno "reconciliation [*Versöhnung*] . . . is very precisely to be taken as a lifting of the tensions and contradictions between the universal and particular," and that "the common understanding that it involves a reconciliation of subject and object is thus erroneous, except to the degree to which object here designates the larger social order and subject the individual or particular" (31–32). While it is true that Adorno's philosophical reflections cannot be detached from his commitment to social justice and that he never imagines reconciliation occurring within individual psychology apart from a changed social order, however, the philosophical tradition of considering the subject-object division as something other than the individual-society opposition alone would make Jameson's statement extraordinarily and misleadingly reductive—even were it not the case that Adorno's writings on the thingness of the work of art (in the *Aesthetic Theory*, especially) leave no doubt that when he refers to the object he means, at least in many pivotal instances, an other to consciousness exemplified most vividly by the discrete material thing.

28. A complaint about the ruining of her country walks by the appearance of a vast cement factory notwithstanding. In a letter to Ethel Smyth of 29 January 1932 she wrote, "No, we're not at Rodmell, and I cant say I ever wish to go there again.

Factories are rising on the river bank [at Ashham]—cement works—huge, vast, about as big as the Albert Hall. . . . I'd much rather stay here [at 52 Tavistock Square, London], or in Whitechapel, or in any suburban slum where theres no down and marsh to be murdered inch by inch by these damnable buggers. Only I generally like buggers; I cant think of a word to fit them—thats all. My walks are ruined for ever" (*Letters* 5: 10).

29. In *The Body in Pain*, Scarry observes that any "artifact (a relocated piece of coal, a sentence, a cup, a piece of lace) is *a fragment of world alteration*" (171), though whereas Sartre stresses the individual's urge to conquer the object world in transforming it, Scarry envisions every act of making as a contribution to the removal of pain from the human community. In spite of her preference for a language of healing over one of domination, however, Scarry too registers making's character of assault on the object world, noting that in it the human "interior gains some small share of the blissful immunity of inert inanimate objecthood; and conversely, by transporting pain out onto the external world, that external environment is deprived of its immunity to, unmindfulness of, and indifference toward the problems of sentience" (285). That the inanimate does not *in fact* become sentient matters a great deal here, of couse, since this distinction marks the difference between a figurative authoring of suffering and a real one, and thus in one sense renders Scarry's celebration of making more credible, pragmatically speaking, than Woolf's and Adorno's doubts. And yet it is worth noting in turn that the major front on which the latter writers' anxieties take on practical force—that of ecological devastation—is one that Scarry strikingly evades, remarking instead, with respect to the fabricating imagination's "tendency toward excess, amplitude, and abundance," that "any problematic manifestation of surfeit . . . can be eliminated by the translation of surfeit into sharability, by, that is, the distribution of the objects to a larger number of persons" (323–24). For an intriguingly related exploration of making and human projection, see Fisher..

30. In a eulogy for Julian Bell written in 1937, Woolf remarks, "We were all C.O.'s in the Great war" (quoted in Bell 2: 258). Lytton Strachey and Duncan Grant both claimed conscientious objector status; Clive Bell did farm duty on Ottoline Morrell's estate in 1916; Leonard Woolf's military service was finally forestalled by medical excuse, though he later partly regretted not serving.

31. On the page of her diary opposite the "effort, effort" comment, Woolf had copied, in Italian, the speech from *Inferno* 26 in which Ulysses explains that not even love for his family could quench his "burning wish," in Mark Musa's translation, "to know the world and have experience / of all man's vices, of all human worth" (308). Certainly, the speech may provoke admiration for effort, effort—it did in Tennyson—and yet its point in the Dantean context is that such struggle is both costly and overreaching.

32. This testimony could certainly suggest that the principal figure for Thoby here is Bernard, whose engagement with death closes the novel. Percival, however, seems more nearly evocative of Woolf's brother in that he dies young and apparently generally beloved, and certainly it is his death upon which the book's energies of mourning seem to converge. Indeed it seems that Bernard is to Percival as Woolf is to Thoby (and Lily to Mrs. Ramsay), and that his author works out her own anxieties about the propriety of objectifying the dead through Bernard's persona. Could she write Julian Thoby Stephen 1881–1906 on the first page? She supposed not.

33. In a chapter from her book on Woolf entitled "Things," Rachel Bowlby argues

that Woolf's way of presenting objects, especially in *Orlando* and *The Years*, suggests a "shift from stable orders of integration between people and things [in the nineteenth century] to the fragmentariness of modernity," but also that Woolf offers this suggestion only by way of furnishing her novels "with the stuff of . . . further questions" designed to unsettle our habit of thinking about the past in terms of coherent periods (*Virginia Woolf* 123). Certainly, Bowlby's argument offers a helpful elucidation of one of the disruptive maneuvers that energize Woolf's later approaches to history; and yet at the same time it clearly underestimates the degree to which Woolf herself regarded "the Victorian" as a coherent entity—and one characterized not merely by stability but by a rigidity of quite astonishing oppressiveness.

34. It is true, of course, that the "object" to which Eleanor points is a pair of human beings, but here Woolf only follows the pattern of *To the Lighthouse* and *The Waves*: like Mrs. Ramsay and Percival, the man and woman alighting from the cab sharpen Woolf's address to the subject-object relation precisely in figuring as both persons and objects for the subject in question. What confirms the promise of this final moment is that it also represents an overcoming of the Victorian social and narrative structures that Woolf found so oppressive. As objects of attention, after all, the man and woman have a peculiar freedom because their identity is so unfixed; they could be married or unmarried, lovers or friends or even colleagues, this very indeterminacy seeming to satisfy Peggy's demand that one "live differently" by marking a highly visible revision of the traditional nuptial ending of the nineteenth-century novel.

35. Woolf began work on what would become *Between the Acts* in the spring of 1938 and finished it in early 1941; German troops invaded Poland on 1 September 1939. As Patricia Joplin notes, the summer of 1939, in which the events of the novel are finally set, marked "the last of interval of 'normal' life before Britain ceased to be a spectator and became an actor in the war" ("Authority" 214).

36. For another aspect of Woolf's reading of Freud in relation to this novel, see Joplin, "Authority" 217. Joplin, incidentally, goes on to charge Leonard with nursing an "easy sense that England represented the forces of civilization over against Germany" (218)—a charge clearly countered by his heavy emphasis on the problem of the barbarian within "our" minds and hearts.

37. Again, this is not to say that Woolf's views changed completely near the end of her life, only that she was beginning to entertain some vigorous doubts. In 1940, she could still ask Lady Simon, in a letter, "How can we alter the crest and the spur of the fighting cock?" (*Letters* 6: 379).

38. In his history of the Hogarth under the Woolfs, J. H. Willis notes that Leonard Woolf "detested nazism and fascism, but it was characteristic of his editorial astuteness to see the usefulness of publishing Mussolini's tract. . . . The original 1,500 copies sold quickly, a reprint of 1,200 copies followed, and eventually the pamphlet went through four impressions before being reset in 1940" (237).

39. Of the Victorians, Mrs. Swithin says, "I don't believe . . . that there ever were such people. Only you and me and William dressed differently," to which William responds, "You don't believe in history" (174–75). He and Isa then imagine her proceeding from harmony and unity to the conclusion that "the agony of the particular sheep, cow, or human being is necessary" (174–75), their speculations couched smugly and patronizingly enough ("Well, if the thought gave her comfort . . . let her

think it" [175]) to make clear that Woolf feels small affection for their soi-disant attunement to brutal reality. This does not mean, however, that she embraces Lucy's complacency; again, *Between the Acts* shows her asking new questions but finding no answers fully satisfactory. At the close of the novel, Mrs. Swithin asks, "Did you feel . . . we act different parts but are the same?" and Isa replies first in the affirmative, then in the negative. "It was Yes, No. Yes, yes, yes, the tide rushed out embracing. No, no, no, it contracted" (215).

40. Joplin, once again: "The English audience that finds it impossible to complete the thought that the Nazis' victims might really be 'people like ourselves' is finally forced to see when La Trobe . . . has the actors confront the audience with 'hand glasses, tin cans, scraps of scullery glass, harness room glass, and heavily embossed silver mirrors'" ("Authority" 220).

CHAPTER TWO
WYNDHAM LEWIS

1. In his introduction to Judith Collins's history of the Omega, Quentin Bell describes the Workshop's operating principle as follows: "The Impressionists (to apply the words of another revolutionary) had merely 'explained the world, the point was to change it'" (ix).

2. On the break between Lewis and Fry, see Lewis's *Letters* 45–53; Meyers 39–50; Collins 54–57, 60–61.

3. Tiffany, once again, argues forcefully that "the transparency of visual experience, epitomized by reflection and observation," becomes under Poundian Imagism not a passive registering of whatever impinges on the eye but "a physiological process that shapes not only perception but 'circumstance' and the external object" (35).

4. In that year he observed in an essay that the Nineties went out "because of their muzziness, because of a softness derived . . . not from books but from impressionist painting" (*Literary* 363), and explained in a letter that the "only reason, or at least a very strong reason for inventing a new term is to have a term with a precise meaning, a term which makes it unnecessary to discuss with every Frank, John and Amy, whether 'hardness' for example is or is not a virtue in itself," having admonished his correspondent, F. S. Flint, "You seem to see no difference between imagisme and impressionism" (quoted in Harmer 59).

5. A page earlier, he remarks, "War, and especially those miles of hideous desert known as 'the Line' in Flanders and France, presented me with a subject-matter so consonant with the austerity of that 'abstract' vision I had developed, that it was an easy transition" back to reality (138). A fuller discussion of Lewis's initial efforts to translate visual priorities into literature can be found in Klein 55ff. For a helpful summary of Lewis's relation to abstraction, see Alan Robinson, who argues forcefully that Lewis's Vorticist polemics embrace neither the antihumanism nor the abstraction advocated by Hulme (140–49), less convincingly that Lewis's aesthetic was premised on an ideal of "empathetic interaction with the environment" (133).

6. On this break see, especially, the beginning of chapter two of David Ayers's *Wyndham Lewis and Western Man*. Years later, Lewis recalled that in attending Bergson's lectures at the Collège de France he had found the philosopher "an excellent lecturer, dry and impersonal" (*Letters* 489).

7. At least in the realm of prose—it having been prevented from exercising its baleful effects on poetry, presumably, by his own efforts and those of Hulme and Pound.

8. Though in this particular case, Lewis is clearly indebted to Hulme, who in the *New Age* in 1911 observed that prior to the ascendancy of the mechanistic conception of the universe that Bergson (rightly, in Hulme's view) combated, "consciousness occupied the position of a rather feeble king who still, by the favour of his troops, retained some power. The change produced by mechanism can be compared to the sudden discovery by the troops that they are self-sufficient and can manage things themselves" (142).

9. Lewis does indulge in something more like the first kind of racism at several points, however, notably in remarks that casually impute to nonwhites a constitutional laziness or indifference. Deploring communist promotion of racial insurgency in Bolivia, he writes in *Paleface*, "we know that the Indian, like the Negro, is politically apathetic and would do little himself" (262), while in *Left Wings over Europe* (1936), he contrasts "the industrious and ingenious Italian" to "the lazy, stupid, and predatory Ethiopian" in defending Mussolini's actions in Africa (164–65). This ambivalence in Lewis's ideas about race is exemplified most clearly, perhaps, in a remark from a typescript of (probably) 1934 or 1935 recently published in *Modernism/Modernity*: "[T]he conquest of the Redskin by the European colonist was not the conquest of a lower type by a higher *necessarily*," Lewis writes, before placing the real triumph with the inventor of the rifle ("Machine" 174, emphasis added).

10. Earlier in *Blasting*, he states bluntly that the "post-war" is "a recrudescence of 'the Nineties'" and recalls one day coming upon his friend Roy Campbell "delivering emphatic thumps upon the table at which he was sitting," shouting, "'I won't be a Nineties man!'" and glaring at someone, probably "Ronald Firbank—who was the very *genius loci* of the 'post-war', and the reincarnation of all the Nineties—Oscar Wilde, Pater, Beardsley, Dawson all rolled into one, and served up with *sauce créole*" (223–24).

11. Lewis has not been alone in finding the Jamesian solid object unusually evanescent. For a consideration of how James's tendency to dematerialize the physical scene while reifying attributes and properties makes him one of consumer culture's great early analysts, see Agnew, above all 96–99.

12. On Wilde, aestheticism, and parodies thereof as sources for Osmond, see Freedman 146–48.

13. The collapse of the division between performers and audience is also the central theme of one of Lewis's long essays of the period, "The Dithyrambic Spectator," an attack on the idea that great art might be produced by collectives rather than individuals. And in *Time and Western Man*, Lewis complains similarly about this "merging of the spectator and the performer" in which "the audience . . . becomes professional, or, worse, semi-professional" and "the employer turns into a rival of his employee" (124–25).

14. An illuminating comparison is provided by a 1915 letter from Pound to John Quinn, the modernist master patron who at Pound's instigation purchased a number of Lewis's works. When the "patron buys from an artist who needs money," writes Pound, "he creates"; but when he "buys even of living artists who are already famous . . . he ceases to create. He sinks back to the rank of a consumer" (*Letters* 53–54). In

1919, Lewis wrote Quinn angrily, "The Englishman accepts the poet or the artist as he accepts a 'native' in a colony, as different & therefore inferior, & proceeds unruffled with his British life, & in most cases treats the native better, & quite inhumanly" (*Letters* 104).

15. In point of fact, the reaction of one Bloomsberry to the creations of another could be strained politeness as soon as swooning. In her article on Woolf and Fry, Broughton comments that Virginia may have "had little but contempt for the 1910 and 1912 Post-Impressionist exhibits and the Omega Workshop," though she purchased anyway, and cites her description of a trip around the latter: "Lord! how tired I got of those sturdy pots and pans, with red billiard balls attached to them! I daresay I am saying all the wrong things—I was taken round by Roger, and felt innumerable eggs crack beneath me" (43; quoting Woolf, *Letters* 2: 130). The "victorian literary splendour" to which Lewis alludes refers most centrally, of course, to Leslie Stephen, father of Virginia Woolf and Vanessa Bell, author of the *Dictionary of National Biography*, and husband in his first marriage to Thackeray's daughter, Minnie.

16. Capturing the essence of Bloomsbury's specific version of the imperative, "We must all do something!" Wicke goes on to write, "If in the nineteenth century 'our' valets did 'our' living for us, Bloomsbury modernism was about a design for living being carried out first by the Bloomsberries and then, perhaps, by a new unvaleted 'us'" (9). We might note also that when Woolf blurs the line between consumption and art production in Mrs. Dalloway's parties or John's object-collecting, she makes a case (albeit an extremely indirect one) for the virtues of Bloomsbury's production practices—a point suggested, in a way, by the casual surfacing of the title of John's story in Woolf's description of Fry at the Omega: "And when he had found out how things are made there was the excitement of trying to make them himself. It seemed a natural division of labour—while his brain spun theories his hands busied themselves with solid objects" (*Fry* 197).

17. In his 1914 lecture on the philosophy of the new art, Hulme had invoked the same remark: Cézanne "wanted, so he said, to make of impressionism something solid and durable like old art" (280).

18. "However antipathetic Woolf, and other modernists, may at times have been toward the small subset of the larger market," Wicke writes, "Woolfian modernism does not target publicity or consumption per se as problems—if anything . . . the market is perceived to be a shadowy common room within which acts of much creative magic or transforming potential can be performed." The Hogarth Press itself, Wicke goes on to note (citing Leonard Woolf via Alex Zwerdling), largely solved for Virginia the problem of "public taste and the pressures of the marketplace" ("*Mrs. Dalloway*" 21).

19. In *Three Guineas*, published the year after *The Revenge for Love*, of course, Woolf would argue pointedly that when leveled by a father who wants to control his daughter, this kind of critique of earning could be and has been a tool of that all too immediately consequential entity known as patriarchy (see, for example 64ff.).

20. On the aunt who actually left Woolf a legacy of £2,500, Caroline Emelia Stephen, see Bell, especially 1: 6–7 and 2: 39; King, especially 25, 113–14, and 146; and Lee 66–68. Caroline Emelia did not in fact die an adventurous death in India, though both Bell and King suggest a very tenuous connection to the subcontinent in noting that the love of her life severed his relationship with her in moving there. Lee

notes elsewhere, incidentally, that Leonard Woolf's "stocks and shares were (in spite of his political convictions) in 'imperial ventures' such as Shell Oil, Federated Selangor Rubber, Ceylon Para Rubber . . . " (557).

21. Complaining about "the swarms of dilettante competitors who make of every art a trifling pastime" in *The Art of Being Ruled*, Lewis ironically praised the Soviet state for "curtailing the impossible freedom of art": "it is a safe prediction," he asserted, "that the time will soon come when a copy of Tolstoi's War and Peace will be read by the person possessing it, if at all, *en cachette*; in the same way that a pornographic book is read to-day" (117–18). It seems, however, that by 1936 (two years after the First All-Union Congress of Soviet Writers all but installed socialist realism as official prescription), Lewis had come to feel less able to indulge in this bitter mirth: in a letter to *The Observer*, he wrote, "A difficult author—Mallarmé, Henry James or Hopkins—would be no hero in Russia today. Indeed it should be self-evident that 'difficulty' (that is, highly individualised expression) must be regarded not only as anti-popular, but, since useless for purposes of propaganda, a sort of affront like an idle man" (*Letters* 235). It is worth adding that after his turn against Fascism, Lewis grew less opposed to the idea of government as patron, writing in July 1942, "All the hostility I felt for the *centralizer* I no longer feel" (*Letters* 328), and nine months later, to another correspondent, "*After* the war, it seems pretty clear to me . . . the painter or other artist will have to depend upon state patronage" (*Letters* 351). A superb summary of the twists and turns of Lewis's positions on the Left, the Right, the British government, and foreign governments in the thirties can be found in chapters five through ten of D. G. Bridson's *Filibuster*.

22. At the end of *Fables of Aggression: Wyndham Lewis, the Modernist as Fascist*, Jameson turns to this notorious book by way of justifying his subtitle, observing that although Lewis had changed his mind about Hitler decisively by the end of the thirties, "*Hitler* is informed by *all* the ideological positions which will remain constant to the end of Lewis' life"—above all, a tendency to view fascism as "the great political expression of *revolutionary* opposition to the status quo" (183). Because Lewis did sometimes explicitly identify his political interests with those of something like the petty bourgeoisie (as we will see), there is clearly a sound basis for Jameson's claim that Lewis's "protofascism" was rooted in a vision of socialism or communism "as the definitive loss of even" the "embattled and precarious, historically threatened status to which the petty bourgeois subject desperately clings" (114); and certainly, Jameson's reading serves as an important reminder that many of Fascism's early sympathizers, including Lewis, felt themselves to be neither clearly central nor clearly marginal to their societies, or rather to oscillate uncomfortably between the two positions. As Jameson himself implies, however, Lewis's enthusiasm for Fascism over a short period hardly made him an essential or lifelong Fascist, to which we might add, first, that Lewis can be represented even as an essential *fascist* (small "f") only if opposition to a putative communist orthodoxy counts as fascism's defining characteristic, and, second, that the extraordinary contempt for the petty bourgeois that Lewis showed at many junctures makes gravely problematic any move to reduce his complexly paranoiac engagement with the power of the thirties Left to an expression of this figure's characteristic anxieties. Jameson's sensational subtitle is especially unfortunate because his remains not only the most widely read study of Lewis, but also the one best known by name to people *who have not read it* and know little

about its subject, which situation has undoubtedly retarded rather than accelerated the renewal of attention to Lewis for which Jameson calls (since few readers and scholars, it seems, are willing to devote substantial energy to writers whose politics they find wholly repellent).

23. Lewis goes on to insist that the British government, faulted elsewhere in *Left Wings* for its attraction to Russia, is in fact controlled by the Banks, and therefore "consents to uphold a system that perpetuates a state of 'want in the midst of plenty' . . . and to back an oppressive international Cabal which presumes to condemn all but a very few nations to a status of economic serfdom and 'inferiority'" (290, 301).

24. By 1948, at the latest, Lewis had grown impatient with Pound's adherence to Social Credit as a positive program: "I understand Social Credit as well as he does," he wrote in some notes of that year, but "do not believe it can *do* anything and is in fact a little silly" (*Letters* 462). As his late fiction and correspondence show, however, he continued to align himself, if only temperamentally, with its vision of a conspiracy of financiers. Writing to Pound's wife Dorothy on the subject of Douglas in 1947, he commented, "I do not consider ours a very rational or ethical world: if I am told that some one is darkly plotting it seems as natural to me as that somebody else is (or was) trying to split the atom" (*Letters* 416). On Douglas's theories, see the sources listed in footnote 16, chapter 3 (below).

25. A routine but necessary footnote to these discussions is that Keynes was a target of Social Credit more because of his prominence than because his views were so sharply antithetical to its own: as many have pointed out, his policy of stimulatory intervention by the state was broadly similar to Social Credit's, though less radical.

26. Lewis's consistent hostility to finance capital and its international reach should not be confused with his opinions about a more literal or statal internationalism, which shifted repeatedly in the course of his career. His most extreme antipathy to internationalism in this sense can be found in *Left Wings*, his most extended promotions of it in the 1929 *Paleface* and the 1948 *America and Cosmic Man*. A fuller charting can be found, once again, in Bridson's *Filibuster*.

27. On the sodomy-usury connection in medieval and Renaissance popular belief and Christian theology, see Boswell 330–32 and Greenberg 294–96.

28. In that story, a seaman duped into believing that he has given birth to a son as a result of intercourse with another man raises the boy successfully, only confessing what he believes to be the truth on his deathbed: "'I am not your fader but your moder,' quod he, / 'Your fader was a rich merchant in Stambouli'" (*Cantos* 56–57).

29. Douglas wrote in 1931, for example, that "an examination of the lesser financial crises" of the century suggests "that there is something in the banking system and its operation, which produces a constitutional inability to look at the industrial system as anything other than the basis of a financial system" (93).

30. The well known paragraph 404 of the report noted testimony to "great difficulty . . . experienced by the smaller and medium-sized businesses in raising the capital which they may from time to time require" (quoted in Thomas 118). On the Macmillan Gap and related questions, see Thomas, along with several of the essays in *Capitalism in a Mature Economy* (especially Cassis, Ross, and Diaper), which reject the general claim that British finance is to be blamed for failing to support industry in favor of more nuanced and situationally specific analyses. On the general fortunes of the City of London in this period and before, see Hobsbawm 152, 210–11, and Cassis 1–3.

31. If Lewis entertains the possibility that discourse is always ideological in this sense, however, he rejects the further implication that political intervention should be understood to be the fundamental springboard of all art production. "[S]ome vitalist impulse," he writes, aping the point of view that he deplores, "drives a man to fiddle or scribble to attract attention—or more obscurely to express an ethos—is not that it? If it is the famous 'personality of the artist' to which expression is given, in the art-form, why then precious 'personality' has been built up out of a number of components, has it not: which, closely enough inspected, would be found to betray a political complexion" (220). A similar passage appears at the close of another essay from 1934 entitled " 'Detachment' and the Fictionist," but this time Lewis speaks in a less clearly ironic register: "You must not," he tells the artist, "be afraid to say, 'In this I am a partisan'. . . . [I]t is . . . the sign that you are an artist if you recognize that the struggles you engage in are a game, in which *vous jouez votre personalité*. You play at being yourself—and so you *are* yourself; it is quite unnecessary to play at being anybody else to be completely the artist" (*Creatures* 228–29).

CHAPTER THREE
EZRA POUND

1. In his well known 1913 essay "The Serious Artist," for example, he refers to the "cult of beauty" as the hygiene of art, that which "reminds one what is worth while" (*Literary* 45), before going on to defend as well the cult of ugliness; in a statement of the year before he calls the poet "the advance guard of the psychologist on the watch for new emotions, new vibrations sensible to faculties as yet ill understood" (*Prose* 361); and as late as 1917 he could be found asserting, in "Provincialism the Enemy," that knowledge is "the enrichment of personality" and (questionably) that "the value of personality" was "constantly" emphasized by Confucius (*Prose* 193).

2. Miller notes that Pound had been using a voice that he himself called "effete and overcivilized" in writing under the pseudonym Walter Villerant for the *Little Review* (963–64). On Villerant, see also Davie 89–90.

3. Walkiewicz and Witemeyer point out that a version of such a bank was finally founded in Venice in 1584, hence the phrase "shelved for a couple of centuries" (91–92).

4. The complexity of this passage is further enhanced by its subject rhyme with the central topic of cantos XLI through XLIV, the Monte dei Paschi ("Mount of the Pastures"), a bank founded in Siena in 1624 that supported its credit with the produce from a plot of public land, the pastures of Maremma (see Terrell 169). In thus starkly opposing the destruction of fertile earth to the public distribution of fruits of the ground, the passage anticipates Pound's eventually pervasive privileging of agriculture as the archetype of legitimate production.

5. This is to say that Pound's devotion to what we might call a mystified politicoeconomics of form undergirded his repression of the possibility that dirty money can pay for excellent things. As Michael André Bernstein has pointed out, the ironies that attend this repression grow especially acute around the matter of usury itself, since "at least until the Counter-Reformation, atonement for usury often provided a crucial impetus for the commissioning of a large number of artworks. . . . [G]uilt

about usury, combined with the wealth amassed through usury, seems to have generated more public art projects than did lives of unparalleled rectitude among Italy's elite" (349).

6. In fact, the historical figure in question was called Hannibal, but Hanno is the name given in the novel.

7. Pound attributed the point about the San Zeno signatures to Edgar Williams, William Carlos's brother, in a 1923 contribution to *The Dial*, and confirmed this attribution in cantos LXXVIII and XCI (*Cantos* 494, 628; see Terrell 419). In canto XLV, the maker is the originary Adam rather than the Matthew of the New Testament: "Came no church of cut stone signed: *Adamo me fecit*" (*Cantos* 230).

8. In his rich and incisive 1981 book, *Critic as Scientist*, Ian F. A. Bell suggests a number of other factors contributing to Pound's overdetermined attention to the scene of the solid object's fashioning, including "a lengthy tradition in American literature . . . of making things that related to the pervasive concern of the nineteenth-century writer to suggest shape and definition for what was still a nebulous civilization" (74) and a British scientific tradition of emphasis on praxis descending from T. H. Huxley and his contemporaries to the anonymous author (probably Dora Marsden) of a number of articles that appeared in the *New Freewoman* alongside Pound's "Serious Artist" (65–74).

9. Pound's encounter with history at this stage of his career has been discussed at length by a number of critics: see, for example, Bush, *Genesis* 211–13 (on cantos V and VI); Longenbach, *Modernist* 96–130, especially 120–30; and North, *Political* 138ff.

10. And he [Tiresias] strong with the blood, said then: "Odysseus
   "Shalt return through spiteful Neptune, over dark seas,
   "Lose all companions." And then Anticlea came.
   Lie quiet, Divus. I mean, that is, Andreas Divus,
   In officina Wecheli, 1538, out of Homer.

(*Cantos* 4–5)

11. These points lie close to the heart of Sherry's major effort in *Ezra Pound, Wyndham Lewis, and Radical Modernism*, which is to situate modernism's privileging of the visual in a theoretical tradition beginning in earnest with the French *idéologues* and culminating, for Pound and Lewis, in Ortega y Gasset, Gourmont, Benda, and Sorel. With a care and insightfulness that has made this one of the more influential studies of high modernist theory and practice to appear in recent years, Sherry charts Pound's and Lewis's changing responses to these other writers' identification of the visual with aristocratic detachment and reflective capacity (and of the aural with mass manipulation), giving ample consideration to the ways in which this identification can also invert or reverse itself—as in the "optical prosody" of *Mauberley*, which arguably ends by producing "only the accumulation of sensuous phrase upon sensuous phrase" (139).

12. A. D. Moody has recently argued that the drafts of the Malatesta cantos reveal Pound working toward a recognition that his own representation of Malatesta's deeds might be as worthy a project as the deeds themselves (86–91); but if this is so, the insight did not seem to carry the implication that other representers might provide heroic subject matter.

13. In April 1929, Yeats wrote to Sturge Moore of Pound, "He is sunk in Frobenius . . . and finds him a most interesting person" (quoted in Carpenter 470).

14. In "Murder by Capital" (1933), Pound had observed that Frobenius is "a bitter pill for the Anglo-Saxon" because he believes "that bad art indicates something more than just bad art" (*Prose* 227), while in *Jefferson and/or Mussolini* (written in that same year), he had followed his claim that "[a]nyone who has seen the furniture at Schönbrunn ought to understand the flop of the Austrian Empire" with the remark that "Frobenius has outstripped other archaeologists and explorers (a) because he does not believe things exist without cause; (b) as corollary, because he considered that the *forms* of pottery, etc., had causes" (83).

15. In a letter of 1939, Pound wrote, "I loathe and always have loathed Indian art. Loathed it long before I got my usury axis. Obnubilated, short curves, muddle, jungle, etc. Waaal, we find the hin-goddam-do is a bloody and voracious usurer" (*Letters* 330).

16. Helpful summaries of Pound's relation to Social Credit can be found in Kenner, *Pound Era* 301–17, Bush, *Genesis* 277–90, and Nicholls, *Ezra Pound* 20–30. The criticism on Pound's economic beliefs in general is extensive, to say the least; other than Nicholls's volume, which is undoubtedly the best resource in this area, the major book-length guide is Earle Davis's pioneering *Vision Fugitive*. Other sources providing useful background—in many cases combined with close analysis of Pound's rhetorical handling of usury, money, gold, and so on—include Bernstein; Flory; Knapp; Murray; Rabaté; Sieburth, "In Pound We Trust"; and Wolfe.

17. Pound here apparently echoes Mussolini's claim, which delighted him, that since the problem of production had been solved, economists might move on to the question of distribution (*Prose* 300); he also makes the same point in the *ABC of Economics* of 1939 (*Prose* 234). As Michael North points out, Pound regarded the supersession of productionism as a quite recent historical development, though we might amend North's specific dating to take into account the passage from *Jefferson and/or Mussolini* quoted here, which suggests that Pound placed the turn (in England, if not in the rest of Europe) in 1918: "Pound seizes on Mussolini's 1934 declaration," writes North, "because it seems to him to represent a historical fulcrum at which production tips and gives way to distribution. . . . In 1934, Mussolini succeeds, through a campaign of modernization, in bringing history to a successful conclusion" (*Political* 171).

18. "Elizabethan Classicists" appeared as a series of notes over several numbers from late 1917 through early 1918; the one quoted here was the third in the series.

19. And it is just here that Tratner's argument becomes problematic. Claiming that modernists virtually across the board adopt the rhetoric of underconsumptionism—that the projects of Eliot, Pound, Joyce, the Dadaists, and many others can be explained by a "general move toward consumption before or without production" (711)—Tratner unjustifiably elides much of the diverseness of the imperatives at work amid the maneuvers and innovations that we label "modernism"; nor does he offer much motivation for this move beyond a gesture toward zeitgeist premised largely on Lawrence Birken's *Consuming Desire*, a provocative study of economics and sexology marred by its own propensity for unfounded generalization (see, for example, Birken 53 and 114). The notable exception in Tratner is, again, the case of Pound, where the invocation of Douglas is obviously well founded; but even here a

certain carelessness prevails. Including no quotations from Pound (no fault in itself, perhaps, since the article in question centers on Joyce), Tratner declares that the poet hated usurers "precisely because they are not interested in consumption" and reads the form of the *Cantos*, highly questionably, as "a model of literary consumption" that happily endorses the continuous stimulation of desires through which capitalism sustains itself (714).

20. Pound makes virtually the same point in a letter to W.H.D. Rouse of 30 October 1937 (*Letters* 298).

21. These matters are complicated somewhat by the fact that Pound was never entirely resolute in denigrating contemplation. In its reference to the twelfth-century scholastic philosopher Richard of St. Victor, this passage itself harks back to a point in the *Guide to Kulchur* at which Pound had suggested setting the passage from *Nicomachean Ethics* VI. iii. in which Aristotle names the five forms of knowledge against "R. St Victor's gradation of processes (1) the aimless flitting of the mind, (2) the systematic circling of the attention around the object, (3) contemplation, the identification of the consciousness WITH the object" (328). That Pound juxtaposes St. Victor and *techne* both in 1938 and a decade and a half later confirms that he found the association between the two compelling, though the earlier passage's apparently benign take on contemplation seems hard to square with canto LXXXV's intimation (in the note that right action includes a movement "from Τέχνη back to σεαυτόν [oneself]" as well as war on contemplatio) that only *techne* allows for a valid connection between subject and object. Nor can the difference be attributed to a simple change of mind over the years intervening, since the "Mang Tsze" essay, in implicating forms of knowledge other than *techne* in the attack on nature, shows that Pound had already taken up the critique of contemplation in the late 1930s.

22. In a 1972 version, also by New Directions, these appear as "CXX"—only one of many complications in the vexed publication history of the late fragments. For the essential resource on these problems, see Bush's "Unstill, Ever Turning" (in which, incidentally, Bush shows why the lines in question are to be assigned the date of 1959).

23. Pound's source for this information, J.–A.–M. de Moyriac Mailla's *Histoire Générale de la Chine*, tells of how "Tching-Tang" received rain for his drought-stricken land after a prayer to the sky, and then,

> après avoir rendu graces au Ciel d'un si grand bienfait, retourna dans son palais, & fit graver sur le bassin dont il se servoit tous les matins pour se laver le visage, ces paroles: *Souviens-toi de te renouveller chaque jour, & plusieurs fois le jour*; afin qu'ayant continuellement cet avertissement devant les yeux, il fût plus attentif à remplir ses devoirs. Que les peuples seroient heureux, si tous les souverains pensoient ainsi! (175)

It is surely worth noting how strikingly Pound's investment in the artist (or politician) as artifex is captured in his transformation of "Souviens-toi de te renouveller" into "Make it new," which not only shifts the locus of newness from subject to object ("it") but adds a suggestion of material fabrication simply absent from Mailla's phrase. (On the genealogy of Mailla's translation from its Chinese sources, see Kenner, *Pound Era* 433, and Gordon 396–98.)

24. This antique charm did not, as it turns out, always confront modern innovation

with perfect satisfaction. In her biography of Fry, Woolf quotes at length from Blunt's diary comment on the 1910 Post-Impressionists exhibit, which concludes, "They are the works of idleness and impotent stupidity, a pornographic show" (157).

25. Reprinted in *Prose* 272–82. The next number of *The Criterion*, incidentally, includes a review of *Jefferson and/or Mussolini* by Montgomery Butchart that suggests how easily readers of publications like Eliot's could assimilate the bizarrerie that makes Pound's writing seem so unassimilable today. To read Butchart's review, which makes no mention of the crazy restlessness of the book's prose or the air of the crank that pervades Pound's meanderings, one would think that *Jefferson* puts forward an utterly reasoned case for the idea that, as Butchart puts it, the modern world needs a "social-catalyst type of individual" (326) along Jeffersonian lines. That same number of *The Criterion* also includes Marianne Moore's review of Stevens's *Ideas of Order*, another volume heavily informed (though in quite different ways, as we will see) by considerations of Fascism's promises.

26. This remark becomes a refrain in the pages immediately following and reappears sporadically through the Pisans thereafter, most notably in LXXX, where its addressee is revealed to be Yeats (*Cantos* 525).

CHAPTER FOUR
WALLACE STEVENS

1. According to Richard Ellmann, America's prior encounters with the stuff of aestheticism had been limited to "women's gowns hung from the shoulders in flowing folds, Queen Anne furniture, Morris wallpaper, Japanese screens—all just beginning to be known" (*Wilde* 152). Freedman, however, calls attention to the popularizing of Ruskin and Morris that had begun in earnest with Charles Eastlake's highly successful *Hints on Household Taste* (first published in the United States in 1872), arguing that Wilde's tour "vividly suggested the extent to which the lower-cultural manifestations of aestheticism, its appearance as a 'mania' or 'craze,' had already made their way into American consciousness" (102; and see 101–32 generally for Freedman's important reconstruction of aestheticism's American career).

2. Townsend notes also that even the writer of the *The Cult of the Purple Rose: A Phase of Harvard Life* insisted that the aesthetic undergraduates portrayed therein represented only "a few extremists," not the college's mainstream (quoted at 143), though Van Wyck Brooks would later defend "the so-called 'aesthetic' side of the college" by insisting that "the word 'aesthetic' indicates . . . the outlook on life of certain clear and sensitive persons who are quite honest and straightforward and by no means effeminate" (quoted at 130). On Charles Flandrau, author of the "Literary Man" portrait mentioned below, see Townsend 143–45.

3. On the development of modern senses of "consumer" and "consumption," see Bowlby, *Shopping* 14–15.

4. This is not to say that the relation between production and degeneration could not be viewed in other lights at the turn of the century. Tom Lutz begins his *American Nervousness, 1903* by considering the case of George M. Beard, "the father of neurasthenia" and author of an 1881 volume also called *American Nervousness*, who found "nerve weakness" epidemic among "leisure-class men and women, artists, and

brain workers of various kinds, those most involved with 'the modern,'" but who for this very reason viewed it as a mark of refinement and advancement in both individuals and civilizations (3–6).

5. Stevens himself wrote in a letter of 1938, "I think that THE COMEDIAN AS THE LETTER C has gathered a good deal of dust" (*Letters* 330), though in 1954 he named it as a possible selection for "a fresh collection" of his poems (*Letters* 831).

6. In the May 1922 issue of *Poetry*: "The initial Blindman Prize of $250 has been awarded by the Poetry Society of South Carolina to Grace Hazard Conkling, for *Variations on a Theme*, which was named by Miss Lowell, the appointed judge, as the best of many poems submitted in a contest open to all poets writing in English" ("Notes" 115).

7. These lines appear only in "From the Journal of Crispin," not in "The Comedian as the Letter C." Except where otherwise noted, quotations from the "Journal" version (now most readily available in the revised edition of the *Opus Posthumous*) differ only trivially from corresponding passages in "The Comedian."

8. By 1941, Filreis notes, "it was assumed that Americans were prepared to acknowledge the reality of the crisis (a campaign against fascism that the United States was ideologically readying itself to enter). . . . But in 1936 there was still plenty of doubt" (*Modernism* 251–52).

9. Filreis offers a memorable reading of "Anglais" as a prologue to the rest of his pathbreaking and exhaustively researched *Modernism from Right to Left*, in which he argues that the numerous and significant cross-currents between "right" and "left" in thirties literary politics have been obscured by later literary history. In accordance with his main thesis, he locates in "Anglais" three different Stevenses: one a lover of apolitical lyric imperiled by changing times, another an admirer of Mussolini hostile to lyric, and the third a " 'middle-ground' writer teaching himself to read the radical cultural position from right to left" (30). As an allegorical approach to Stevens's thirties ambivalences, this reading can hardly be excelled, but it should be clear from the foregoing that such a tripartite division obscures precisely the work of naturalization so essential to the political operations of *Ideas*—obscures, that is to say, the fact that any support for Mussolini expressed in this poem depends upon an argument that lyric (engaged or otherwise) and the police *both* respond to *la condition humaine*.

10. These debates are helpfully summarized in B. J. Leggett's *Wallace Stevens and Poetic Theory*.

11. Lengthy and involved as the debates on Stevens's take on reality have been, it is clear that his position on the question of knowledge of the thing itself remained virtually constant from the beginning of his career to the end. A passage from the 1943 essay, "The Figure of the Youth as Virile Poet," sums up this position as well as any:

It is easy to suppose that few people realize on that occasion, which comes to all of us, when we look at the blue sky for the first time, that is to say: not merely see it, but look at it and experience it . . .—few people realize that they are looking at the world of their own thoughts and the world of their own feelings. (*Necessary* 65–66)

12. See, for example, Bloom 197; Hines 148; Longenbach, *Wallace Stevens* 256; Morrison 97; Riddel, *Clairvoyant* 169.

13. As though in long-delayed response to Williams's remarks on the falsity of sentimental value, Stevens wrote in his well known 1934 preface to Williams's *Collected Poems, 1921–1931* of the latter's "sentimental side," of how his poetry shows "a little sentiment, very little, together with acute reaction"—which reaction he then described, much to Williams's annoyance, as "anti-poetic" (*Opus* 213).

14. We can also discern a version of this problem at work in the Stein of the *Tender Buttons* period, who made writings far from mimetic out of words that things suggested to her while regarding this operation (arguably no more than a recording of associations) as a discovery of those things' names. "I began to discover the names of things," she remarked when looking back on this phase later, "the things to look at and in so doing I had of course to name them not to give them new names but to see that I could find out how to know that they were there by their names or by replacing their names. . . . I called them by their names with passion and that made poetry . . . it made the Tender Buttons . . . " (235).

15. Reading this poem together with "A Primitive Like an Orb," Judith Butler cogently reminds us that Stevens's claims for the mind's conferring of value on Being almost inevitably modulate into something like an affirmation of the absolute value of Being after all. Having noted that for Stevens meaning seems to come "first from the acts of the mind," that "the domain of particular beings receives its meaning only after being filtered through the cognitive grid of a rational agent," Butler adds that "there are clearly moments" in Stevens when "what 'is' has its meaning in virtue of a kind of primary precognitive 'isness,'" according to an effect in which "not being" finally "allows for the poetic affirmation of mere being" (283). Stevens himself suggests something of the kind in his 1948 note on (appropriately) John Crowe Ransom, remarking that as Ransom became an "outsider" to his home state of Tennessee, "without ceasing to be an insider, it was as if everything to which he was native took on a special quality, an exact identity, a microscopic reality, which, only for what it was, had a value because it was wholly free from his outsidedness. This is what happens to things we love" (*Opus* 249).

16. This tradition (and, incidentally, its ability to absorb and redispose the elements even of religious culture) is casually in evidence in a sonnet that Santayana wrote in response to one by Stevens in 1899. To the undergraduate's "Cathedrals are not built along the sea," Santayana replied with "For aeons had the self-responsive tide," in which the world of sea and moon finds its needed completion only when the earth raises a "cross-shaped temple to the Crucified" (quoted in Richardson 1: 533).

17. The number of the *Partisan Review* that contained the second half of "The New Failure of Nerve" also included Allen Tate's "Ode: To Our Young Pro-Consuls of the Air," Stevens's reaction to which Filreis discusses in *Wallace Stevens and the Actual World* 78–80. (Filreis points out that Tate's poem would certainly have caught Stevens's eye in another of its appearances—in *New Poems 1943*, a collection that also carried five poems by Stevens.)

18. In one of the late conversations recorded by Simone de Beauvoir in *Adieux: A Farewell to Sartre*, Sartre does follow a reference to "the in-itself for-itself perceived as the being of God," an "impossibility," with the remark, "And then again there is the in-itself for-itself link of the consciousness and the thing, which is another form of the in-itself for-itself and which exists at every moment. At this particular moment I am conscious of a mass of things that are here before me, that really exist . . . "

(442). Sartre thus cannot be said to ignore completely the meeting of consciousness and Being in the moment of perception; and thus his difference from Stevens is perhaps better described as a striking and widely consequential difference in emphasis than as an absolute disagreement on basic ontology.

19. This conclusion's best allegory, perhaps, is the seventh canto of "An Ordinary Evening in New Haven," in which, as Helen Vendler notes, Stevens finds the architects of chapels and schools "made visible and rock-like" in those buildings: "In turning into things," she writes, "men lose the power to be self-deprecatory and down-to-earth, 'practical' . . . ; in spite of themselves, their fantasy breaks out everywhere" (301). Here again, however, the virtue of production depends eminently on perception rather than on solidification as such—it being not the rocklike facticity of the buildings that makes them good, but rather what they disclose, to their observer, of "[c]onceptions of new mornings of new worlds, / The tips of cock-cry pinked out pastily, / As that which was incredible becomes, / In misted contours, credible day again" (*Poems* 470).

WORKS CITED

Abbott, Reginald. "What Miss Kilman's Petticoat Means: Virginia Woolf, Shopping, and Spectacle." *Modern Fiction Studies* 38 (1992): 193–216.

Adorno, Theodor W. *Aesthetic Theory*. Trans. C. Lenhardt. Ed. Gretel Adorno and Rolf Tiedemann. London: Routledge, 1984.

———. *Negative Dialectics*. Trans. E. B. Ashton. New York: Continuum, 1990.

Agnew, Jean-Christophe. "The Consuming Vision of Henry James." *The Culture of Consumption: Critical Essays in American History 1880–1980*. Ed. Richard Wightman Fox and T. J. Jackson Lears. New York: Pantheon, 1983. 65–100.

Althusser, Louis. *Lenin and Philosophy and Other Essays*. Trans. Ben Brewster. New York: Monthly Review Press, 1971.

Annan, Noel. "Bloomsbury and the Leavises." *Virginia Woolf and Bloomsbury*. Ed. Jane Marcus. Houndmills: Macmillan, 1987. 23–38.

Arendt, Hannah. Introduction. *Illuminations*. By Walter Benjamin. Trans. Harry Zohn. New York: Schocken, 1969.

Armstrong, Isobel. *Language as Living Form in Nineteenth-Century Poetry*. Brighton: Harvester, 1982.

Ayers, David. *Wyndham Lewis and Western Man*. Houndmills: Macmillan, 1992.

Barthes, Roland. *The Rustle of Language*. Trans. Richard Howard. Oxford: Basil Blackwell, 1986.

Bate, W. Jackson. *The Burden of the Past and the English Poet*. New York: Norton, 1972.

Bates, Milton J. *Wallace Stevens: A Mythology of Self*. Berkeley: University of California Press, 1985.

Baudrillard, Jean. *The Mirror of Production*. Trans. Mark Poster. St. Louis: Telos, 1975.

———. *The System of Objects*. Trans. James Benedict. London: Verso, 1996. Trans. of *Système des Objets*. Paris: Gallimard, 1968.

Beauvoir, Simone de. *Adieux: A Farewell to Sartre*. Trans. Patrick O'Brian. New York: Pantheon, 1984.

Bell, Clive. *Since Cézanne*. New York: Harcourt, 1922.

———. "Wilcoxism" (article). *Athenaeum* 4688 (5 March 1920): 311–12.

———. "Wilcoxism" (letter). *Athenaeum* 4690 (19 March 1920): 379.

Bell, Ian F. A. *Critic as Scientist: The Modernist Poetics of Ezra Pound*. London: Methuen, 1981.

———. "'Speaking in Figures': The Mechanical Thomas Jefferson of Canto 31." *Ezra Pound: Tactics for Reading*. Ed. Ian F. A. Bell. London: Vision, 1982. 148–86.

Bell, Quentin. Foreword. *The Omega Workshops*. By Judith Collins. Chicago: University of Chicago Press, 1984.

———. *Virginia Woolf*. 2 vols. New York: Harcourt, 1972.

Benjamin, Walter. *Illuminations*. Ed. Hannah Arendt. Trans. Harry Zohn. New York: Schocken, 1969.

Bergson, Henri. *Creative Evolution*. 1907. Trans. Arthur Mitchell. New York: Henry Holt, 1911.

———. *Matter and Memory*. 1896. Trans. N. M. Paul and W. S. Palmer. New York: Zone, 1991.

Bernstein, Michael André. "Image, Word, and Sign: The Visual Arts as Evidence in Ezra Pound's *Cantos*." *Critical Inquiry* 12 (1985–86): 347–64.

Birken, Lawrence. *Consuming Desire: Sexual Science and the Emergence of a Culture of Abundance, 1871–1914*. Ithaca: Cornell University Press, 1988.

Blackmur, R. P. "Examples of Wallace Stevens." *Hound and Horn* 5 (1932). Reprinted in *The Achievement of Wallace Stevens*. Ed. Ashley Brown and Robert S. Haller. New York: Gordian, 1973. 52–80.

Bloom, Harold. *The Anxiety of Influence: A Theory of Poetry*. London: Oxford University Press, 1973.

———. *Wallace Stevens: The Poems of Our Climate*. Ithaca: Cornell University Press, 1977.

Boris, Eileen. *Art and Labor: Ruskin, Morris, and the Craftsman Ideal in America*. Philadelphia: Temple University Press, 1980.

Boswell, John. *Christianity, Social Tolerance, and Homosexuality*. Chicago: University of Chicago Press, 1980.

Bowlby, Rachel. *Just Looking: Consumer Culture in Dreiser, Gissing and Zola*. New York: Methuen, 1985.

———. *Shopping with Freud*. London: Routledge, 1993.

———. *Virginia Woolf: Feminist Destinations*. Oxford: Basil Blackwell, 1988.

Bradley, F. H. *Appearance and Reality*. 1897. Oxford: Clarendon Press, 1951.

Bridson, D. G. *The Filibuster: A Study of the Political Ideas of Wyndham Lewis*. London: Cassell, 1972.

Briggs, Asa. *Victorian Things*. London: B. T. Batsford, 1988.

Brooks, Cleanth. *The Well Wrought Urn*. New York: Harcourt, 1947.

———. *Modern Poetry and the Tradition*. 1939. Chapel Hill: University of North Carolina Press, 1967.

Broughton, Panthea Reid. "The Blasphemy of Art: Fry's Aesthetics and Woolf's Non-'Literary' Stories." *The Multiple Muses of Virginia Woolf*. Ed. Diane F. Gillespie. Columbia: University of Missouri Press, 1993. 36–57.

Buck-Morss, Susan. *The Dialectics of Seeing: Walter Benjamin and the Arcades Project*. Cambridge: MIT Press, 1989.

Burdett, Osbert. *The Beardsley Period: An Essay in Perspective*. 1925. New York: Cooper Square, 1969.

Bürger, Peter. *Theory of the Avant-Garde*. Trans. Michael Shaw. Minneapolis: University of Minnesota Press, 1984.

Burke, Kenneth. *A Grammar of Motives*. New York: Prentice-Hall, 1945.

Bush, Ronald. *The Genesis of Ezra Pound's Cantos*. Princeton: Princeton University Press, 1976.

———. "'Unstill, Ever Turning': The Composition of Ezra Pound's *Drafts & Fragments*." *Ezra Pound and Europe*. Ed. Richard Taylor and Claus Melchior. Amsterdam: Rodopi, 1993. 223–42.

Butchart, Montgomery. "*Jefferson and/or Mussolini*." *Criterion* 15 (1936): 323–26.

Butler, Judith. "The Nothing That Is: Wallace Stevens' Hegelian Affinities." *Theoriz-*

ing American Literature: Hegel, the Sign, and History. Ed. Bainard Cowan and Joseph G. Kronick. Baton Rouge: Louisiana State University Press, 1991. 269–87.

Carpenter, Humphrey. *A Serious Character: The Life of Ezra Pound.* New York: Delta, 1988.

Casillo, Robert. *The Genealogy of Demons: Anti-Semitism, Fascism, and the Myths of Ezra Pound.* Evanston: Northwestern University Press, 1988.

Cassis, Youssef. "British Finance: Success and Controversy." *Capitalism in a Mature Economy.* Ed. J. J. van Helten and Y. Cassis. Aldershot: Edward Elgar, 1990. 1–22.

Caughie, Pamela L. *Virginia Woolf and Postmodernism: Literature in Quest and Question of Itself.* Urbana: University of Illinois Press, 1991.

Chai, Leon. *Aestheticism.* New York: Columbia University Press, 1990.

Chamberlin, Henry Harmon. "The Ballade of Beardsley." *Harvard Advocate* 58 (1894): 128.

Cohen-Salal, Annie. *Sartre: A Life.* Trans. Anna Cancogni. New York: Pantheon, 1987.

Collins, Judith. *The Omega Workshops.* Chicago: University of Chicago Press, 1984.

Damon, S. Foster. *Amy Lowell: A Chronicle.* Boston: Houghton Mifflin, 1935.

Dante Alighieri. *Inferno.* Trans. Mark Musa. Harmondsworth: Penguin, 1984. Vol. 1 of *The Divine Comedy.*

Dasenbrock, Reed Way. *The Literary Vorticism of Ezra Pound and Wyndham Lewis.* Baltimore: Johns Hopkins University Press, 1985.

———. "Wyndham Lewis's Fascist Imagination and the Fiction of Paranoia." *Fascism, Aesthetics, and Culture.* Ed. Richard J. Golsan. Hanover, New Hampshire: University Press of New England, 1992. 81–97.

Davie, Donald. *Studies in Ezra Pound.* Manchester: Carcanet, 1991.

Davis, Earle. *Vision Fugitive.* Lawrence: University Press of Kansas, 1968.

DeKoven, Marianne. *Rich and Strange: Gender, History, Modernism.* Princeton: Princeton University Press, 1991.

Descombes, Vincent. *Objects of All Sorts: A Philosophical Grammar.* Trans. Lorna Scott-Fox and Jeremy Harding. Baltimore: Johns Hopkins University Press, 1986.

Dewey, John. "Anti-Naturalism in Extremis." *Partisan Review* 10 (1943): 24–39.

Diaper, Stefanie. "The Sperling Combine and the Shipbuilding Industry: Merchant Banking and Industrial Finance in the 1920s." *Capitalism in a Mature Economy.* Ed. J. J. van Helten and Y. Cassis. Aldershot: Edward Elgar, 1990. 71–94.

Dickens, Charles. *Hard Times.* 1854. London: Penguin, 1985.

Editorial. *Harvard Advocate* 60 (1896): 129–30.

Eliot, T. S. *The Complete Poems and Plays 1909–1950.* New York: Harcourt, 1952.

———. *Knowledge and Experience in the Philosophy of F. H. Bradley.* New York: Farrar, 1964.

———. *Selected Prose of T. S. Eliot.* Ed. Frank Kermode. New York: Harcourt, 1975.

Ellmann, Richard. *James Joyce.* Rev. ed. New York: Oxford University Press, 1983.

———. *Oscar Wilde.* New York: Vintage, 1988.

Felski, Rita. *The Gender of Modernity.* Cambridge: Harvard University Press, 1995.

Filreis, Alan. *Modernism from Right to Left: Wallace Stevens, the Thirties, and Literary Radicalism.* New York: Cambridge University Press, 1994.

———. *Wallace Stevens and the Actual World*. Princeton: Princeton University Press, 1991.

Fisher, Philip. *Making and Effacing Art: Modern Art in a Culture of Museums*. New York: Oxford University Press, 1991.

Flandrau, C. M. "Harvard Types III: The Undergraduate Literary Man." *Harvard Advocate* 56 (1891): 19–20.

Flaubert, Gustave. *Salammbo*. 1862. Trans. A. J. Krailsheimer. London: Penguin, 1977.

Fleishman, Avrom. "Woolf and McTaggart." *ELH* 36 (1969): 719–38.

Flory, Wendy Stallard. *The American Ezra Pound*. New Haven: Yale University Press, 1989.

Forster, E.M. *Abinger Harvest*. New York: Harcourt, 1936.

———. *A Passage to India*. San Diego: Harcourt, 1924.

Foucault, Michel. *The Order of Things: An Archaeology of the Human Sciences*. New York: Vintage, 1973.

Fox, Richard Wightman and T. J. Jackson Lears. Introduction. *The Culture of Consumption: Critical Essays in American History 1880–1980*. Ed. Richard Wightman Fox and T. J. Jackson Lears. New York: Pantheon, 1983. vii–xvii.

Freedman, Jonathan. *Professions of Taste: Henry James, British Aestheticism, and Commodity Culture*. Stanford: Stanford University Press, 1990.

Freud, Sigmund. *Civilization and Its Discontents*. 1930. Trans. James Strachey. New York: Norton, 1962.

Géfin, Laszlo. *Ideogram: History of a Poetic Method*. Austin: University of Texas Press, 1982.

Gilbert, Bentley G. Introduction. *The Heart of the Empire*. 1901. Ed. C. F. G. Masterman. Brighton: Harvester, 1973.

Gilbert, Sandra M. and Susan Gubar. *No Man's Land: The Place of the Woman Writer in the Twentieth Century*. New Haven: Yale University Press, 1988.

Gordon, David. "'Confucius, Philosophe': An Introduction to the Chinese Cantos 52–61." *Paideuma* 5 (1976): 387–403.

Graves, Robert. *The Long Week-End: A Social History of Great Britain, 1918–1939*. London: Faber, 1950.

Greenberg, David F. *The Construction of Homosexuality*. Chicago: University of Chicago Press, 1988.

Hamilton, Paul. *Coleridge's Poetics*. Oxford: Basil Blackwell, 1983.

Harmer, J. B. *Victory in Limbo: Imagism 1908–1917*. London: Secker and Warburg, 1975.

H. D. *Tribute to Freud*. New York: New Directions, 1984.

Hegel, G.W.F. *Phenomenology of Spirit*. Trans. A. V. Miller. Oxford: Oxford University Press, 1977.

Hines, Thomas J. *The Later Poetry of Wallace Stevens: Phenomenological Parallels with Husserl and Heidegger*. Lewisburg: Bucknell University Press, 1976.

Hobsbawm, E. J. *Industry and Empire*. Harmondsworth: Penguin, 1969. Vol. 3 of *The Pelican Economic History of Britain*.

Horkheimer, Max and Theodor W. Adorno. *Dialectic of Enlightenment*. Trans. John Cumming. New York: Continuum, 1994. Trans. of *Dialektik der Aufklärung*. New York: Social Studies Association, 1944.

Hulme, T. E. *Collected Writings*. Ed. Karen Csengeri. Oxford: Clarendon, 1994.

Huysmans, J.-K. *Against Nature*. Trans. Robert Baldick. London: Penguin, 1959. Trans. of *A rebours*. Paris, 1884.

Huyssen, Andreas. *After the Great Divide: Modernism, Mass Culture, Postmodernism*. Bloomington: Indiana University Press, 1986.

Hynes, Samuel. *The Edwardian Turn of Mind*. Princeton: Princeton University Press, 1968.

Jackson, Holbrook. *The Eighteen Nineties: A Review of Art and Ideas at the Close of the Nineteenth Century*. Rev. ed. New York: Knopf, 1923.

Jacobus, Mary. "'The Third Stroke': Reading Woolf with Freud." *Virginia Woolf*. Ed. Rachel Bowlby. London: Longman, 1992.

Jameson, Fredric. *Fables of Aggression: Wyndham Lewis, the Modernist as Fascist*. Berkeley: University of California Press, 1979.

——. *Late Marxism: Adorno, or the Persistence of the Dialectic*. London: Verso, 1990.

——. *Postmodernism: or, The Cultural Logic of Late Capitalism*. Durham: Duke University Press, 1991.

Johnston, Judith L. "The Remediable Flaw: Revisioning Cultural History in *Between the Acts*." *Virginia Woolf and Bloomsbury*. Ed. Jane Marcus. Bloomington: Indiana University Press, 1987. 253–77.

Joplin, Patricia Klindienst. "The Authority of Illusion: Feminism and Fascism in Virginia Woolf's *Between the Acts*." *Virginia Woolf: A Collection of Critical Essays*. Ed. Margaret Homans. Englewood Cliffs: Prentice Hall, 1993. 210–226.

——. Lecture series. Yale University. New Haven. Spring 1991.

Joyce, James. *A Portrait of the Artist as a Young Man*. 1916. Harmondsworth: Penguin, 1976.

Kenner, Hugh. *A Homemade World: The American Modernist Writers*. New York: Knopf, 1975.

——. *The Pound Era*. Berkeley: University of California Press, 1971.

King, James. *Virginia Woolf*. London: Hamish Hamilton, 1994.

Klein, Scott W. *The Fictions of James Joyce and Wyndham Lewis*. Cambridge: Cambridge University Press, 1994.

Knapp, James. F. *Literary Modernism and the Transformation of Work*. Evanston: Northwestern University Press, 1988.

Knoblauch, Edward G. "Letters of Theodore Bumford Greene." *Harvard Advocate* 58 (1893): 44–45.

Lacoue-Labarthe, Philippe. *Heidegger, Art and Politics: The Fiction of the Political*. Trans. Chris Turner. Oxford: Basil Blackwell, 1990.

Larrissy, Edward. *Reading Twentieth-Century Poetry: The Language of Gender and Objects*. Oxford: Basil Blackwell, 1990.

Lears, T. J. Jackson. "From Salvation to Self-Realization: Advertising and the Therapeutic Roots of Consumer Culture, 1880–1930." *The Culture of Consumption: Critical Essays in American History 1880–1980*. Ed. Richard Wightman Fox and T. J. Jackson Lears. New York: Pantheon, 1983. 1–38.

Lee, Hermione. *Virginia Woolf*. London: Chatto and Windus, 1996.

Lee, Judith. "'This Hideous Shaping and Molding': War and *The Waves*." *Virginia Woolf and War*. Ed. Mark Hussey. Syracuse: Syracuse University Press, 1991. 180–202.

Leggett, B. J. *Wallace Stevens and Poetic Theory*. Chapel Hill: University of North Carolina Press, 1987.

Lentricchia, Frank. *After the New Criticism*. Chicago: University of Chicago Press, 1980.

———. *Modernist Quartet*. Cambridge: Cambridge University Press, 1994.

Levenson, Michael H. *A Genealogy of Modernism*. Cambridge: Cambridge University Press, 1984.

Lewis, Wyndham. *America and Cosmic Man*. London: Nicholson and Watson, 1948.

———. *The Apes of God*. 1930. Santa Barbara: Black Sparrow, 1984.

———. *The Art of Being Ruled*. 1926. New York: Haskell House, 1972.

———. Ed. *Blast 1*. 1914. Santa Rosa: Black Sparrow, 1992.

———. Ed. *Blast 2*. 1915. Santa Barbara: Black Sparrow, 1981.

———. *Blasting and Bombardiering*. 1937. London: John Calder, 1982.

———. *The Caliph's Design*. 1919. Santa Barbara: Black Sparrow, 1986.

———. *The Complete Wild Body*. Ed. Bernard Lafourcade. Santa Barbara: Black Sparrow, 1982.

———. *Creatures of Habit and Creatures of Change: Essays on Art, Literature and Society 1914–1956*. Ed. Paul Edwards. Santa Rosa: Black Sparrow, 1989.

———. *The Diabolical Principle and the Dithyrambic Spectator*. London: Chatto and Windus, 1931.

———. *Hitler*. London: Chatto and Windus, 1931.

———. *Left Wings over Europe: or, How to Make a War about Nothing*. London: Jonathan Cape, 1936.

———. *The Letters of Wyndham Lewis*. Ed. W. K. Rose. Norfolk: New Directions, 1963.

———. "The Machine." *Modernism/Modernity* 4 (1997): 171–74.

———. *Malign Fiesta*. 1955. London: Jupiter, 1966.

———. *Men without Art*. 1934. Santa Barbara: Black Sparrow, 1987.

———. "Mr. Clive Bell and 'Wilcoxism'" (first letter). *Athenaeum* 4689 (12 March 1920): 349.

———. "Mr. Clive Bell and 'Wilcoxism'" (second letter). *Athenaeum* 4691 (26 March 1920): 425.

———. "Note for Catalogue." *Vorticist Exhibition*. (Catalogue, Doré Galleries.) London: 1915.

———. *Paleface: The Philosophy of the "Melting-Pot."* London: Chatto and Windus, 1929.

———. *The Revenge for Love*. 1937. Santa Rosa: Black Sparrow, 1991.

———. *Rude Assignment*. 1950. Santa Barbara: Black Sparrow, 1984.

———. *Self Condemned*. 1954. Santa Barbara: Black Sparrow, 1983.

———. *Snooty Baronet*. 1932. Santa Barbara: Black Sparrow, 1984.

———. *Tarr: The 1918 Version*. 1918. Santa Rosa: Black Sparrow, 1990.

———. *Time and Western Man*. 1927. Santa Rosa: Black Sparrow, 1993.

———. *The Vulgar Streak*. 1941. Santa Barbara: Black Sparrow, 1985.

Litz, A. Walton. *Introspective Voyager: The Poetic Development of Wallace Stevens*. New York: Oxford University Press, 1972.

Longenbach, James. *Modernist Poetics of History*. Princeton: Princeton University Press, 1987.

————. *Wallace Stevens: The Plain Sense of Things*. New York: Oxford University Press, 1991.

Lukács, Georg. *History and Class Consciousness: Studies in Marxist Dialectics*. 1922. Trans. Rodney Livingstone. Cambridge: MIT Press, 1971.

Lutz, Tom. *American Nervousness, 1903: An Anecdotal History*. Ithaca: Cornell University Press, 1991.

Lyotard, Jean-François. *The Postmodern Condition*. Trans. Geoff Bennington and Brian Massumi. Minneapolis: University of Minnesota Press, 1984.

MacCarthy, Desmond. "The Post-Impressionists." *Manet and the Post-Impressionists*. (Exhibition Catalogue, Grafton Galleries.) London: Ballantyne, 1910.

MacLeod, Glen G. *Wallace Stevens and Company: The Harmonium Years, 1913–1932*. Ann Arbor: UMI Research Press, 1983.

Macy, John Albert. "Ballade of Decadency." *Harvard Advocate* 64 (1900): 77.

Mailla, Joseph-Anne-Marie de Moyriac de. *Histoire Générale de la Chine, ou Annales de Cet Empire*. Paris, 1777. 13 vols.

Man, Paul de. *The Rhetoric of Romanticism*. New York: Columbia University Press, 1984.

Mares, Cheryl. "Reading Proust: Woolf and the Painter's Perspective." *The Multiple Muses of Virginia Woolf*. Ed. Diane F. Gillespie. Columbia: University of Missouri Press, 1993. 58–89.

Martz, Louis. "'From the Journal of Crispin': An Early Version of 'The Comedian as the Letter C.'" *Wallace Stevens: A Celebration*. Ed. Frank Doggett and Robert Buttel. Princeton: Princeton University Press, 1980. 3–29.

Marx, Karl. *Economic and Philosophic Manuscripts of 1844*. 1932. Trans. Martin Milligan. New York: International, 1964.

Masterman, C.F.G. Preface. *The Heart of the Empire*. 1901. Ed. C.F.G. Masterman. Brighton: Harvester, 1973.

————. "Realities at Home." *The Heart of the Empire*. 1901. Ed. C.F.G. Masterman. Brighton: Harvester, 1973.

McGrath, F. C. *The Sensible Spirit: Walter Pater and the Modernist Paradigm*. Tampa: University Press of Florida, 1986.

Meisel, Perry. *The Absent Father: Virginia Woolf and Walter Pater*. New Haven: Yale University Press, 1980.

Meyers, Jeffrey. *The Enemy: A Biography of Wyndham Lewis*. London: Routledge, 1980.

Michaels, Walter Benn. *The Gold Standard and the Logic of Naturalism*. Berkeley: University of California Press, 1987.

Miller, J. Hillis. "*Mrs. Dalloway*: Repetition as the Raising of the Dead." *Virginia Woolf's Mrs. Dalloway*. Ed. Harold Bloom. New York: Chelsea House, 1988. 79–101.

————. *Poets of Reality*. Cambridge: Harvard University Press, 1965.

Miller, Vincent. "Mauberley and His Critics." *ELH* 57 (1990): 961–76.

Mills, Elliot. *The Decline and Fall of the British Empire*. Oxford: Alden, 1906.

Mitchell, W.J.T. "Ekphrasis and the Other." *South Atlantic Quarterly* 91 (1992): 695–719.

Montresor, C. A. *Some Hobby Horses: or, How to Collect Stamps, Coins, Seals, Crests, and Scraps*. 2nd ed. London: W. H. Allen, 1890.

Moody, A. D. "*Bel Esprit* and the Malatesta Cantos: A Post-*Waste Land* Conjunction of Pound and Eliot." *Ezra Pound and Europe.* Ed. Richard Taylor and Claus Melchior. Amsterdam: Rodopi, 1993. 79–91.

Moore, G. E. *Philosophical Studies.* London: Routledge, 1922.

———. *Principia Ethica.* 1903. Cambridge: Cambridge University Press, 1960.

Moore, Marianne. "Well Moused, Lion." *Dial* 76 (1924). Reprinted in *The Achievement of Wallace Stevens.* Ed. Ashley Brown and Robert S. Haller. New York: Gordian, 1973. 21–28.

Morrison, Paul. "The Fat Girl in Paradise: Stevens, Wordsworth, Milton, and the Proper Name." *Wallace Stevens and the Feminine.* Ed. Melita Schaum. Tuscaloosa: University of Alabama Press, 1993. 80–114.

Munson, Gorham. "The Dandyism of Wallace Stevens." *Dial* 79 (1925). Reprinted in *The Achievement of Wallace Stevens.* Ed. Ashley Brown and Robert S. Haller. New York: Gordian, 1973. 41–45.

Murray, David. "Pound-signs: Money and Representation in Ezra Pound." *Ezra Pound: Tactics for Reading.* Ed. Ian F. A. Bell. London: Vision, 1982. 50–78.

Mussolini, Benito. *The Political and Social Doctrine of Fascism.* Trans. Jane Soames. London: Hogarth, 1933.

Naremore, James. *The World without a Self: Virginia Woolf and the Novel.* New Haven: Yale University Press, 1973.

Nicholls, Peter. "Apes and Familiars: Modernism, Mimesis and the Work of Wyndham Lewis." *Textual Practice* 6 (1992): 421–38.

———. *Ezra Pound: Politics, Economics and Writing.* Atlantic Highlands: Humanities Press, 1984.

———. "Lost Object(s): Ezra Pound and the Idea of Italy." *Ezra Pound and Europe.* Ed. Richard Taylor and Claus Melchior. Amsterdam: Rodopi, 1993. 165–75.

———. *Modernisms: A Literary Guide.* Houndmills: Macmillan, 1995.

Nordau, Max. *Degeneration.* New York: D. Appleton, 1895.

North, Michael. *The Final Sculpture: Public Monuments and Modern Poets.* Ithaca: Cornell University Press, 1985.

———. *The Political Aesthetic of Yeats, Eliot, and Pound.* Cambridge: Cambridge University Press, 1991.

Norton, Charles Eliot. *Letters.* Vol. 2. Boston: Houghton Mifflin, 1913.

"Notes." *Poetry* 20 (1922): 115.

Nussbaum, Martha. "The Window: Knowledge of Other Minds in Virginia Woolf's *To the Lighthouse.*" *New Literary History* 26 (1995): 731–53.

O'Hara, Patricia. "'The Willow Pattern that We Knew': The Victorian Literature of Blue Willow." *Victorian Studies* (1993): 421–42.

Omega Workshops Limited. Prospectus. London: 1913.

Orvell, Miles. *The Real Thing: Imitation and Authenticity in American Culture, 1880–1940.* Chapel Hill: University of North Carolina Press, 1989.

Pater, Walter. *Marius the Epicurean.* 1885. Harmondsworth: Penguin, 1985.

———. *Selected Writings of Walter Pater.* New York: Columbia University Press, 1974.

Patten, Simon N. *The New Basis of Civilization.* 1907. Cambridge: Harvard University Press, 1968.

Perelman, Bob. *The Trouble with Genius: Reading Pound, Joyce, Stein, and Zukofsky.* Berkeley: University of California Press, 1994.

Perloff, Marjorie. "Pound/Stevens: Whose Era?" *New Literary History* 13 (1982): 485–510.

Pietz, William. "Fetishism and Materialism: The Limits of Theory in Marx." *Fetishism as Cultural Discourse.* Ed. Emily Apter and William Pietz. Ithaca: Cornell University Press, 1993. 119–51.

Plarr, Victor. *In the Dorian Mood.* London: John Lane, 1896.

Porter, Bernard. "The Edwardians and their Empire." *Edwardian England.* Ed. Donald Read. New Brunswick: Rutgers University Press, 1982. 128–44.

Pound, Ezra. *ABC of Reading.* 1934. New York: New Directions, 1960.

———. *Cantos.* New York: New Directions, 1970.

———. *Collected Early Poems.* Ed. Michael John King. New York: New Directions, 1976.

———. *Ezra Pound's Poetry and Prose: Contributions to Periodicals.* Ed. Lee Baechler, A. Walton Litz, and James Longenbach. 11 vols. New York: Garland, 1991.

———. *Gaudier-Brzeska.* 1916. New York: New Directions, 1970.

———. *Guide to Kulchur.* 1938. New York: New Directions, 1970.

———. *Jefferson and/or Mussolini.* London: Stanley Nott, 1935.

———. *Literary Essays.* Ed. T. S. Eliot. New York: New Directions, 1968.

———. *Personae: The Shorter Poems of Ezra Pound.* Ed. Lea Baechler and A. Walton Litz. New York: New Directions, 1990.

———. *Polite Essays.* London: Faber, 1937.

———. *Selected Letters 1907–1941.* Ed. D. D. Paige. London: Faber, 1950.

———. *Selected Prose 1909–1965.* Ed. William Cookson. New York: New Directions, 1973.

———. *The Spirit of Romance.* London: J. M. Dent, 1910.

Rabaté, Jean-Michel. *Language, Sexuality, and Ideology in Ezra Pound's Cantos.* Albany: State University of New York Press, 1986.

Rainey, Lawrence. *Ezra Pound and the Monument of Culture: Text, History, and the Malatesta Cantos.* Chicago: University of Chicago Press, 1991.

Ransom, John Crowe. "Art and the Human Economy." *Kenyon Review* 7 (1945): 683–88.

———. *Poems and Essays.* New York: Vintage, 1955.

———. *The World's Body.* New York: Scribner's, 1938.

Rebel Art Centre. Prospectus. London: 1914.

Richardson, Joan. *Wallace Stevens: A Biography.* 2 vols. New York: William Morrow, 1986–88.

Riddel, Joseph N. *The Clairvoyant Eye.* Baton Rouge: Louisiana State University Press, 1965.

———. "Neo-Nietzschean Clatter: Speculation and/on Pound's Poetic Image." *Ezra Pound: Tactics for Reading.* Ed. Ian F. A. Bell. London: Vision, 1982. 187–220.

Rilke, Rainer Maria. *New Poems.* 1907. Trans. Edward Snow. San Francisco: North Point, 1984.

Robinson, Alan. *Symbol to Vortex: Poetry, Painting and Ideas, 1885–1914.* New York: St. Martin's, 1985.

Robinson, Frederick S. *The Connoisseur: Essays on the Romantic and Picturesque Associations of Art and Artists*. London: George Redway, 1897.

Rosenbaum, S. P. "The Philosophical Realism of Virginia Woolf." *English Literature and British Philosophy*. Ed. S. P. Rosenbaum. Chicago: University of Chicago Press, 1971. 316–56.

Rosenfeld, Paul. "Wallace Stevens." *Men Seen*. New York: Dial, 1925. Reprinted in *The Achievement of Wallace Stevens*. Ed. Ashley Brown and Robert S. Haller. New York: Gordian, 1973. 35–40.

Ross, Duncan M. "The Clearing Banks and Industry—New Perspectives on the Interwar Years." *Capitalism in a Mature Economy*. Ed. J. J. van Helten and Y. Cassis. Aldershot: Edward Elgar, 1990. 52–70.

Ruotolo, Lucio. *The Interrupted Moment: A View of Virginia Woolf's Novels*. Stanford: Stanford University Press, 1980.

———. *Six Existential Heroes: The Politics of Faith*. Cambridge: Harvard University Press, 1973.

Ruskin, John. *The Works of John Ruskin*. London: George Allen, 1903–12. 39 vols.

Santayana, George. *Interpretations of Poetry and Religion*. 1900. Cambridge: MIT Press, 1989. Vol. 3 of *The Works of George Santayana*.

———. *Persons and Places: Fragments of Autobiography*. 1944–1953. Cambridge: MIT Press, 1986. Vol. 1 of *The Works of George Santayana*.

———. *The Sense of Beauty: Being the Outlines of an Aesthetic Theory*. 1896. Cambridge: MIT Press, 1988. Vol. 2 of *The Works of George Santayana*.

Sartre, Jean-Paul. *Being and Nothingness*. 1943. Trans. Hazel E. Barnes. New York: Washington Square-Pocket, 1956.

———. *Critique of Dialectical Reason*. 1960. Trans. Alan Sheridan-Smith. London: Verso, 1976.

———. *Nausea*. 1938. Trans. Lloyd Alexander. New York: New Directions, 1969.

———. *Oeuvres romanesques*. Paris: Gallimard, 1981.

Saussure, Ferdinand de. *Course in General Linguistics*. 1915. New York: McGraw-Hill, 1966.

Scarry, Elaine. *The Body in Pain: The Making and Unmaking of the World*. New York: Oxford University Press, 1985.

Sears, Sallie. "Theater of War: Virginia Woolf's *Between the Acts*." *Virginia Woolf: A Feminist Slant*. Ed. Jane Marcus. Lincoln: University of Nebraska Press, 1983. 212–235.

Sekora, John. *Luxury: The Concept in Western Thought, Eden to Smollett*. Baltimore: Johns Hopkins University Press, 1977.

Shakespeare, William. *The Riverside Shakespeare*. Boston: Houghton Mifflin, 1974.

Sherry, Vincent. *Ezra Pound, Wyndham Lewis, and Radical Modernism*. New York: Oxford University Press, 1993.

Shetley, Vernon. *After the Death of Poetry*. Durham: Duke University Press, 1993.

Shi, David E. *The Simple Life: Plain Living and High Thinking in American Culture*. New York: Oxford University Press, 1985.

Sieburth, Richard. "In Pound We Trust." *Critical Inquiry* 14 (1987): 142–72.

———. Introduction. *A Walking Tour in Southern France*. By Ezra Pound. New York: New Directions, 1992. vii–xxi.

Simpson, David. *Fetishism and Imagination*. Baltimore: Johns Hopkins University Press, 1982.

Sinfield, Alan. *The Wilde Century: Effeminacy, Oscar Wilde, and the Queer Moment*. London: Cassell, 1994.

Spencer, Herbert. *Education: Intellectual, Moral, and Physical*. London: G. Manwaring, 1861.

Stein, Gertrude. *Lectures in America*. 1935. Boston: Beacon, 1957.

Steiner, Wendy. *The Scandal of Pleasure: Art in an Age of Fundamentalism*. Chicago: University of Chicago Press, 1995.

Stevens, Holly. *Souvenirs and Prophecies: The Young Wallace Stevens*. New York: Knopf, 1977.

Stevens, Wallace. *The Collected Poems*. 1954. New York: Vintage, 1982.

———. "The Higher Life." *Harvard Advocate* 67 (1899): 123–24.

———. *Letters of Wallace Stevens*. Ed. Holly Stevens. New York: Knopf, 1966.

———. *The Necessary Angel*. New York: Vintage, 1951.

———. *Opus Posthumous*. 1957. Rev. ed. New York: Vintage, 1989.

———. "Part of His Education." *Harvard Advocate* 67 (1899): 35–37.

Street, G. S. *The Autobiography of a Boy*. London: Elkin Mathews and John Lane, 1894.

Taylor, A.J.P. "Prologue: The Year 1906." *Edwardian England*. Ed. Donald Read. New Brunswick: Rutgers University Press, 1982. 1–13.

Terrell, Carroll F. *A Companion to the Cantos of Ezra Pound*. Berkeley: University of California Press, 1980.

Thomas, W. A. *The Finance of British Industry 1918–1976*. London: Methuen, 1978.

Tiffany, Daniel. *Radio Corpse: Imagism and the Cryptaesthetic of Ezra Pound*. Cambridge: Harvard University Press, 1995.

Townsend, Kim. *Manhood at Harvard: William James and Others*. New York: Norton, 1996.

Tratner, Michael. "Sex and Credit: Consumer Capitalism in *Ulysses*." *James Joyce Quarterly* 30–31 (1993): 695–716.

Veblen, Thorstein. *The Theory of the Leisure Class*. 1899. Boston: Houghton Mifflin, 1973.

Vendler, Helen. *On Extended Wings: Wallace Stevens' Longer Poems*. Cambridge: Harvard University Press, 1969.

Walkiewicz, E. P., and Hugh Witemeyer. "A Public Bank in Canto 40." *Paideuma* 19 (1990): 91–98.

Waller, Edmund and John Denham. *The Poetical Works of Edmund Waller and Sir John Denham*. Edinburgh: James Nichol, 1857.

Webb, Caroline. "Life After Death: The Allegorical Progress of *Mrs. Dalloway*." *Modern Fiction Studies* 40 (1994): 279–98.

Wicke, Jennifer. *Advertising Fictions: Literature, Advertisement, and Social Reading*. New York: Columbia University Press, 1988.

———. "*Mrs. Dalloway* Goes to Market: Woolf, Keynes, and Modern Markets." *Novel* 28 (Fall 1994): 5–23.

———. "'Who's She When She's at Home?': Molly Bloom and the Work of Consumption." *James Joyce Quarterly* 28 (1991): 749–63.

Wilde, Oscar. *Intentions*. 1891. New York: AMS, 1980. Vol. 10 of *The Works of Oscar Wilde*.

———. *The Picture of Dorian Gray*. 1891. New York: AMS, 1980. Vol. 2 of *The Works of Oscar Wilde*.

Williams, William Carlos. *Autobiography*. New York: Random House, 1951.

———. *Paterson*. New York: New Directions, 1963.

———. *Selected Essays*. 1954. New York: New Directions, 1969.

———. *Selected Letters*. New York: McDowell, 1957.

Willis, J. H., Jr. *Leonard and Virginia Woolf as Publishers: The Hogarth Press, 1917–41*. Charlottesville: University Press of Virginia, 1992.

Wolfe, Cary. *The Limits of American Literary Ideology in Pound and Emerson*. Cambridge: Cambridge University Press, 1993.

Woolf, Leonard. *Barbarians Within and Without*. New York: Harcourt, 1939.

Woolf, Virginia. "Anon." Ed. Brenda R. Silver. *Twentieth Century Literature* 25 (1979): 380–426.

———. *Between the Acts*. San Diego: Harcourt, 1941.

———. *Collected Essays*. 4 vols. London: Hogarth, 1966–67.

———. *The Complete Shorter Fiction of Virginia Woolf*. San Diego: Harcourt, 1985.

———. *The Diary of Virginia Woolf*. Ed. Anne Olivier Bell. 5 vols. San Diego: Harcourt, 1977–84.

———. *The Hours: The British Museum Manuscript of Mrs. Dalloway*. Ed. Helen M. Wussow. New York: Pace University Press, 1996.

———. *Jacob's Room*. San Diego: Harcourt, 1922.

———. *The Letters of Virginia Woolf*. Ed. Nigel Nicolson and Joanne Trautman. 6 vols. New York: Harcourt, 1975–80.

———. *Moments of Being*. Ed. Jeanne Schulkind. 2nd ed. San Diego: Harcourt, 1976.

———. *Mrs. Dalloway*. 1925. San Diego: Harcourt, 1990.

———. *Night and Day*. San Diego: Harcourt, 1919.

———. *Orlando*. San Diego: Harcourt, 1928.

———. *Roger Fry: A Biography*. London: Hogarth, 1940.

———. *A Room of One's Own*. San Diego: Harcourt, 1929.

———. *Three Guineas*. San Diego: Harcourt, 1938.

———. *To the Lighthouse*. 1927. San Diego: Harcourt, 1989.

———. *To the Lighthouse: The Original Holograph Draft*. Ed. Susan Dick. Toronto: University of Toronto Press, 1982.

———. *The Voyage Out*. San Diego: Harcourt, 1915.

———. *The Waves*. San Diego: Harcourt, 1931.

———. *The Years*. San Diego: Harcourt, 1937.

Wordsworth, William. *The Fourteen-Book Prelude*. Ithaca: Cornell University Press, 1985.

———. *The Prose Works of William Wordsworth*. Vol. 1. Oxford: Clarendon, 1974.

Zwerdling, Alex. *Virginia Woolf and the Real World*. Berkeley: University of California Press, 1986.

INDEX

abstraction: in art, 15–16, 94–95, 106, 235, 250, 255, 271n.5; versus concreteness, 6–7, 15–16, 25, 129, 175, 179, 181–82, 212, 235, 250, 255, 271n.5

absurdity, 44–45, 135–37, 156, 250–51, 266–67n.14

Adams, John, 171, 175, 180

Adorno, Theodor W., 7–8, 11, 18, 22, 64–69, 76–77, 87, 101, 160, 181–82, 191–92, 268–69nn. 27 and 29

aesthetes. *See* aestheticism

aesthetic, 6, 8, 26–30, 36–38, 47–48, 50, 56, 124–25, 176, 193, 196–212, 216, 239–40, 268n.23. *See also* aesthetes; aestheticism

aestheticism, 18–19, 21, 26–38, 42–43, 58, 90, 93, 103–108, 111–12, 114, 131, 140, 142–43, 145, 147–48, 152–53, 160–66, 169, 179, 186, 193–213, 231, 253–54, 263–64n.11, 265–66nn. 6, 7, and 9, 271–72nn. 4, 10, and 12, 276n.1, 280nn. 1 and 2. *See also* decadence

Agnew, Jean-Christophe, 272n.16

Alberti, Leon Battista, 167

Aldington, Richard, 186, 262n.7

alienation of labor, 127, 147–48, 182

Althusser, Louis, 9, 216

Annan, Noel, 67

architecture, 90, 119–20, 123, 137, 283n.19

Arendt, Hannah, 7

Aristotle, 181–82, 192, 279n.21

Armstrong, Isobel, 263n.10

art (*see also* artist; production, artistic; work of art): autonomy of, 39–40, 71, 167, 196–99, 211, 221, 237, 258; evaluation of, 111–16, 119–22, 126, 143–45, 149, 169, 174–76, 180, 278n.14; financial support for, 109, 115, 121–23, 145–47 (*see also* patronage); role of, in society, 7, 10, 25, 38–42, 65–66, 70, 76–78, 80, 87–88, 90–96, 107–108, 119–24, 131–39, 160–80, 184–86, 196–240, 246, 249–59 (*see also* poetry, role and nature of); versus life. *See* life

artist (*see also* art; production, artistic; work of art): amateur or leisure-class, 109–22, 125, 131, 255, 272n.13; consumer as, 40–

41, 63, 107–108, 111, 266n.11; lifestyle of, 26–27, 30, 40–43, 108–111, 161–65, 177, 200, 210–12, 280–81n.4; professional, 110–17, 120–26, 177, 255, 272–73nn. 13 and 14; role of, in society, 39–40, 93–96, 104, 107, 115, 122–33, 147–50, 162–76, 203, 211–22, 230–40, 246, 276n.31

Arts and Crafts, 92, 201–202

association, 46, 221–24, 229–31, 246, 282n.14

Athenaeum, 26, 112–13

Auden, W. H., 16

aura, 6, 22, 121–22, 126

Ayers, David, 271n. 6

Babbitt, Irving, 15

Barthes, Roland, 13, 59

Bataille, Georges, 22

Bate, W. J., 151, 157

Bates, Milton, 194–95

Baudelaire, Charles, 26, 30, 38, 108

Baudrillard, Jean, 22, 76, 101

Beard, George M., 280–81n.4

Beardsley, Aubrey, 108, 189, 193, 195

Beauvoir, Simone de, 41, 43, 45, 282–83n.18

Beckett, Samuel, 53

Behn, Aphra, 116

Being, 4, 17, 20, 23, 43–45, 48, 53, 56–58, 67, 137, 182, 215–16, 228–29, 233–47, 256, 282–83nn. 15 and 18. See also *object world*

Bell, Clive, 35, 46, 112–15, 269n.30

Bell, Ian, 174–75, 181, 277n.8

Bell, Julian, 269n.30

Bell, Quentin, 271n.1

Bell, Vanessa, 35, 112, 273n.15

Benjamin, Walter, 5–7, 25, 28, 117, 121

Bennett, Arnold, 37, 59, 161–62

Bergson, Henri, 15–16, 20–21, 36, 97–98, 107, 133, 263–64nn. 8 and 14, 271–72nn. 6 and 8

Berkeley, George, 137

Bernstein, Michael André, 276–77n.5

Birken, Lawrence, 19, 278–79n.19

DATE DUE
